STOP!

This is the back of the book.
You wouldn't want to spoil a great ending!

This book is printed "manga-style," in the authentic Japanese right-to-left format. Since none of the artwork has been flipped or altered, readers get to experience the story just as the creator intended. You've been asking for it, so TOKYOPOP® delivered: authentic, hot-off-the-press, and far more fun!

DIRECTIONS

1
2
3
4
5
6
7
8
9
10

If this is your first time reading manga-style, here's a quick guide to help you understand how it works.

It's easy... just start in the top right panel and follow the numbers. Have fun, and look for more 100% authentic manga from TOKYOPOP®!

100% AUTHENTIC MANGA
品質第一公式商品

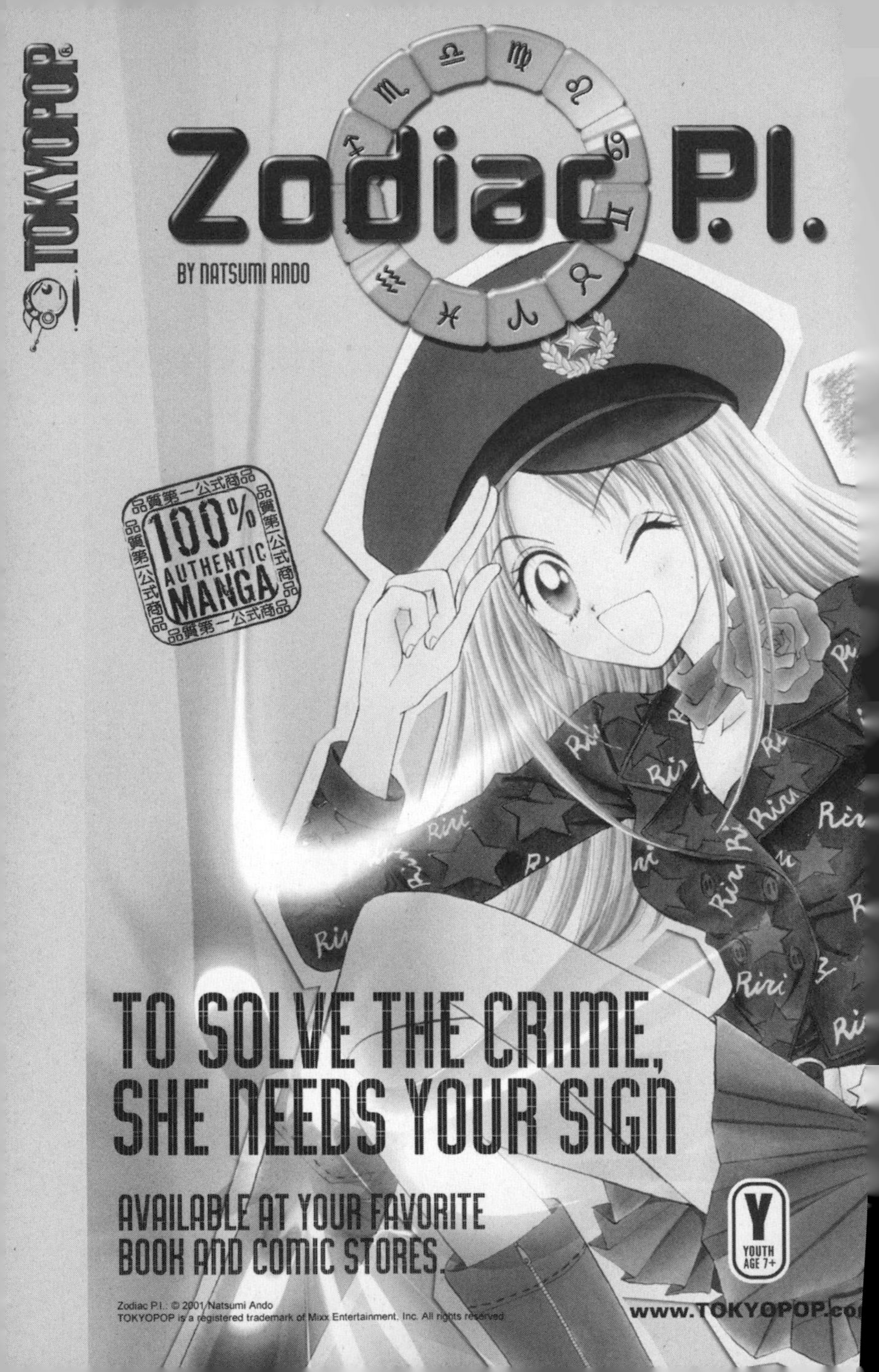
TOKYOPOP®
Zodiac P.I.
BY NATSUMI ANDO
100% AUTHENTIC MANGA
品質第一公式商品
TO SOLVE THE CRIME, SHE NEEDS YOUR SIGN
AVAILABLE AT YOUR FAVORITE BOOK AND COMIC STORES.
Y YOUTH AGE 7+
Zodiac P.I.: © 2001 Natsumi Ando
TOKYOPOP is a registered trademark of Mixx Entertainment, Inc. All rights reserved
www.TOKYOPOP.co

Forbidden Dance

ALSO AVAILABLE FROM  TOKYOPOP®

Forbidden Dance

Volume 2

Written and Illustrated by
Hinako Ashihara

TOKYOPOP®

Los Angeles • Tokyo • London

Translator - Takae Brewer
English Adaptation - Tisha Ford
Contributing Editor - Jodi Bryson
Retouch and Lettering - Jen Nunn
Cover Layout - Aaron Suhr
Graphic Designer - James Lee

Editor - Julie Taylor
Managing Editor - Jill Freshney
Production Coordinator - Antonio DePietro
Production Manager - Jennifer Miller
Art Director - Matt Alford
Editorial Director - Jeremy Ross
VP of Production - Ron Klamert
President & C.O.O. - John Parker
Publisher & C.E.O. - Stuart Levy

Email: editor@TOKYOPOP.com
Come visit us online at www.TOKYOPOP.com

A  Manga

TOKYOPOP Inc.
5900 Wilshire Blvd. Suite 2000
Los Angeles, CA 90036

ISBN: 1-59182-346-3

First TOKYOPOP® printing: October 2003

10 9 8 7 6 5 4 3 2 1
Printed in the USA

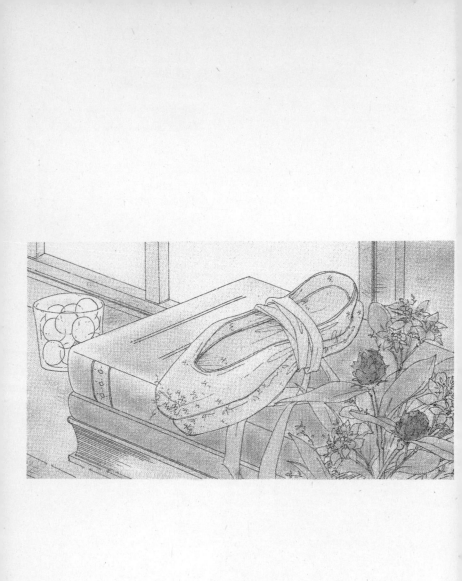

FORBIDDEN DANCE 2

CONTENTS

AYA FUJI
HIGH SCHOOL STUDENT.
SHE HAS BEEN TRAINING IN
CLASSICAL BALLET SINCE
SHE WAS VERY YOUNG.

AKIRA HIBIYA
LEADER OF THE ALL-
MALE DANCE TROUPE
"COOL."

NACHAN
AYA'S "BEST FRIEND."
NACHAN IS JEALOUS OF
AYA'S DANCING TALENT.

STORY

AYA IS A HIGH SCHOOL STUDENT WHO LOVES BALLET. AT A BALLET
COMPETITION, SHE INJURED HER FOOT IN FRONT OF AN AUDIENCE AND
DEVELOPED A MORBID FEAR OF DANCING ON THE STAGE. SHE QUIT
DANCING BECAUSE OF HER NOW ACUTE STAGE FRIGHT. ONE DAY,
AYA SEES A BALLET PERFORMANCE BY THE DANCE TROUPE COOL AND
BECOMES DEEPLY MOVED BY AKIRA'S STYLE OF DANCING. THIS INSPIRES
AYA TO START DANCING AGAIN. AYA WANTS NOTHING MORE THAN
TO DANCE WITH AKIRA, AND ASKS AKIRA TO LET HER JOIN COOL. AKIRA
TELLS AYA THAT HE WILL ALLOW HER TO JOIN COOL ONLY IF SHE WINS
FIRST PLACE AT THE NATIONAL BALLET COMPETITION. NOW AYA IS
MORE SERIOUS ABOUT HER TRAINING THAN EVER BEFORE. BUT AYA BARELY
PASSES THE PRELIMINARY ROUND AT THE COMPETITION WHEN A JUDGE
INTERRUPTS HER PERFORMANCE BECAUSE HE HATES AYA'S ATHLETIC
STYLE OF DANCING. THEN, ON THE DAY OF THE FINALS, SHE LEARNS
THAT HER FRIEND NACHAN IS MISSING. AYA LEAVES THE COMPETITION
SITE TO HELP NACHAN'S MOTHER LOOK FOR HER. AYA DISCOVERS
NACHAN AT HER OLD BALLET SCHOOL, AND DISCOVERS THAT NACHAN
IS RESPONSIBLE FOR PUTTING THE GLASS IN HER BALLET SHOES—
IT WASN'T AYA'S RIVAL, YOSHINO, AFTER ALL! NACHAN THEN THREATENS TO
KILL HERSELF TO PREVENT AYA FROM RETURNING TO THE COMPTETITION.
WHAT WILL AYA DO?!

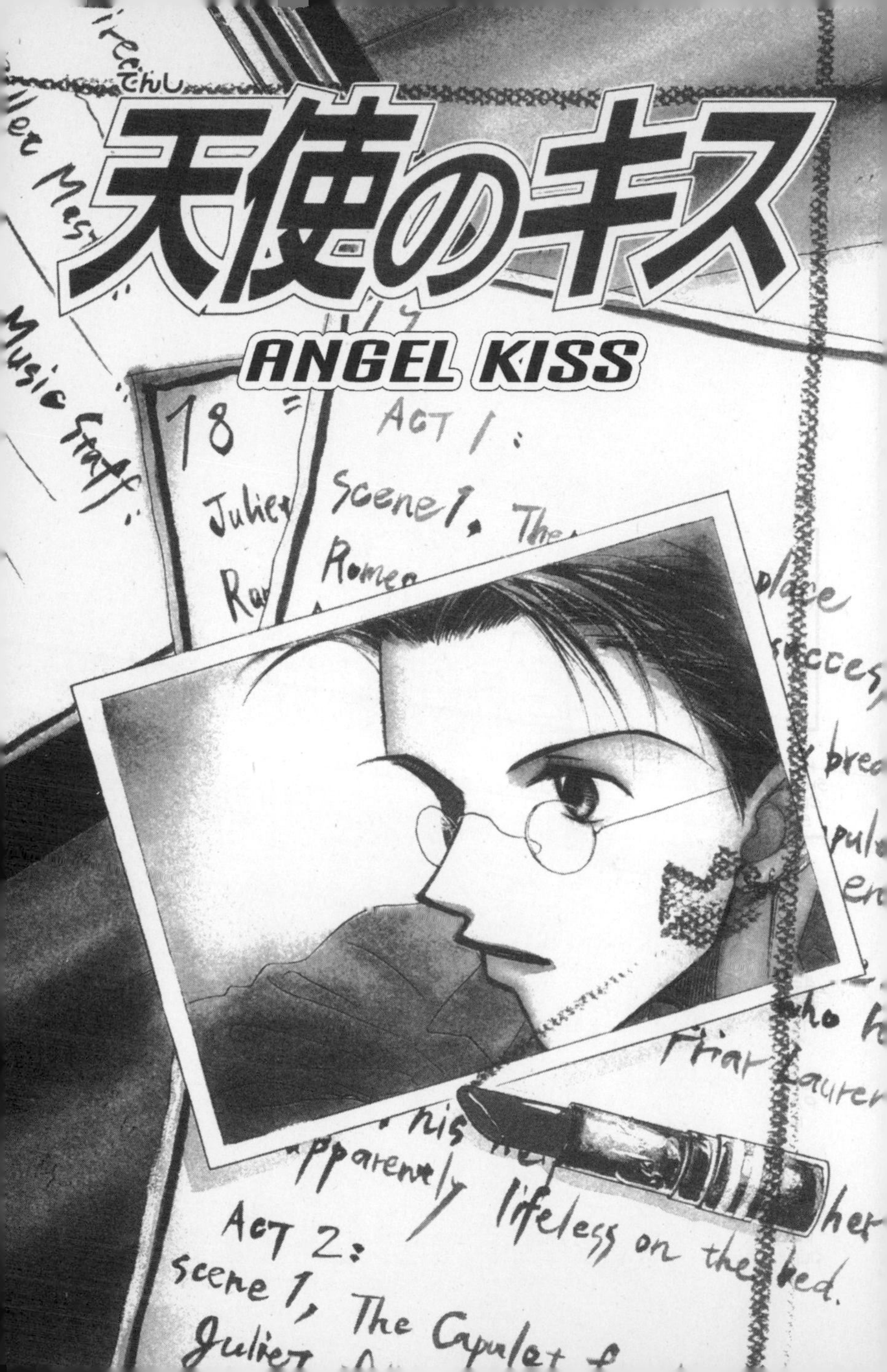
天使のキス
ANGEL KISS
Music Staff:
18
ACT 1:
Scene 1, The
Romeo
lifeless on the bed.
ACT 2:
scene 1, The Capulet
Friar Lauren

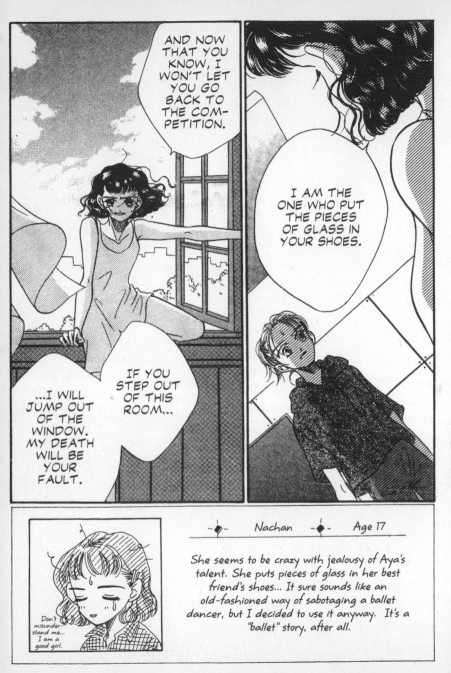

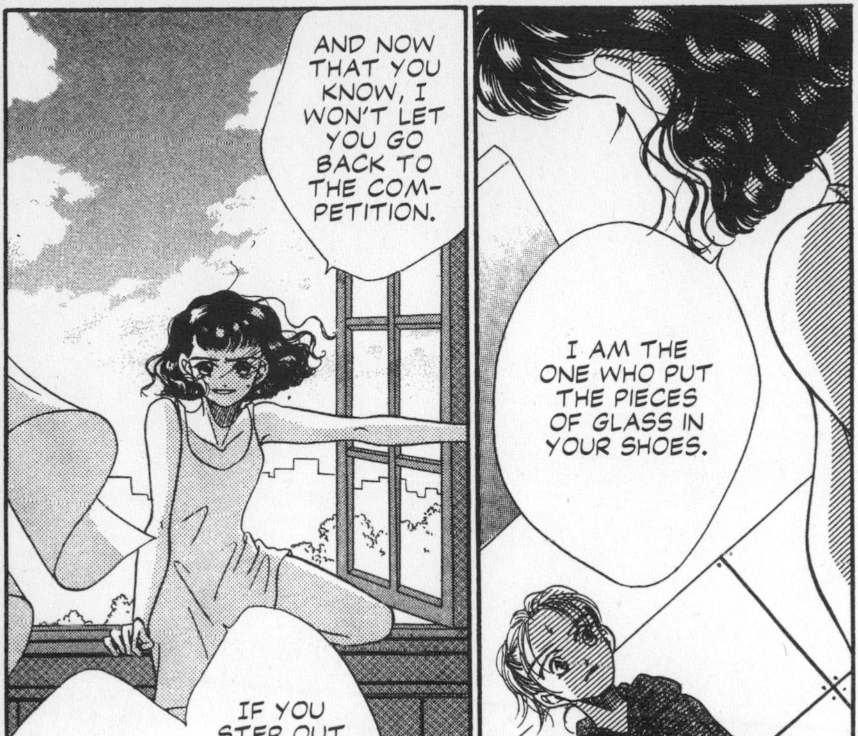
I AM THE ONE WHO PUT THE PIECES OF GLASS IN YOUR SHOES.
AND NOW THAT YOU KNOW, I WON'T LET YOU GO BACK TO THE COM-PETITION.
IF YOU STEP OUT OF THIS ROOM...
...I WILL JUMP OUT OF THE WINDOW. MY DEATH WILL BE YOUR FAULT.

Nachan — Age 17

She seems to be crazy with jealousy of Aya's talent. She puts pieces of glass in her best friend's shoes... It sure sounds like an old-fashioned way of sabotaging a ballet dancer, but I decided to use it anyway. It's a "ballet" story, after all.

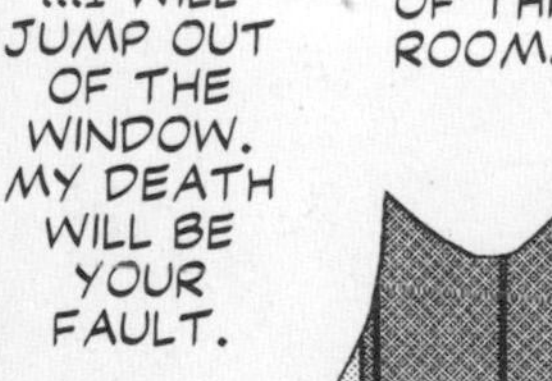
Don't misunder-stand me... I am a good girl.

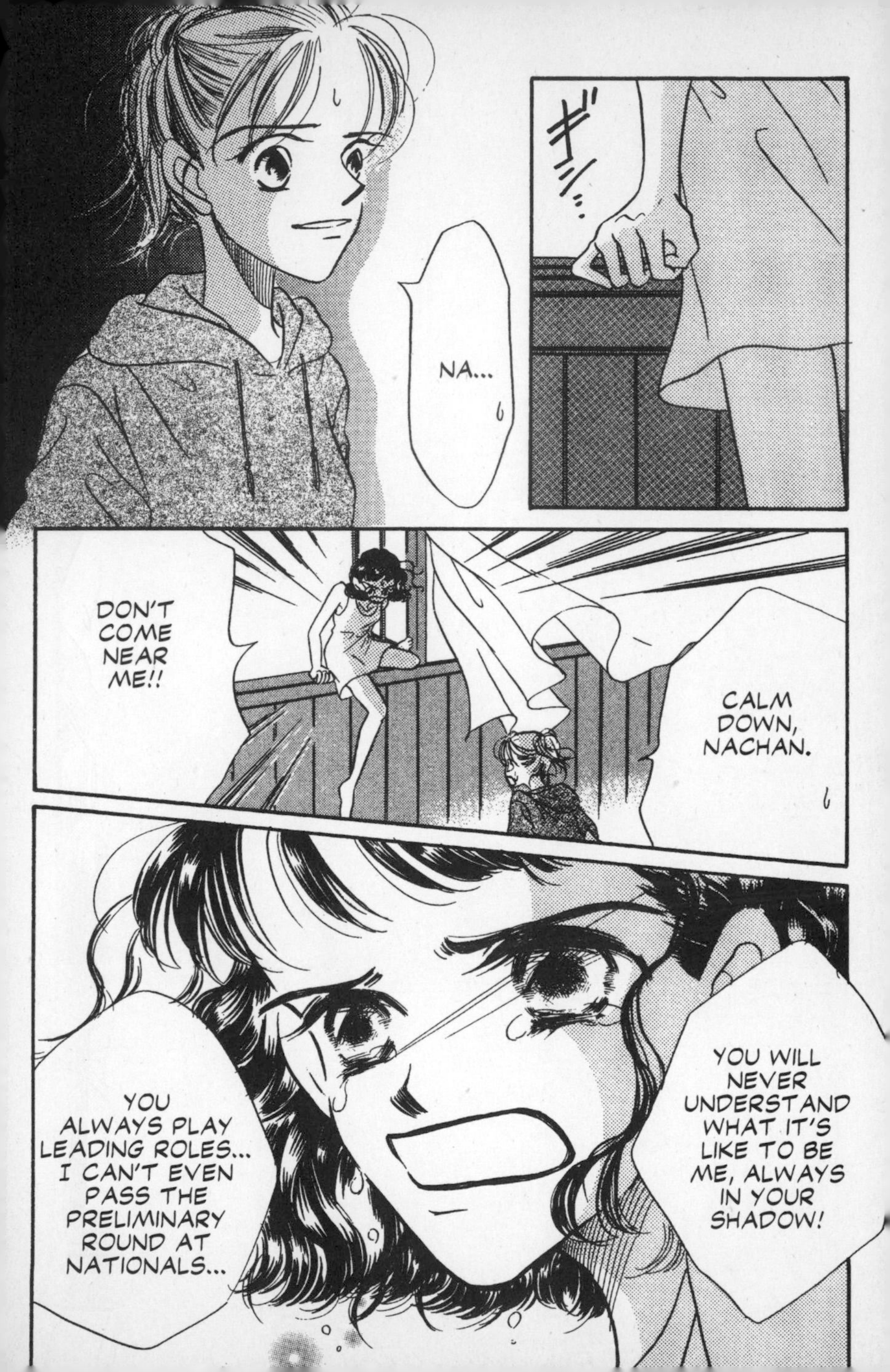
NA...
CALM DOWN, NACHAN.
DON'T COME NEAR ME!!
YOU WILL NEVER UNDERSTAND WHAT IT'S LIKE TO BE ME, ALWAYS IN YOUR SHADOW!
YOU ALWAYS PLAY LEADING ROLES... I CAN'T EVEN PASS THE PRELIMINARY ROUND AT NATIONALS...

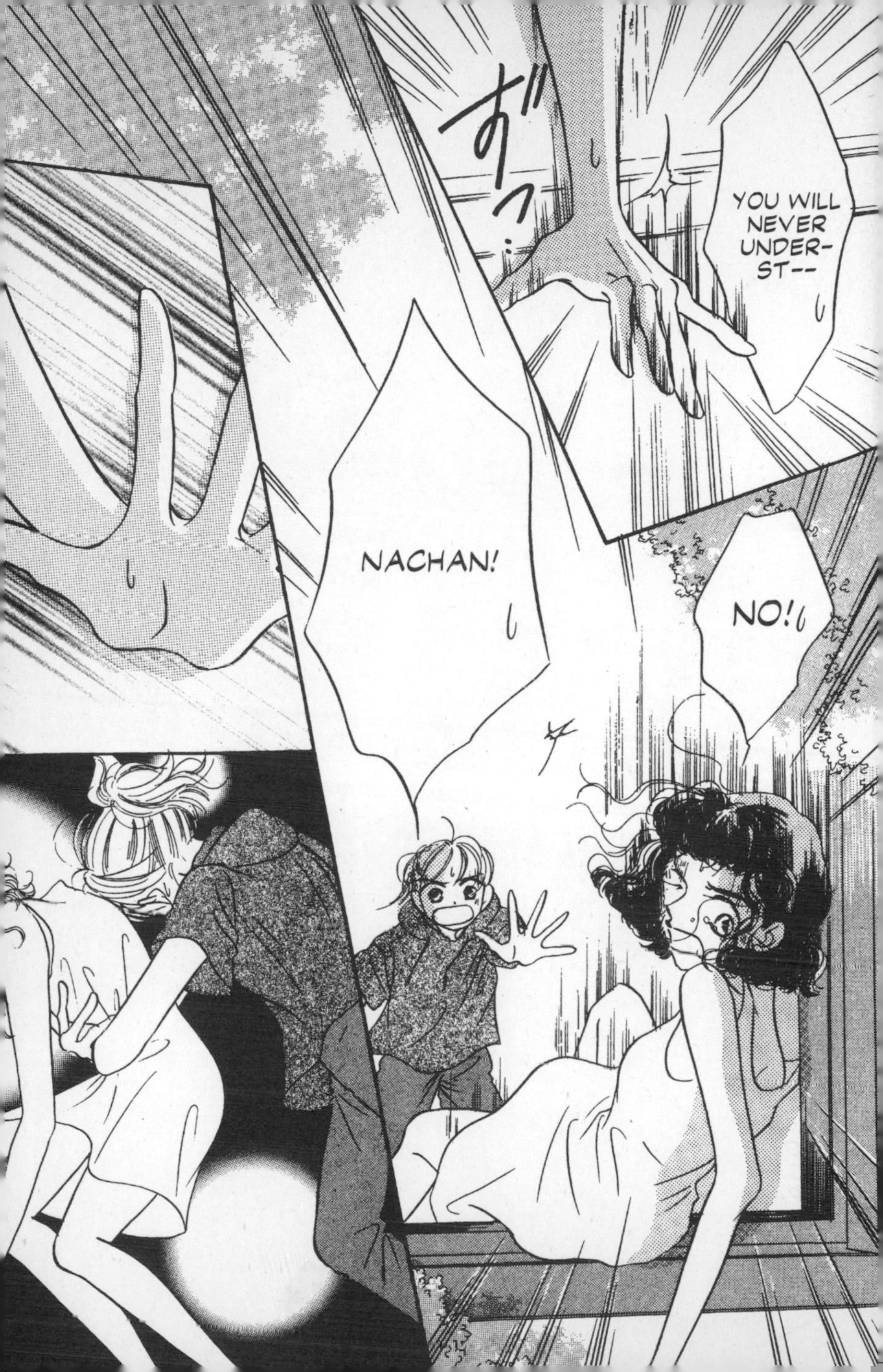
YOU WILL NEVER UNDER-ST--
ずっ…
NACHAN!
NO!

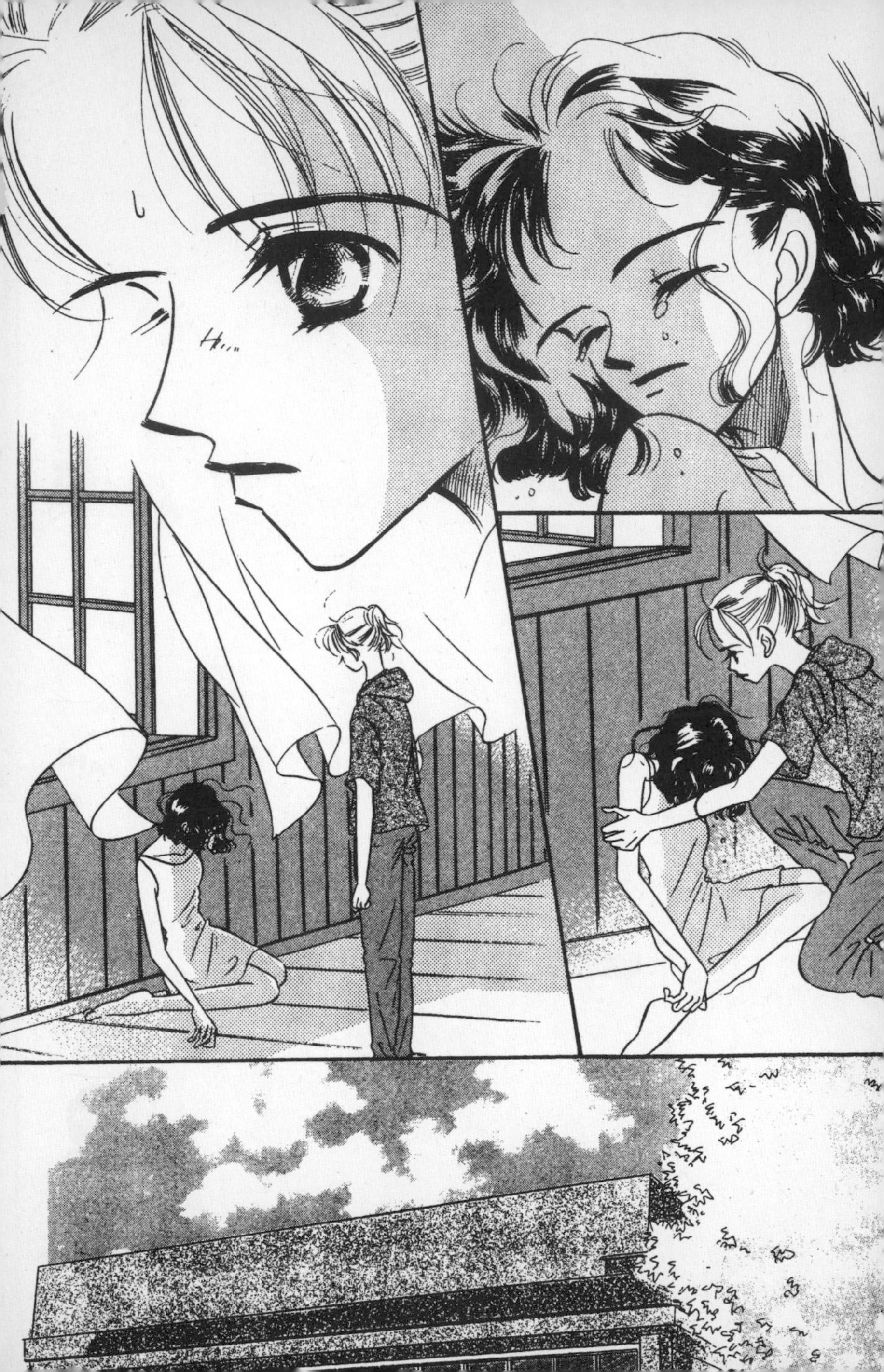
H...

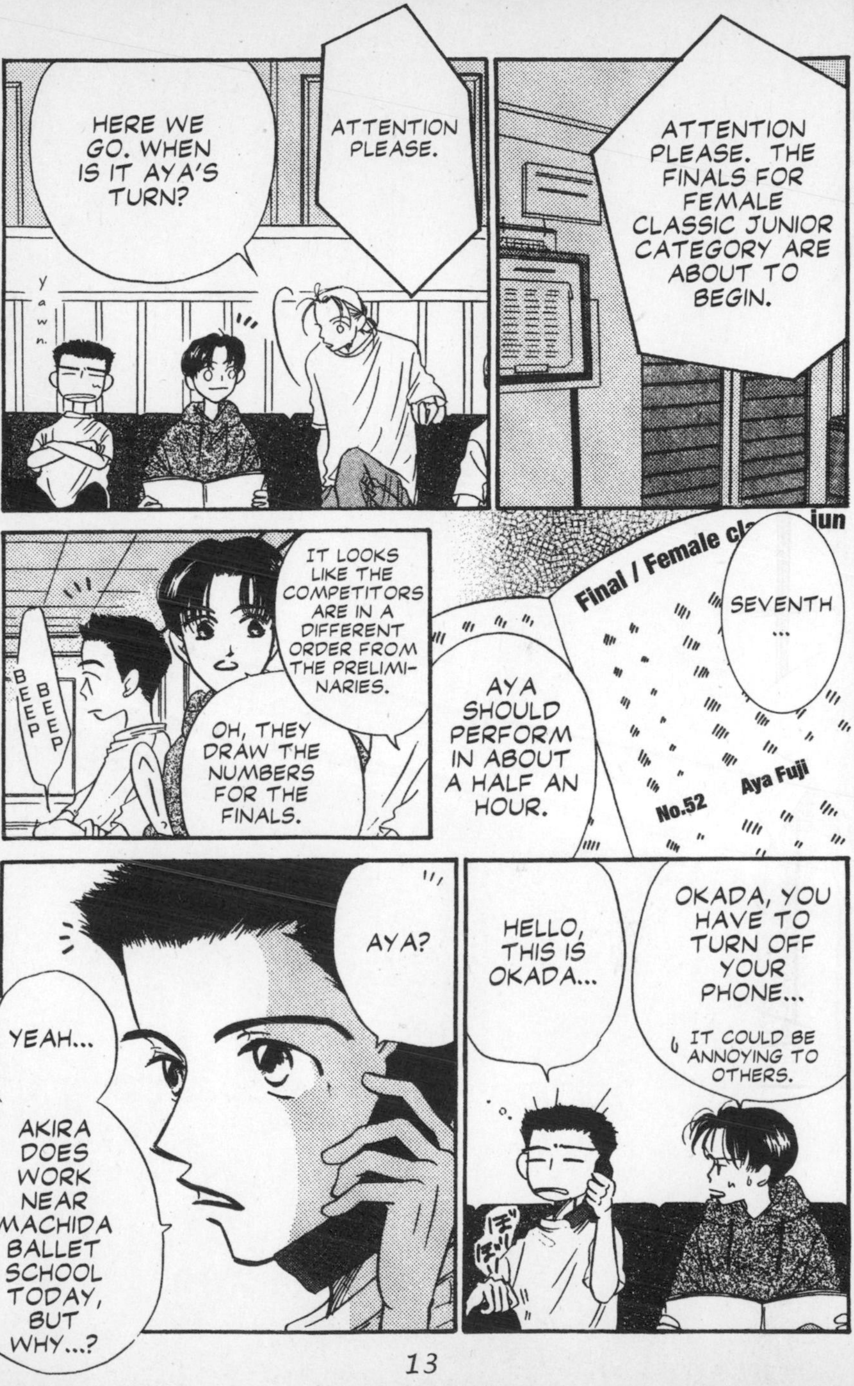

ATTENTION PLEASE. THE FINALS FOR FEMALE CLASSIC JUNIOR CATEGORY ARE ABOUT TO BEGIN.
ATTENTION PLEASE.
HERE WE GO. WHEN IS IT AYA'S TURN?
yawn.
Final / Female
SEVENTH ...
Aya Fuji
No.52
AYA SHOULD PERFORM IN ABOUT A HALF AN HOUR.
IT LOOKS LIKE THE COMPETITORS ARE IN A DIFFERENT ORDER FROM THE PRELIMINARIES.
OH, THEY DRAW THE NUMBERS FOR THE FINALS.
BEEP BEEP
OKADA, YOU HAVE TO TURN OFF YOUR PHONE...
IT COULD BE ANNOYING TO OTHERS.
HELLO, THIS IS OKADA...
AYA?
YEAH...
AKIRA DOES WORK NEAR MACHIDA BALLET SCHOOL TODAY, BUT WHY...?

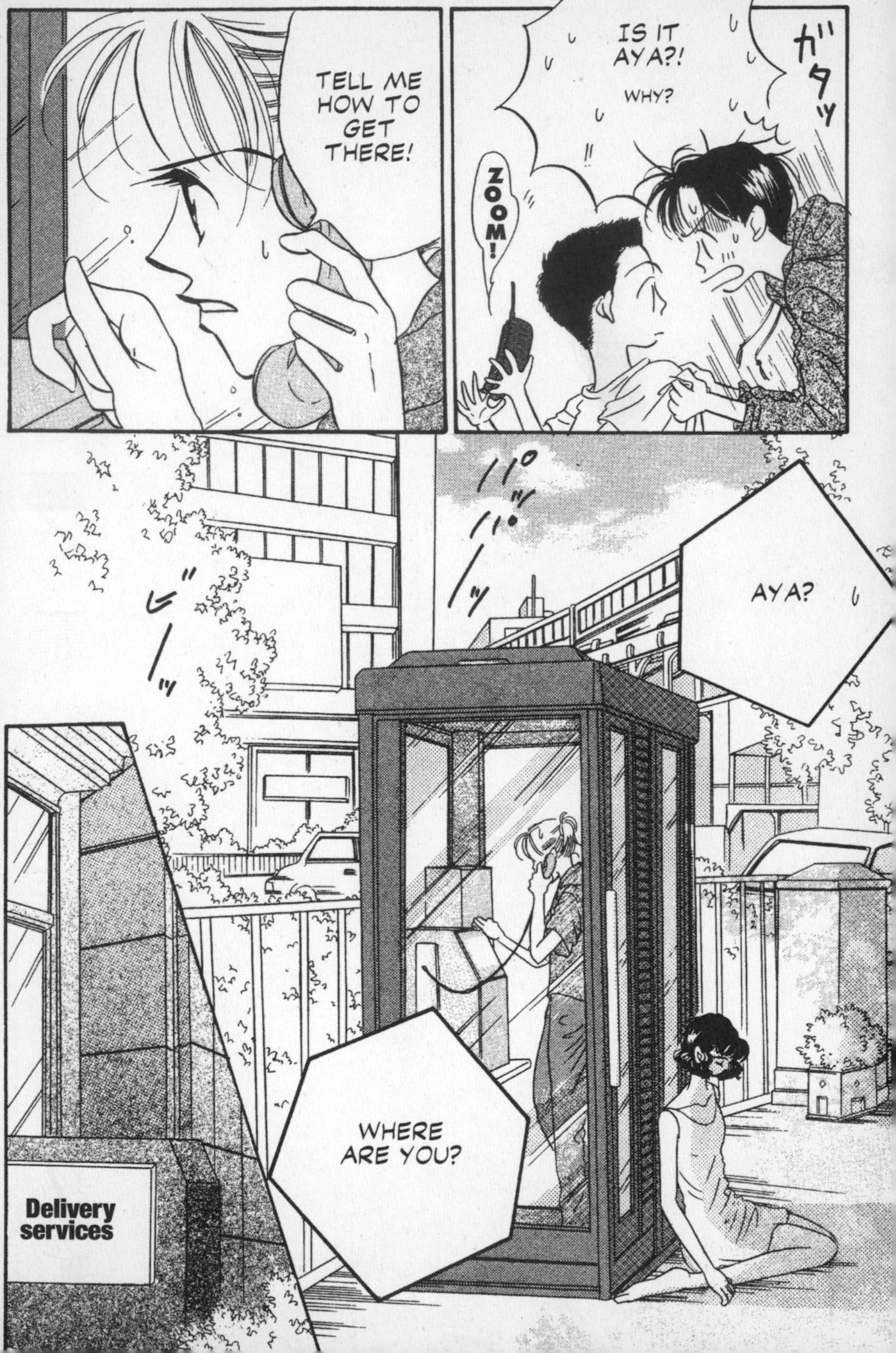
IS IT AYA?!
WHY?
ガタッ
ZOOM!
TELL ME HOW TO GET THERE!
AYA?
WHERE ARE YOU?
Delivery services

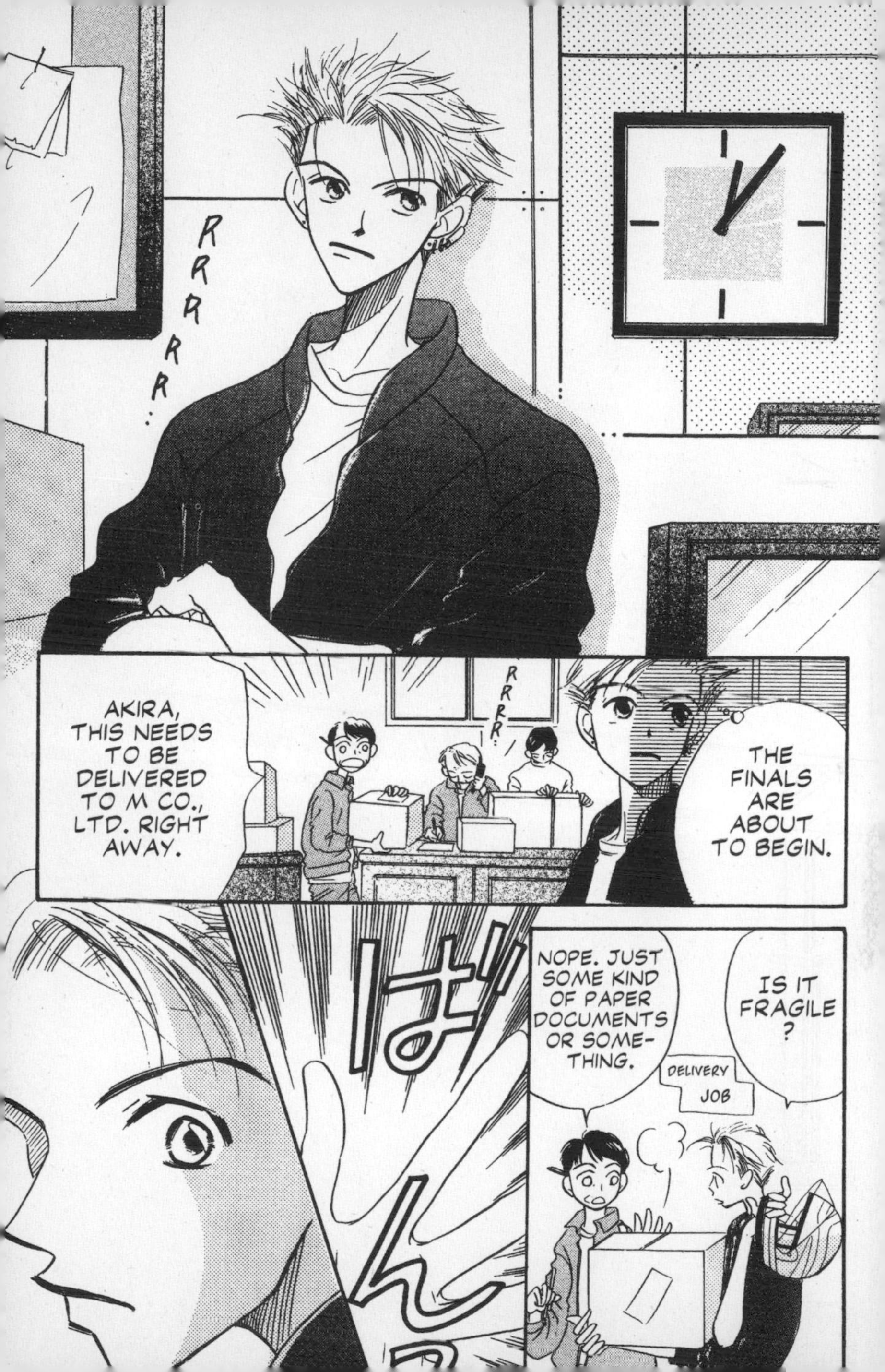
RRRRR...
THE FINALS ARE ABOUT TO BEGIN.
RRRR...
AKIRA, THIS NEEDS TO BE DELIVERED TO M CO., LTD. RIGHT AWAY.
IS IT FRAGILE?
NOPE. JUST SOME KIND OF PAPER DOCUMENTS OR SOME-THING.
DELIVERY JOB
ばん

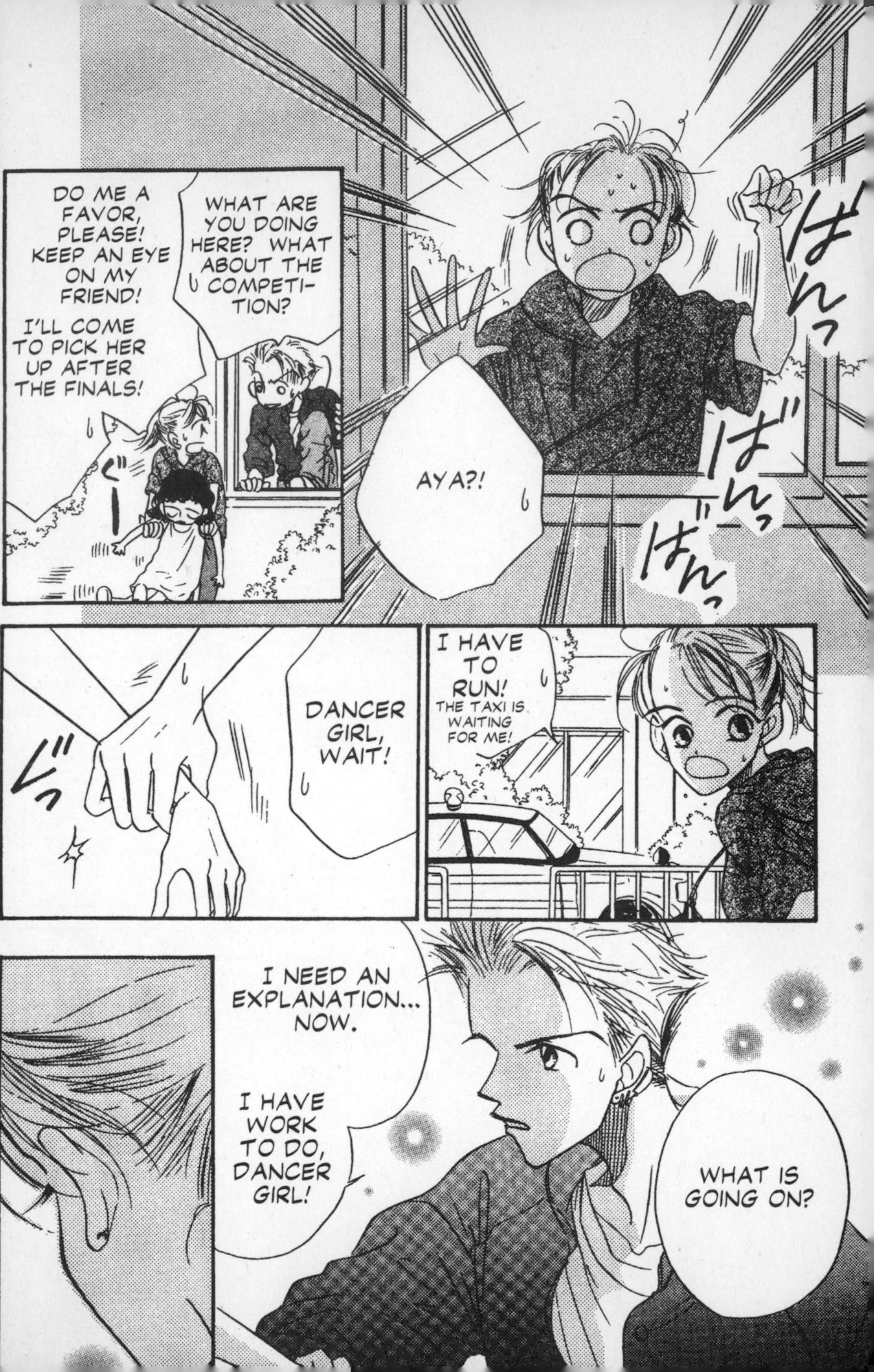
はんっ
ばんっ
ばんっ
AYA?!
WHAT ARE YOU DOING HERE? WHAT ABOUT THE COMPETITION?
DO ME A FAVOR, PLEASE! KEEP AN EYE ON MY FRIEND!
I'LL COME TO PICK HER UP AFTER THE FINALS!
ぐー
I HAVE TO RUN! THE TAXI IS WAITING FOR ME!
DANCER GIRL, WAIT!
ぐっ
WHAT IS GOING ON?
I NEED AN EXPLANATION... NOW.
I HAVE WORK TO DO, DANCER GIRL!

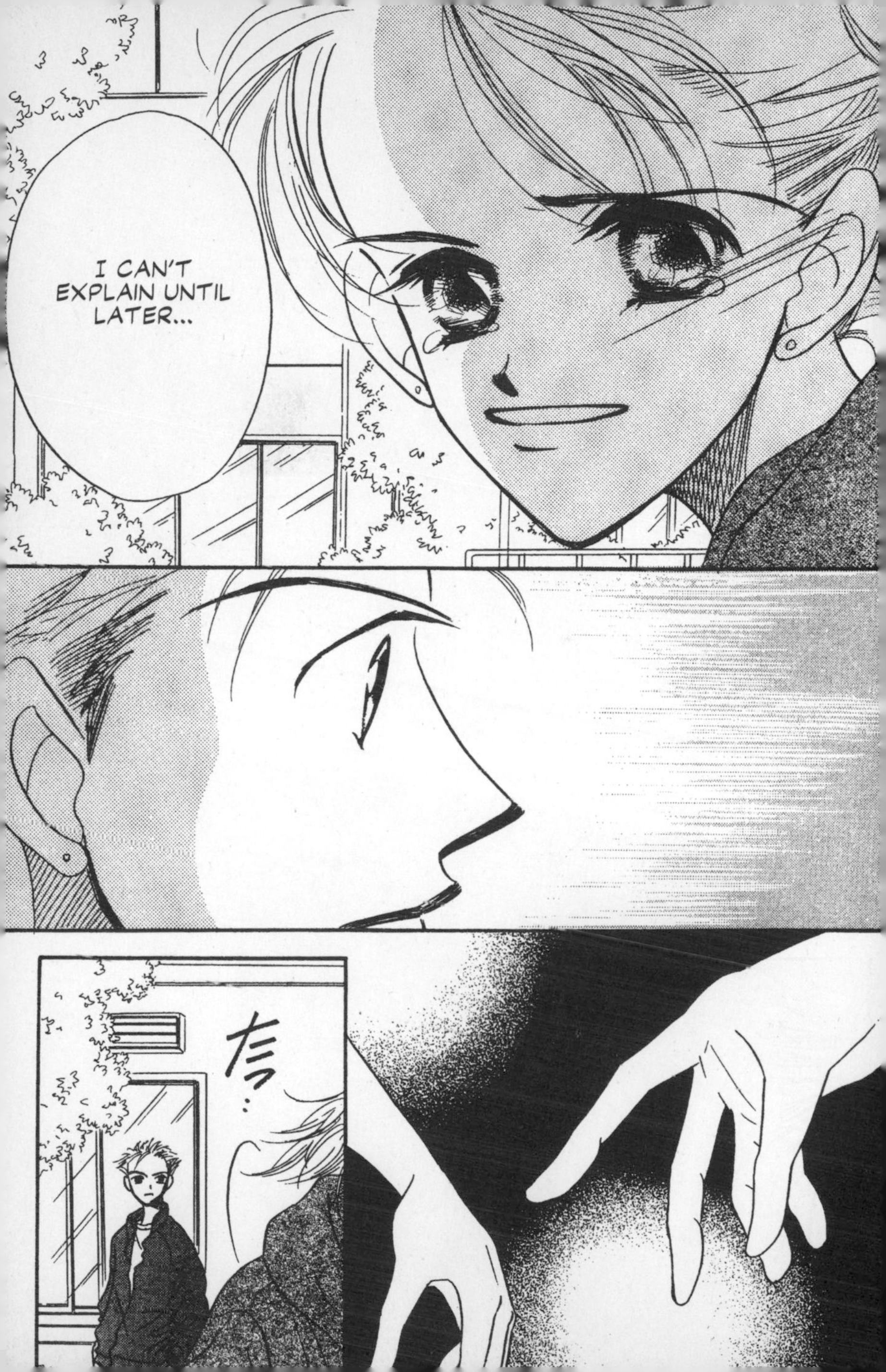
I CAN'T EXPLAIN UNTIL LATER...
たっ

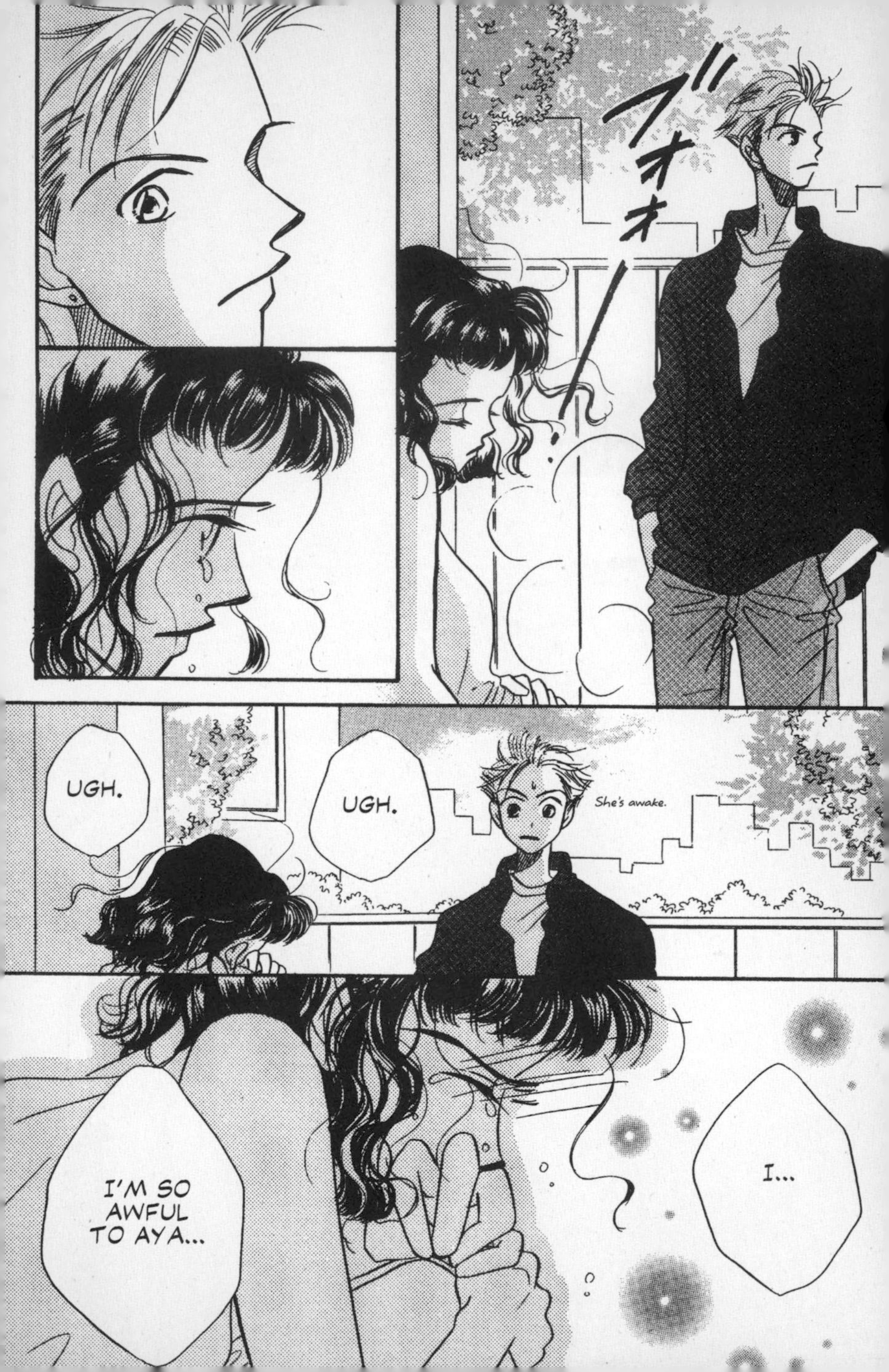
ブォォ
She's awake.
UGH.
UGH.
I...
I'M SO AWFUL TO AYA...

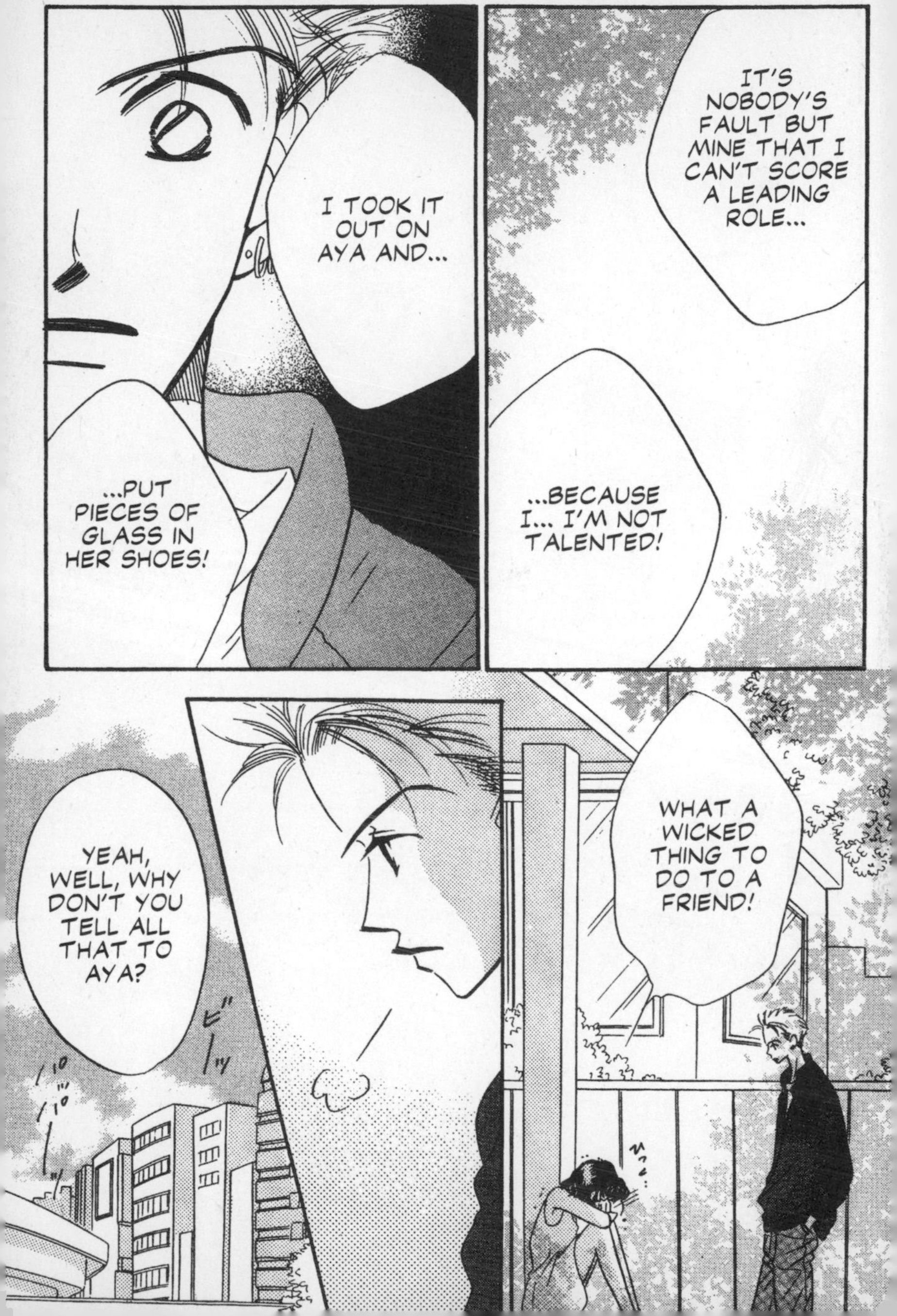
IT'S NOBODY'S FAULT BUT MINE THAT I CAN'T SCORE A LEADING ROLE...
...BECAUSE I... I'M NOT TALENTED!
I TOOK IT OUT ON AYA AND...
...PUT PIECES OF GLASS IN HER SHOES!
WHAT A WICKED THING TO DO TO A FRIEND!
YEAH, WELL, WHY DON'T YOU TELL ALL THAT TO AYA?

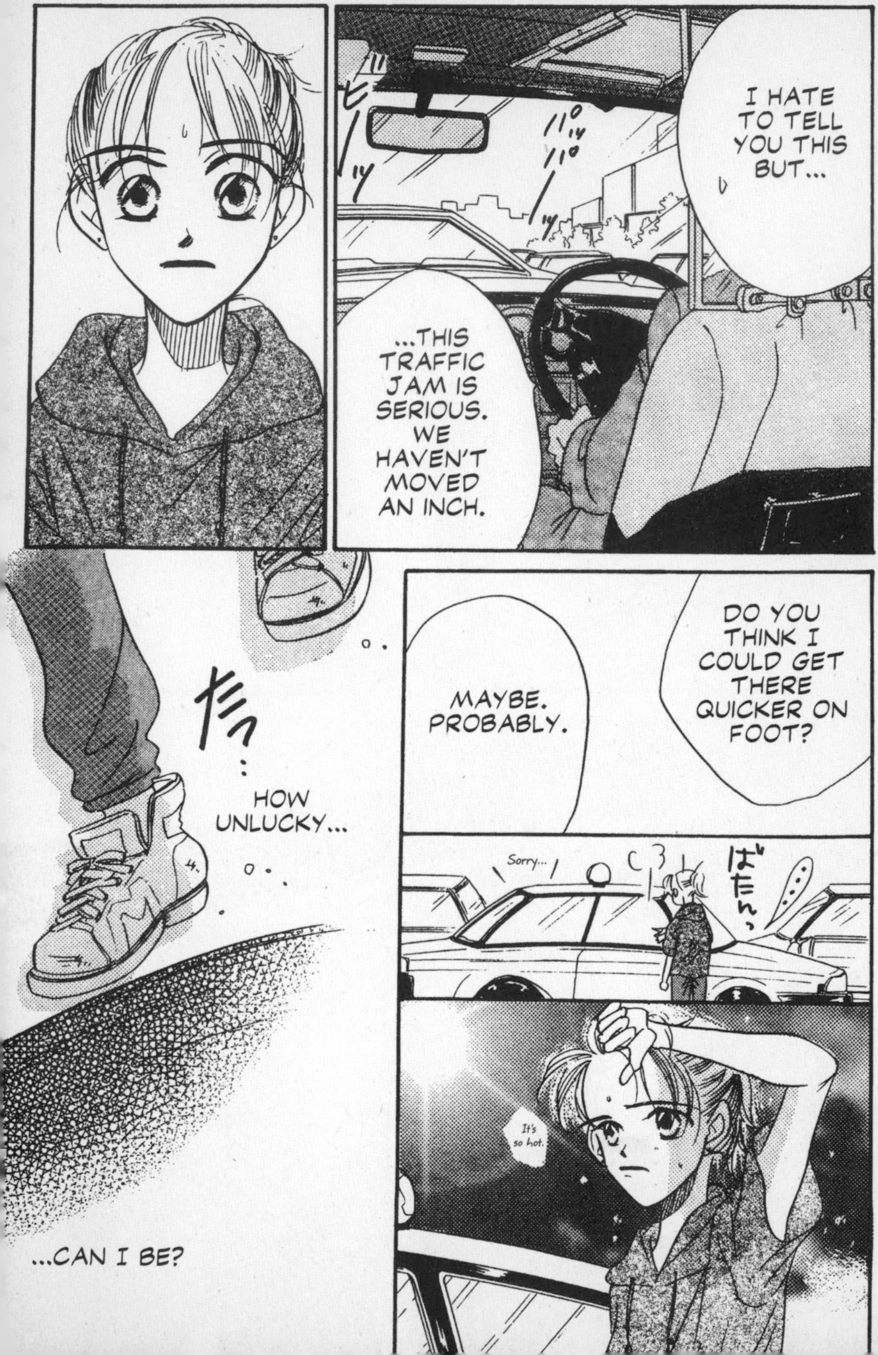

I HATE TO TELL YOU THIS BUT...
...THIS TRAFFIC JAM IS SERIOUS. WE HAVEN'T MOVED AN INCH.
DO YOU THINK I COULD GET THERE QUICKER ON FOOT?
MAYBE. PROBABLY.
ばたんっ
Sorry...
It's so hot.
たっ
HOW UNLUCKY...
...CAN I BE?

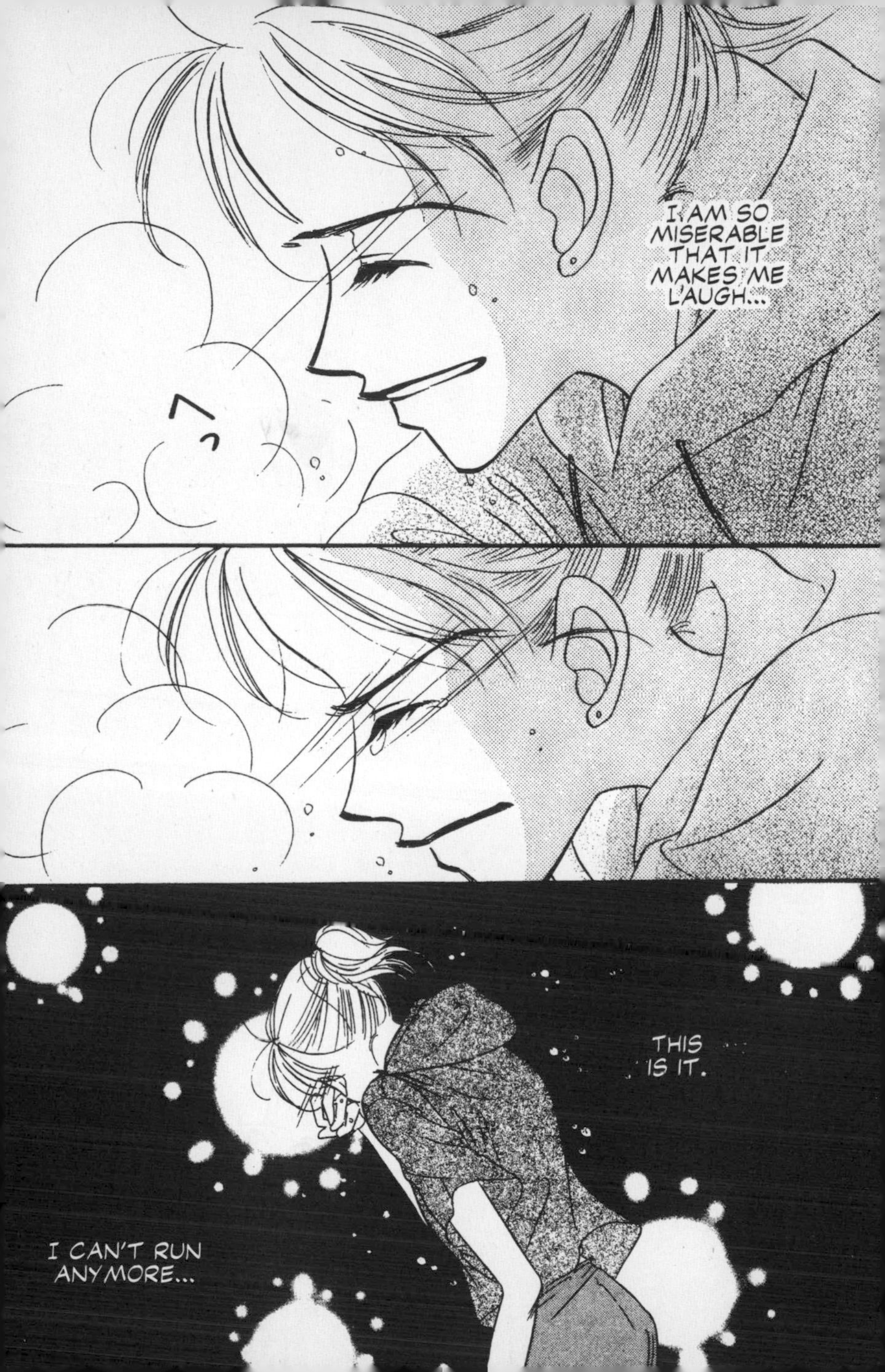
I AM SO MISERABLE THAT IT MAKES ME LAUGH...
THIS... IS IT.
I CAN'T RUN ANYMORE...

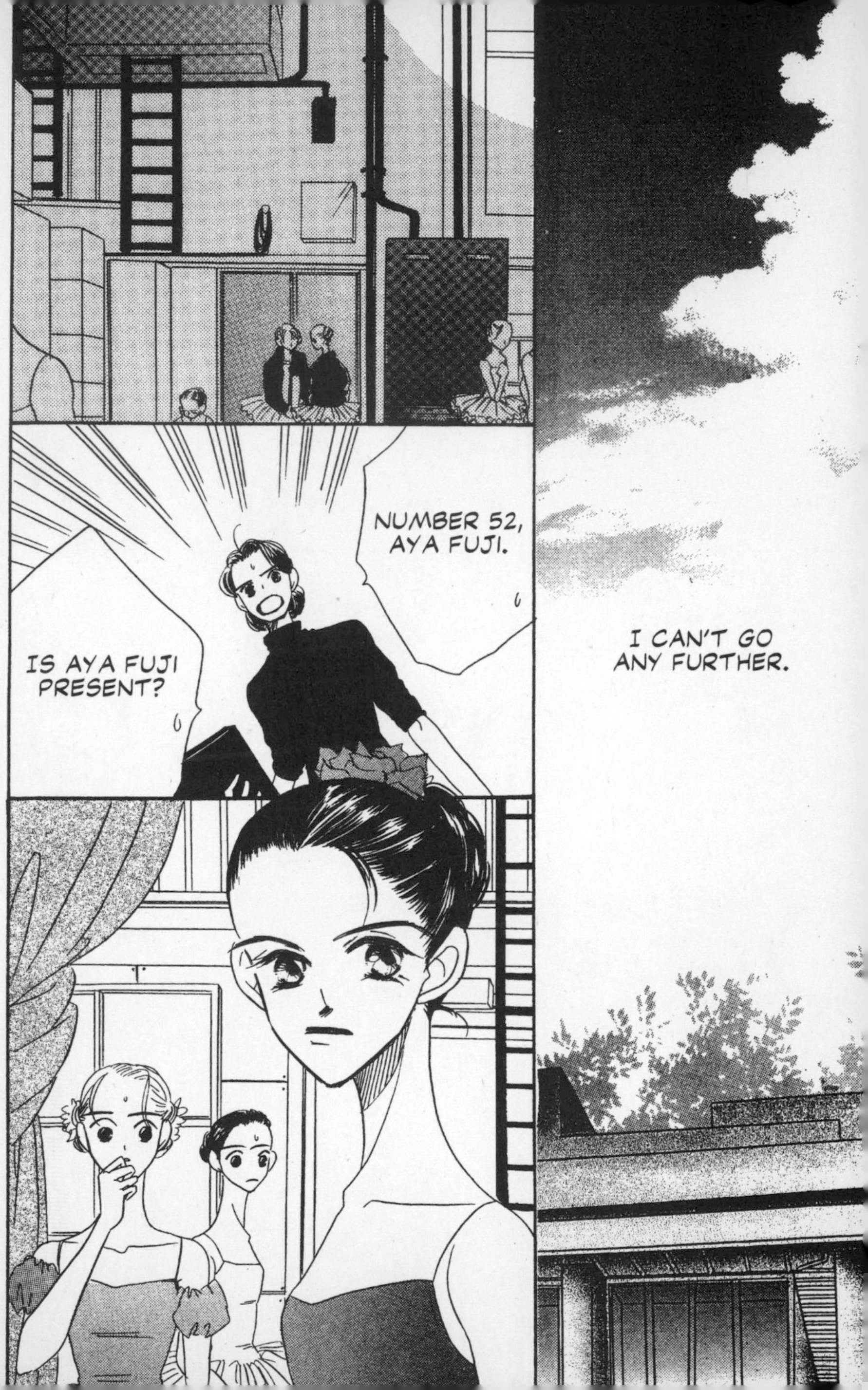
I CAN'T GO ANY FURTHER.
NUMBER 52, AYA FUJI.
IS AYA FUJI PRESENT?

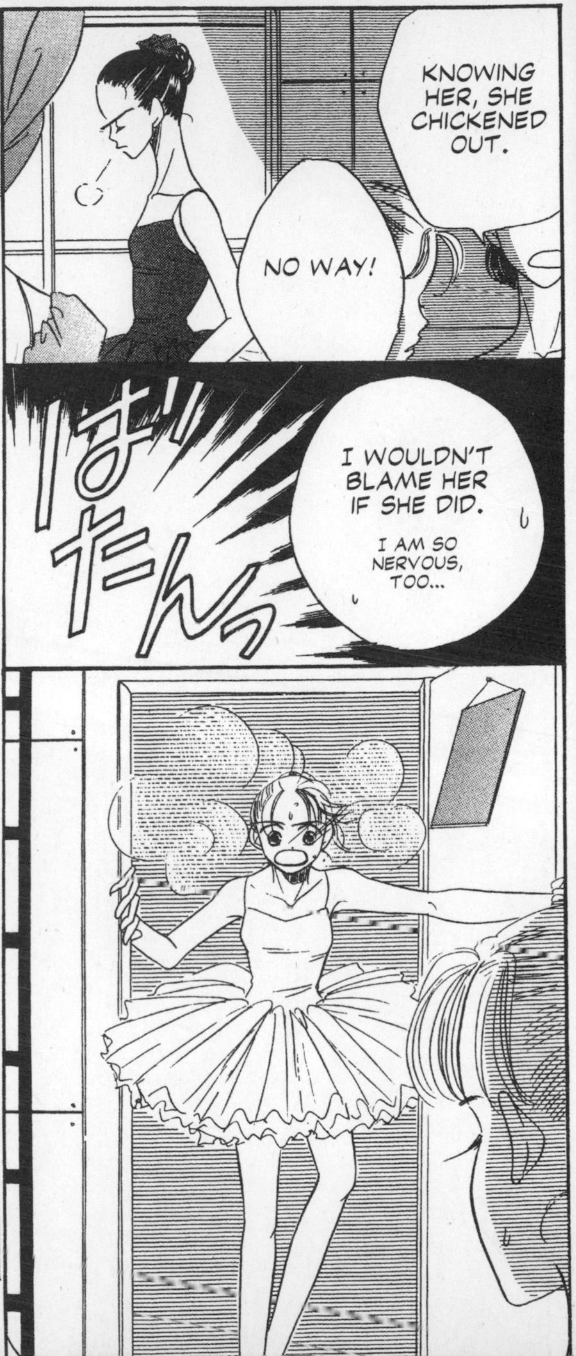
KNOWING HER, SHE CHICKENED OUT.
NO WAY!
I WOULDN'T BLAME HER IF SHE DID.
I AM SO NERVOUS, TOO...
ばたんっ

Ashihara's Diary

No. 1

Hello everyone. This is Ashihara. Thank you for reading Forbidden Dance volume 2, which is my seventh book. Forbidden Dance was supposed to be a six-episode series, but it ended up being much longer. I'm surprised that it's lasting long enough to publish volume 2! I am so happy about that. I would like to express my appreciation to everyone who has been helping me.

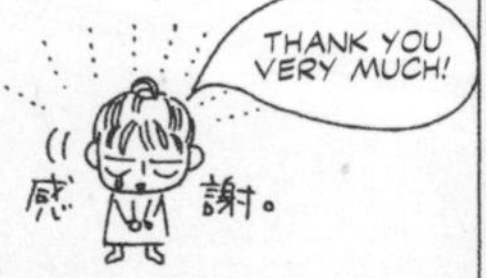
THANK YOU VERY MUCH!
感謝。

When I started Forbidden Dance, I was at a loss for what to do because I had no knowledge of ballet. There is still much to learn! But I'm doing a lot of research and trying my best to make the series cool for you. Okay, bye!

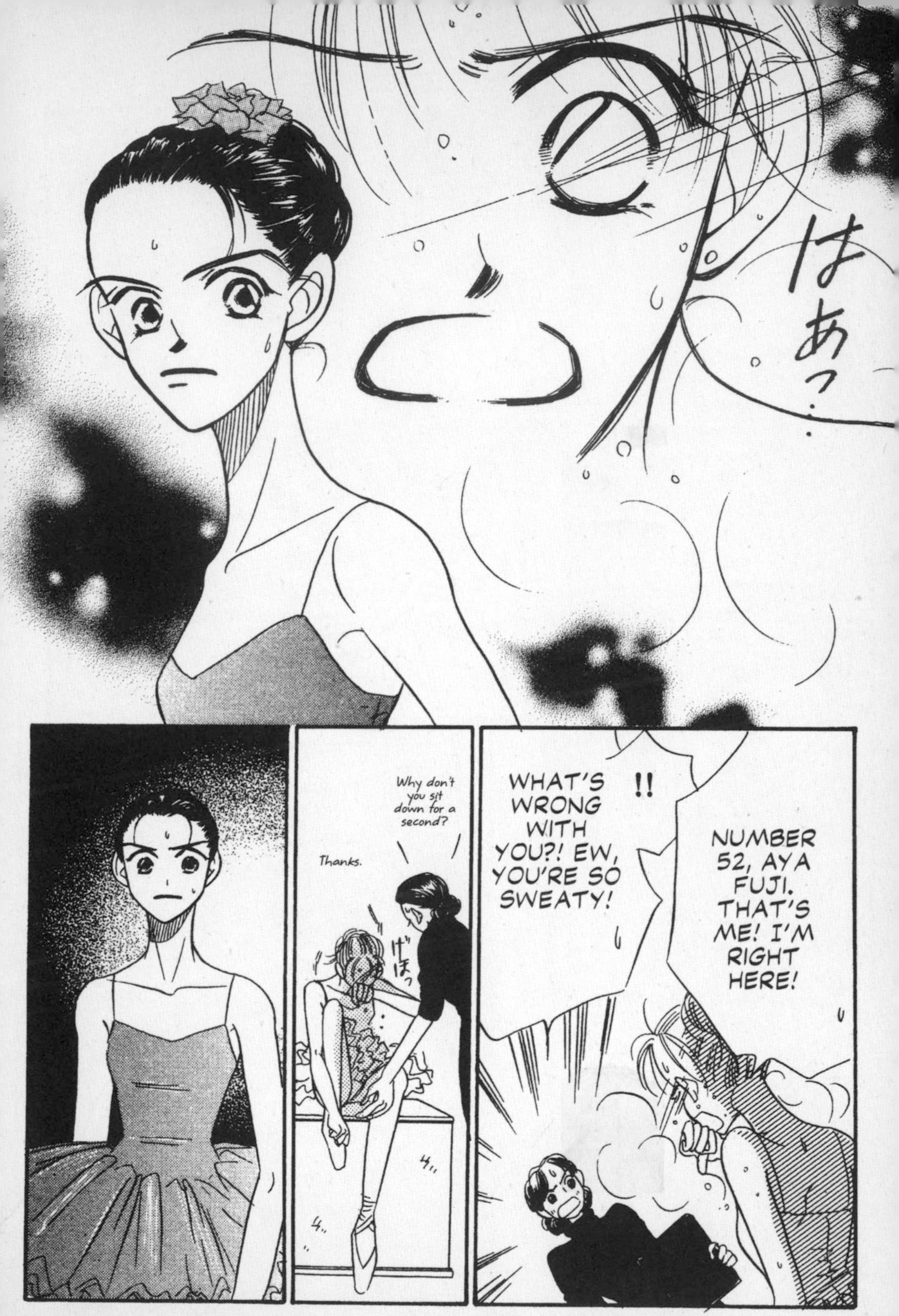
はあっ…
NUMBER 52, AYA FUJI. THAT'S ME! I'M RIGHT HERE!
!!
WHAT'S WRONG WITH YOU?! EW, YOU'RE SO SWEATY!
Why don't you sit down for a second?
Thanks.
げほっ

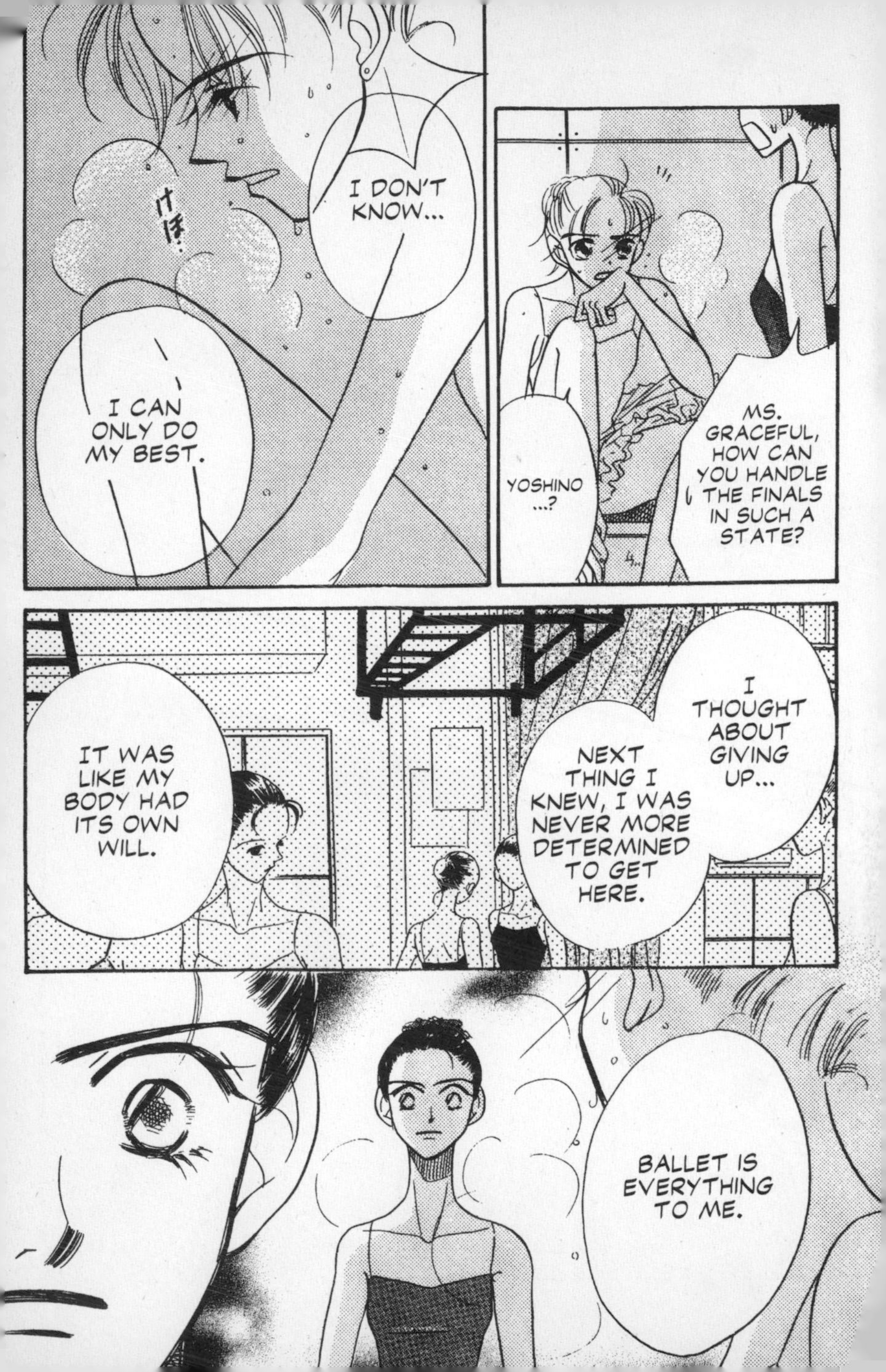
MS. GRACEFUL, HOW CAN YOU HANDLE THE FINALS IN SUCH A STATE?
YOSHINO ...?
I DON'T KNOW...
けほ…
I CAN ONLY DO MY BEST.
I THOUGHT ABOUT GIVING UP...
NEXT THING I KNEW, I WAS NEVER MORE DETERMINED TO GET HERE.
IT WAS LIKE MY BODY HAD ITS OWN WILL.
BALLET IS EVERYTHING TO ME.

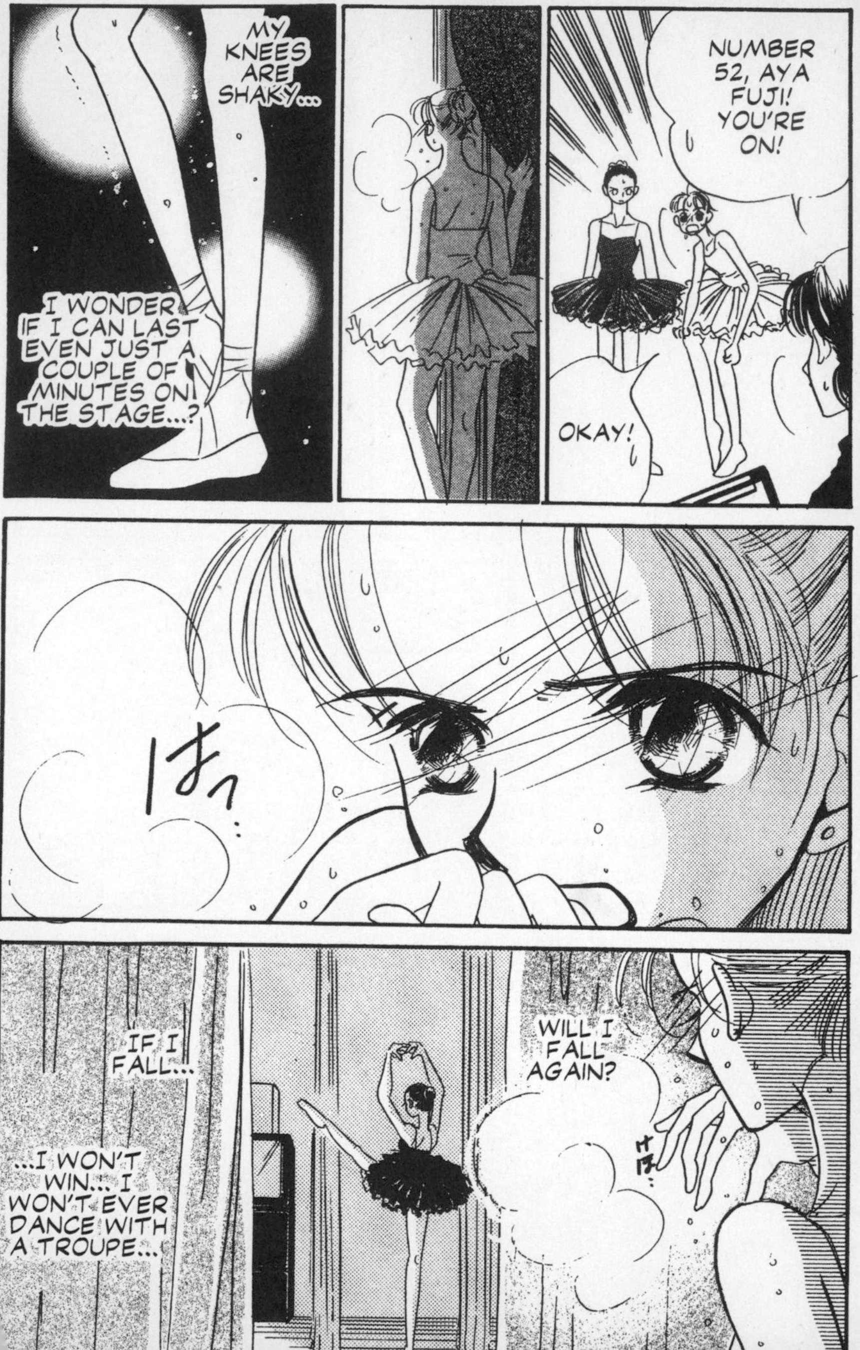
NUMBER 52, AYA FUJI! YOU'RE ON!
OKAY!
MY KNEES ARE SHAKY...
I WONDER IF I CAN LAST EVEN JUST A COUPLE OF MINUTES ON THE STAGE...?
はっ
WILL I FALL AGAIN?
けほ
IF I FALL...
...I WON'T WIN... I WON'T EVER DANCE WITH A TROUPE...

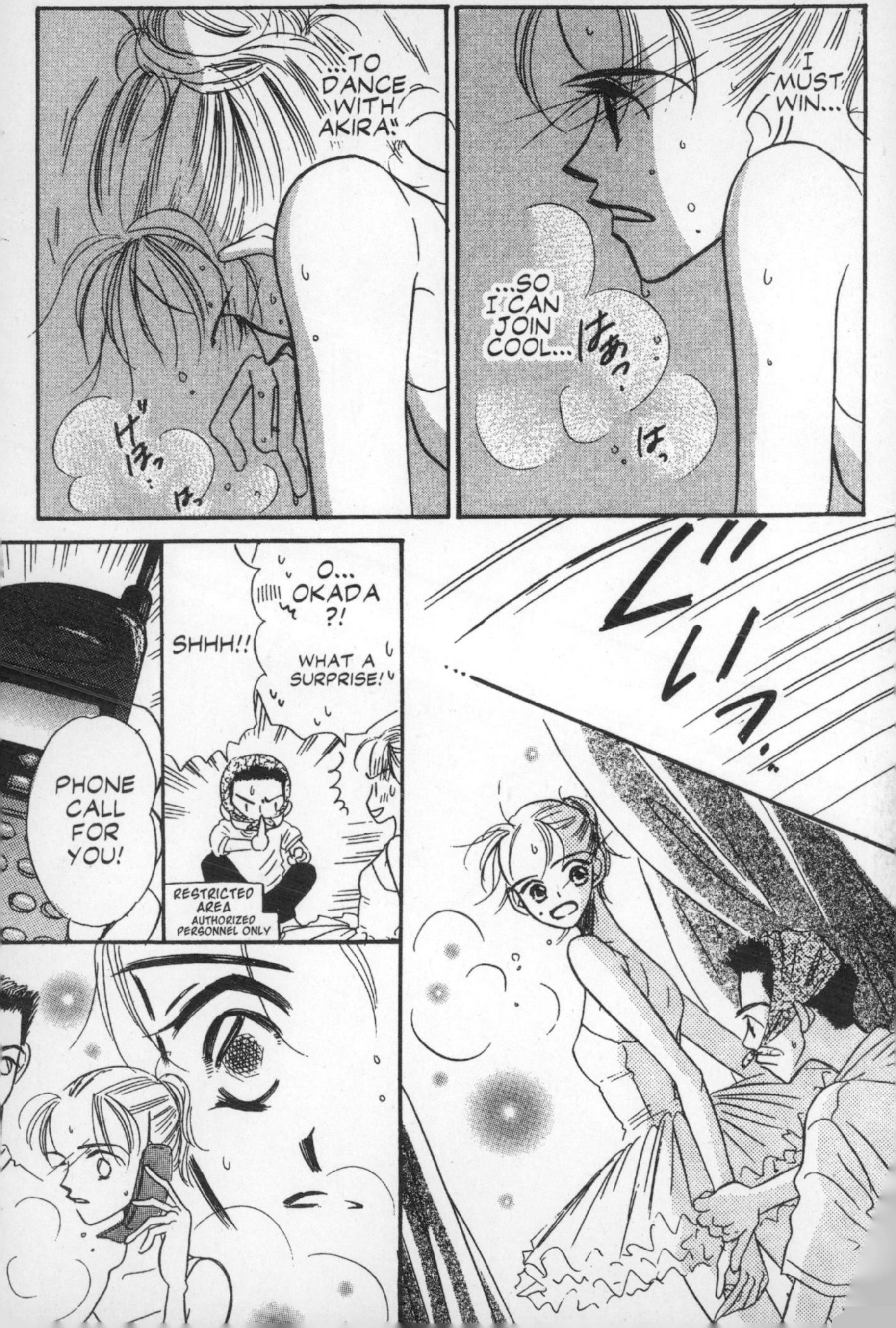
I MUST WIN...
...SO I CAN JOIN COOL...
はあっ
はっ
...TO DANCE WITH AKIRA!!
ゲほっ
はっ
ぐいっ
...
O... OKADA?!
WHAT A SURPRISE!
SHHH!!
RESTRICTED AREA AUTHORIZED PERSONNEL ONLY
PHONE CALL FOR YOU!

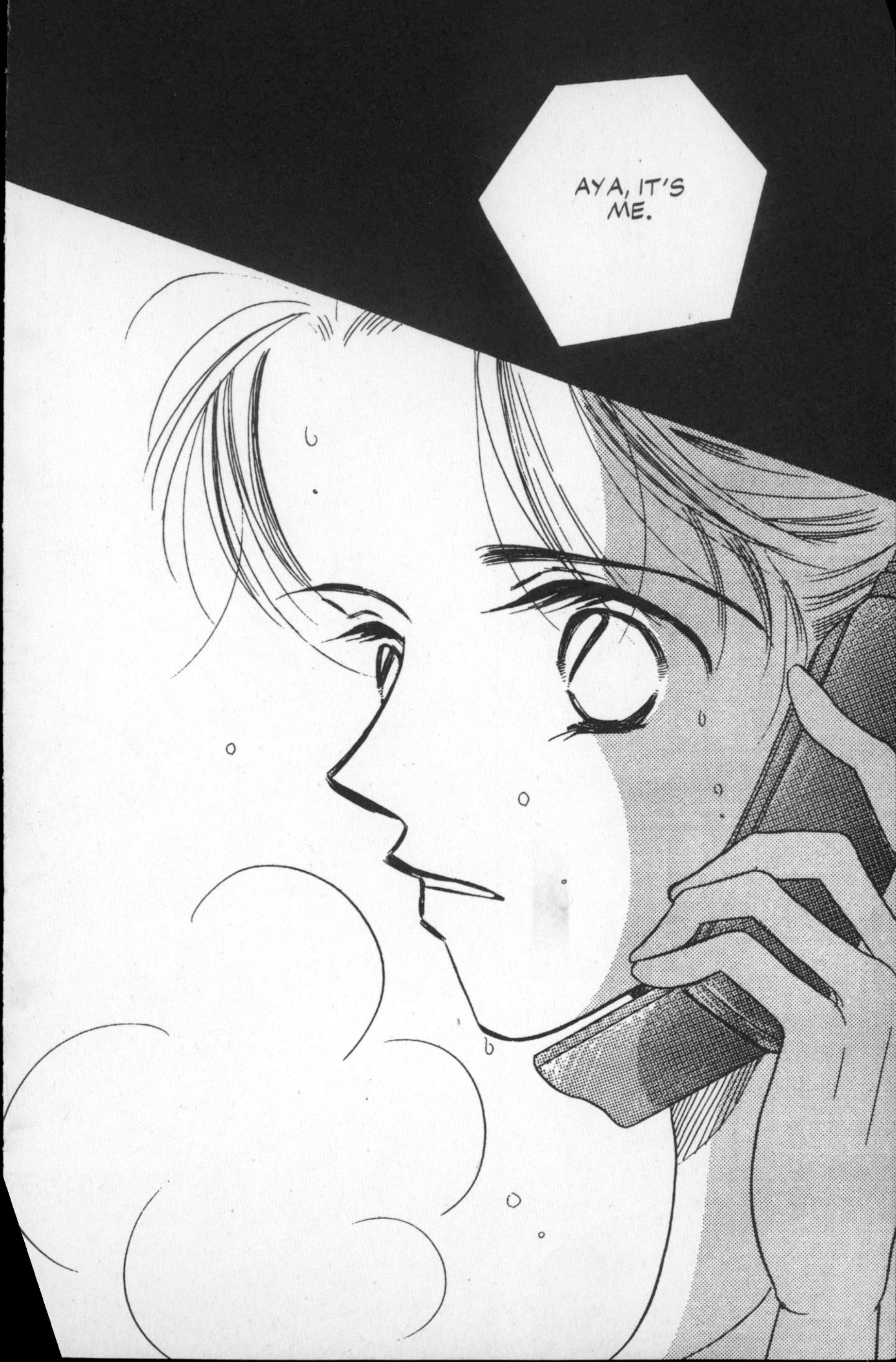
AYA, IT'S ME.

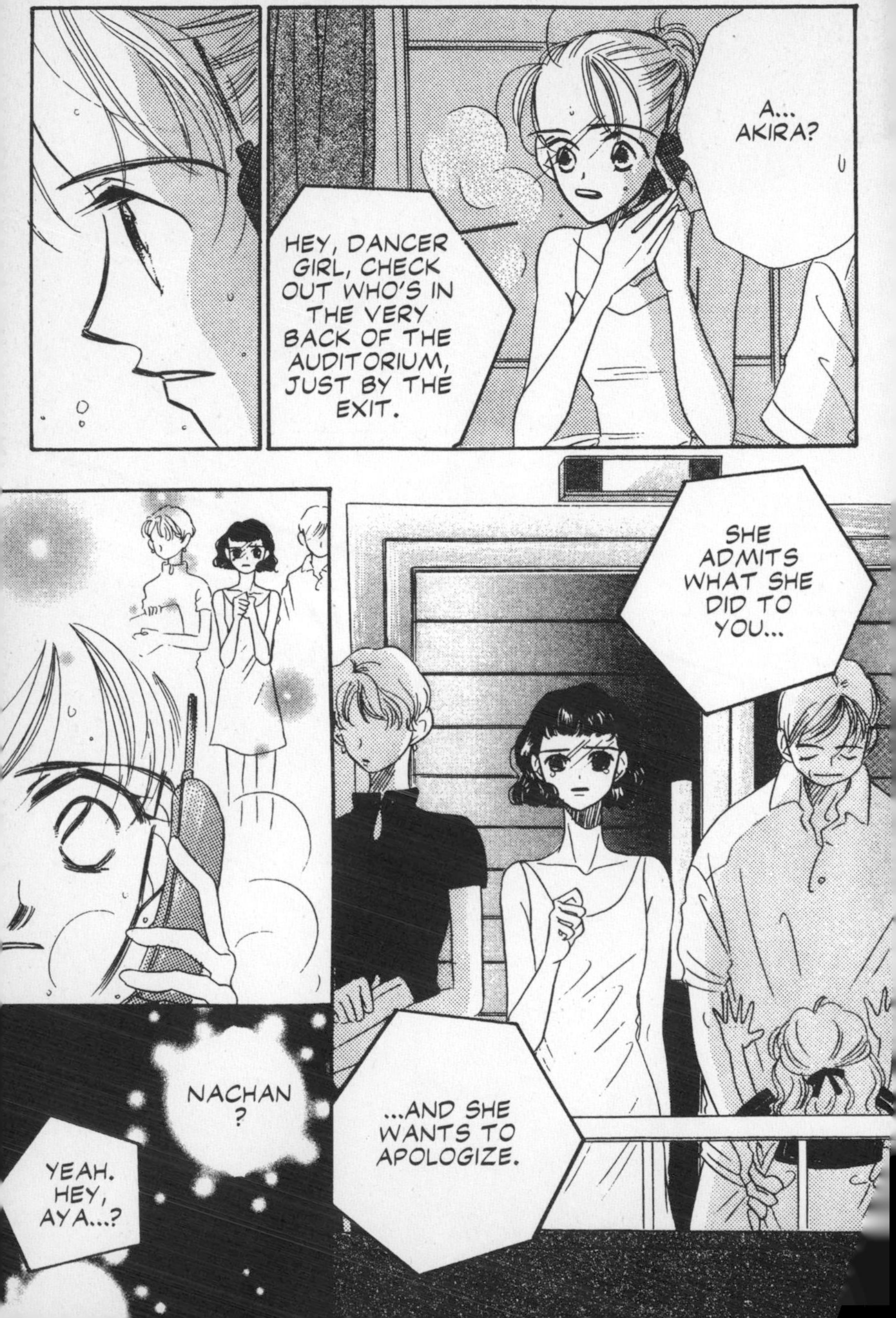
A... AKIRA?
HEY, DANCER GIRL, CHECK OUT WHO'S IN THE VERY BACK OF THE AUDITORIUM, JUST BY THE EXIT.
SHE ADMITS WHAT SHE DID TO YOU...
...AND SHE WANTS TO APOLOGIZE.
NACHAN?
YEAH. HEY, AYA...?

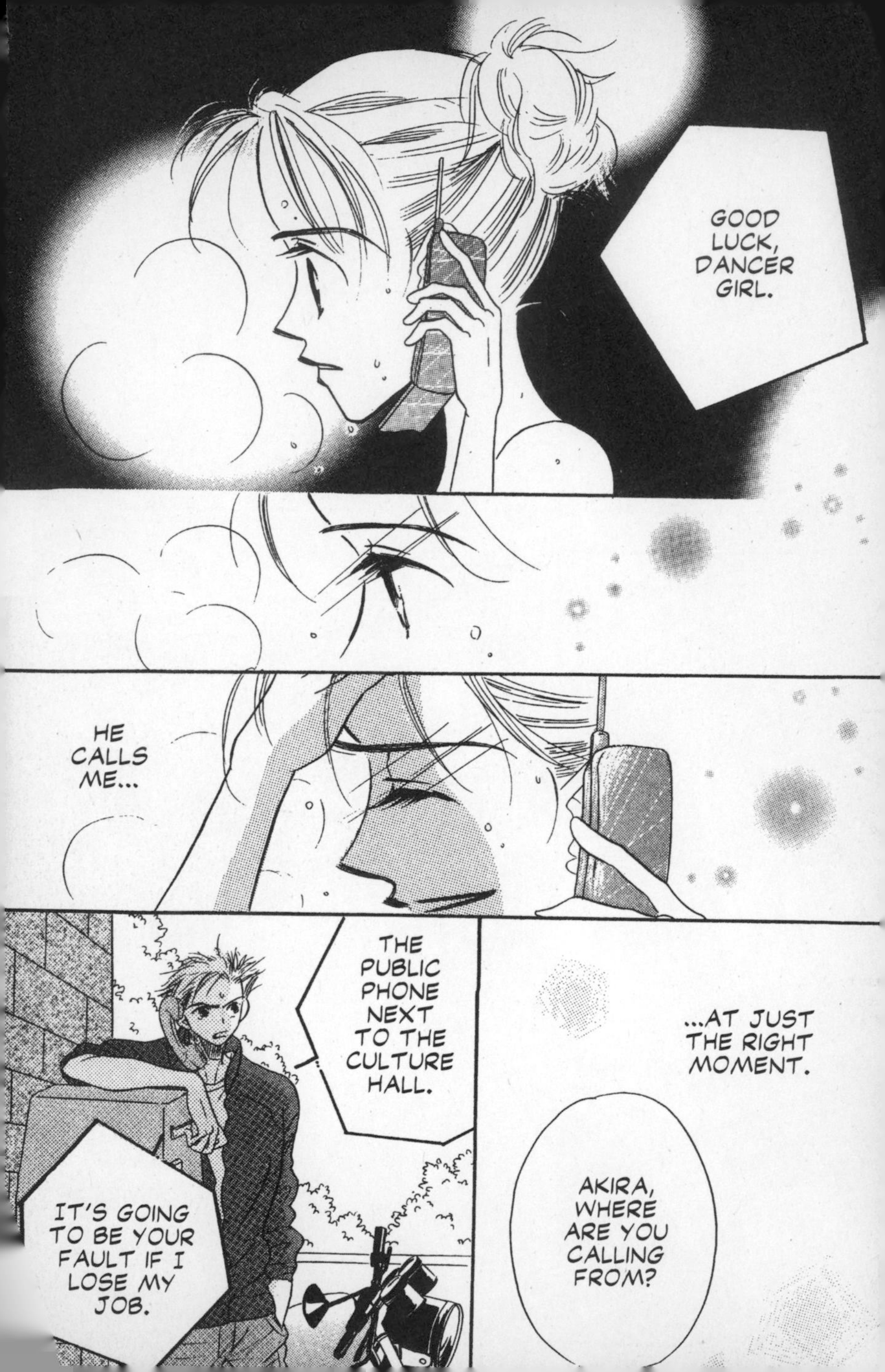
GOOD LUCK, DANCER GIRL.
HE CALLS ME...
...AT JUST THE RIGHT MOMENT.
AKIRA, WHERE ARE YOU CALLING FROM?
THE PUBLIC PHONE NEXT TO THE CULTURE HALL.
IT'S GOING TO BE YOUR FAULT IF I LOSE MY JOB.

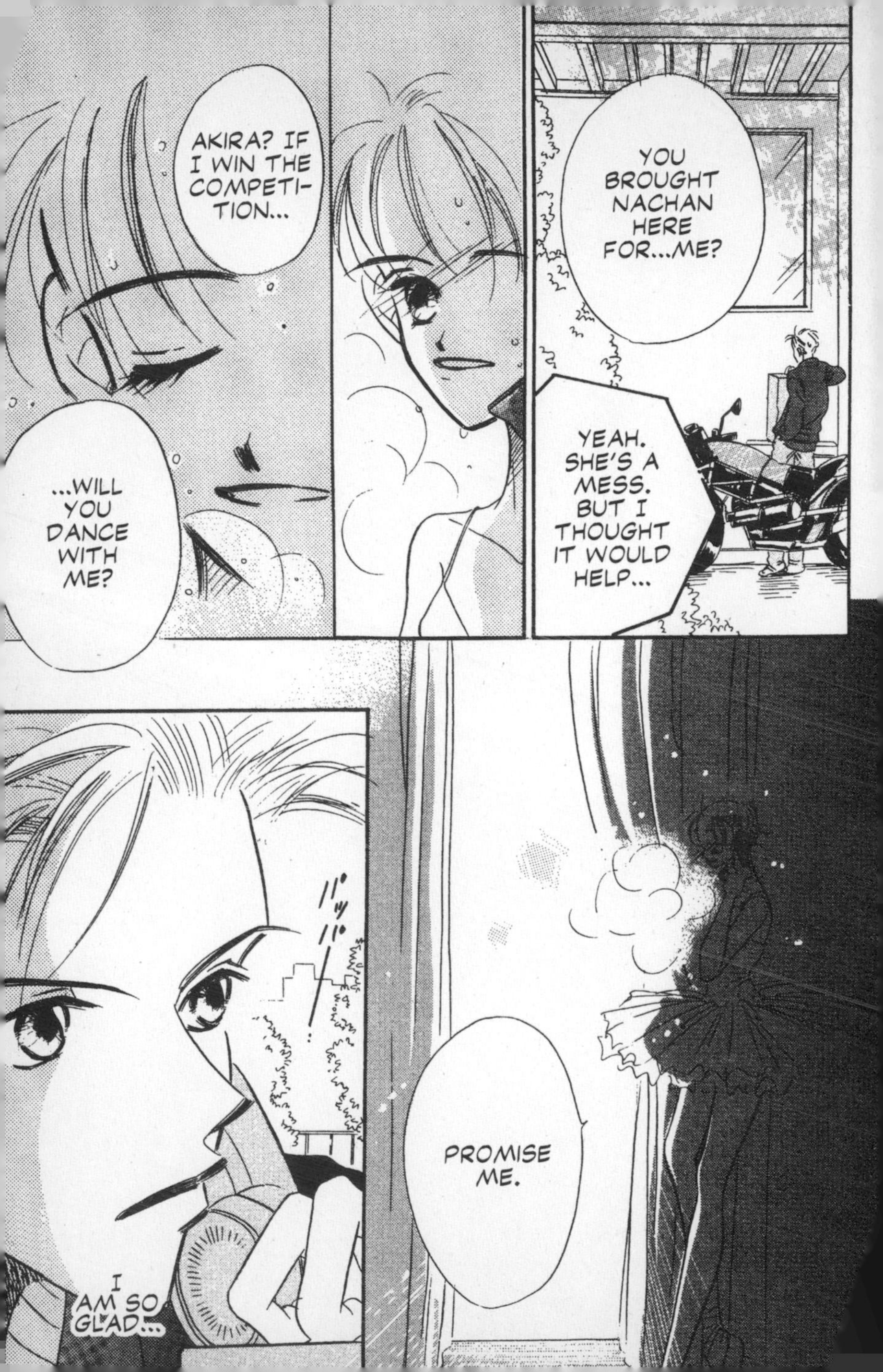
YOU BROUGHT NACHAN HERE FOR...ME?
YEAH. SHE'S A MESS. BUT I THOUGHT IT WOULD HELP...
AKIRA? IF I WIN THE COMPETI-TION...
...WILL YOU DANCE WITH ME?
PROMISE ME.
I AM SO GLAD...

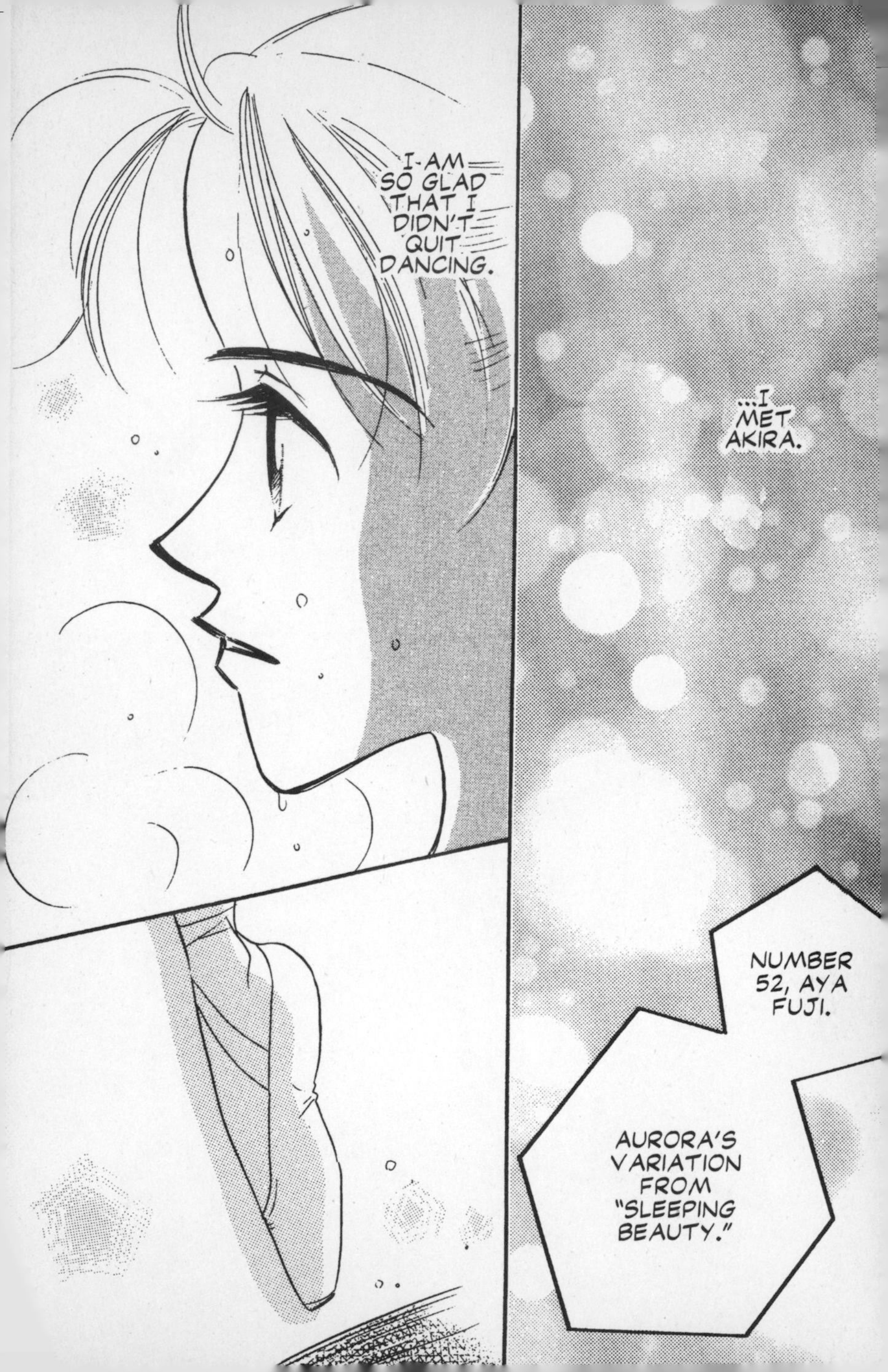
...I MET AKIRA.
NUMBER 52, AYA FUJI.
AURORA'S VARIATION FROM "SLEEPING BEAUTY."
I AM SO GLAD THAT I DIDN'T QUIT DANCING.

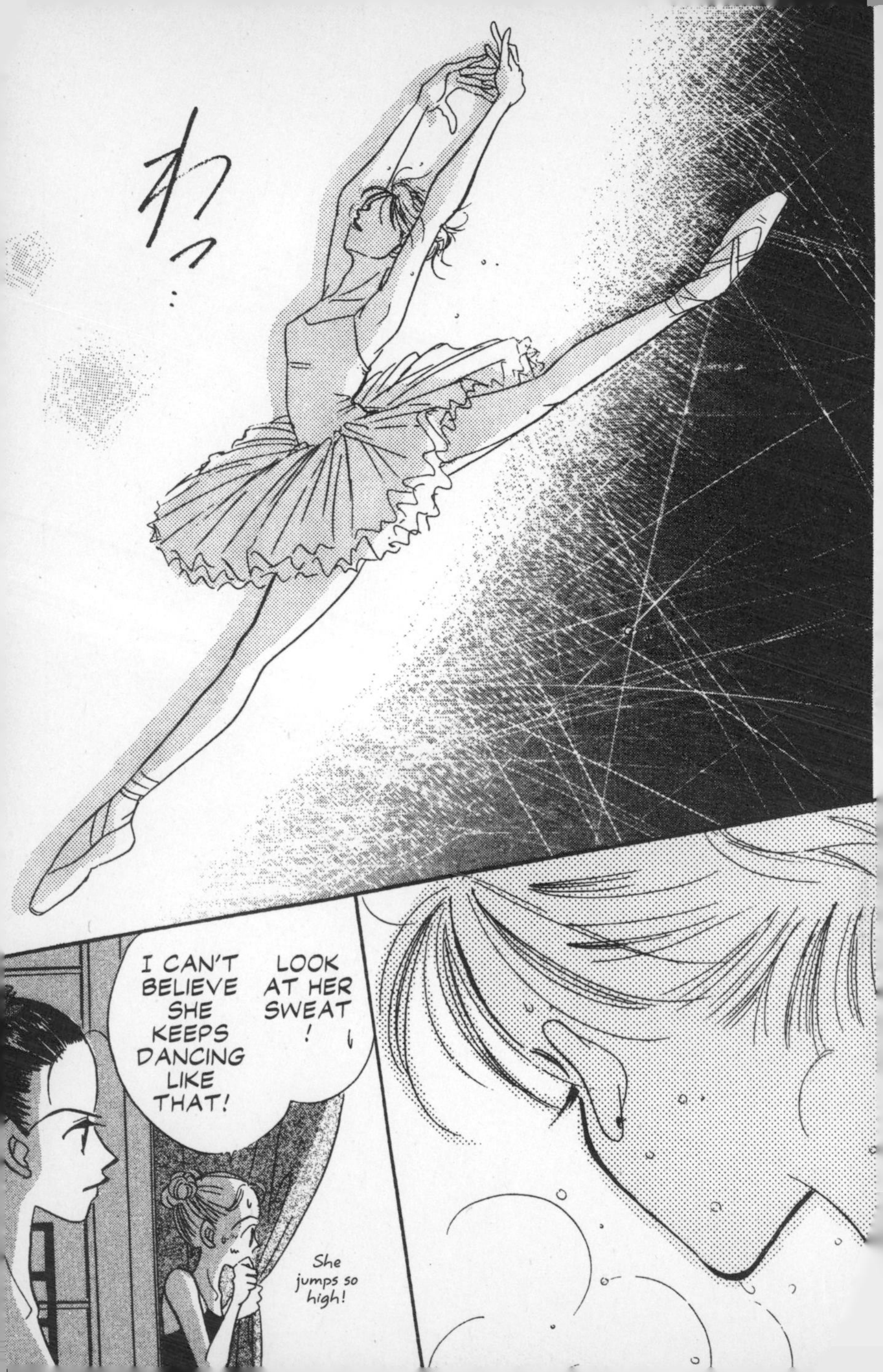
わっ
LOOK AT HER SWEAT!
I CAN'T BELIEVE SHE KEEPS DANCING LIKE THAT!
She jumps so high!

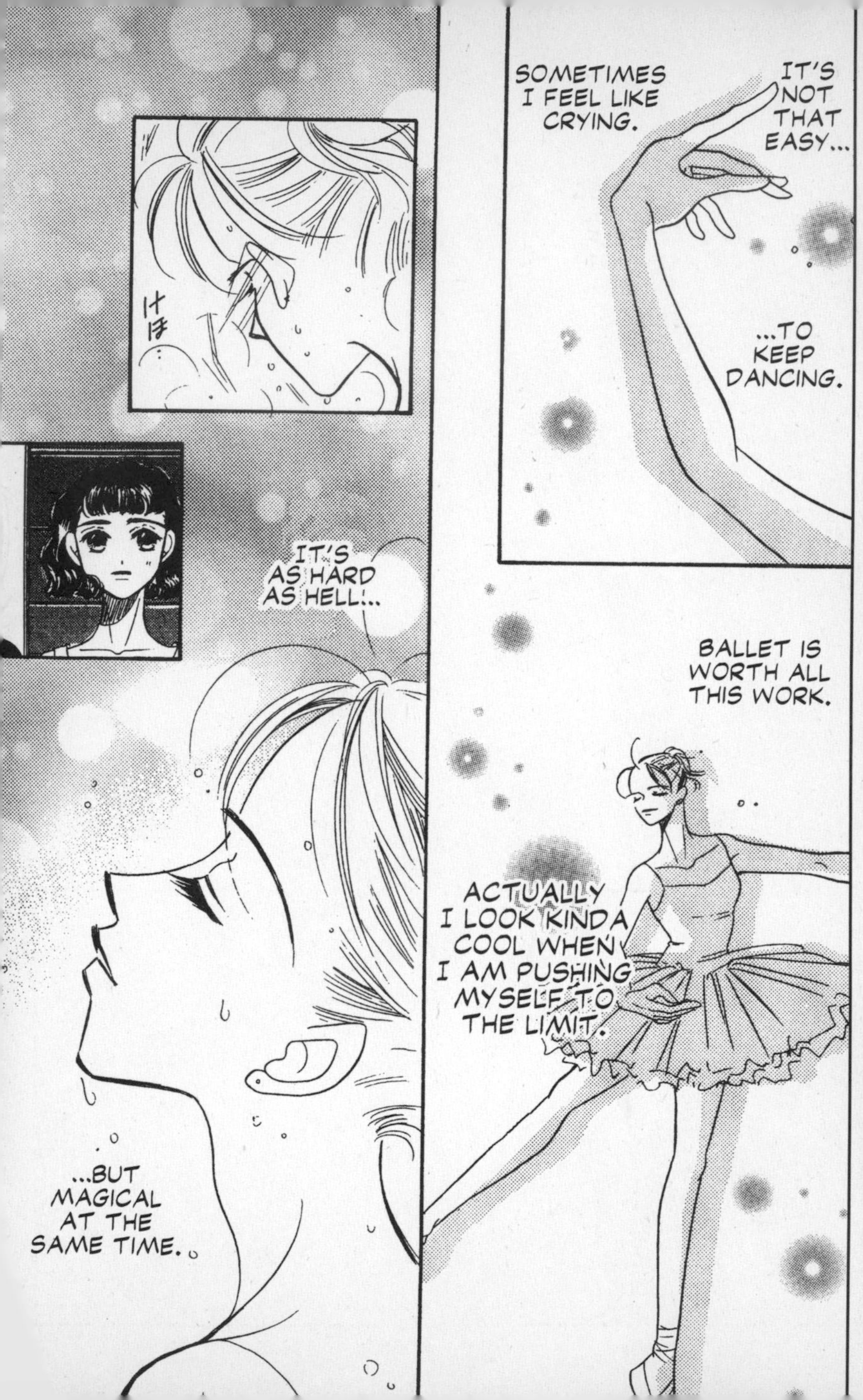
IT'S NOT THAT EASY...
SOMETIMES I FEEL LIKE CRYING.
...TO KEEP DANCING.
BALLET IS WORTH ALL THIS WORK.
ACTUALLY I LOOK KINDA COOL WHEN I AM PUSHING MYSELF TO THE LIMIT.
けほ…
IT'S AS HARD AS HELL!...
...BUT MAGICAL AT THE SAME TIME.

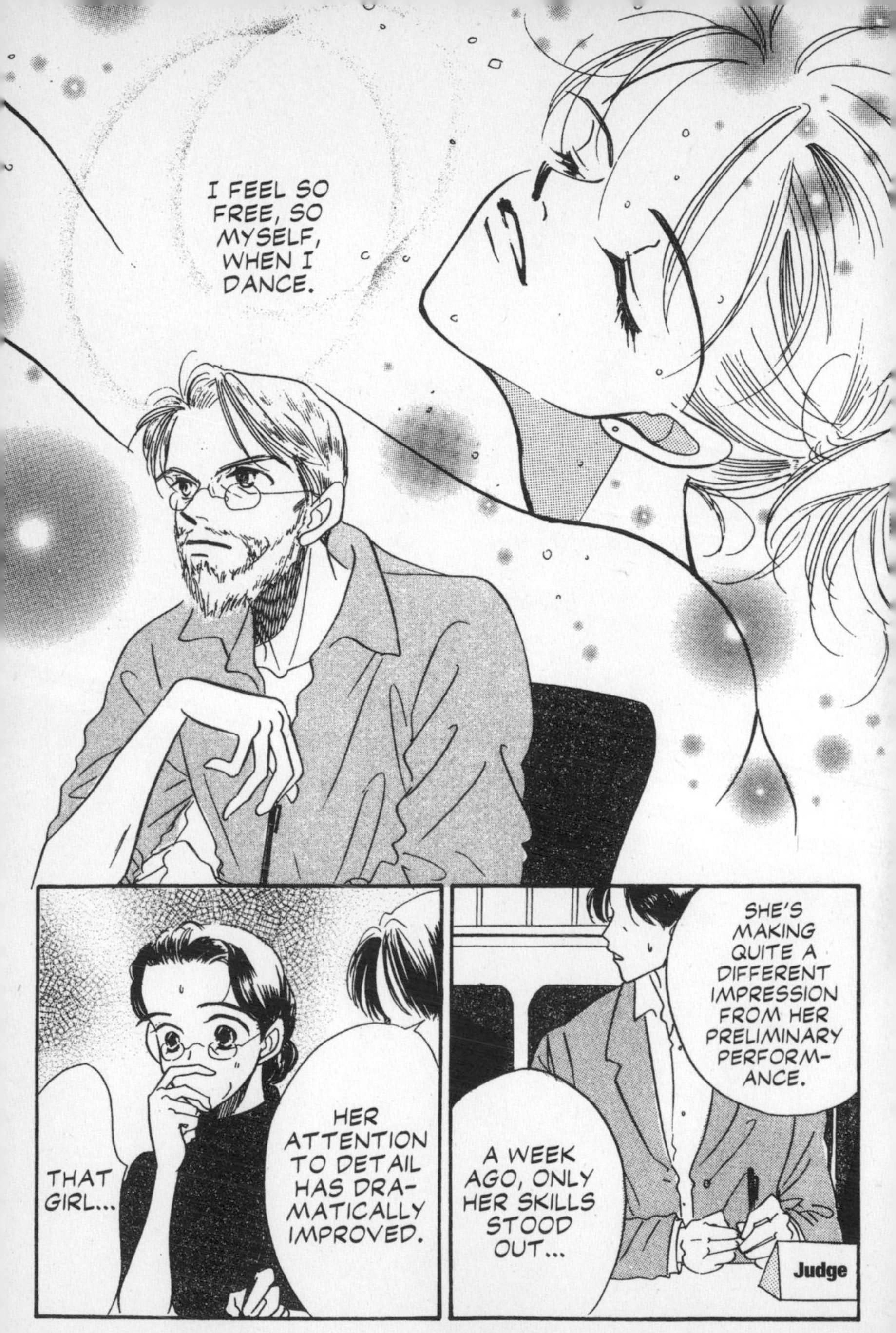
I FEEL SO FREE, SO MYSELF, WHEN I DANCE.
SHE'S MAKING QUITE A DIFFERENT IMPRESSION FROM HER PRELIMINARY PERFORM-ANCE.
A WEEK AGO, ONLY HER SKILLS STOOD OUT...
Judge
HER ATTENTION TO DETAIL HAS DRA-MATICALLY IMPROVED.
THAT GIRL...

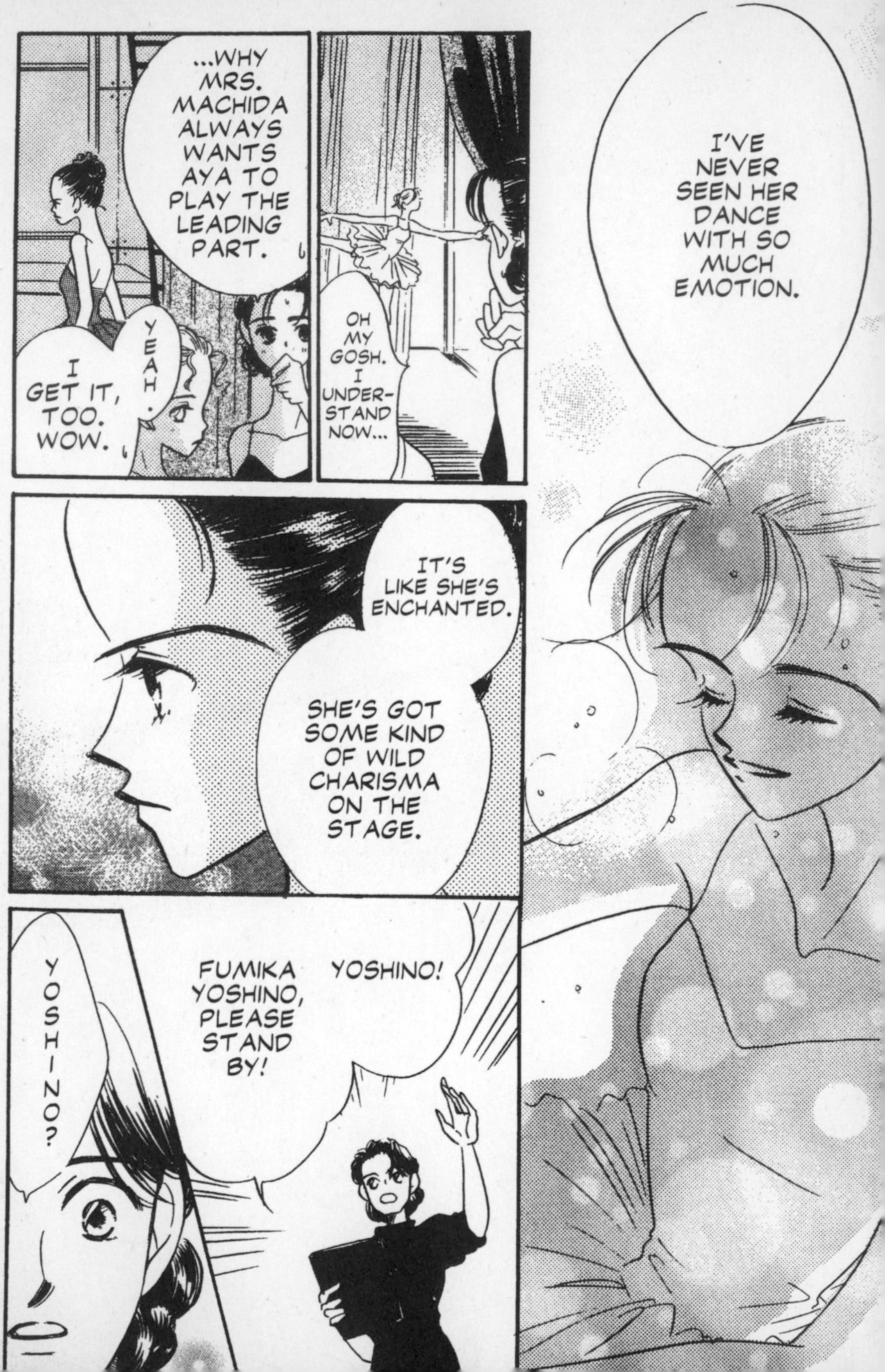
I'VE NEVER SEEN HER DANCE WITH SO MUCH EMOTION.
OH MY GOSH. I UNDERSTAND NOW...
...WHY MRS. MACHIDA ALWAYS WANTS AYA TO PLAY THE LEADING PART.
YEAH.
I GET IT, TOO. WOW.
IT'S LIKE SHE'S ENCHANTED.
SHE'S GOT SOME KIND OF WILD CHARISMA ON THE STAGE.
FUMIKA YOSHINO, PLEASE STAND BY! YOSHINO!
YOSHINO?

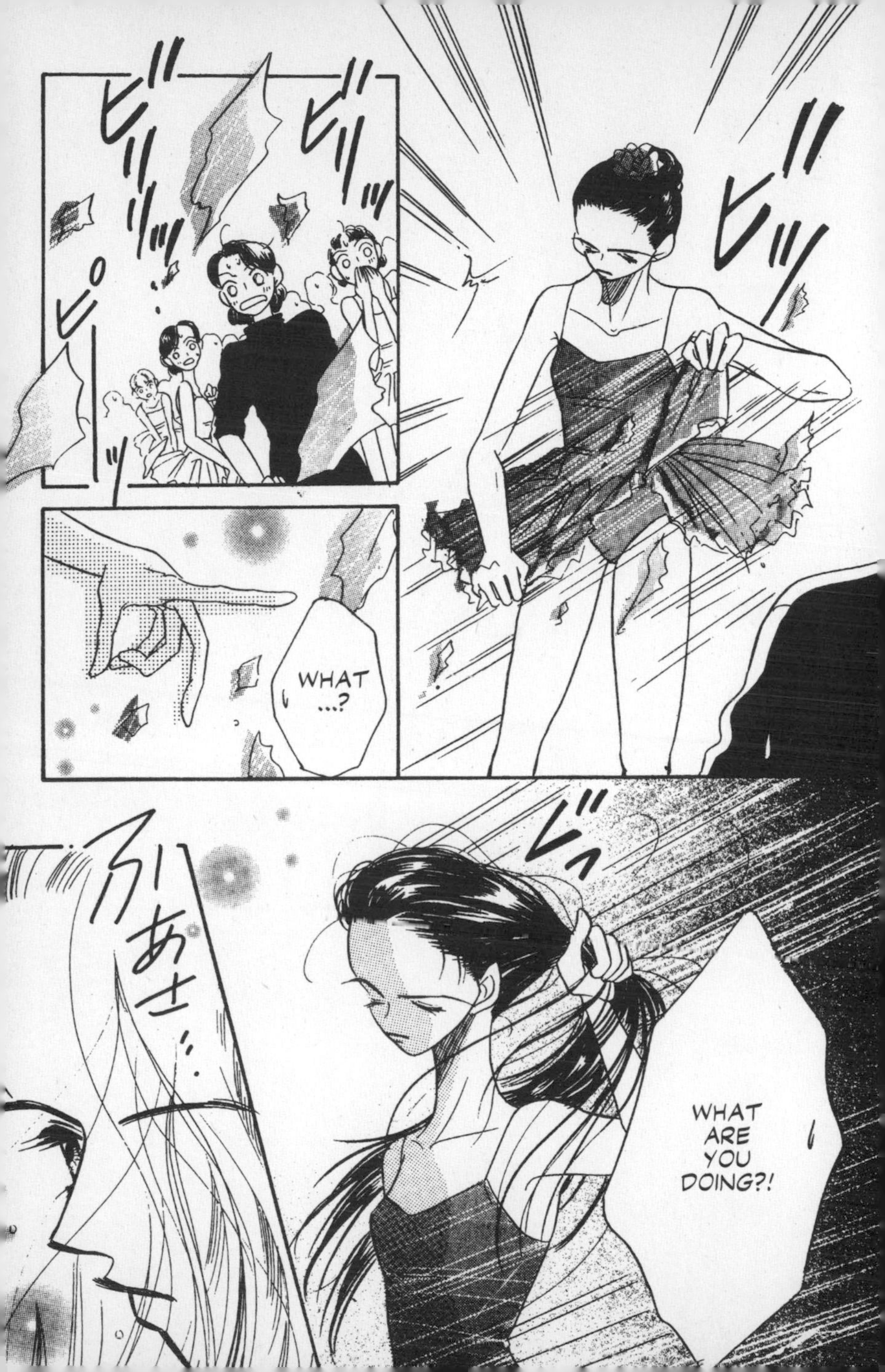
ビッ
WHAT ...?
ぐっ
ふぁさ…
WHAT ARE YOU DOING?!

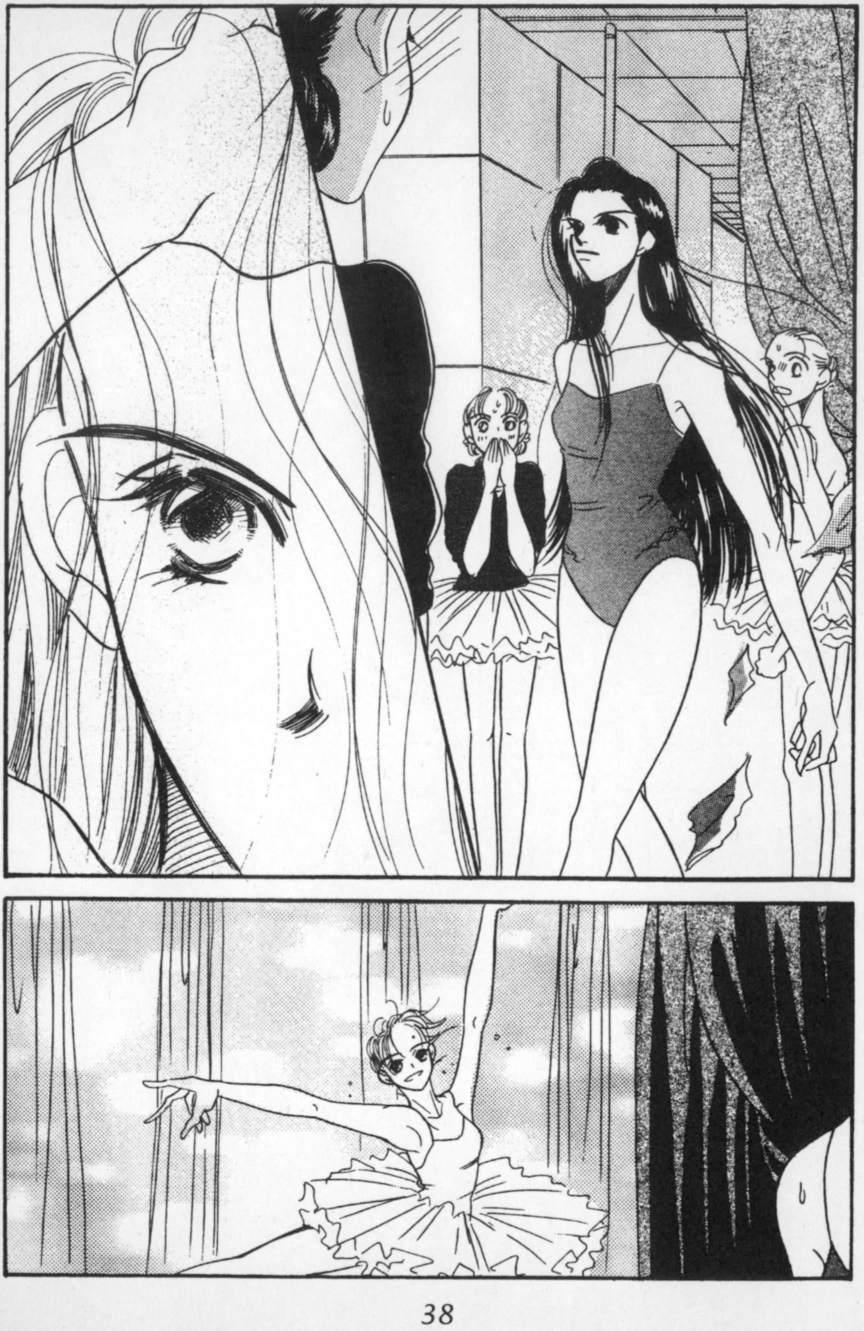

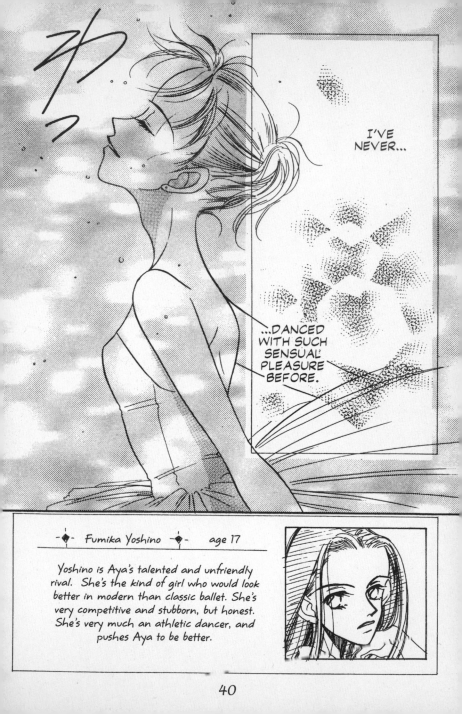

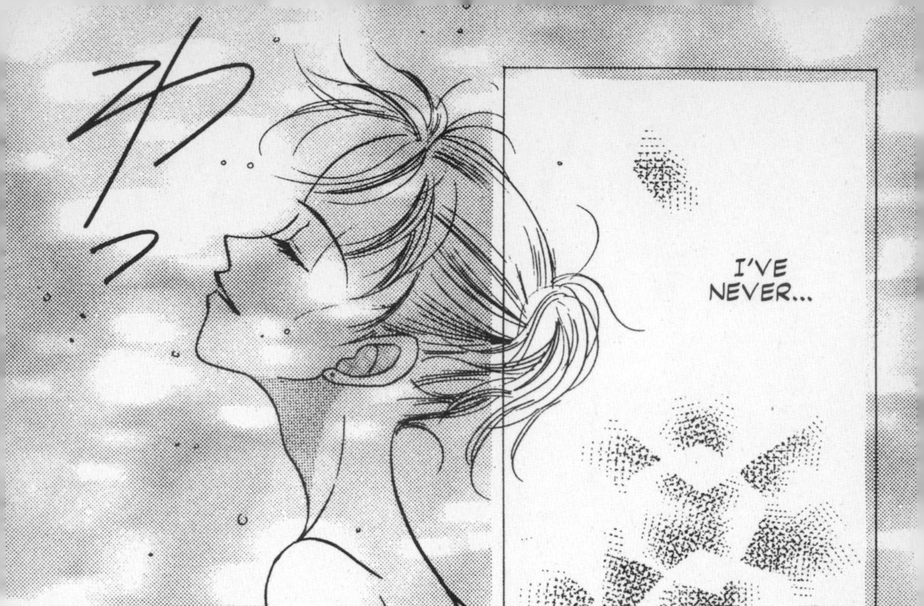
I'VE NEVER...
...DANCED WITH SUCH SENSUAL PLEASURE BEFORE.

-◆- Fumika Yoshino -◆- age 17

Yoshino is Aya's talented and unfriendly rival. She's the kind of girl who would look better in modern than classic ballet. She's very competitive and stubborn, but honest. She's very much an athletic dancer, and pushes Aya to be better.

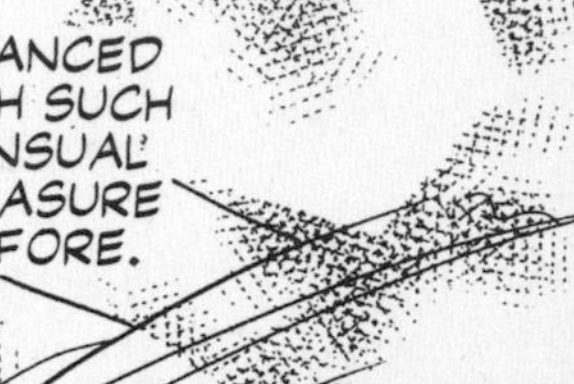

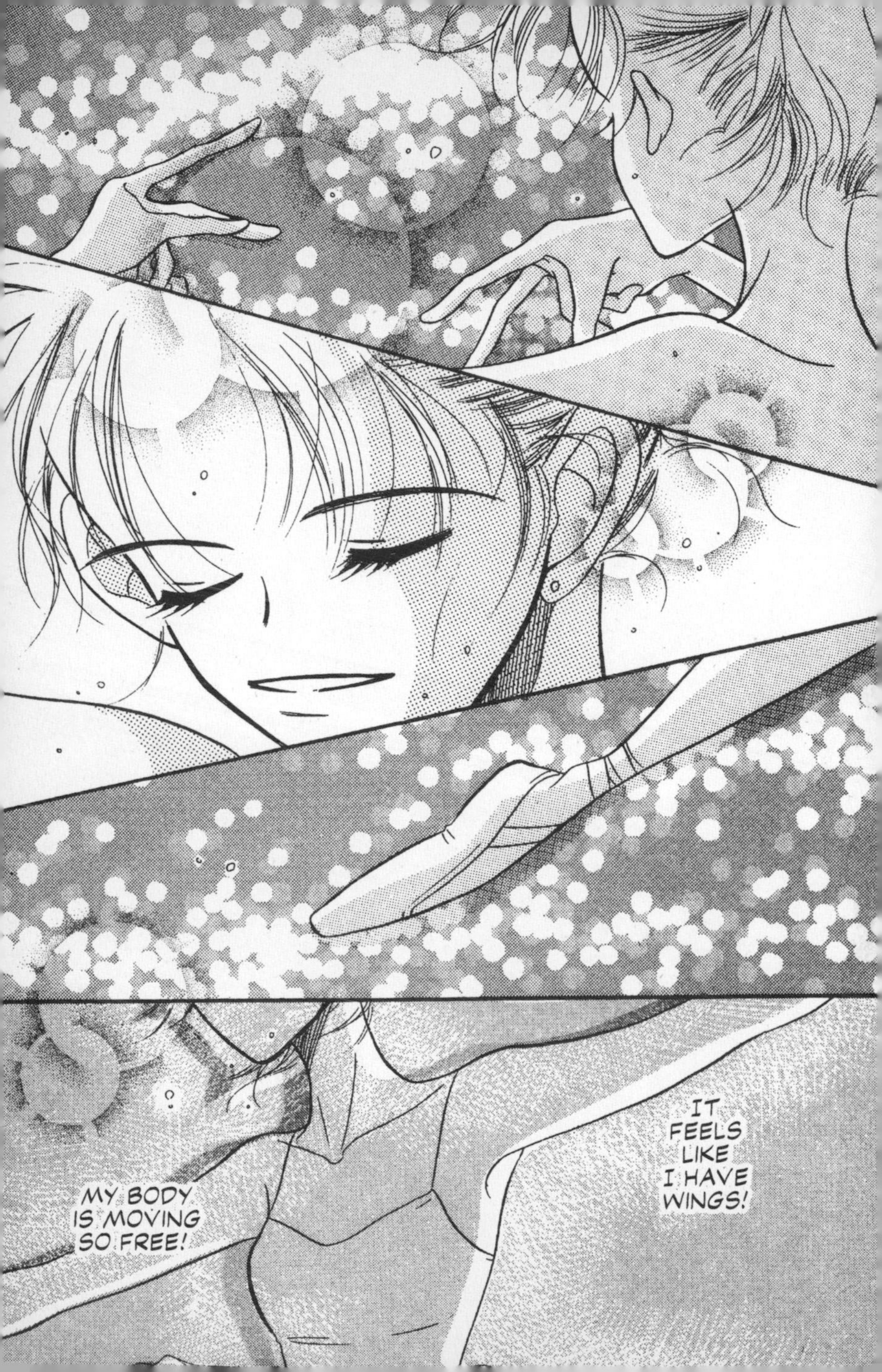
IT FEELS LIKE I HAVE WINGS!
MY BODY IS MOVING SO FREE!

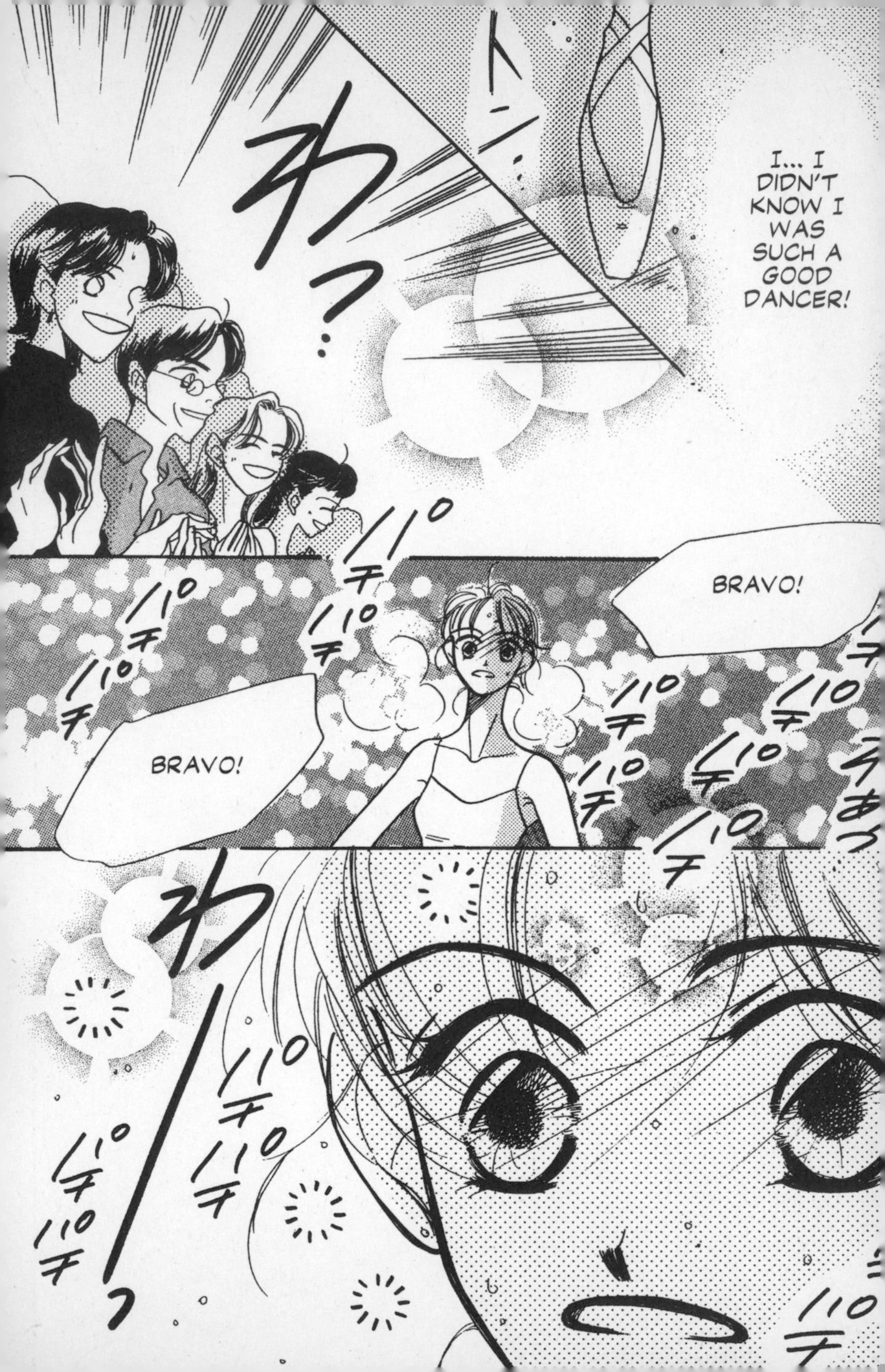
I... I DIDN'T KNOW I WAS SUCH A GOOD DANCER!
わっ…
パチパチ
BRAVO!
BRAVO!
わっ
パチパチ

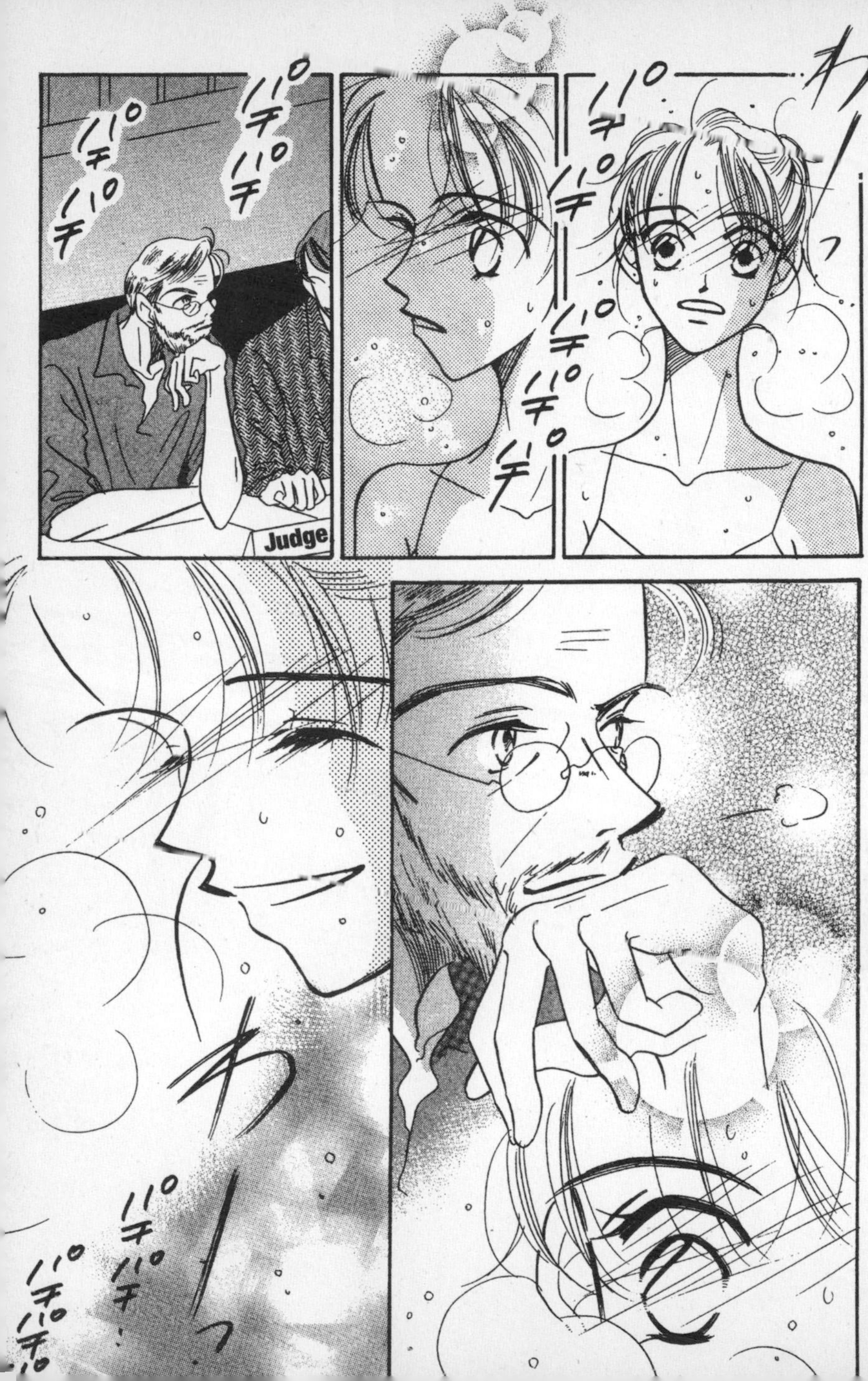
わーっ
パ――チパチ
パチパチパチ
パチパチパチ
パチパチ
Judge
パチパチパチ
わーっ
パチパチ！
パチパチパチ

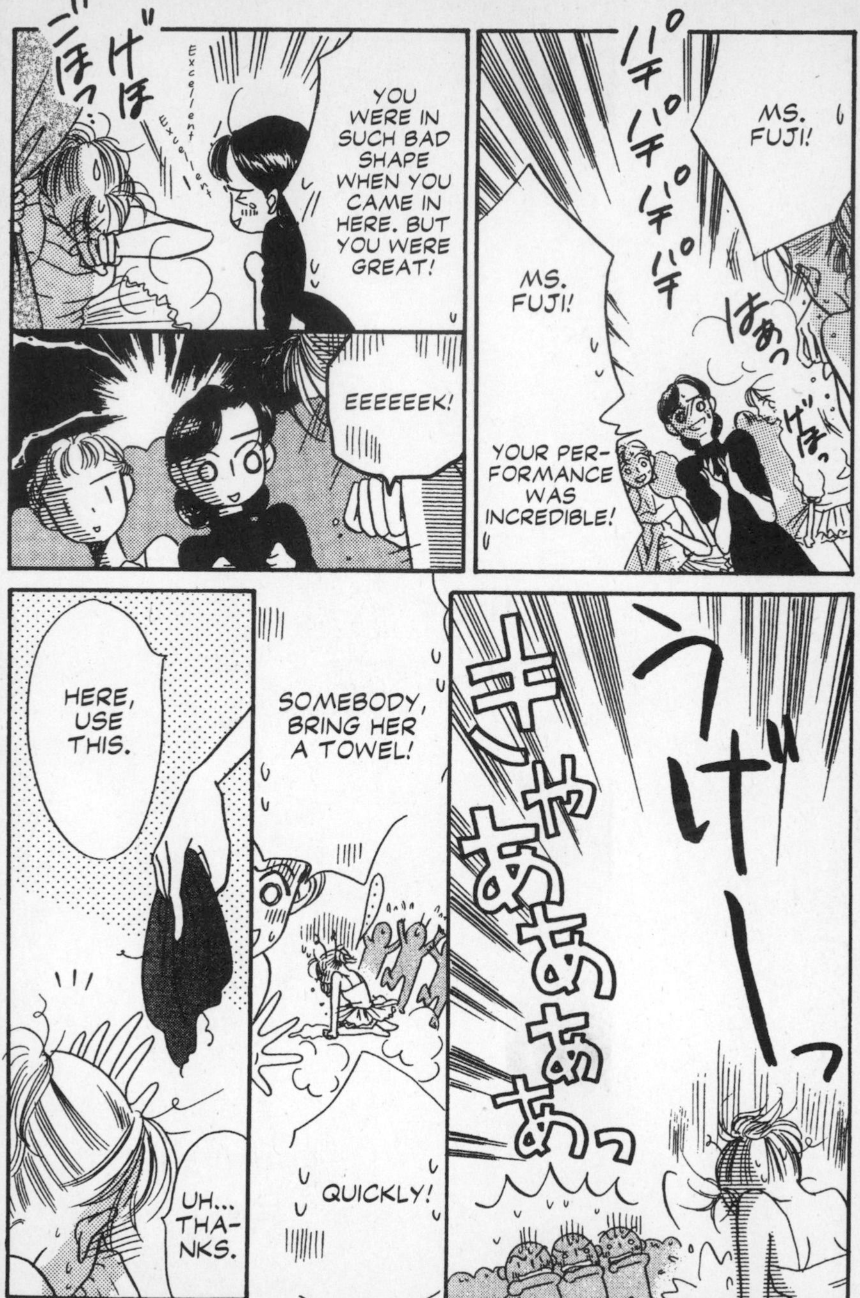
パチパチパチパチ
MS. FUJI!
MS. FUJI!
はあっ
げほっ
YOUR PER-FORMANCE WAS INCREDIBLE!
げほ ごほっ
Excellent Excellent
YOU WERE IN SUCH BAD SHAPE WHEN YOU CAME IN HERE. BUT YOU WERE GREAT!
EEEEEEK!
うげーっ
キャあああっ
SOMEBODY, BRING HER A TOWEL!
QUICKLY!
HERE, USE THIS.
UH... THA-NKS.

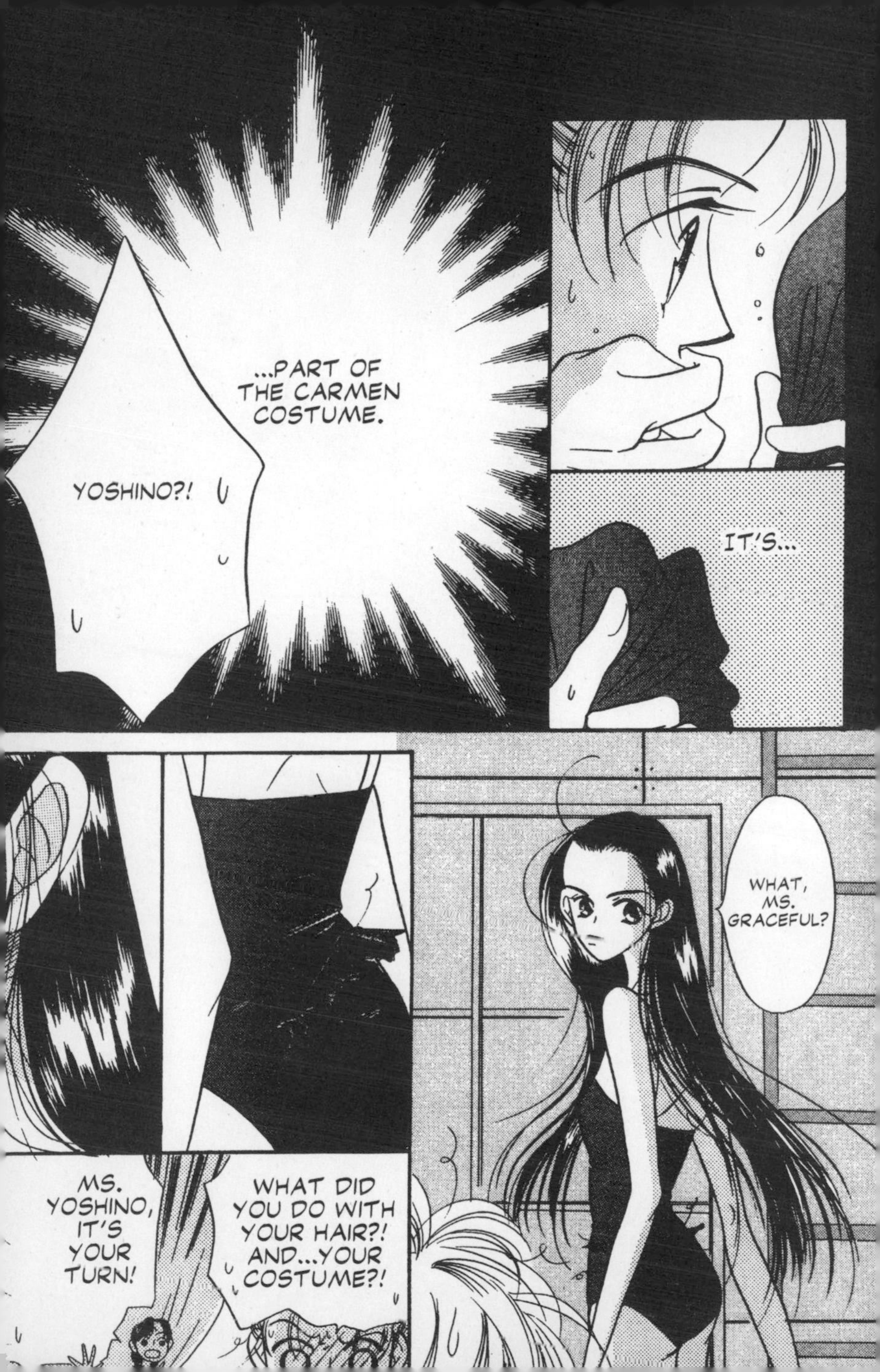
IT'S...
...PART OF THE CARMEN COSTUME.
YOSHINO?!
WHAT, MS. GRACEFUL?
WHAT DID YOU DO WITH YOUR HAIR?! AND...YOUR COSTUME?!
MS. YOSHINO, IT'S YOUR TURN!

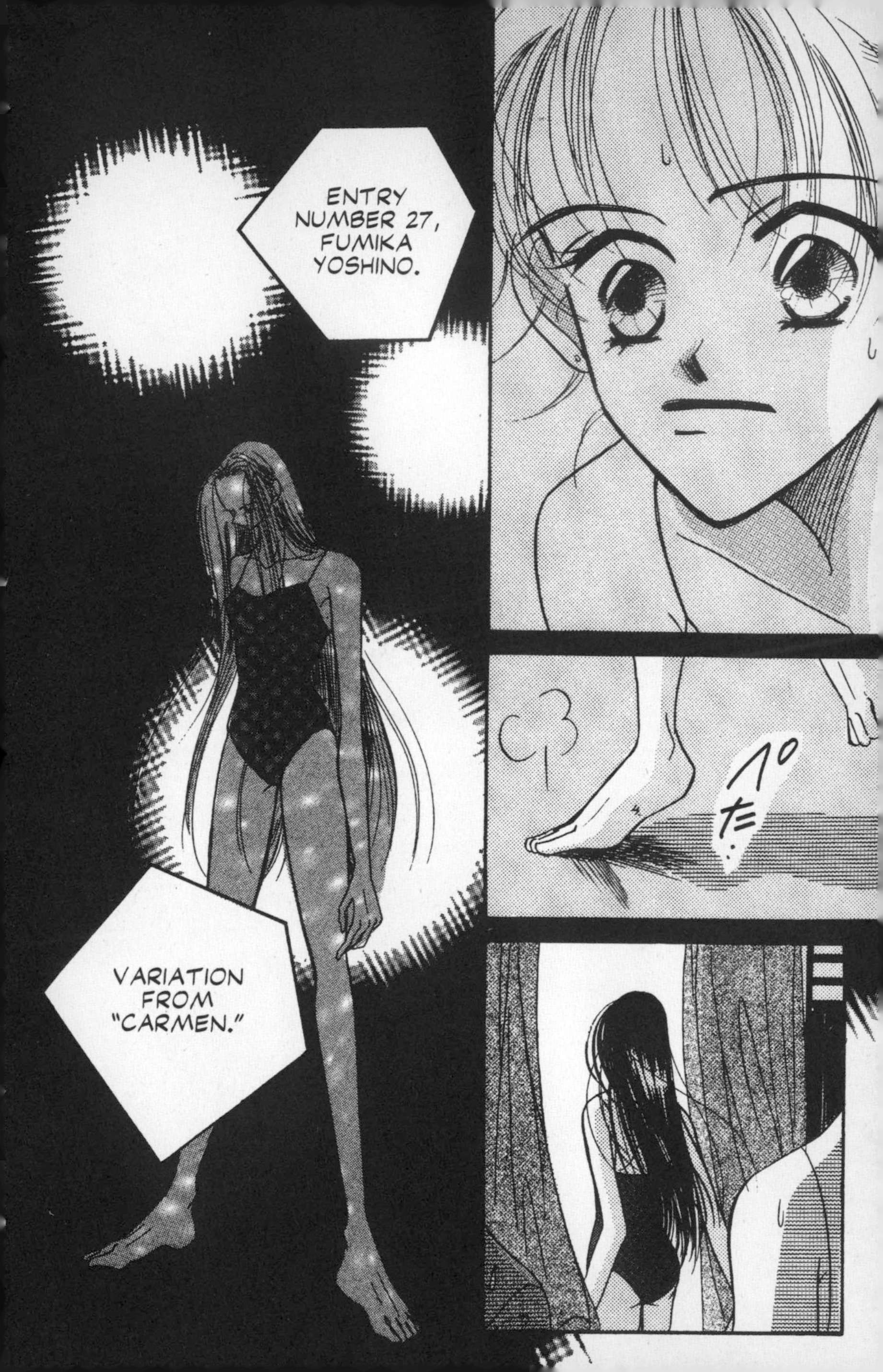
ぺた
ENTRY NUMBER 27, FUMIKA YOSHINO.
VARIATION FROM "CARMEN."

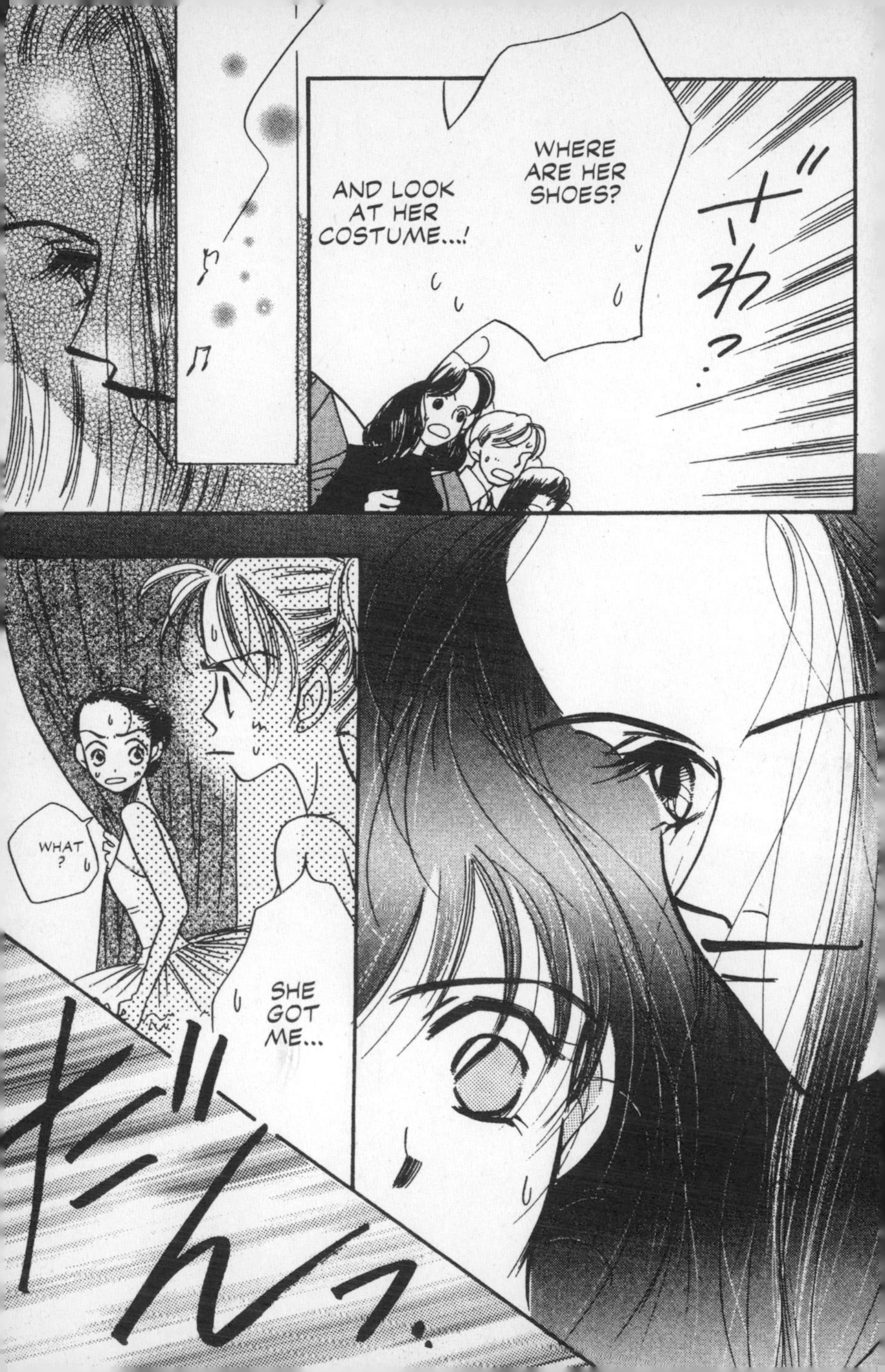
WHERE ARE HER SHOES?
AND LOOK AT HER COSTUME...!
ザわっ
WHAT ?
SHE GOT ME...
ギんっ

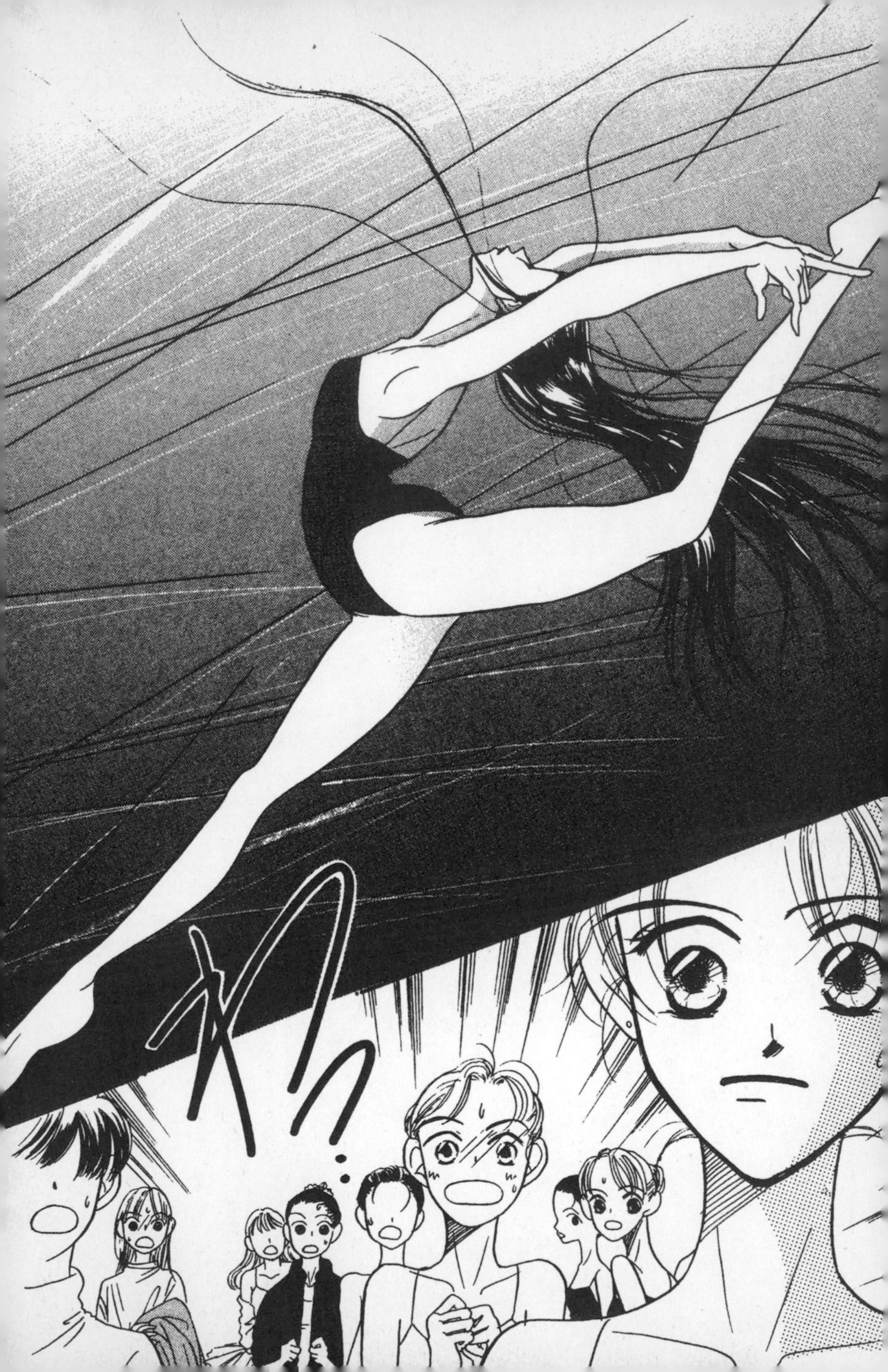

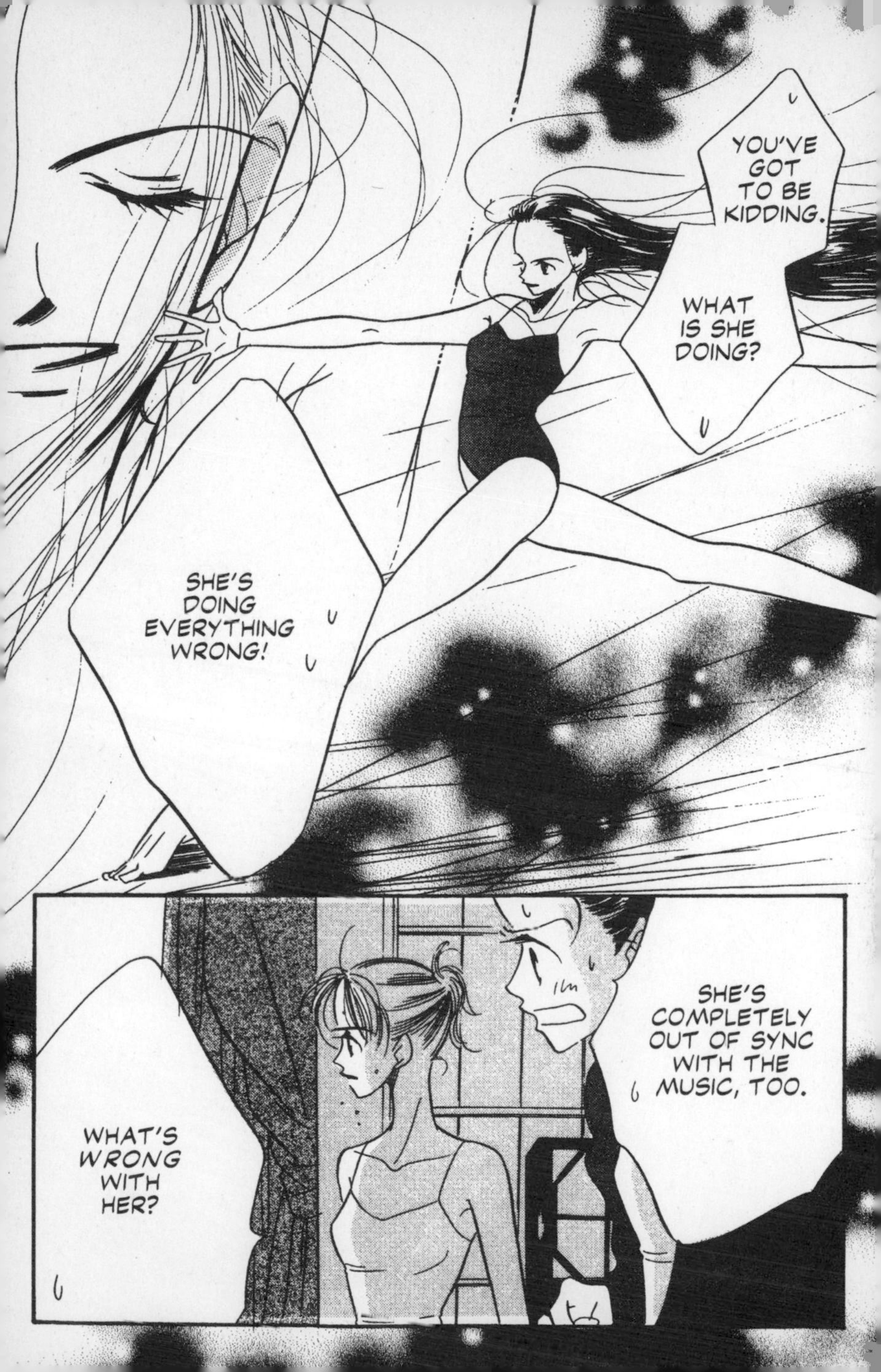
YOU'VE GOT TO BE KIDDING.
WHAT IS SHE DOING?
SHE'S DOING EVERYTHING WRONG!
SHE'S COMPLETELY OUT OF SYNC WITH THE MUSIC, TOO.
WHAT'S WRONG WITH HER?

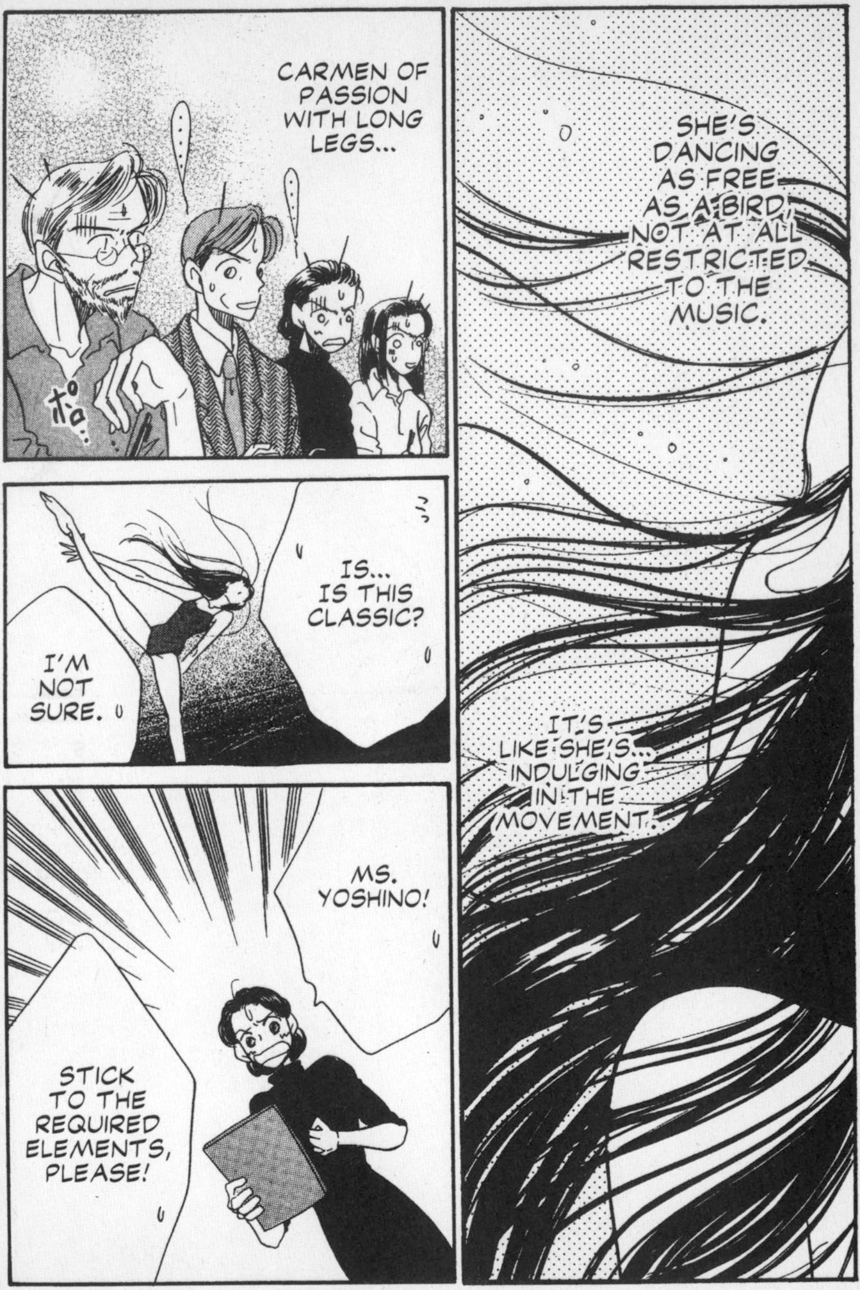
SHE'S DANCING AS FREE AS A BIRD, NOT AT ALL RESTRICTED TO THE MUSIC.
IT'S LIKE SHE'S... INDULGING IN THE MOVEMENT.
CARMEN OF PASSION WITH LONG LEGS...
ポロ...
IS... IS THIS CLASSIC?
I'M NOT SURE.
MS. YOSHINO!
STICK TO THE REQUIRED ELEMENTS, PLEASE!

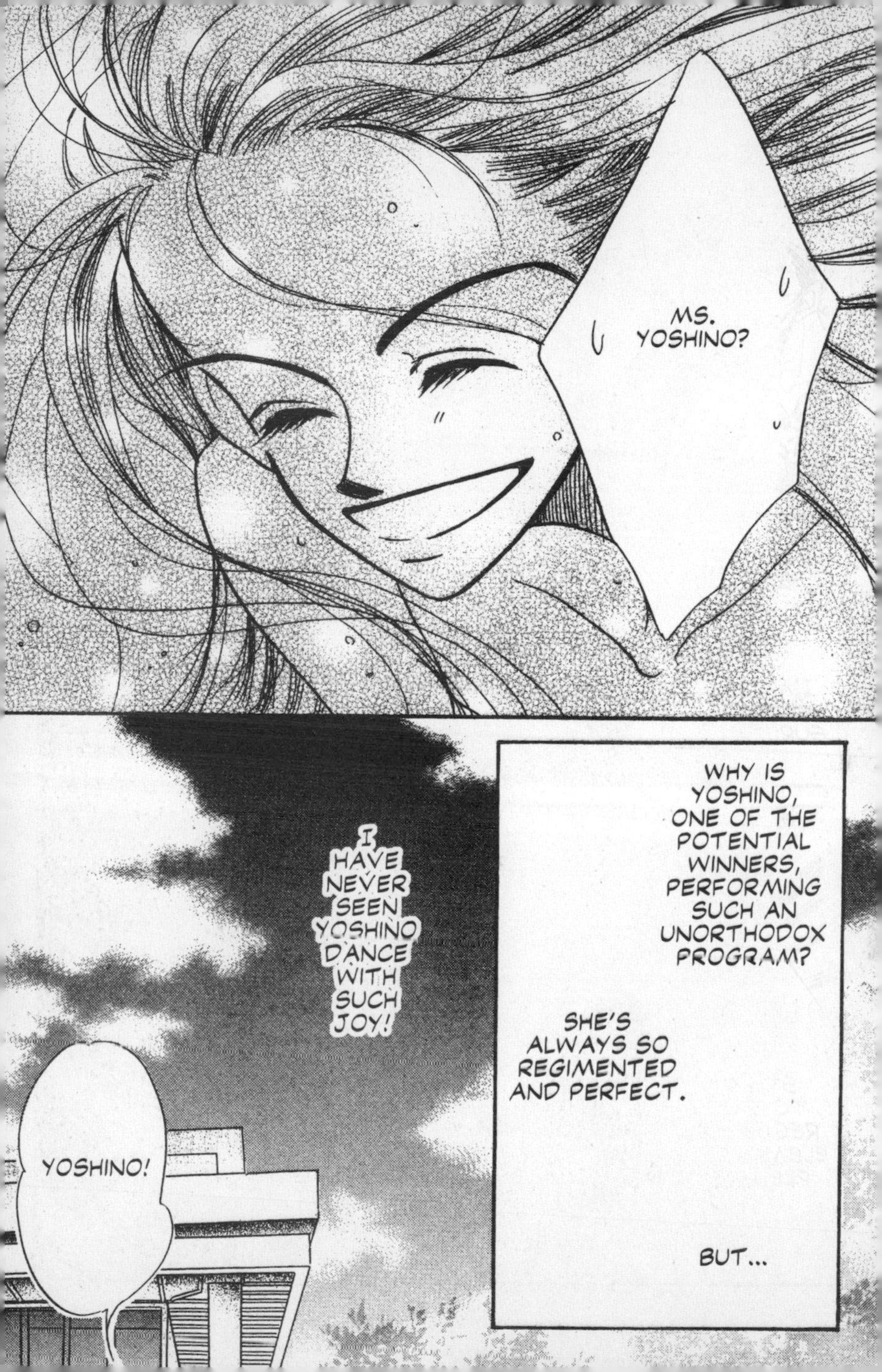
MS. YOSHINO?
WHY IS YOSHINO, ONE OF THE POTENTIAL WINNERS, PERFORMING SUCH AN UNORTHODOX PROGRAM?
SHE'S ALWAYS SO REGIMENTED AND PERFECT.
BUT...
I HAVE NEVER SEEN YOSHINO DANCE WITH SUCH JOY!
YOSHINO!

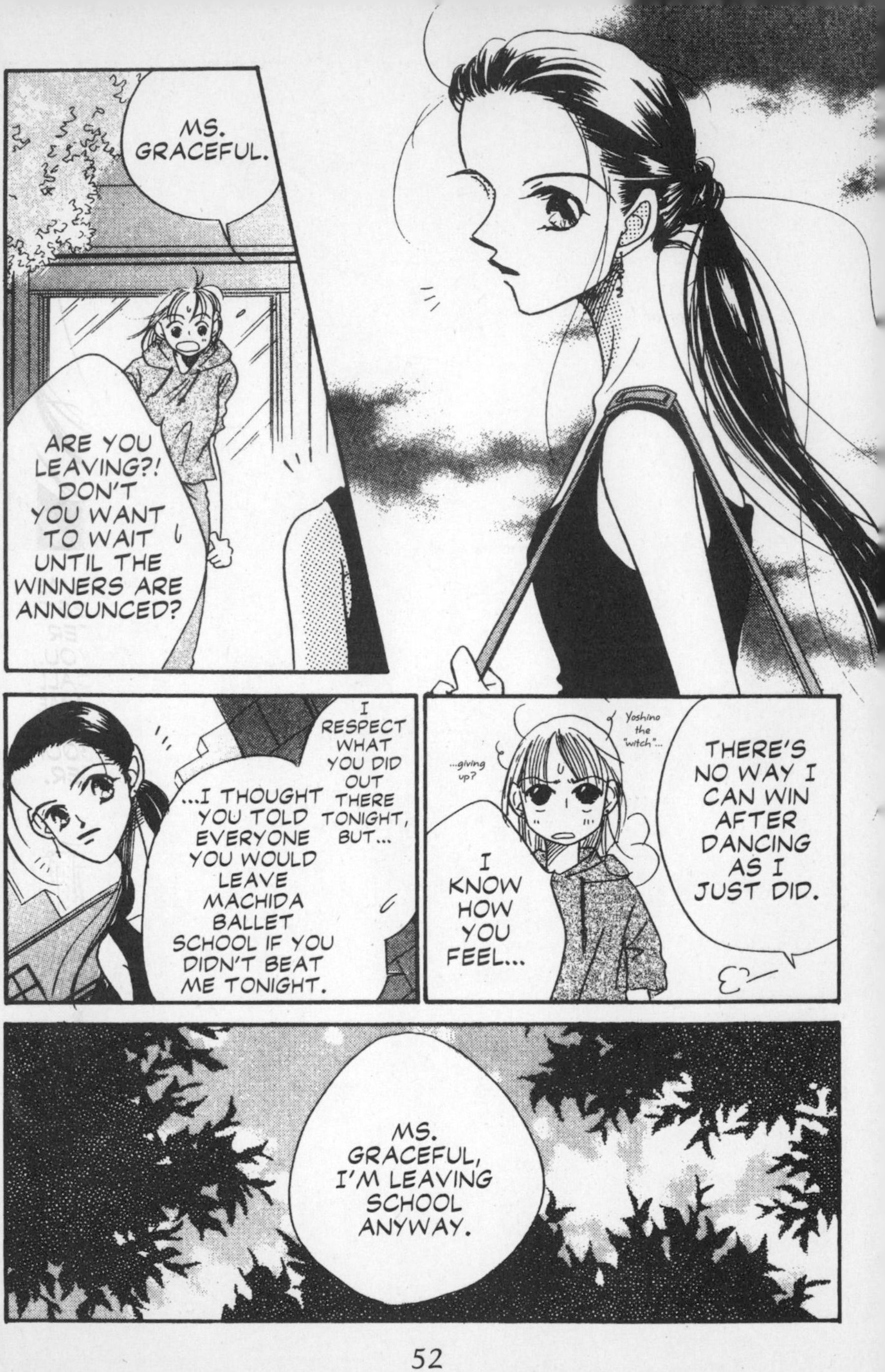
MS. GRACEFUL.
ARE YOU LEAVING?! DON'T YOU WANT TO WAIT UNTIL THE WINNERS ARE ANNOUNCED?
THERE'S NO WAY I CAN WIN AFTER DANCING AS I JUST DID.
Yoshino the "witch"...
...giving up?
I KNOW HOW YOU FEEL...
I RESPECT WHAT YOU DID OUT THERE TONIGHT, BUT...
...I THOUGHT YOU TOLD EVERYONE YOU WOULD LEAVE MACHIDA BALLET SCHOOL IF YOU DIDN'T BEAT ME TONIGHT.
MS. GRACEFUL, I'M LEAVING SCHOOL ANYWAY.

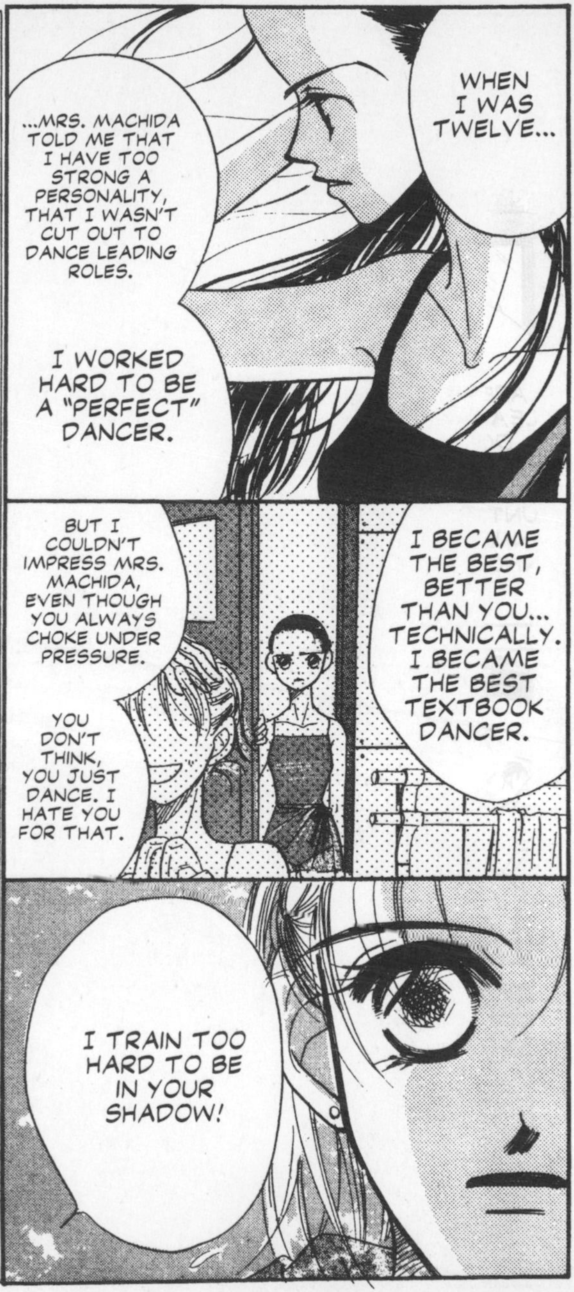
WHEN I WAS TWELVE...
...MRS. MACHIDA TOLD ME THAT I HAVE TOO STRONG A PERSONALITY, THAT I WASN'T CUT OUT TO DANCE LEADING ROLES.
I WORKED HARD TO BE A "PERFECT" DANCER.
I BECAME THE BEST, BETTER THAN YOU... TECHNICALLY. I BECAME THE BEST TEXTBOOK DANCER.
BUT I COULDN'T IMPRESS MRS. MACHIDA, EVEN THOUGH YOU ALWAYS CHOKE UNDER PRESSURE.
YOU DON'T THINK, YOU JUST DANCE. I HATE YOU FOR THAT.
I TRAIN TOO HARD TO BE IN YOUR SHADOW!

Ashihara's Diary

No. 2

Since I was very clueless when it comes to ballet, my chief editor took me to a lot of ballet performances.

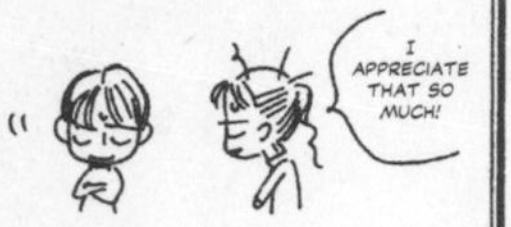
I APPRECIATE THAT SO MUCH!

I also went to see a lot of performances by myself. I've seen performances by Matsuyama Ballet, Bolshoi, Royal, Leningrad, Trockadero, and Alvin Ailey, just to name a few. I also saw Tetsuya Kumakawa's performances. He is one of the most popular Japanese male dancers today. Now, I see anything—solo, classic, modern, whatever. I've even seen flamenco dance (it's not ballet, but anyway...). Some might say all types of ballet are just ballet, but even I can see that each performance is totally unique.

To be continued in - No.3 - ↗

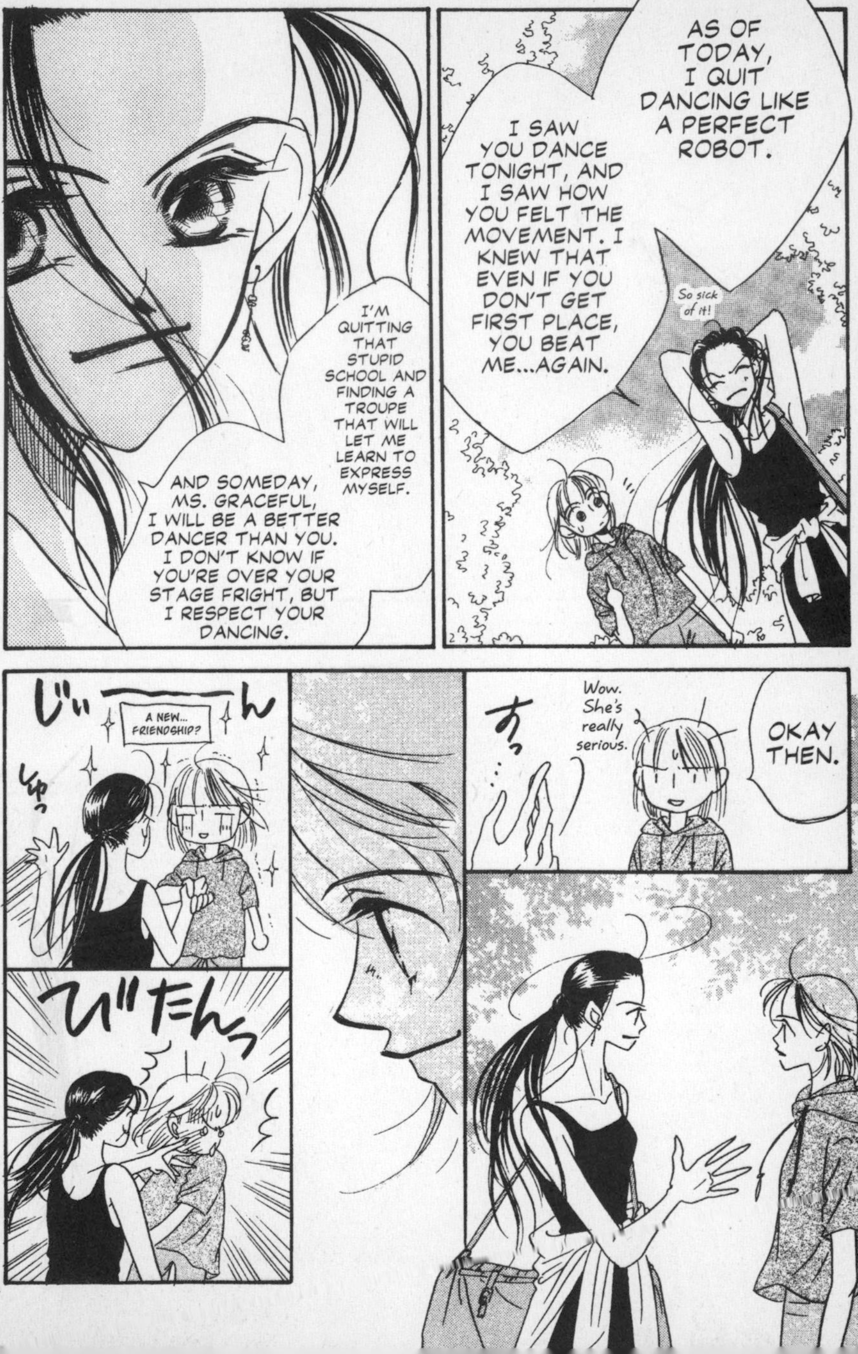
AS OF TODAY, I QUIT DANCING LIKE A PERFECT ROBOT.
I SAW YOU DANCE TONIGHT, AND I SAW HOW YOU FELT THE MOVEMENT. I KNEW THAT EVEN IF YOU DON'T GET FIRST PLACE, YOU BEAT ME...AGAIN.
So sick of it!
I'M QUITTING THAT STUPID SCHOOL AND FINDING A TROUPE THAT WILL LET ME LEARN TO EXPRESS MYSELF.
AND SOMEDAY, MS. GRACEFUL, I WILL BE A BETTER DANCER THAN YOU. I DON'T KNOW IF YOU'RE OVER YOUR STAGE FRIGHT, BUT I RESPECT YOUR DANCING.
OKAY THEN.
Wow. She's really serious.
すっ
じぃーーーん
A NEW... FRIENDSHIP?
しゅっ
びたんっ

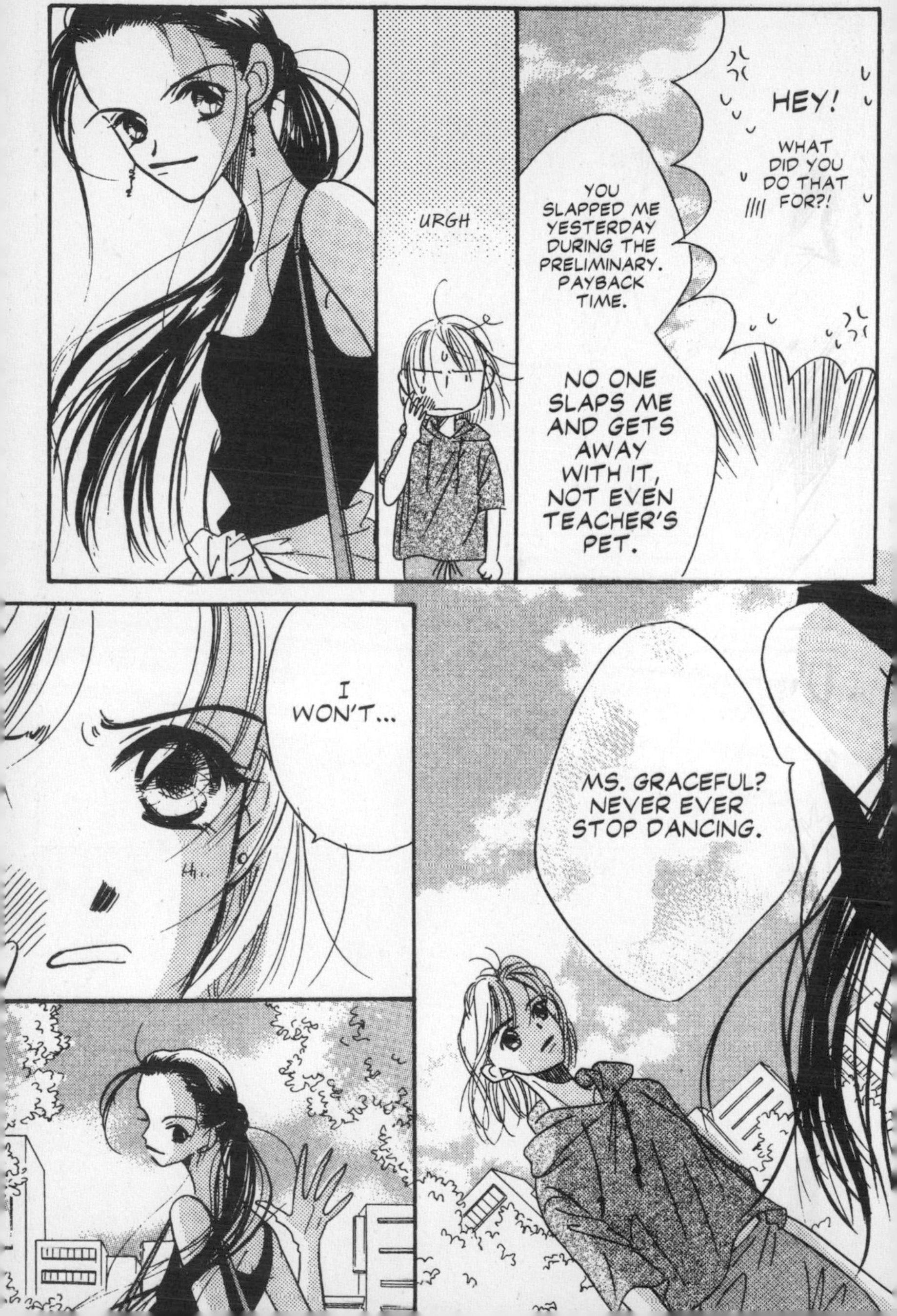
HEY!
WHAT DID YOU DO THAT FOR?!
YOU SLAPPED ME YESTERDAY DURING THE PRELIMINARY. PAYBACK TIME.
NO ONE SLAPS ME AND GETS AWAY WITH IT, NOT EVEN TEACHER'S PET.
URGH
MS. GRACEFUL? NEVER EVER STOP DANCING.
I WON'T...

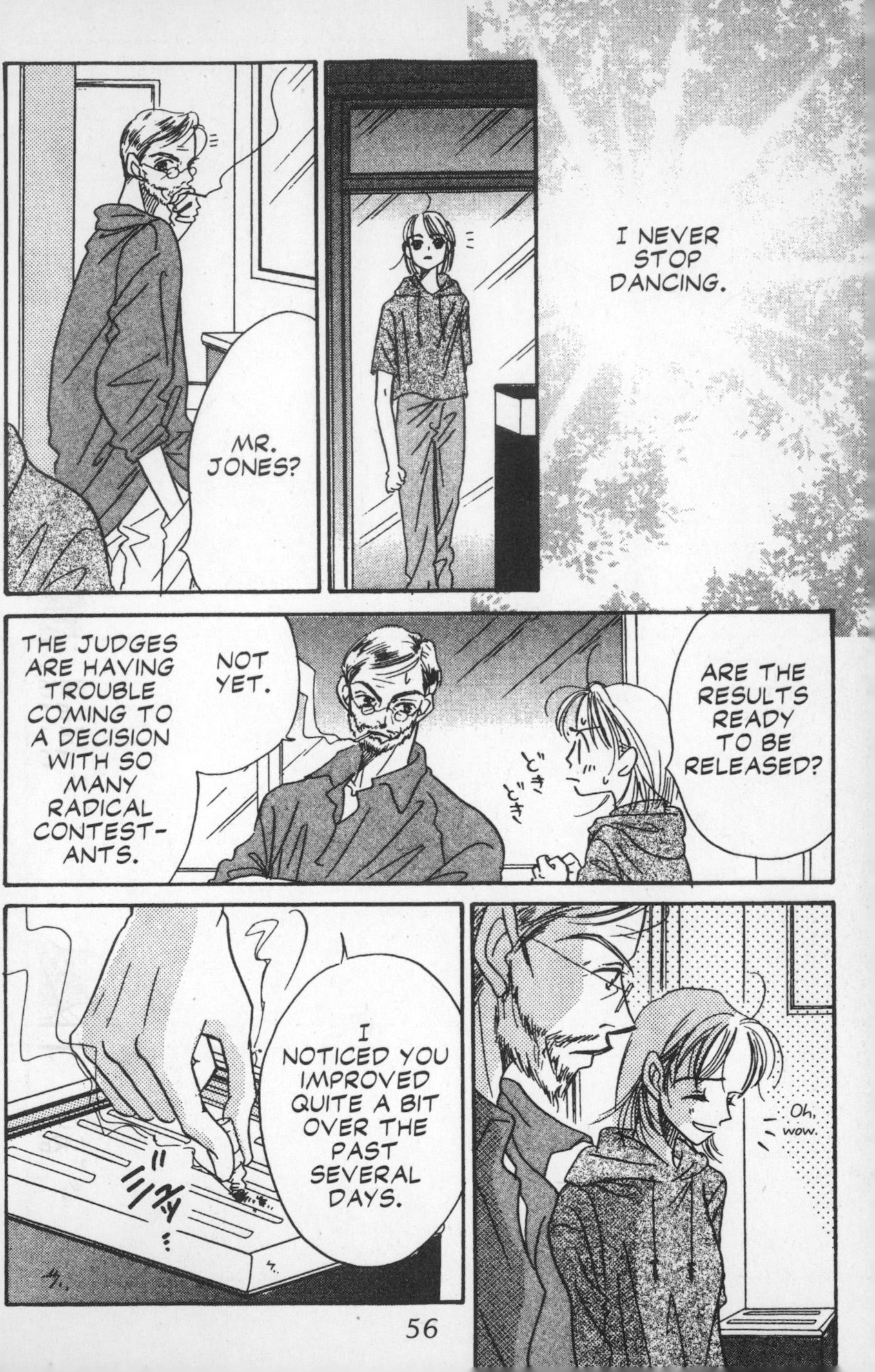
I NEVER STOP DANCING.
MR. JONES?
ARE THE RESULTS READY TO BE RELEASED?
どき どき
NOT YET.
THE JUDGES ARE HAVING TROUBLE COMING TO A DECISION WITH SO MANY RADICAL CONTEST-ANTS.
Oh, wow.
I NOTICED YOU IMPROVED QUITE A BIT OVER THE PAST SEVERAL DAYS.

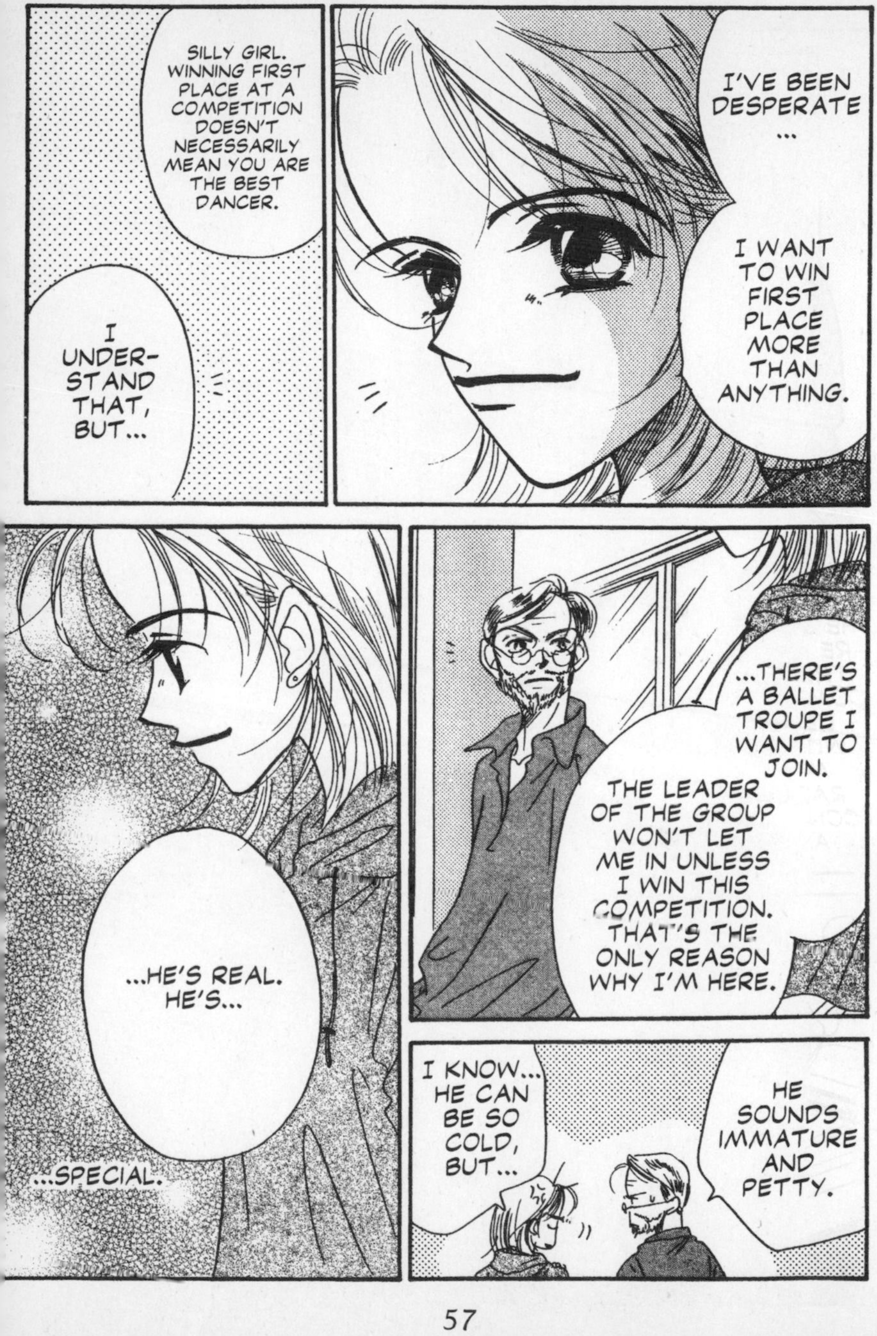
I'VE BEEN DESPERATE ...
I WANT TO WIN FIRST PLACE MORE THAN ANYTHING.
SILLY GIRL. WINNING FIRST PLACE AT A COMPETITION DOESN'T NECESSARILY MEAN YOU ARE THE BEST DANCER.
I UNDER-STAND THAT, BUT...
...THERE'S A BALLET TROUPE I WANT TO JOIN.
THE LEADER OF THE GROUP WON'T LET ME IN UNLESS I WIN THIS COMPETITION. THAT'S THE ONLY REASON WHY I'M HERE.
HE SOUNDS IMMATURE AND PETTY.
I KNOW... HE CAN BE SO COLD, BUT...
...HE'S REAL. HE'S...
...SPECIAL.

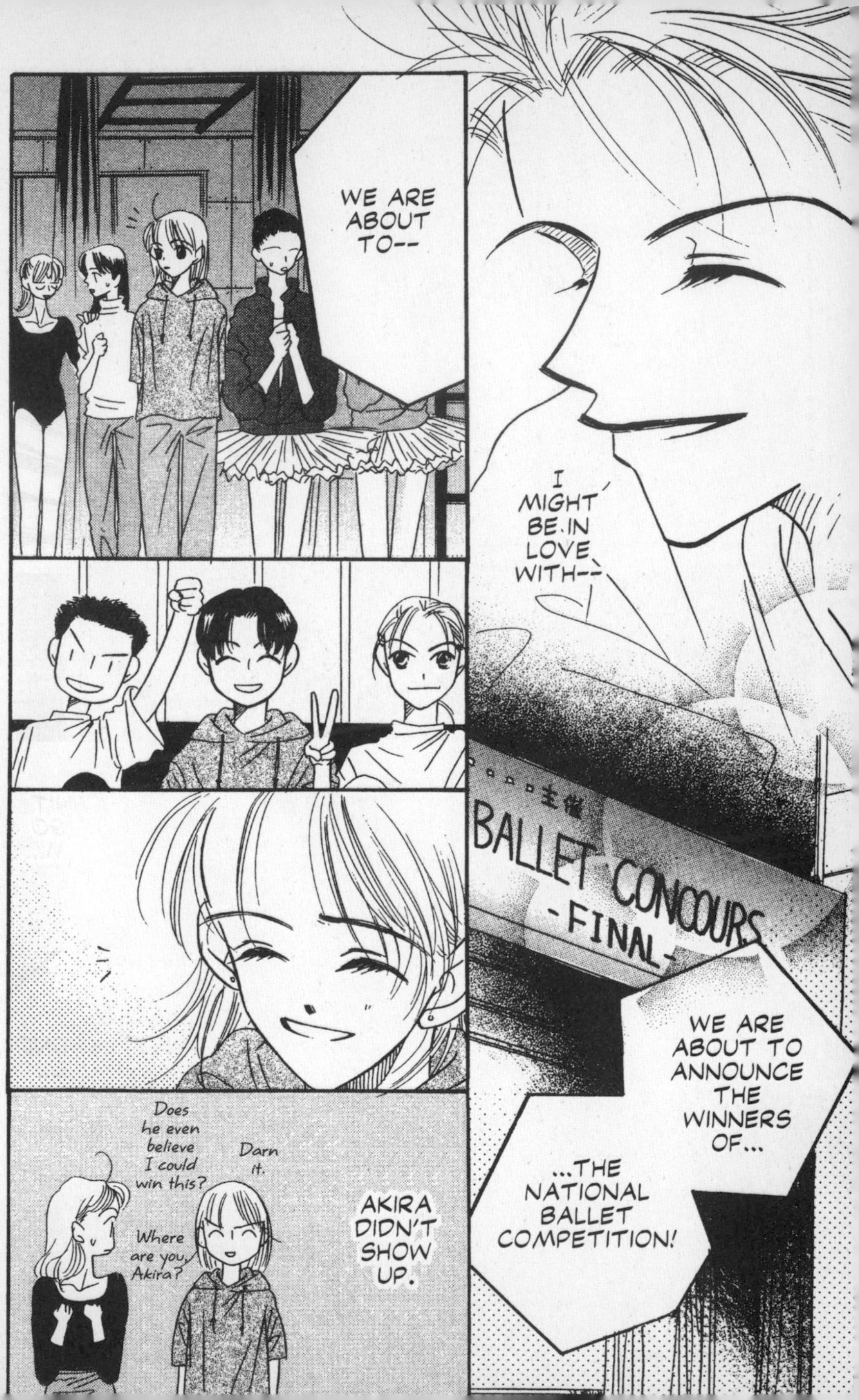
I MIGHT BE IN LOVE WITH--
BALLET CONCOURS
-FINAL-
WE ARE ABOUT TO ANNOUNCE THE WINNERS OF...
...THE NATIONAL BALLET COMPETITION!
WE ARE ABOUT TO--
AKIRA DIDN'T SHOW UP.
Darn it.
Does he even believe I could win this?
Where are you, Akira?

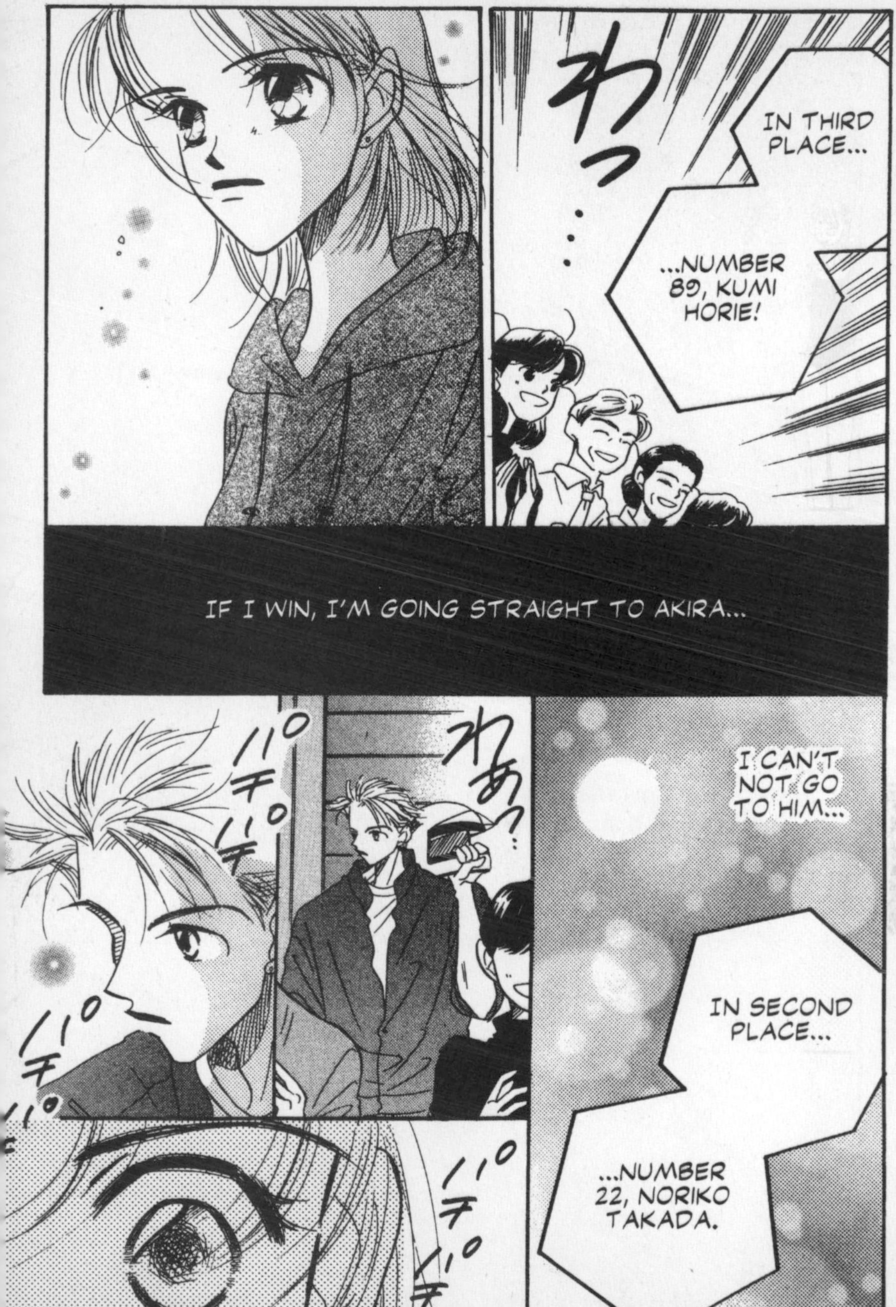
IN THIRD PLACE...
...NUMBER 89, KUMI HORIE!
わっ
IF I WIN, I'M GOING STRAIGHT TO AKIRA...
I CAN'T NOT GO TO HIM...
IN SECOND PLACE...
...NUMBER 22, NORIKO TAKADA.
わあっ
パチパチ
パチパチ
パチパチ

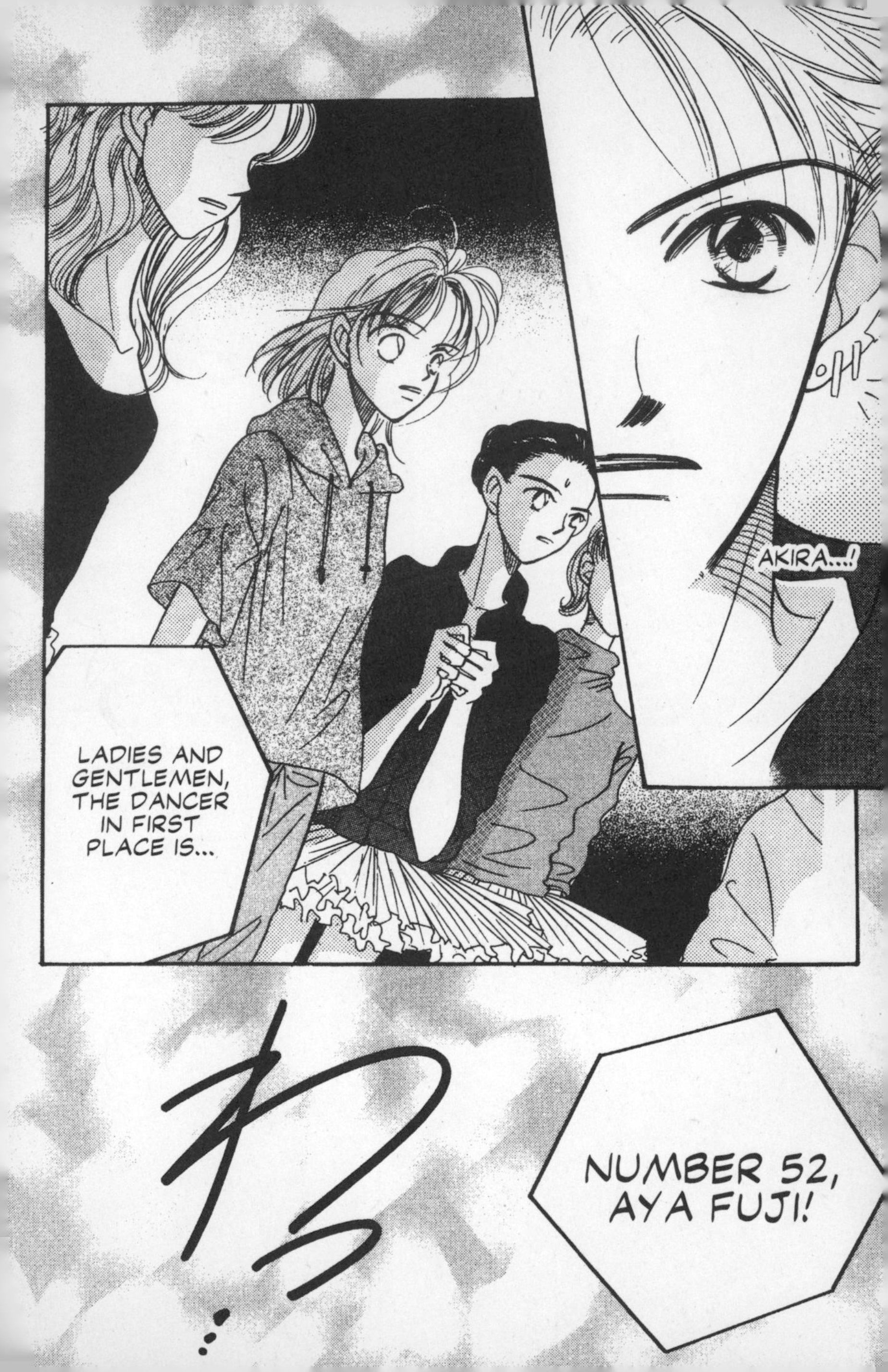
AKIRA...!
LADIES AND GENTLEMEN, THE DANCER IN FIRST PLACE IS...
NUMBER 52, AYA FUJI!

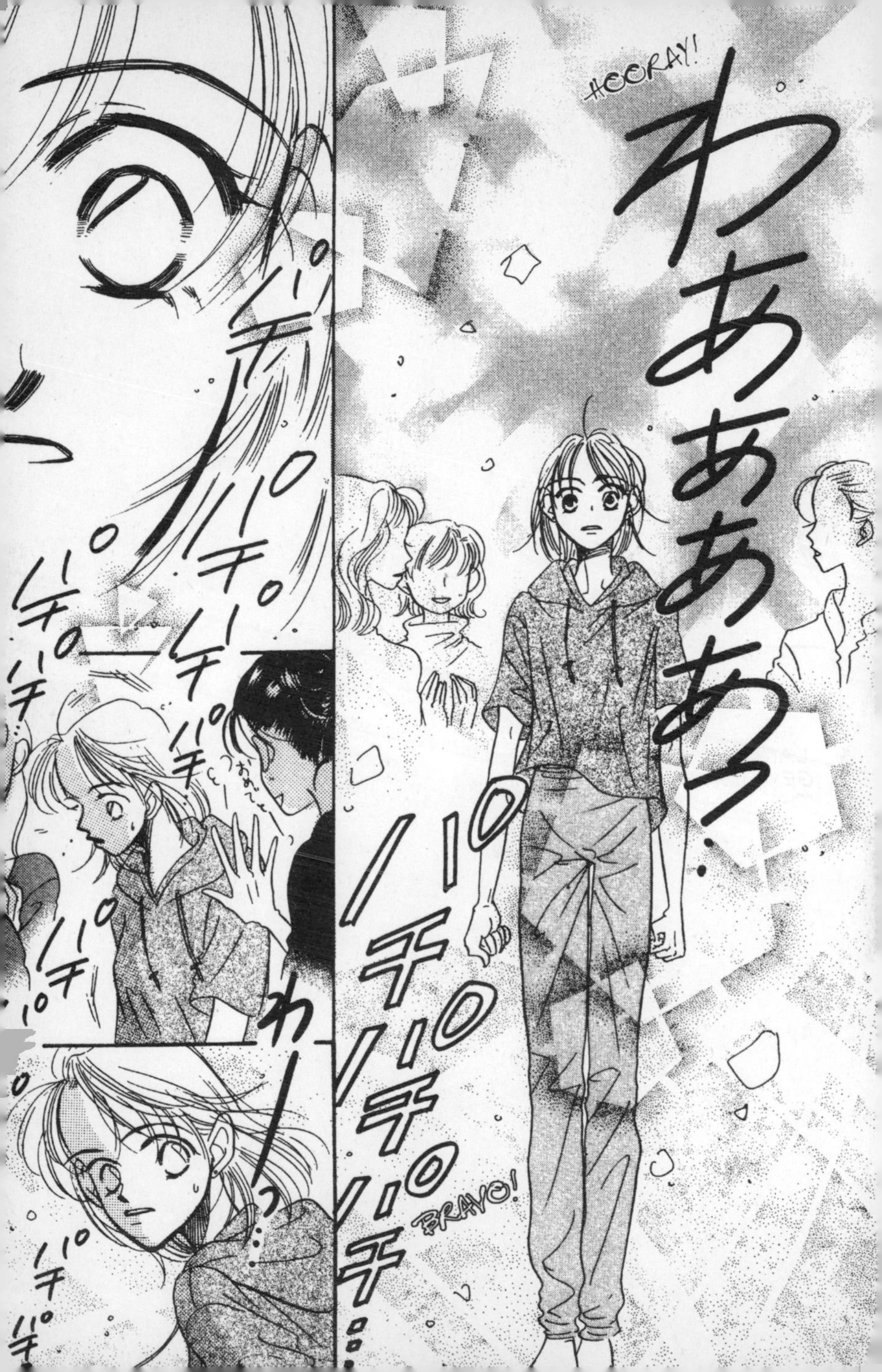
わあああああっ
HOORAY!
パチパチパチ…
BRAVO!
パチパチパチパチ
パチパチパチ…
おめでとーっ
パチパチパ
わーっ…
パチパ

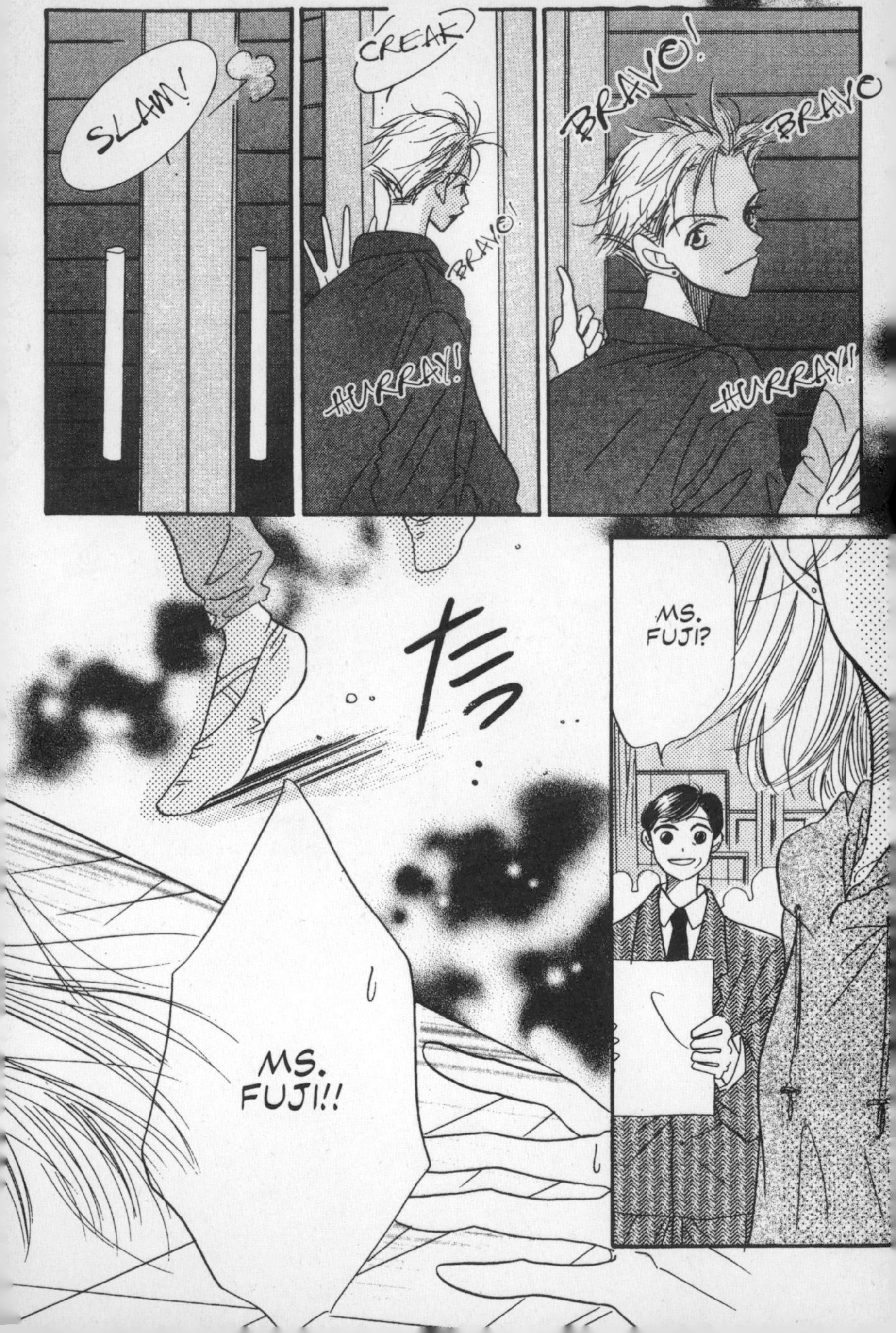
BRAVO!
BRAVO
HURRAY!
CREAK
BRAVO!
HURRAY!
SLAM!
MS. FUJI?
MS. FUJI!!

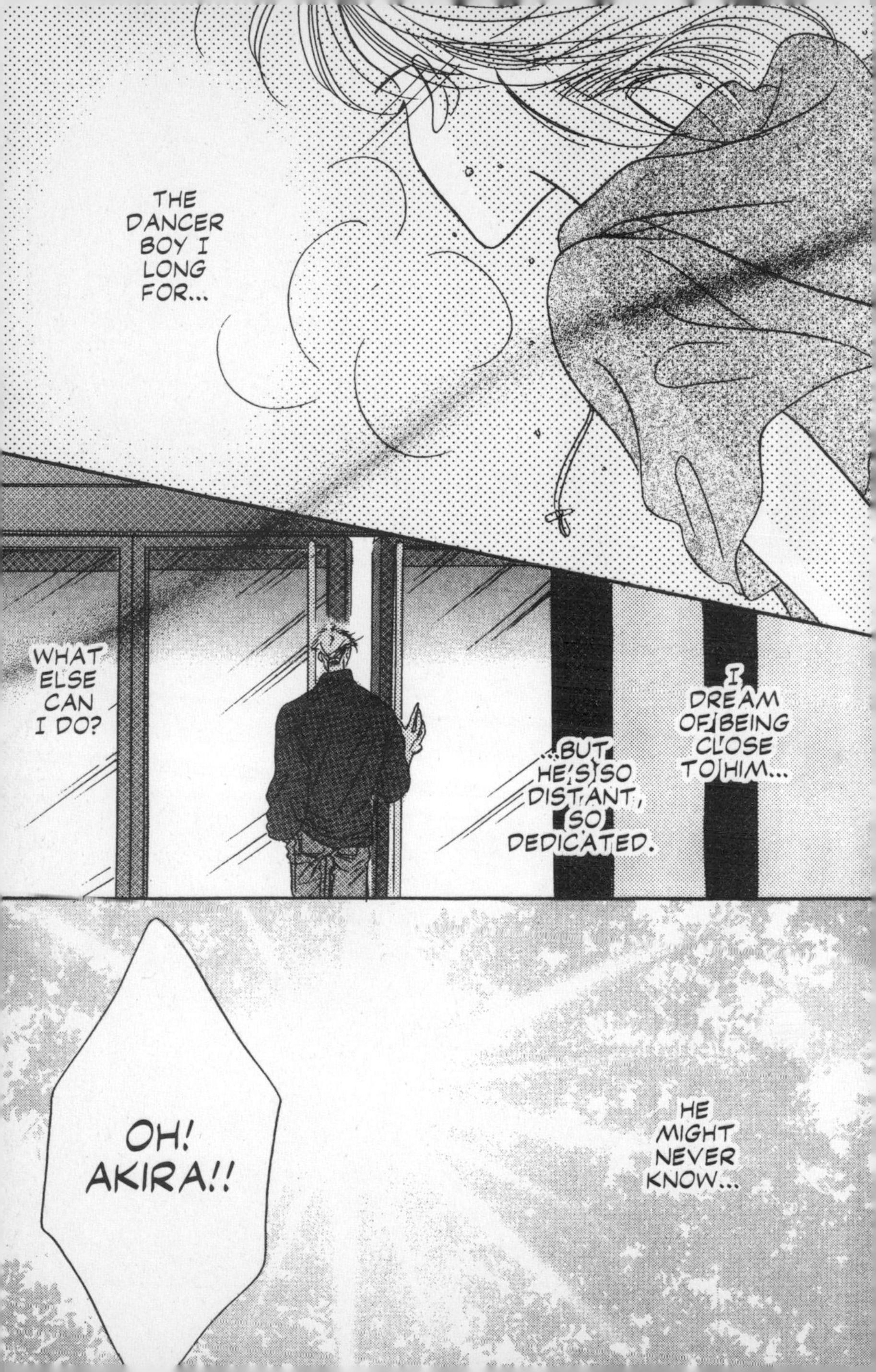
THE DANCER BOY I LONG FOR...
I DREAM OF BEING CLOSE TO HIM...
...BUT HE'S SO DISTANT, SO DEDICATED.
WHAT ELSE CAN I DO?
HE MIGHT NEVER KNOW...
OH! AKIRA!!

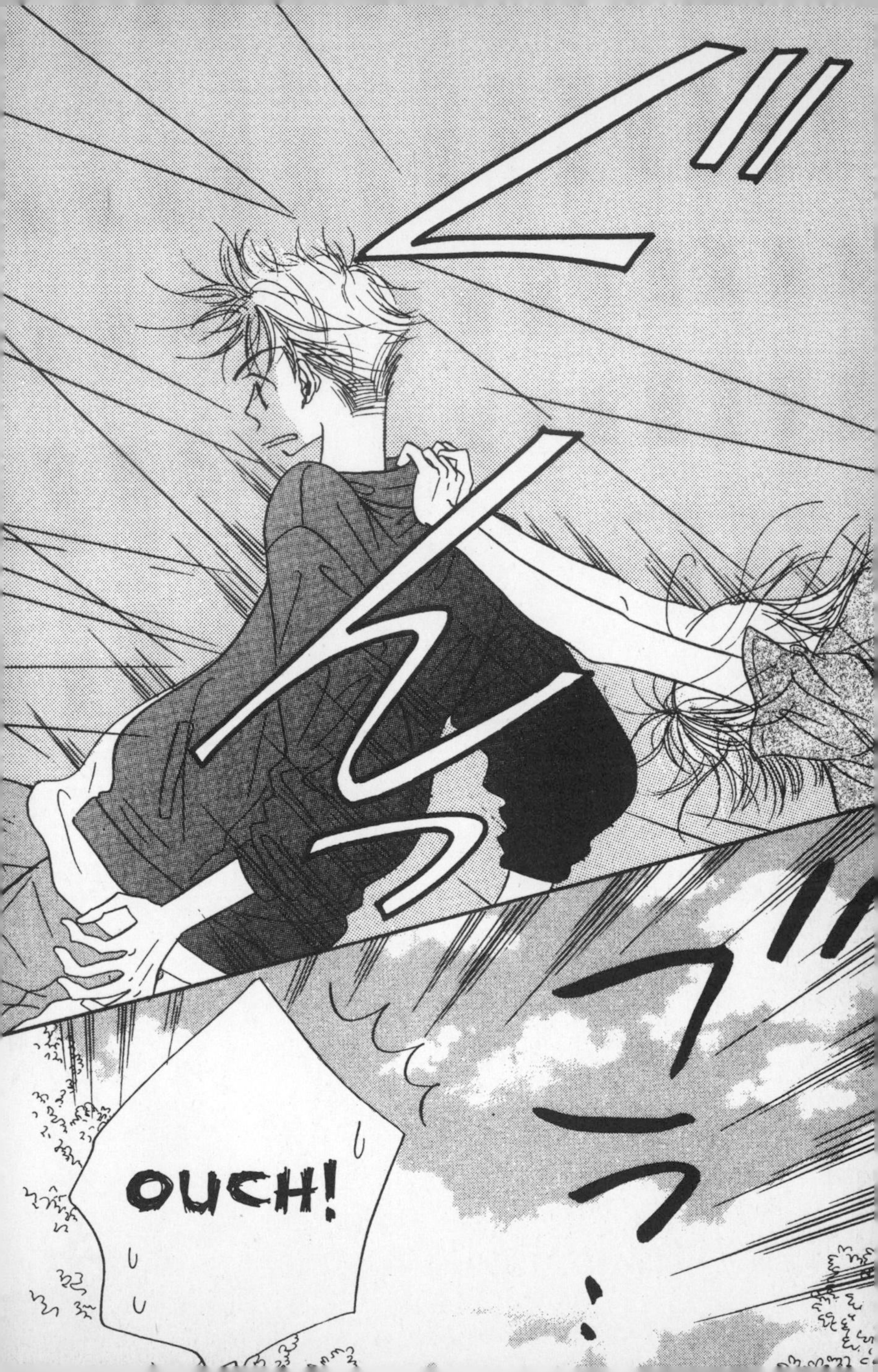
OUCH!

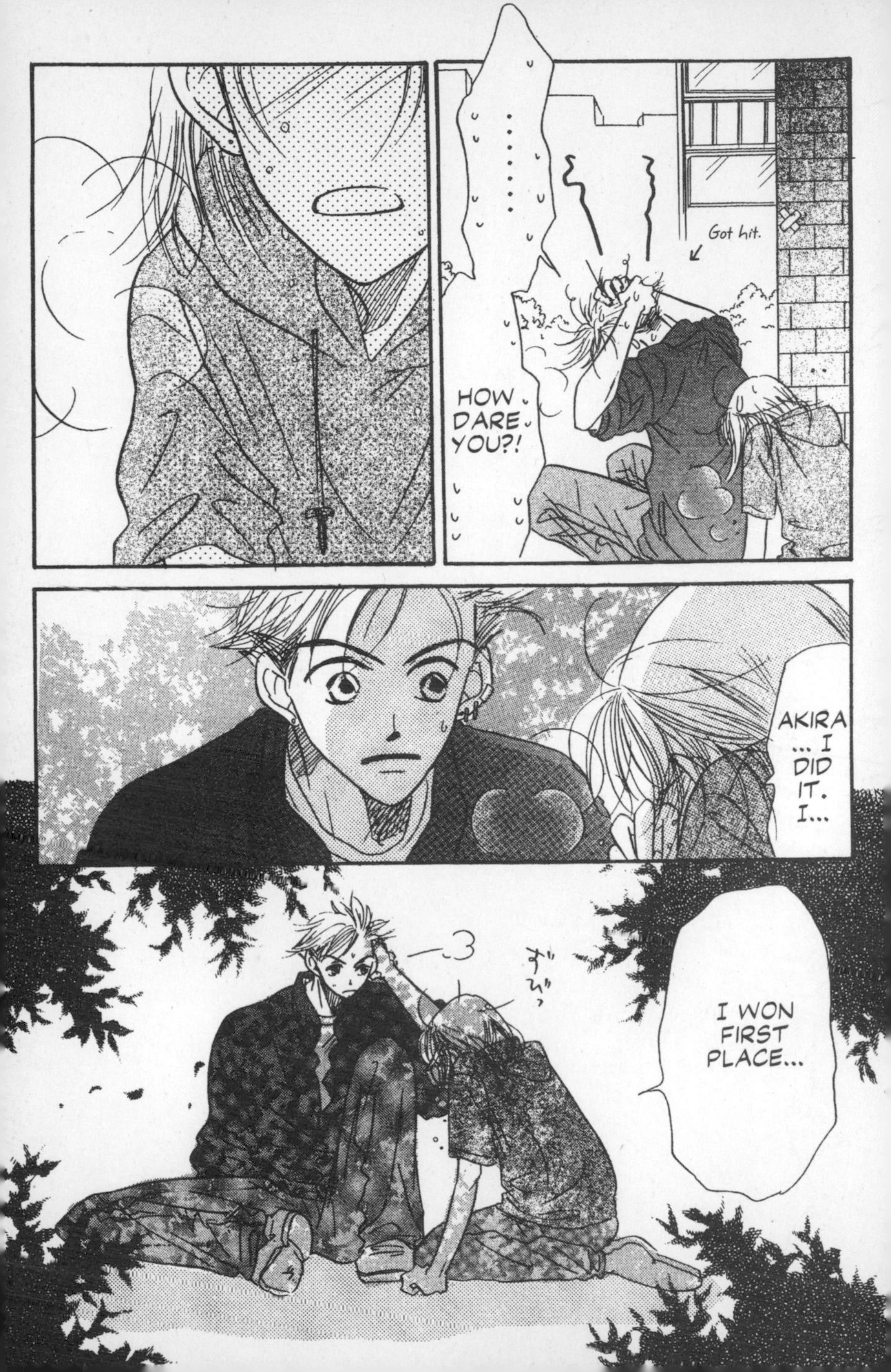
......
HOW DARE YOU?!
Got hit.
AKIRA ... I DID IT. I...
ずびっ
I WON FIRST PLACE...

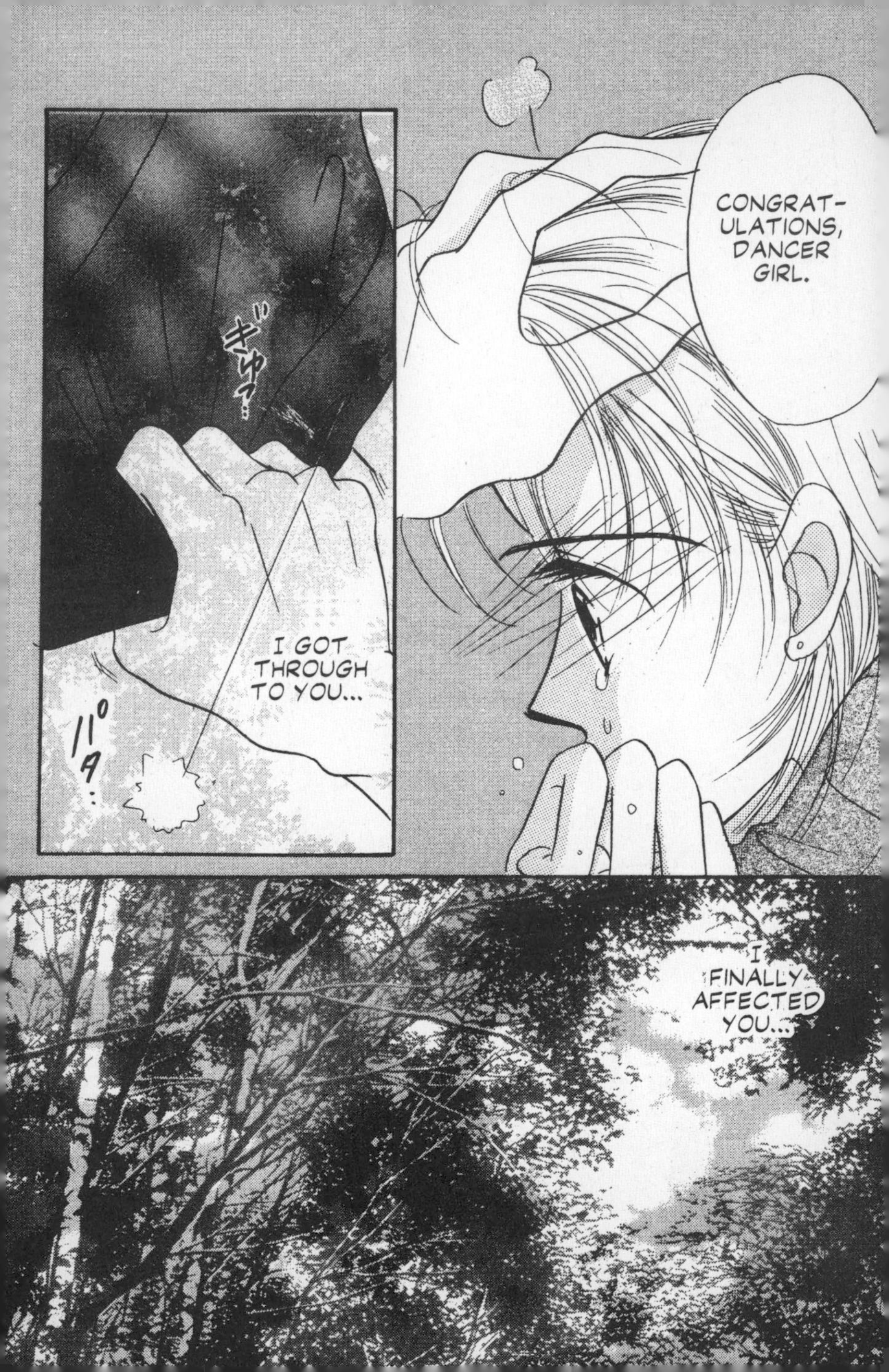
CONGRAT-ULATIONS, DANCER GIRL.
ぎゅア…
I GOT THROUGH TO YOU...
パタ…
I FINALLY AFFECTED YOU...

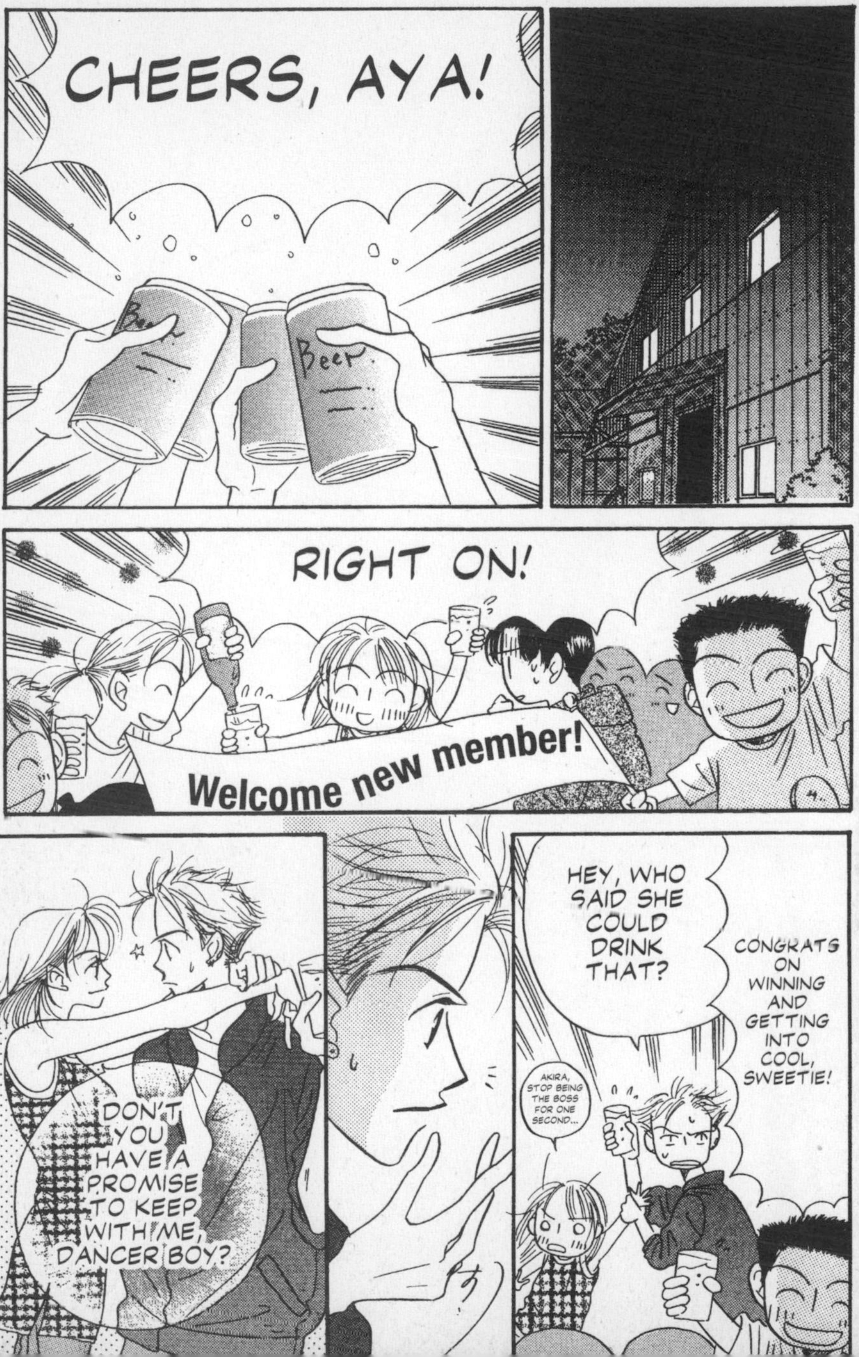
CHEERS, AYA!
Beer
RIGHT ON!
Welcome new member!
CONGRATS ON WINNING AND GETTING INTO COOL, SWEETIE!
HEY, WHO SAID SHE COULD DRINK THAT?
AKIRA, STOP BEING THE BOSS FOR ONE SECOND...
DON'T YOU HAVE A PROMISE TO KEEP WITH ME, DANCER BOY?

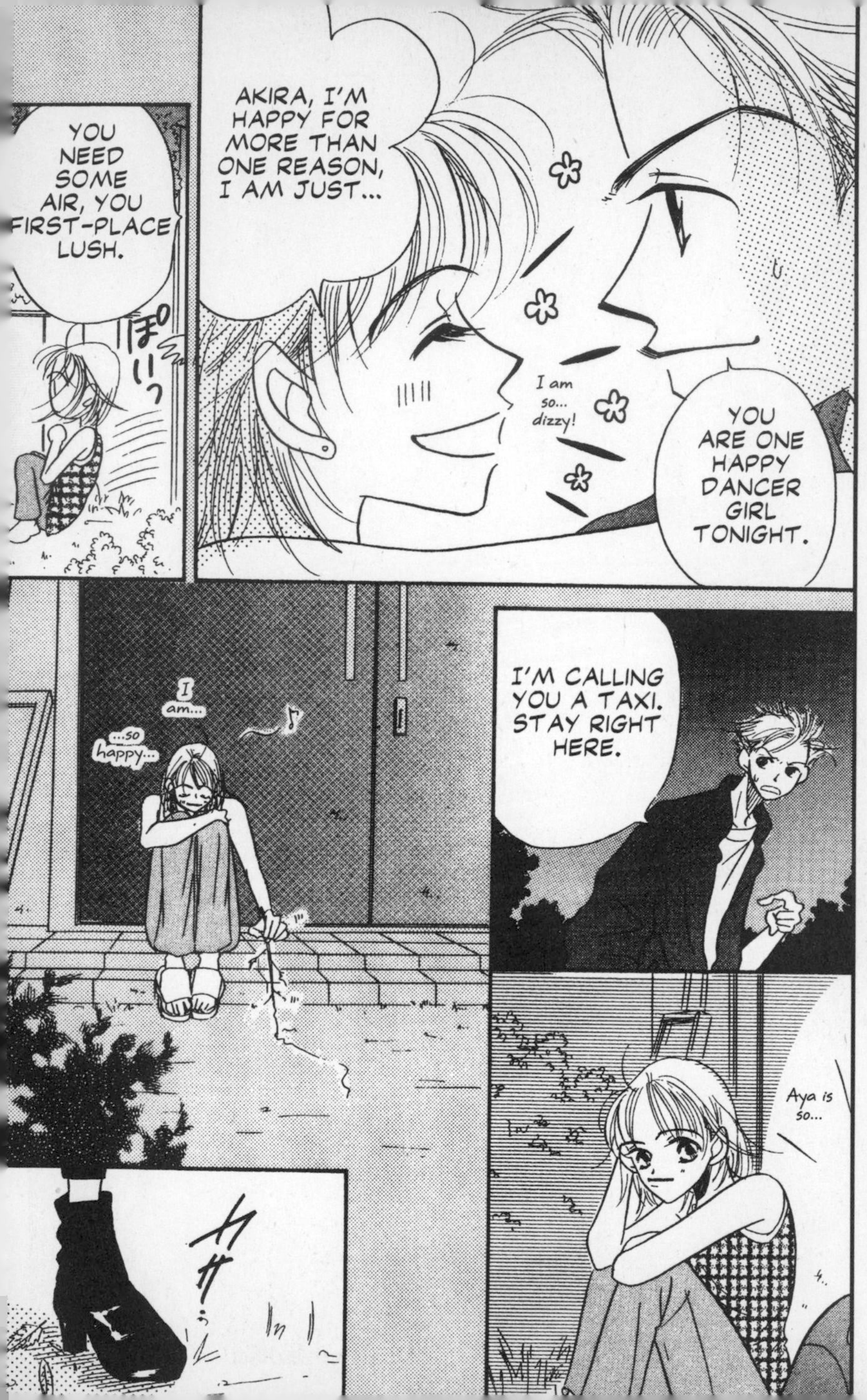
AKIRA, I'M HAPPY FOR MORE THAN ONE REASON, I AM JUST...
I am so... dizzy!
YOU ARE ONE HAPPY DANCER GIRL TONIGHT.
YOU NEED SOME AIR, YOU FIRST-PLACE LUSH.
ぽいっ
I'M CALLING YOU A TAXI. STAY RIGHT HERE.
I am...
...so happy...
Aya is so...

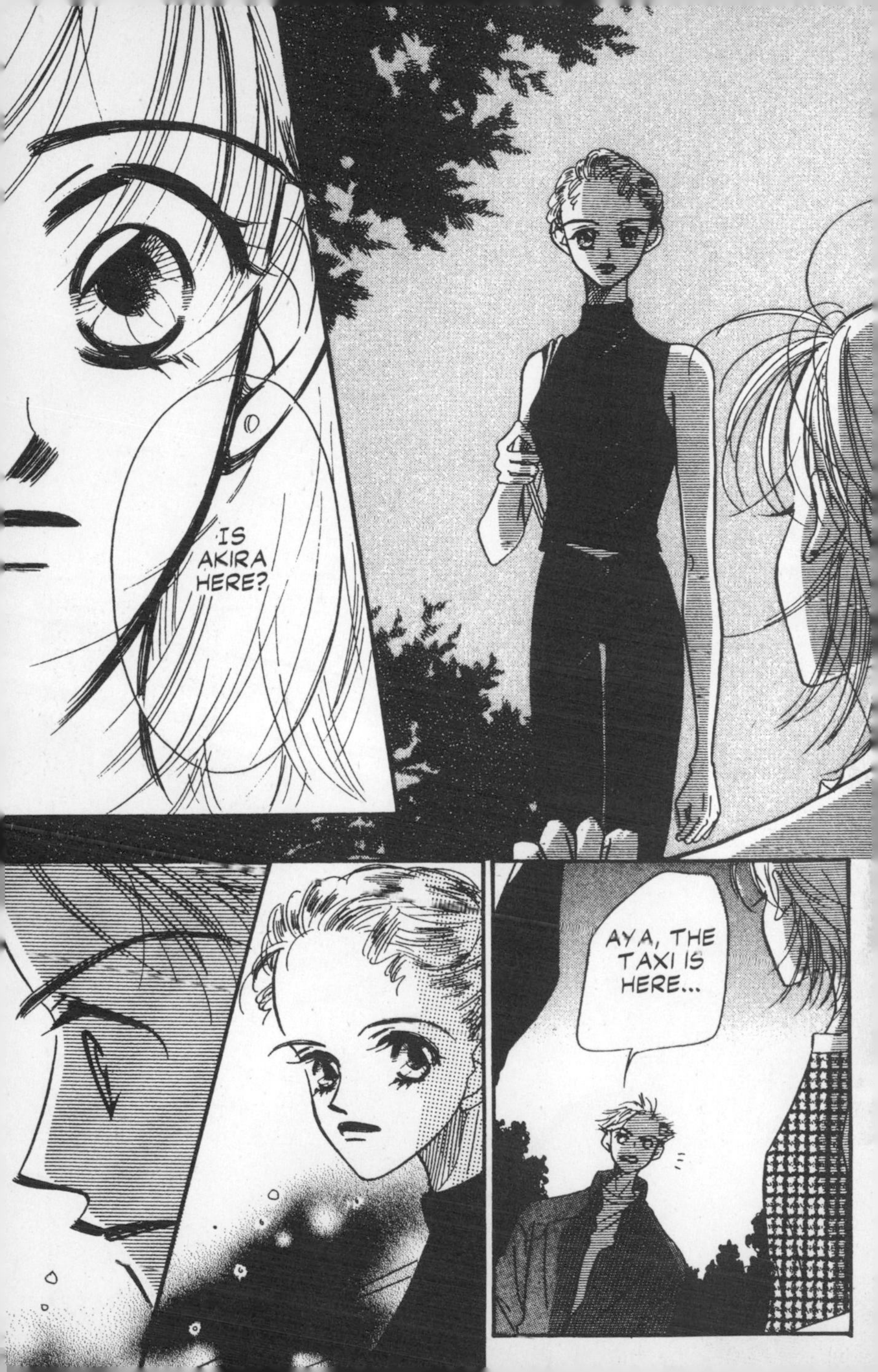
IS AKIRA HERE?
AYA, THE TAXI IS HERE...

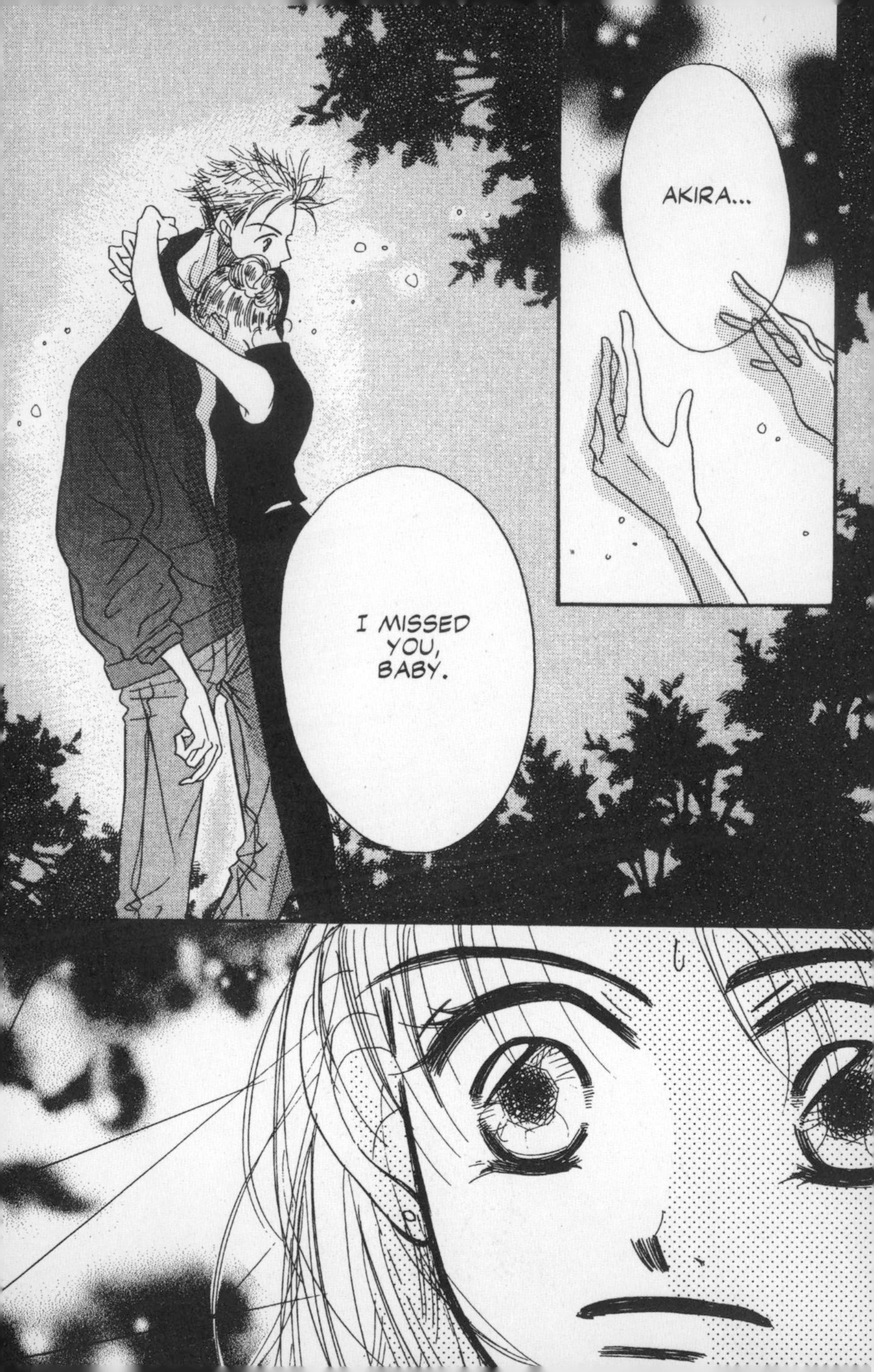
AKIRA...
I MISSED YOU, BABY.

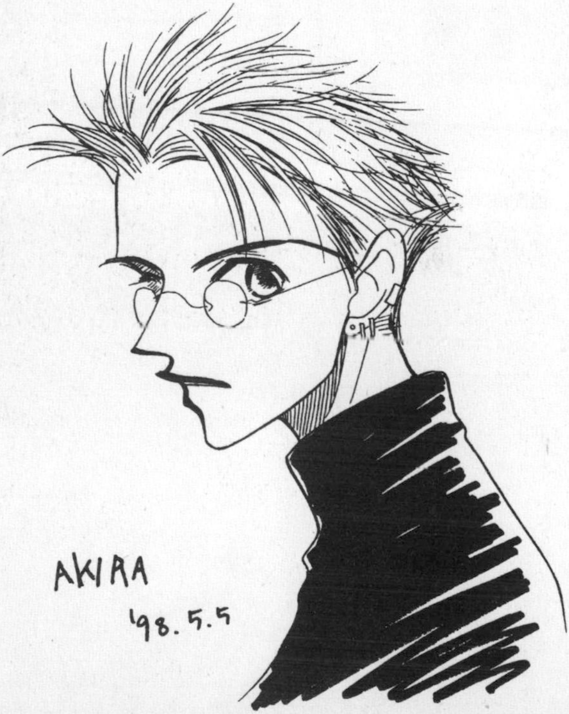
AKIRA
'98.5.5

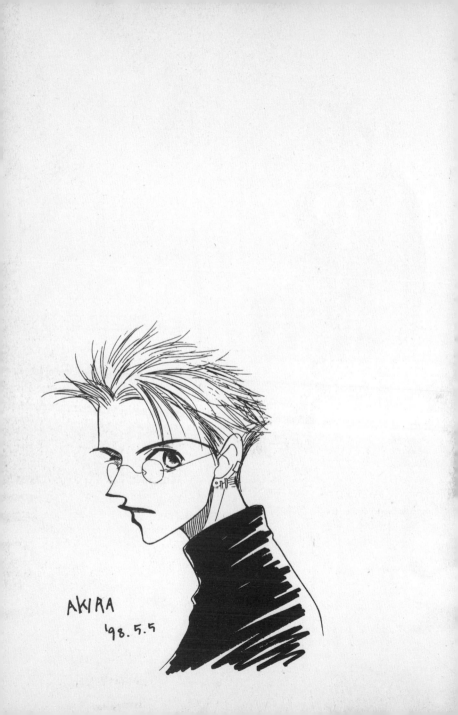

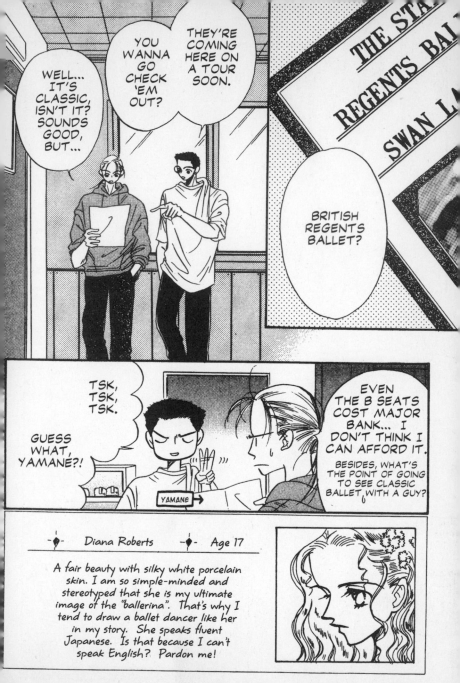

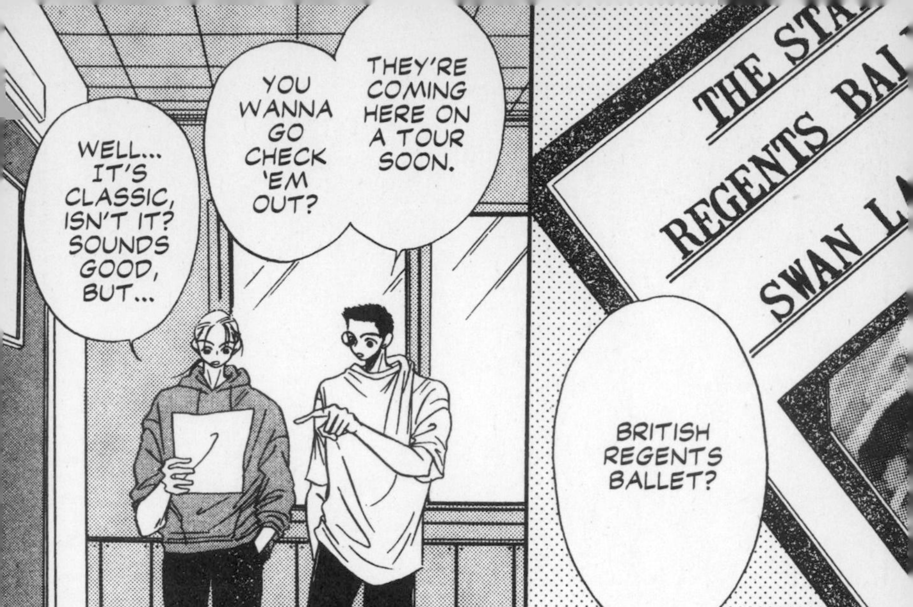
BRITISH REGENTS BALLET?
THEY'RE COMING HERE ON A TOUR SOON.
YOU WANNA GO CHECK 'EM OUT?
WELL... IT'S CLASSIC, ISN'T IT? SOUNDS GOOD, BUT...
EVEN THE B SEATS COST MAJOR BANK... I DON'T THINK I CAN AFFORD IT.
BESIDES, WHAT'S THE POINT OF GOING TO SEE CLASSIC BALLET WITH A GUY?
TSK, TSK, TSK.
GUESS WHAT, YAMANE?!
YAMANE

Diana Roberts — Age 17

A fair beauty with silky white porcelain skin. I am so simple-minded and stereotyped that she is my ultimate image of the "ballerina". That's why I tend to draw a ballet dancer like her in my story. She speaks fluent Japanese. Is that because I can't speak English? Pardon me!

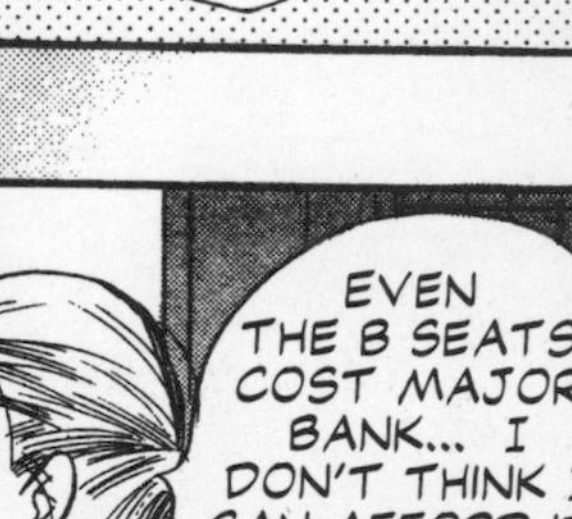

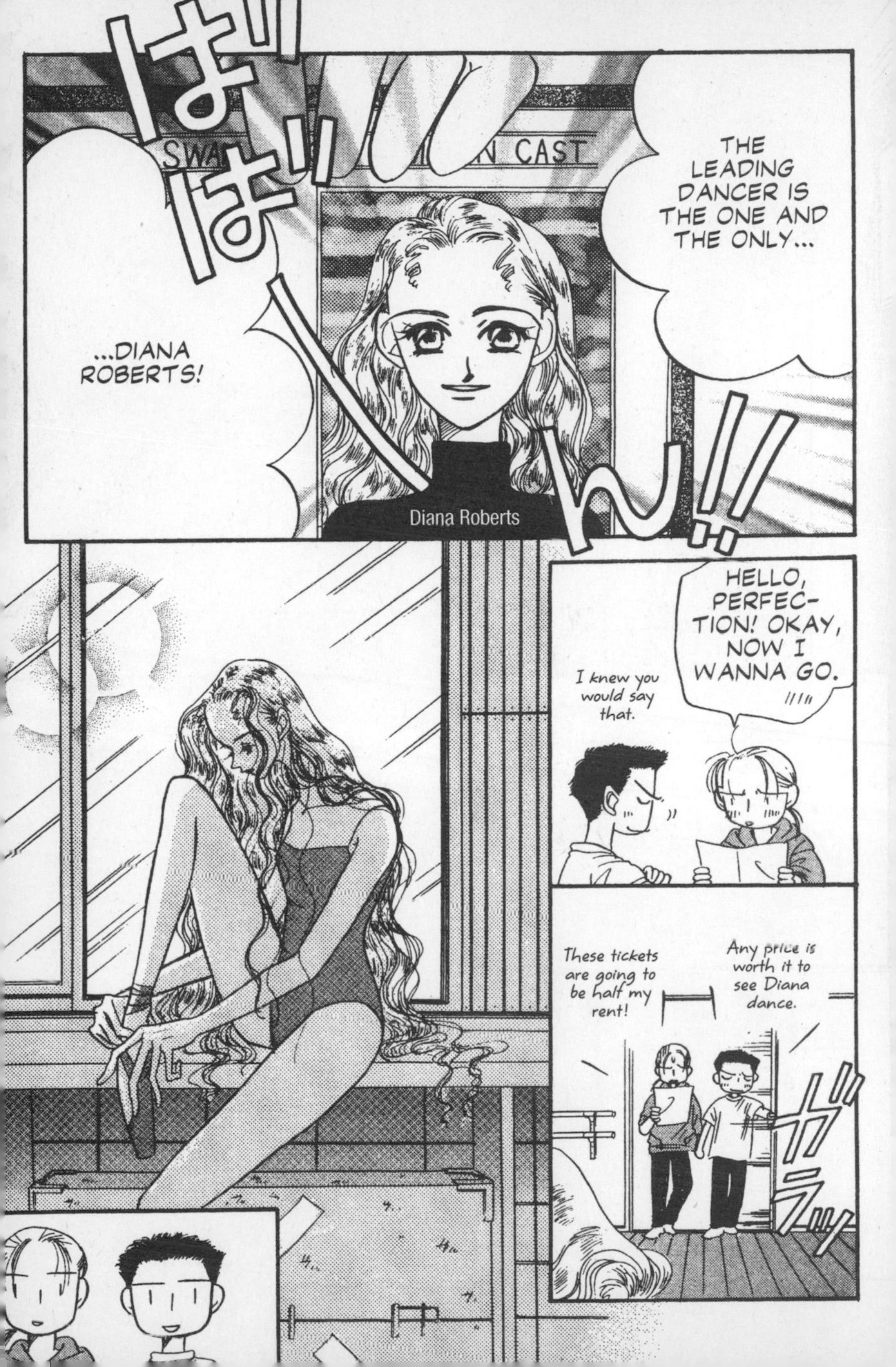
THE LEADING DANCER IS THE ONE AND THE ONLY...
...DIANA ROBERTS!
ばばーん!!
Diana Roberts
HELLO, PERFECTION! OKAY, NOW I WANNA GO.
I knew you would say that.
Any price is worth it to see Diana dance.
These tickets are going to be half my rent!
ガラッ

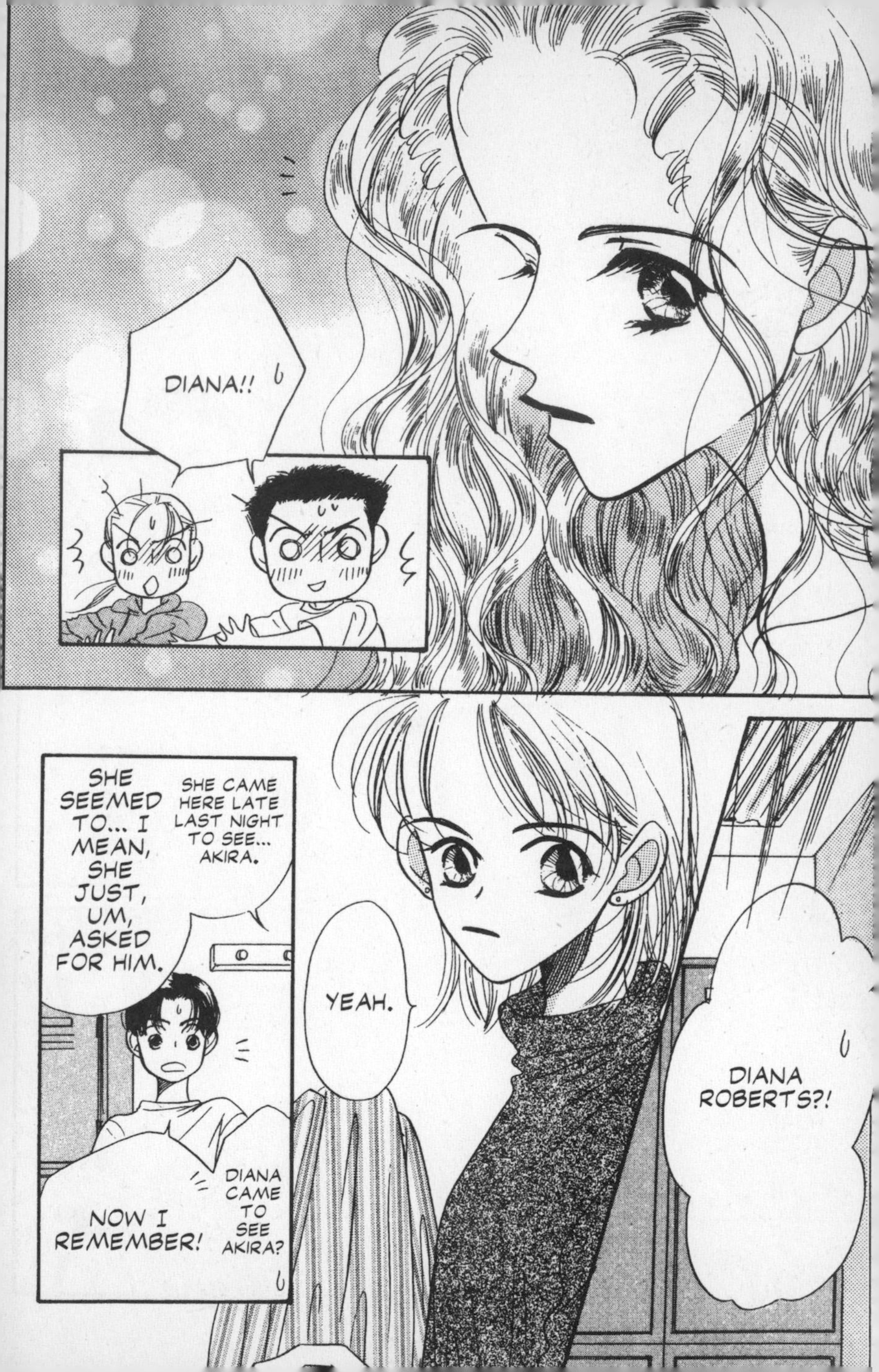
DIANA!!
DIANA ROBERTS?!
YEAH.
SHE CAME HERE LATE LAST NIGHT TO SEE... AKIRA.
SHE SEEMED TO... I MEAN, SHE JUST, UM, ASKED FOR HIM.
DIANA CAME TO SEE AKIRA?
NOW I REMEMBER!

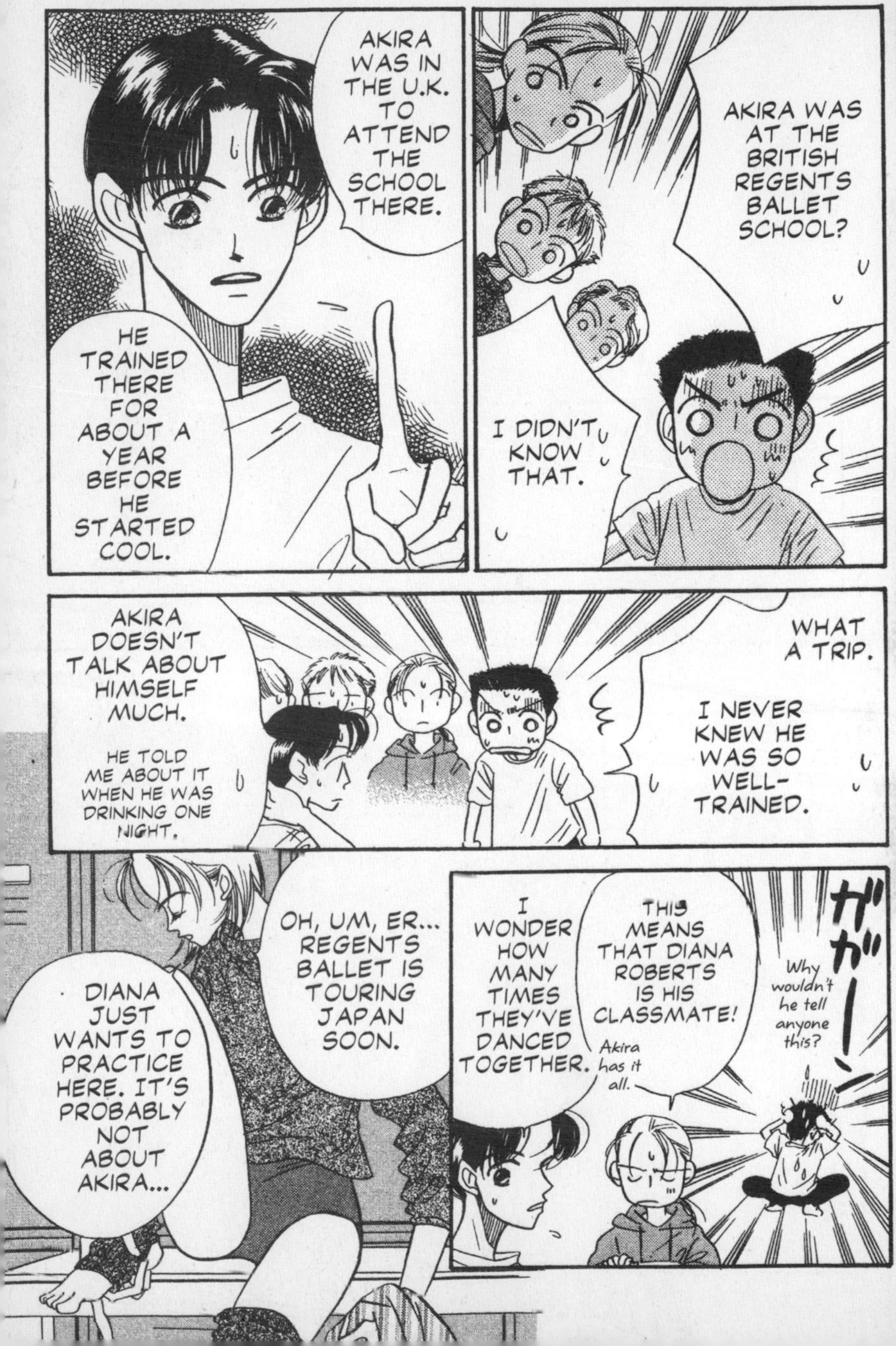
AKIRA WAS AT THE BRITISH REGENTS BALLET SCHOOL?
I DIDN'T KNOW THAT.
AKIRA WAS IN THE U.K. TO ATTEND THE SCHOOL THERE.
HE TRAINED THERE FOR ABOUT A YEAR BEFORE HE STARTED COOL.
WHAT A TRIP.
I NEVER KNEW HE WAS SO WELL-TRAINED.
AKIRA DOESN'T TALK ABOUT HIMSELF MUCH.
HE TOLD ME ABOUT IT WHEN HE WAS DRINKING ONE NIGHT.
ガガー！
Why wouldn't he tell anyone this?
THIS MEANS THAT DIANA ROBERTS IS HIS CLASSMATE!
Akira has it all.
I WONDER HOW MANY TIMES THEY'VE DANCED TOGETHER.
OH, UM, ER... REGENTS BALLET IS TOURING JAPAN SOON.
DIANA JUST WANTS TO PRACTICE HERE. IT'S PROBABLY NOT ABOUT AKIRA...

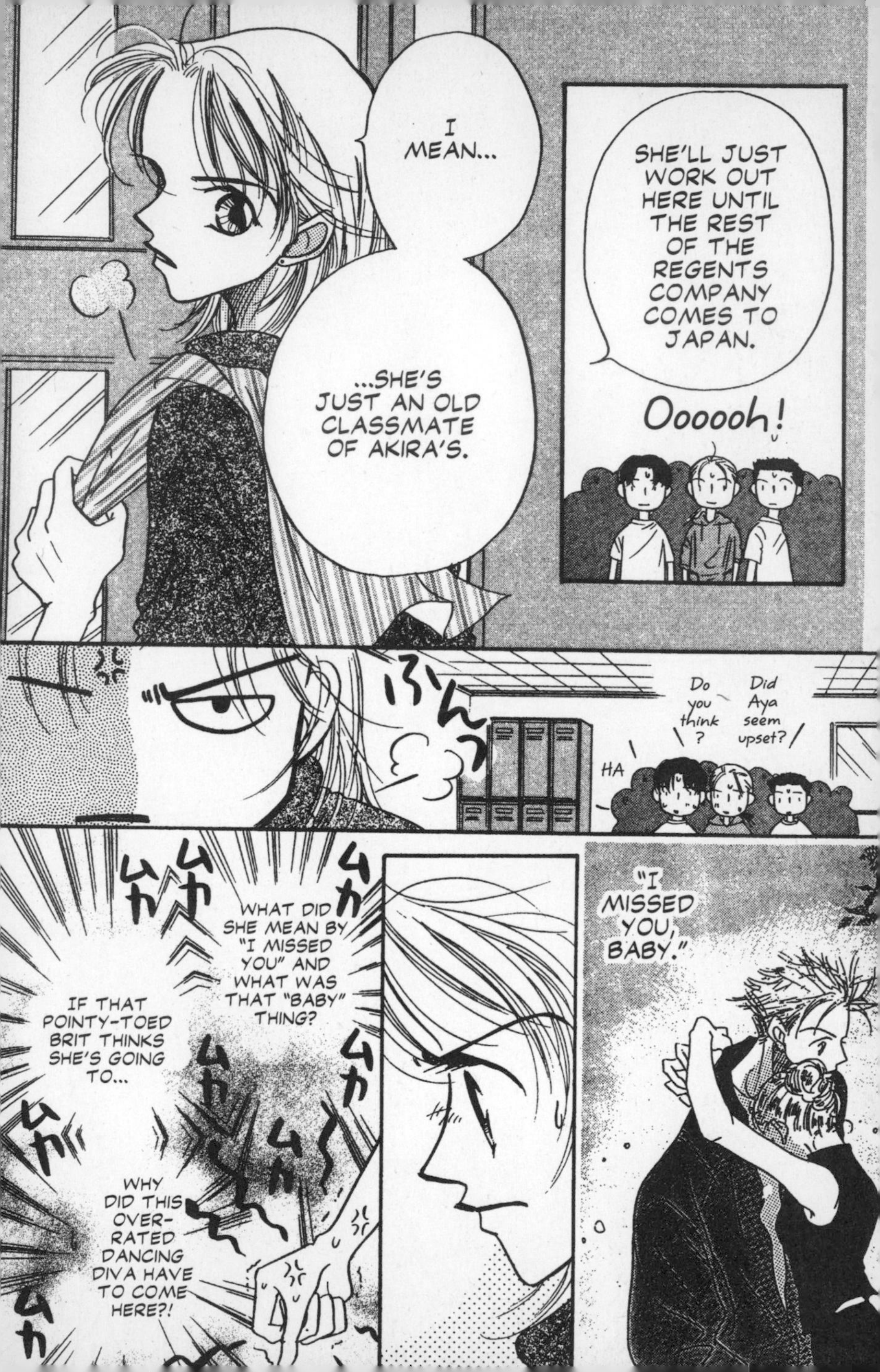
SHE'LL JUST WORK OUT HERE UNTIL THE REST OF THE REGENTS COMPANY COMES TO JAPAN.
Oooooh!
I MEAN...
...SHE'S JUST AN OLD CLASSMATE OF AKIRA'S.
Did Aya seem upset?
Do you think?
HA
ふんっ
"I MISSED YOU, BABY."
ムカ
WHAT DID SHE MEAN BY "I MISSED YOU" AND WHAT WAS THAT "BABY" THING?
ムカムカ
IF THAT POINTY-TOED BRIT THINKS SHE'S GOING TO...
WHY DID THIS OVER-RATED DANCING DIVA HAVE TO COME HERE?!
ムカ

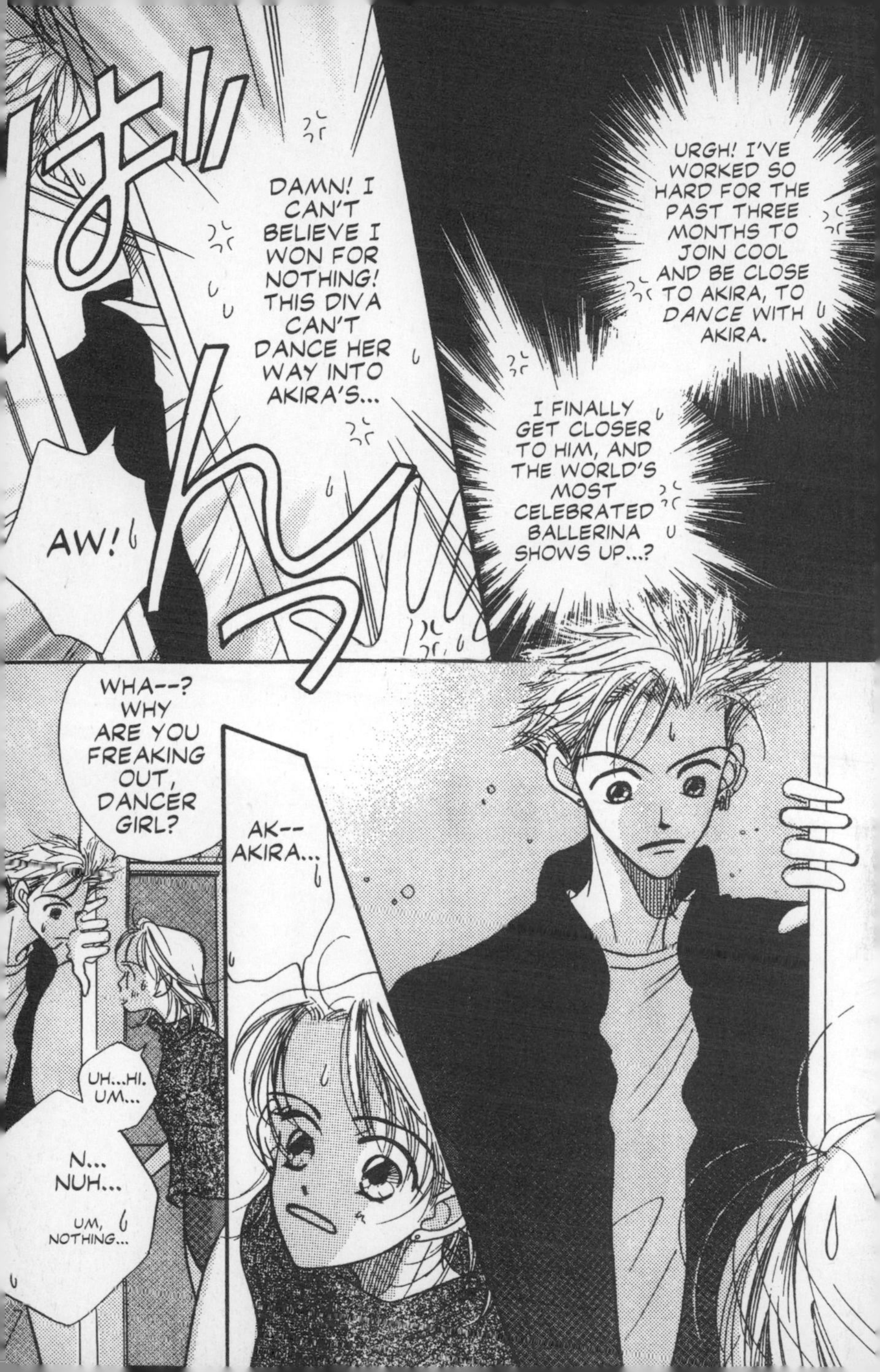
URGH! I'VE WORKED SO HARD FOR THE PAST THREE MONTHS TO JOIN COOL AND BE CLOSE TO AKIRA, TO *DANCE* WITH AKIRA.
I FINALLY GET CLOSER TO HIM, AND THE WORLD'S MOST CELEBRATED BALLERINA SHOWS UP...?
DAMN! I CAN'T BELIEVE I WON FOR NOTHING! THIS DIVA CAN'T DANCE HER WAY INTO AKIRA'S...
AW!
AK-- AKIRA...
WHA--? WHY ARE YOU FREAKING OUT, DANCER GIRL?
UH...HI. UM...
N... NUH...
UM, NOTHING...

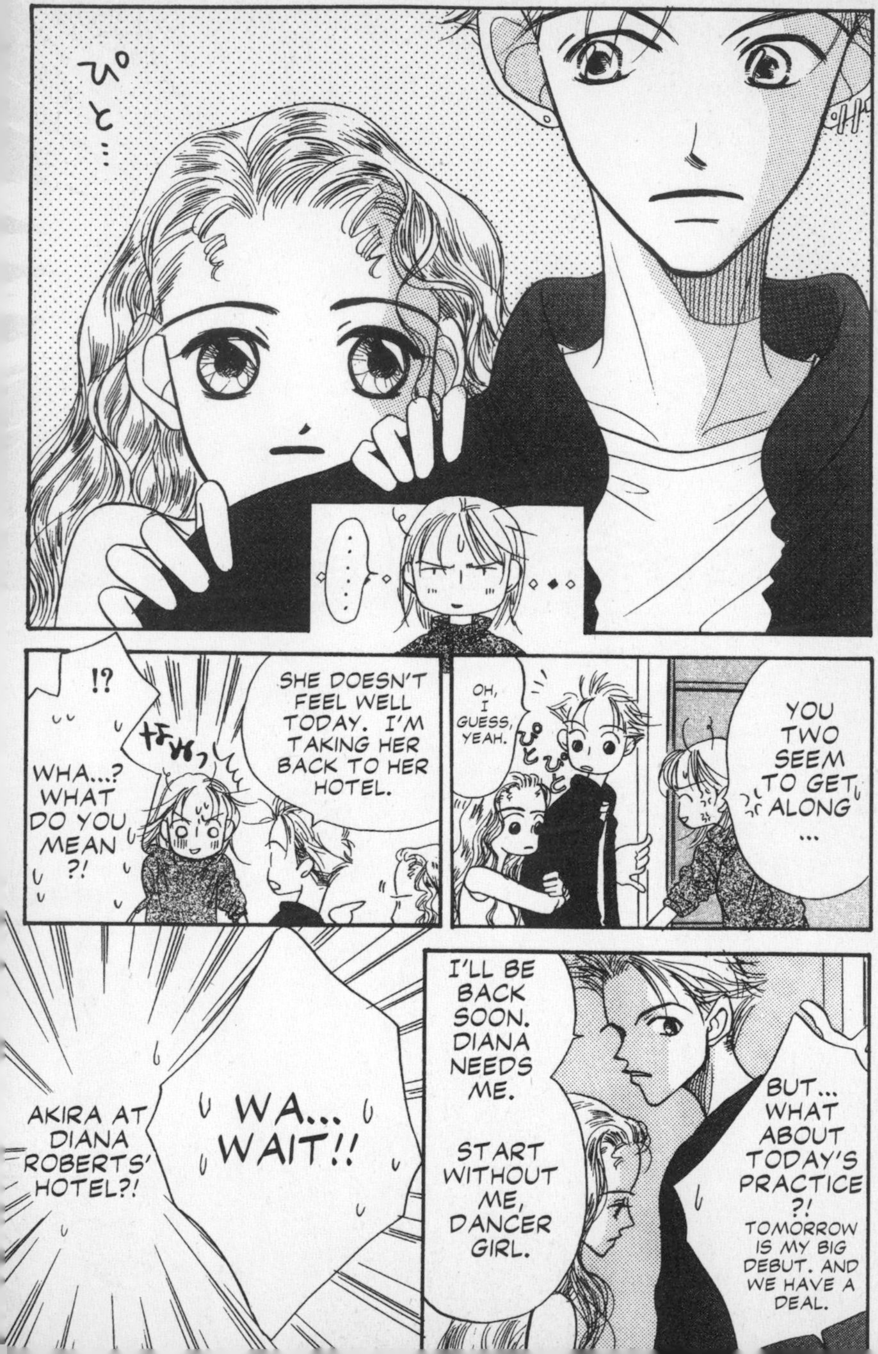
ぴと…
……
YOU TWO SEEM TO GET ALONG ...
OH, I GUESS, YEAH.
ぴとぴと
SHE DOESN'T FEEL WELL TODAY. I'M TAKING HER BACK TO HER HOTEL.
!?
WHA...? WHAT DO YOU MEAN ?!
I'LL BE BACK SOON. DIANA NEEDS ME.
BUT... WHAT ABOUT TODAY'S PRACTICE ?! TOMORROW IS MY BIG DEBUT. AND WE HAVE A DEAL.
START WITHOUT ME, DANCER GIRL.
WA... WAIT!!
AKIRA AT DIANA ROBERTS' HOTEL?!

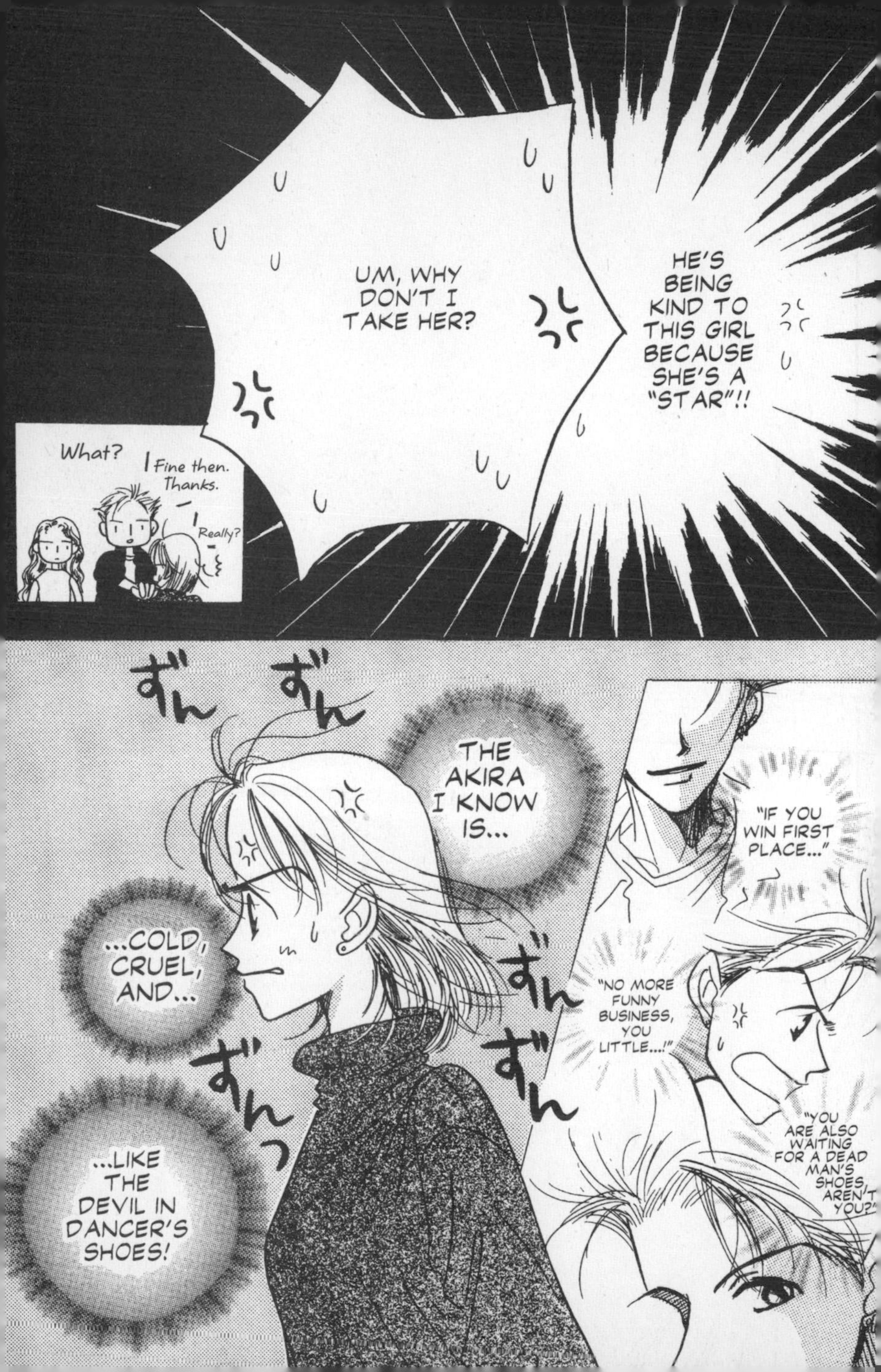
HE'S BEING KIND TO THIS GIRL BECAUSE SHE'S A "STAR"!!
UM, WHY DON'T I TAKE HER?
Fine then. Thanks.
Really?
What?
"IF YOU WIN FIRST PLACE..."
"NO MORE FUNNY BUSINESS, YOU LITTLE...!"
"YOU ARE ALSO WAITING FOR A DEAD MAN'S SHOES, AREN'T YOU?"
ずん
ずん
THE AKIRA I KNOW IS...
...COLD, CRUEL, AND...
ずん
ずん
ずんっ
...LIKE THE DEVIL IN DANCER'S SHOES!

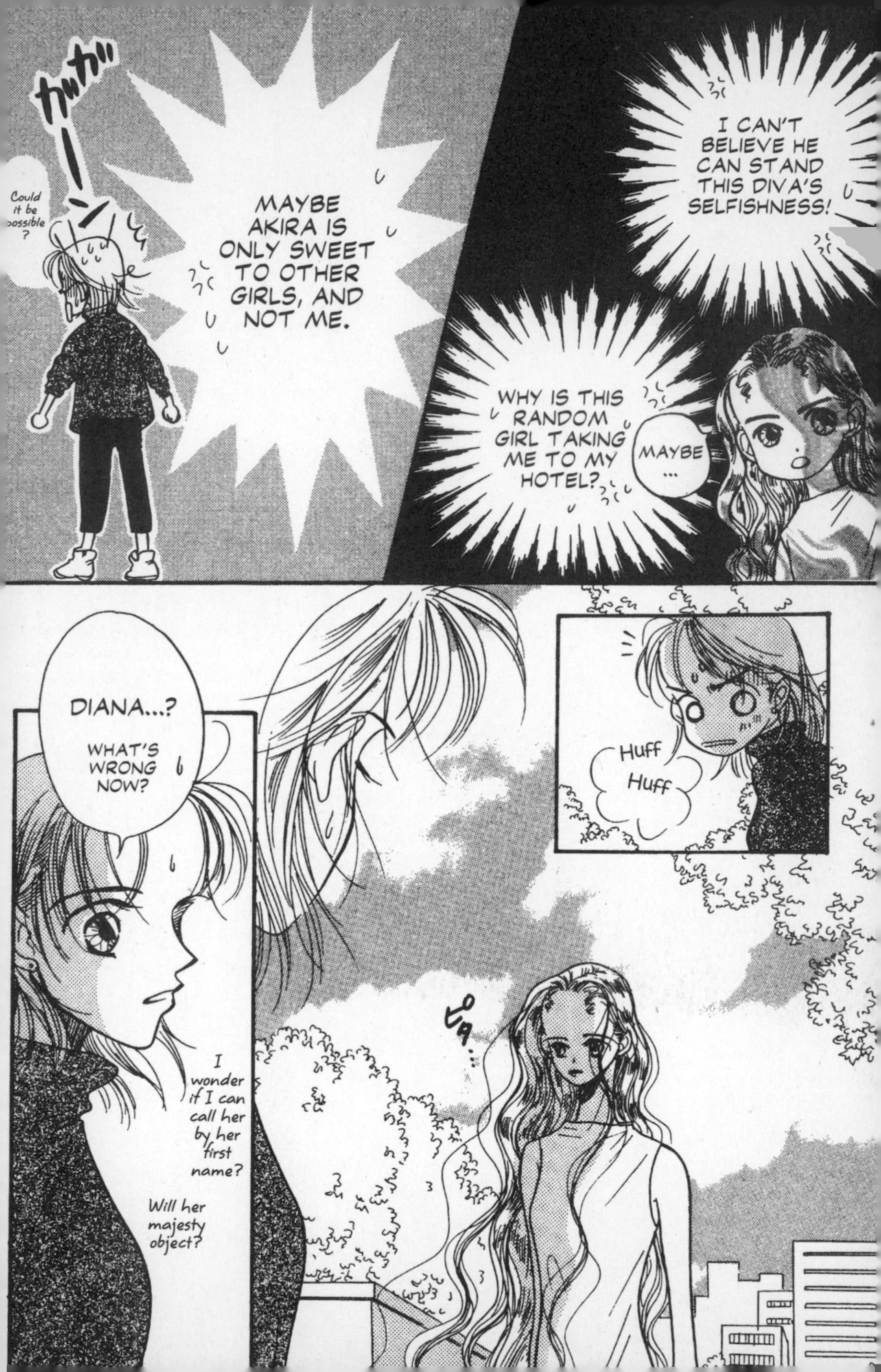
I CAN'T BELIEVE HE CAN STAND THIS DIVA'S SELFISHNESS!
WHY IS THIS RANDOM GIRL TAKING ME TO MY HOTEL?
MAYBE ...
MAYBE AKIRA IS ONLY SWEET TO OTHER GIRLS, AND NOT ME.
Could it be possible?
Huff Huff
DIANA...? WHAT'S WRONG NOW?
I wonder if I can call her by her first name?
Will her majesty object?

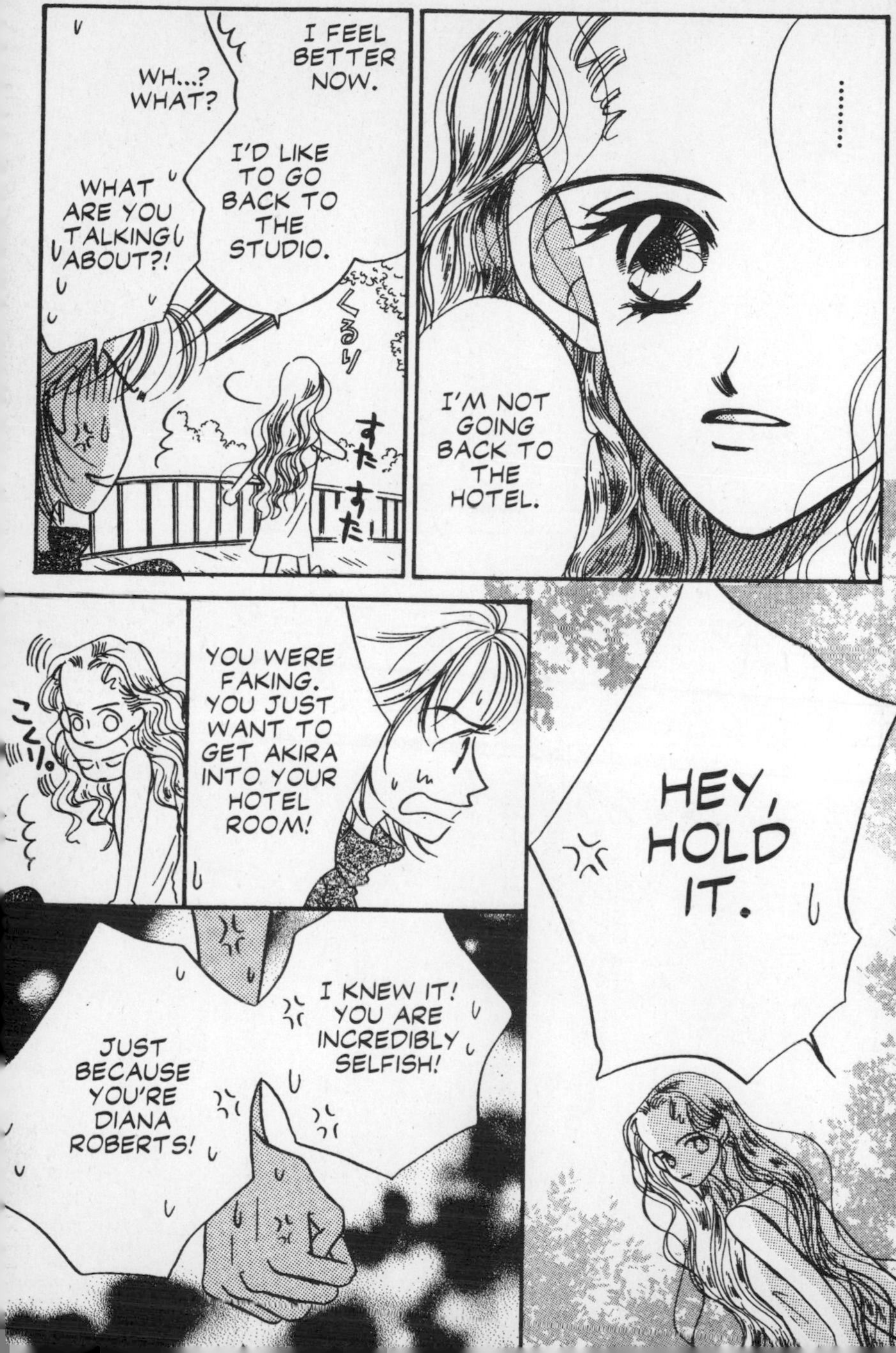
......
I'M NOT GOING BACK TO THE HOTEL.
I FEEL BETTER NOW.
I'D LIKE TO GO BACK TO THE STUDIO.
くるり
WH...? WHAT?
WHAT ARE YOU TALKING ABOUT?!
すたすた
HEY, HOLD IT.
YOU WERE FAKING. YOU JUST WANT TO GET AKIRA INTO YOUR HOTEL ROOM!
I KNEW IT! YOU ARE INCREDIBLY SELFISH!
JUST BECAUSE YOU'RE DIANA ROBERTS!

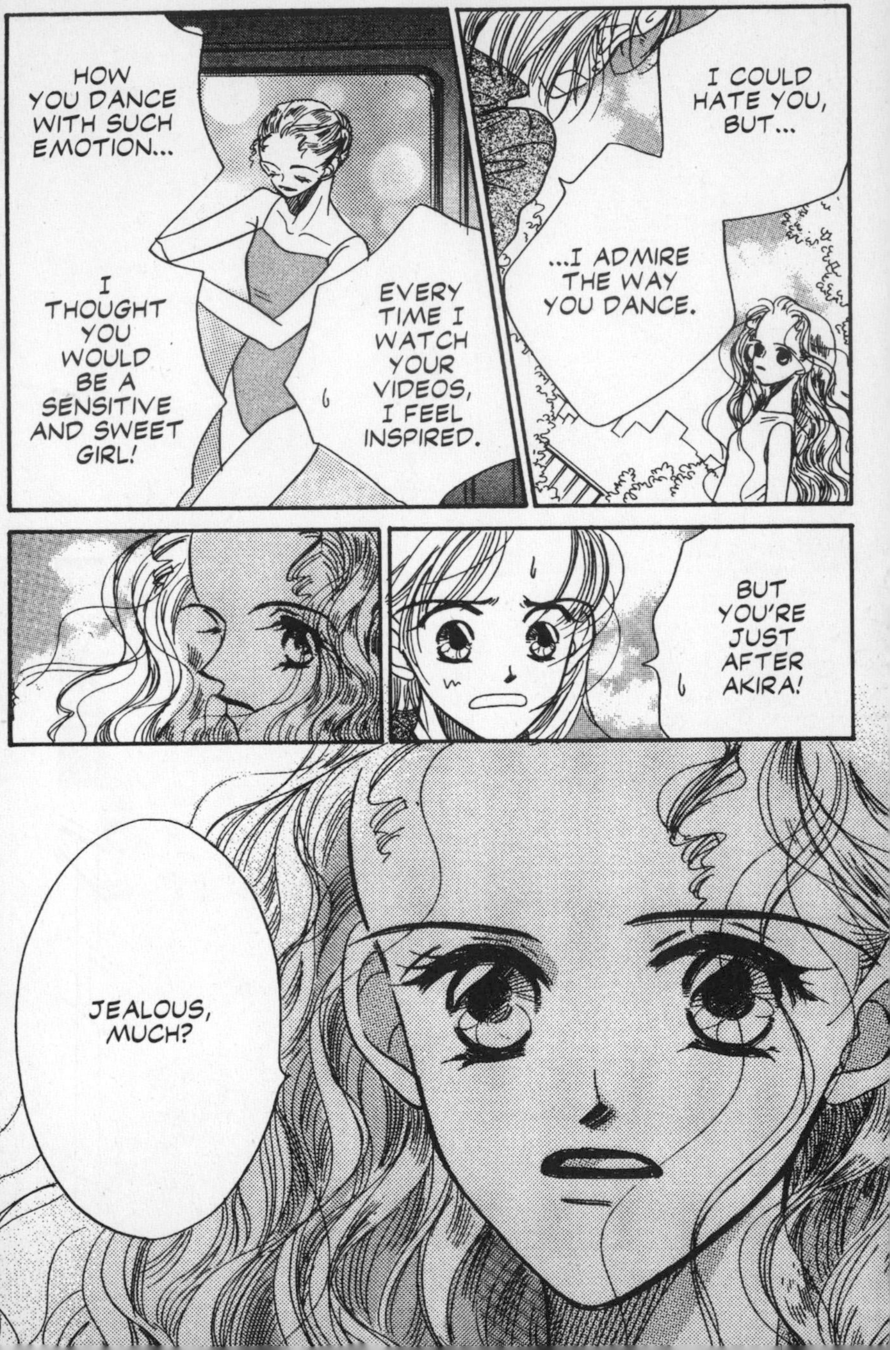
I COULD HATE YOU, BUT...
...I ADMIRE THE WAY YOU DANCE.
EVERY TIME I WATCH YOUR VIDEOS, I FEEL INSPIRED.
HOW YOU DANCE WITH SUCH EMOTION...
I THOUGHT YOU WOULD BE A SENSITIVE AND SWEET GIRL!
BUT YOU'RE JUST AFTER AKIRA!
JEALOUS, MUCH?

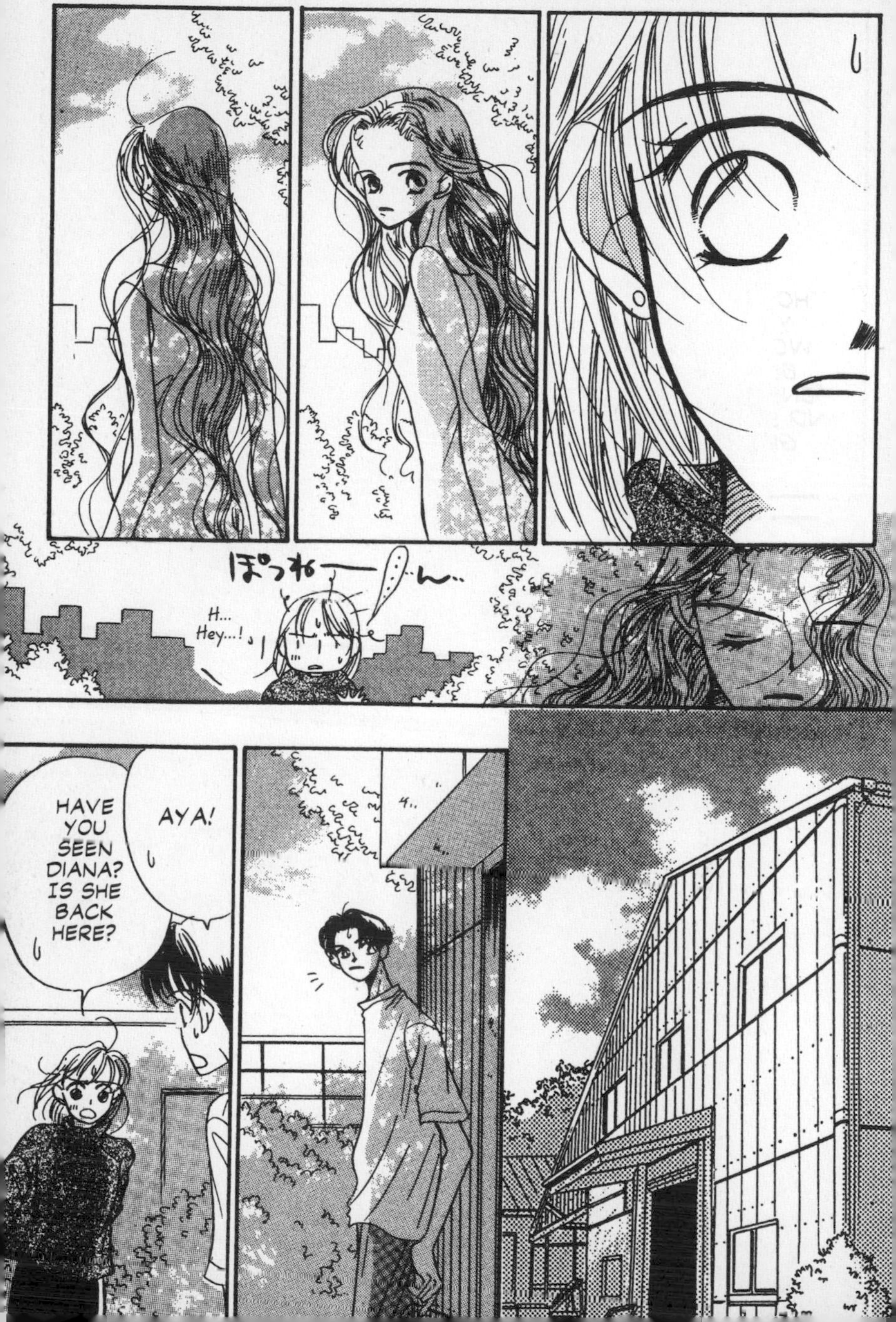
ぽつねーーん
H... Hey...!
AYA!
HAVE YOU SEEN DIANA? IS SHE BACK HERE?

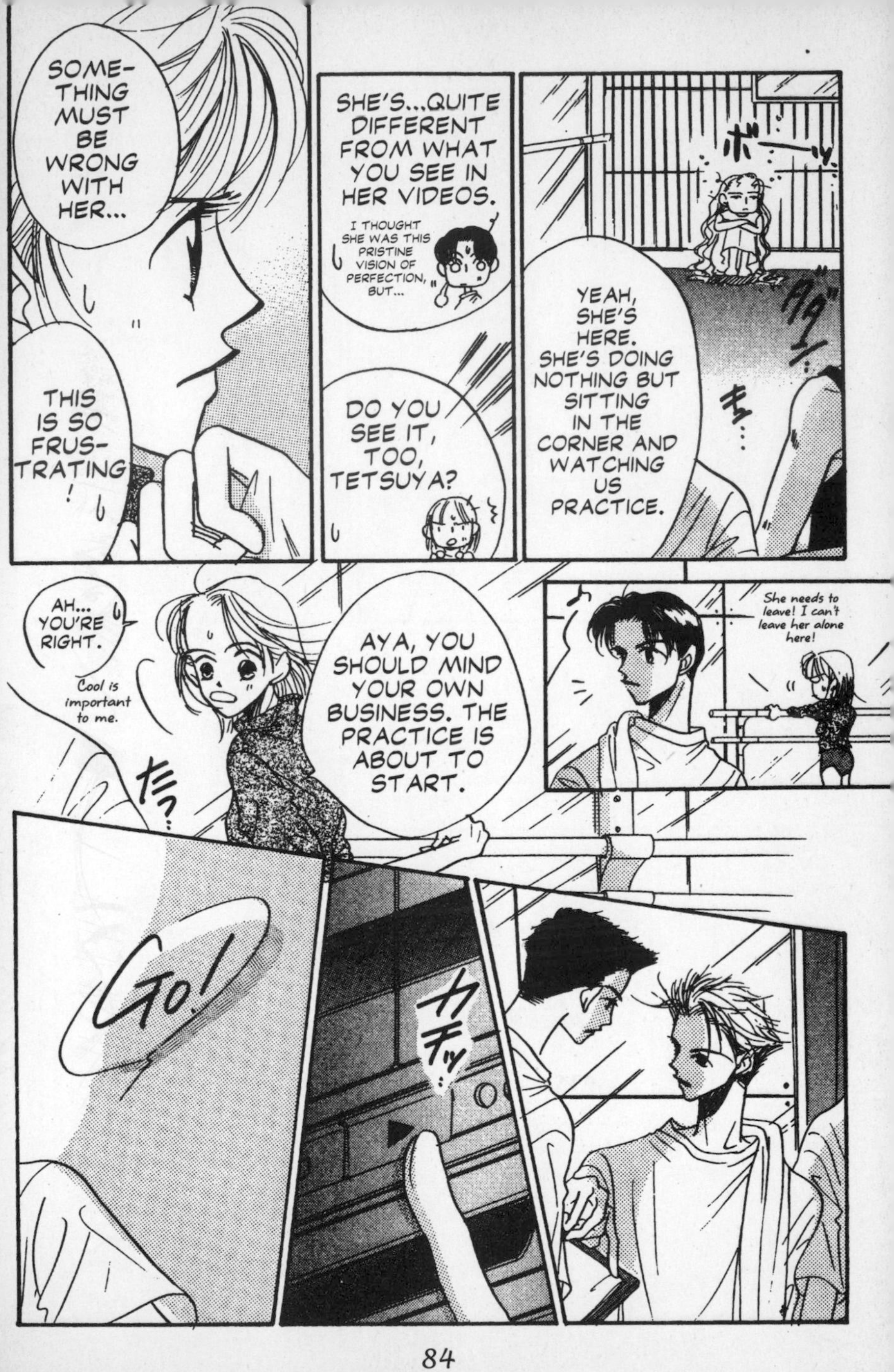
YEAH, SHE'S HERE. SHE'S DOING NOTHING BUT SITTING IN THE CORNER AND WATCHING US PRACTICE.
SHE'S...QUITE DIFFERENT FROM WHAT YOU SEE IN HER VIDEOS.
I THOUGHT SHE WAS THIS PRISTINE VISION OF PERFECTION, BUT...
DO YOU SEE IT, TOO, TETSUYA?
SOME-THING MUST BE WRONG WITH HER...
THIS IS SO FRUS-TRATING!
She needs to leave! I can't leave her alone here!
AYA, YOU SHOULD MIND YOUR OWN BUSINESS. THE PRACTICE IS ABOUT TO START.
AH... YOU'RE RIGHT.
Cool is important to me.
GO!

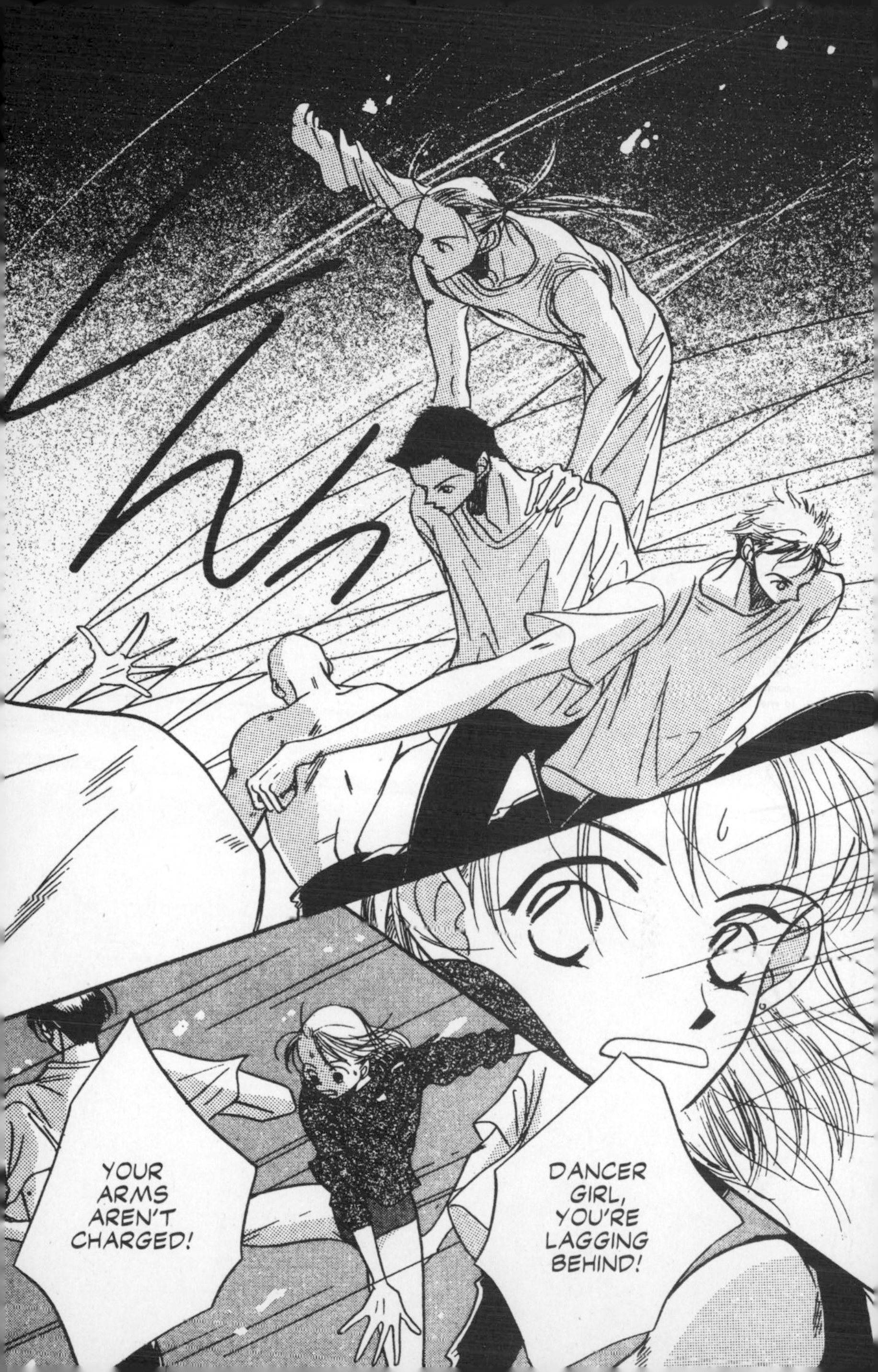
DANCER GIRL, YOU'RE LAGGING BEHIND!
YOUR ARMS AREN'T CHARGED!

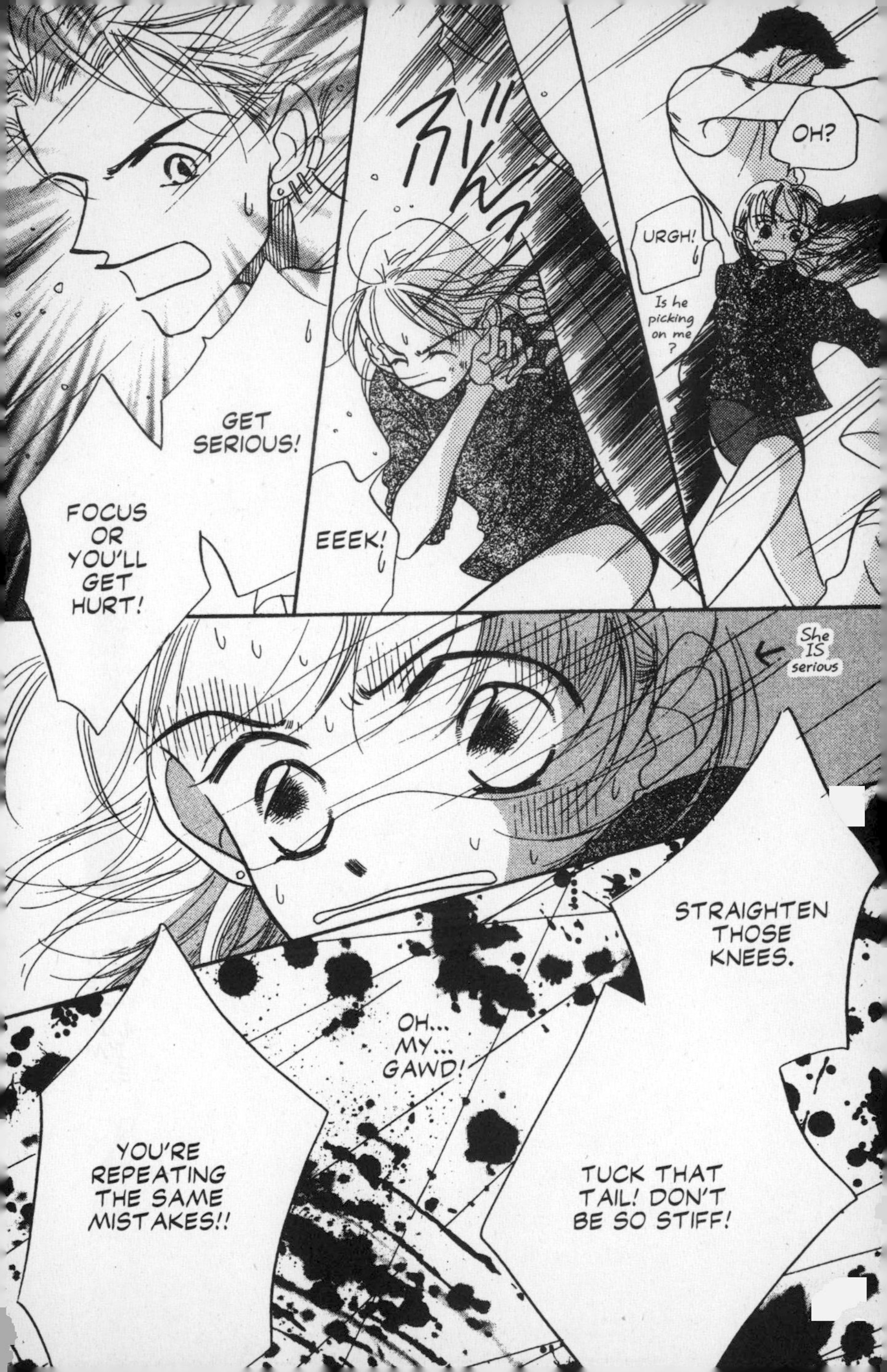
OH?
URGH!
Is he picking on me?
EEEK!
GET SERIOUS!
FOCUS OR YOU'LL GET HURT!
She IS serious
STRAIGHTEN THOSE KNEES.
OH... MY... GAWD!
TUCK THAT TAIL! DON'T BE SO STIFF!
YOU'RE REPEATING THE SAME MISTAKES!!

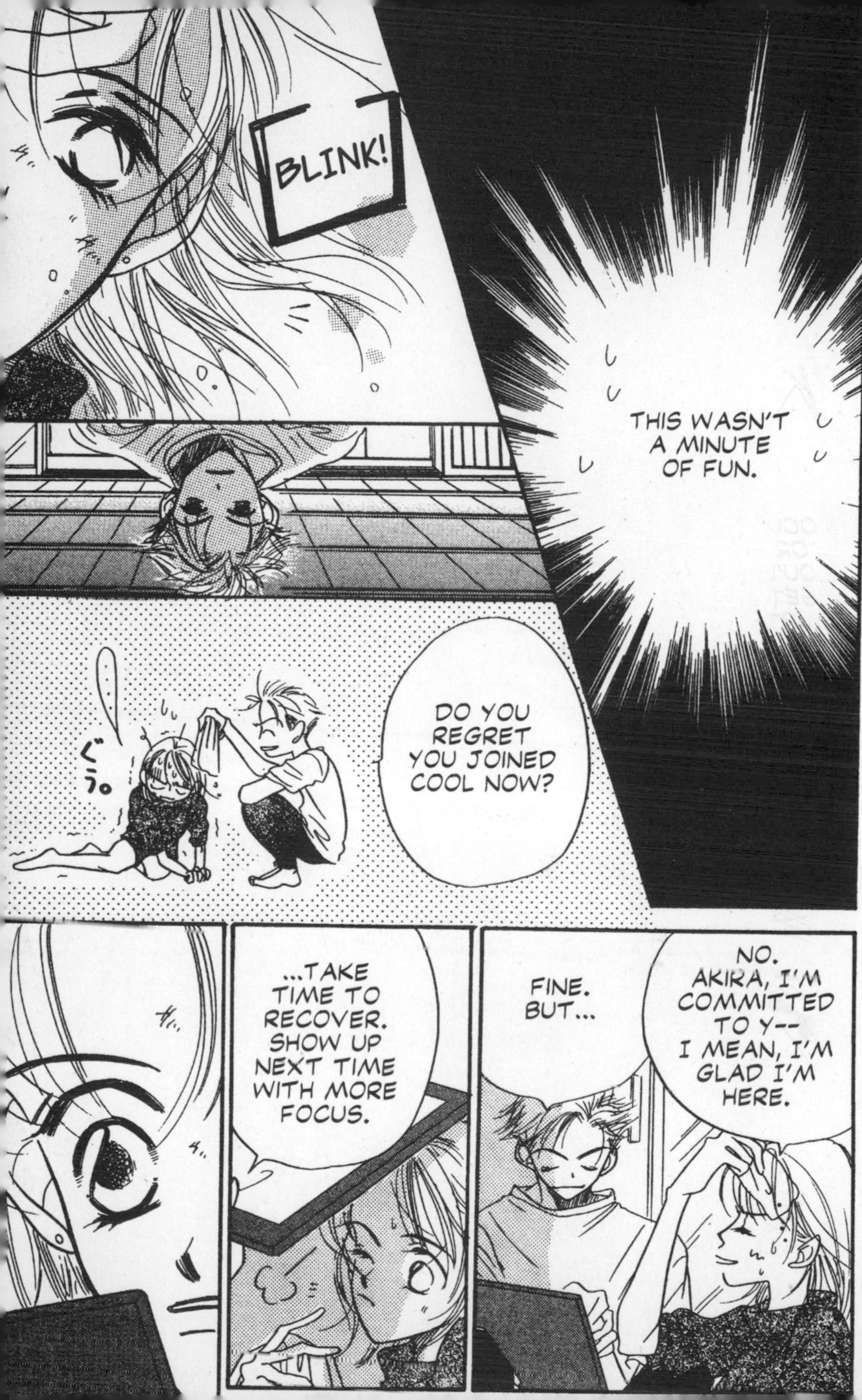
THIS WASN'T A MINUTE OF FUN.
BLINK!
DO YOU REGRET YOU JOINED COOL NOW?
NO. AKIRA, I'M COMMITTED TO Y-- I MEAN, I'M GLAD I'M HERE.
FINE. BUT...
...TAKE TIME TO RECOVER. SHOW UP NEXT TIME WITH MORE FOCUS.

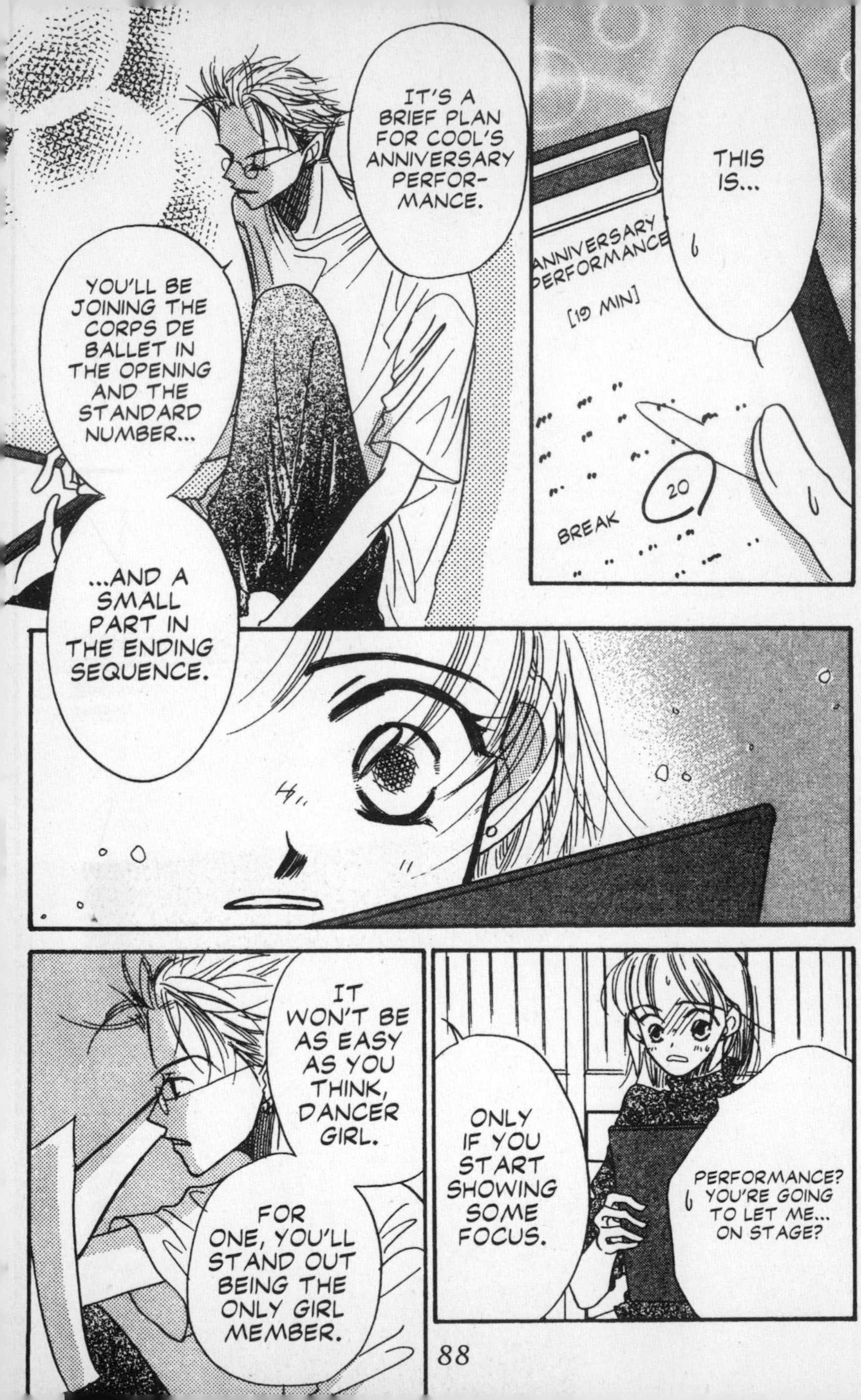
THIS IS...
ANNIVERSARY PERFORMANCE
[19 MIN]
20
BREAK
IT'S A BRIEF PLAN FOR COOL'S ANNIVERSARY PERFORMANCE.
YOU'LL BE JOINING THE CORPS DE BALLET IN THE OPENING AND THE STANDARD NUMBER...
...AND A SMALL PART IN THE ENDING SEQUENCE.
PERFORMANCE? YOU'RE GOING TO LET ME... ON STAGE?
ONLY IF YOU START SHOWING SOME FOCUS.
IT WON'T BE AS EASY AS YOU THINK, DANCER GIRL.
FOR ONE, YOU'LL STAND OUT BEING THE ONLY GIRL MEMBER.

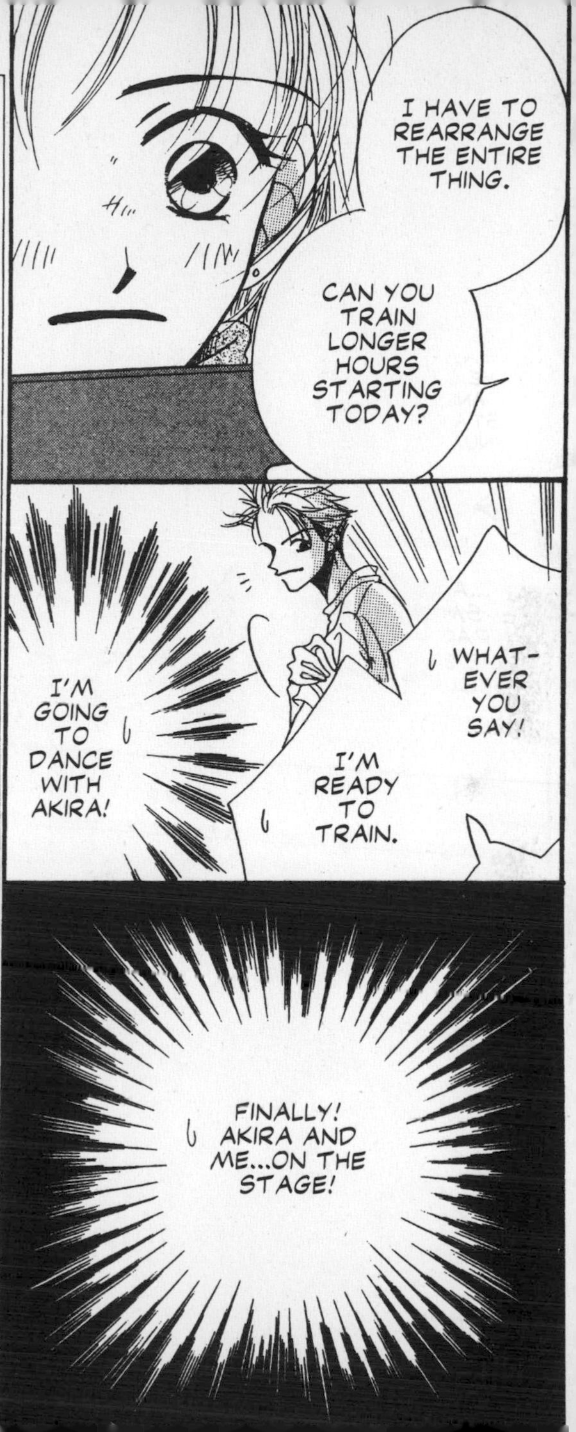
I HAVE TO REARRANGE THE ENTIRE THING.
CAN YOU TRAIN LONGER HOURS STARTING TODAY?
WHAT-EVER YOU SAY!
I'M READY TO TRAIN.
I'M GOING TO DANCE WITH AKIRA!
FINALLY! AKIRA AND ME...ON THE STAGE!

Ashihara's Diary

No. 3

It's interesting to see how each ballet troupe is different, even if they all do classic ballet. For example, each ballet group does "Swan Lake" in their own way and gives a different impression. I am sure each viewer also interprets the same ballet differently. To be honest, I am not an expert of ballet yet, and sometimes feel tired and sleepy in the middle of the performance. I often find out that some critics rave about the scenes I found boring! When that happens, I tend to think "no kidding?" But I've learned how to appreciate ballet differently by reading the reviews. Ballet is an art and it's only natural that each person has her own unique way of interpreting it. Although I might not have a deep understanding, I realized that it's okay to enjoy ballet in my own way.

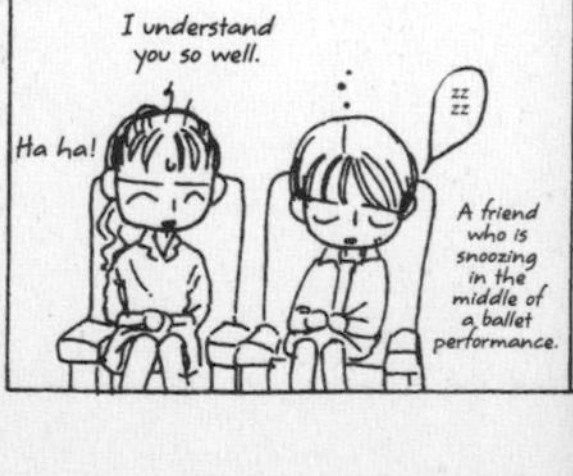
I understand you so well.
Ha ha!
ZZ ZZ
A friend who is snoozing in the middle of a ballet performance.

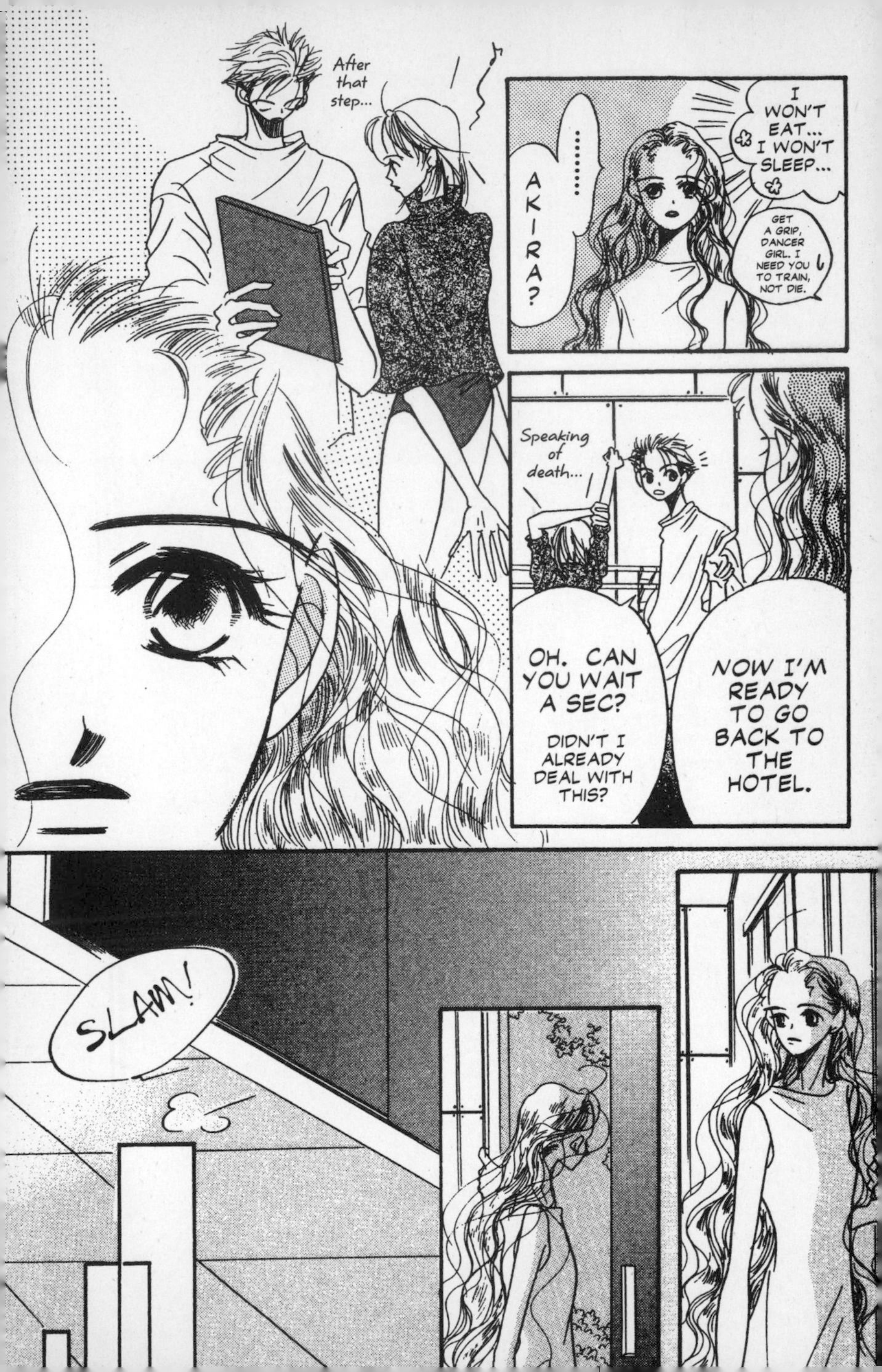
I WON'T EAT... I WON'T SLEEP...
GET A GRIP, DANCER GIRL. I NEED YOU TO TRAIN, NOT DIE.
...... AKIRA?
NOW I'M READY TO GO BACK TO THE HOTEL.
OH. CAN YOU WAIT A SEC?
DIDN'T I ALREADY DEAL WITH THIS?
Speaking of death...
After that step...
SLAM!

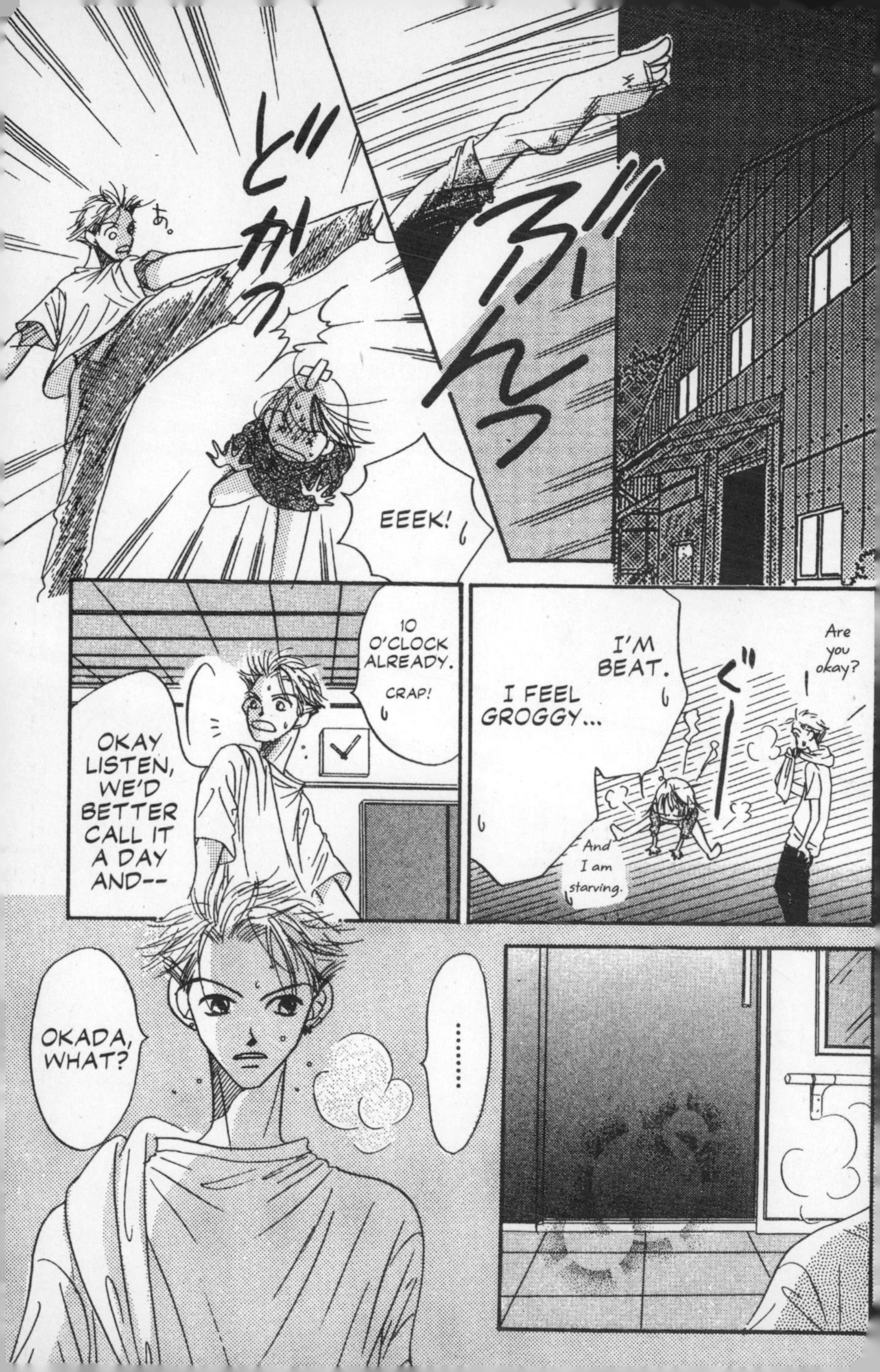
ぶんっ
どかっ
あ。
EEEK!
Are you okay?
ぐー
I'M BEAT.
I FEEL GROGGY...
And I am starving.
10 O'CLOCK ALREADY.
CRAP!
OKAY LISTEN, WE'D BETTER CALL IT A DAY AND--
....
OKADA, WHAT?

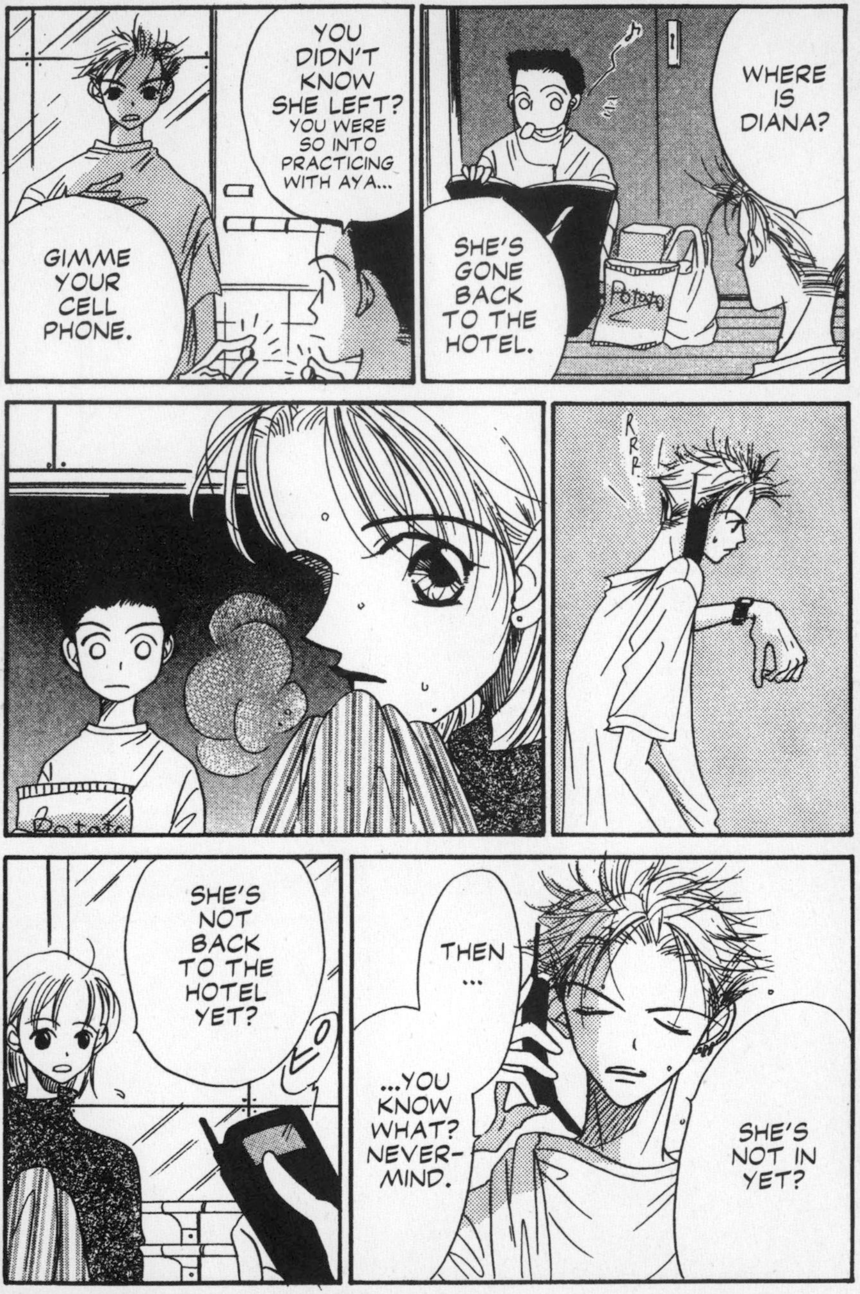
WHERE IS DIANA?
SHE'S GONE BACK TO THE HOTEL.
YOU DIDN'T KNOW SHE LEFT? YOU WERE SO INTO PRACTICING WITH AYA...
GIMME YOUR CELL PHONE.
RRR
SHE'S NOT IN YET?
THEN...
...YOU KNOW WHAT? NEVER-MIND.
SHE'S NOT BACK TO THE HOTEL YET?

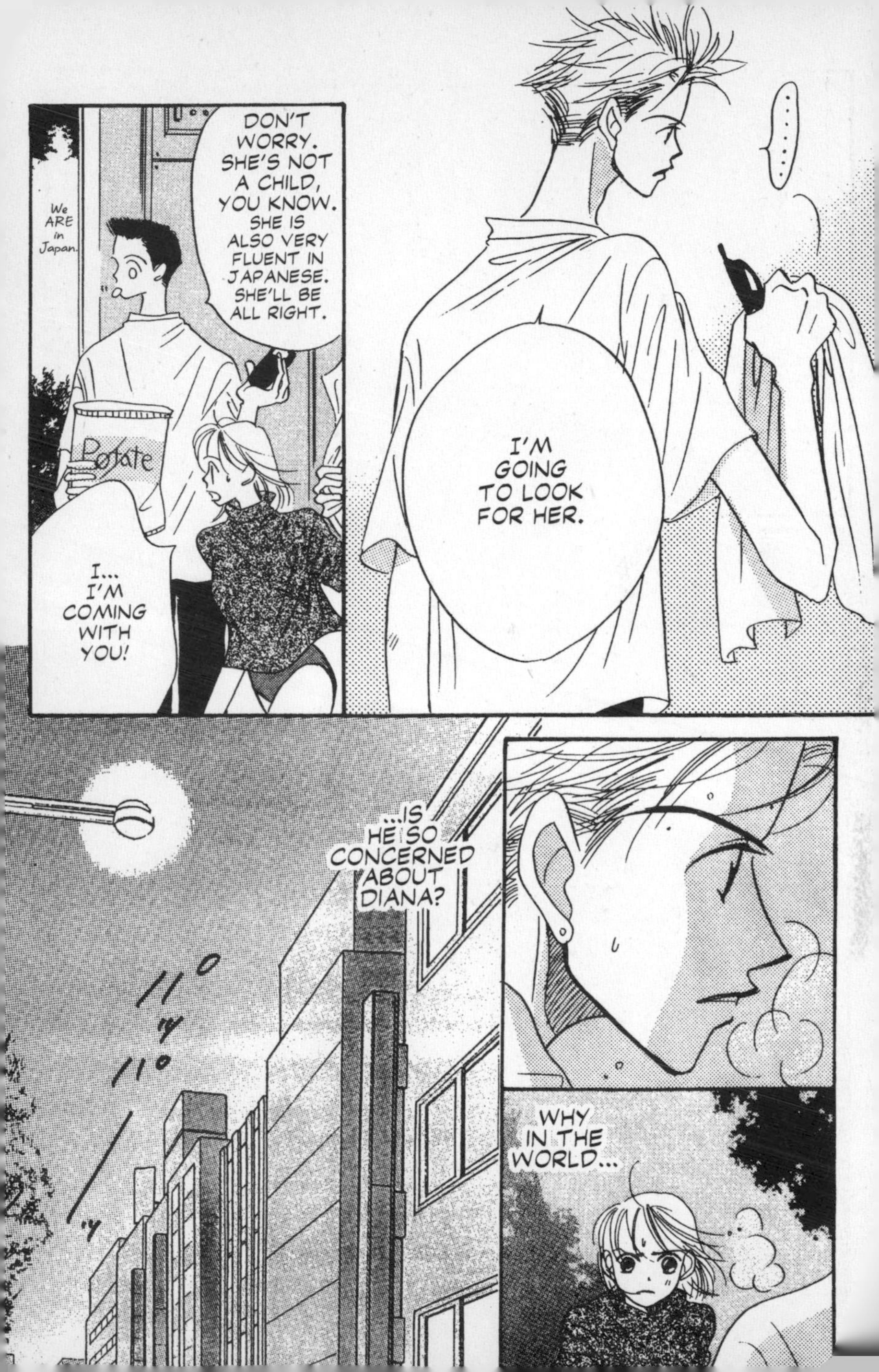
. . . . . .
I'M GOING TO LOOK FOR HER.
DON'T WORRY. SHE'S NOT A CHILD, YOU KNOW. SHE IS ALSO VERY FLUENT IN JAPANESE. SHE'LL BE ALL RIGHT.
We ARE in Japan.
Potate
I... I'M COMING WITH YOU!
WHY IN THE WORLD...
...IS HE SO CONCERNED ABOUT DIANA?

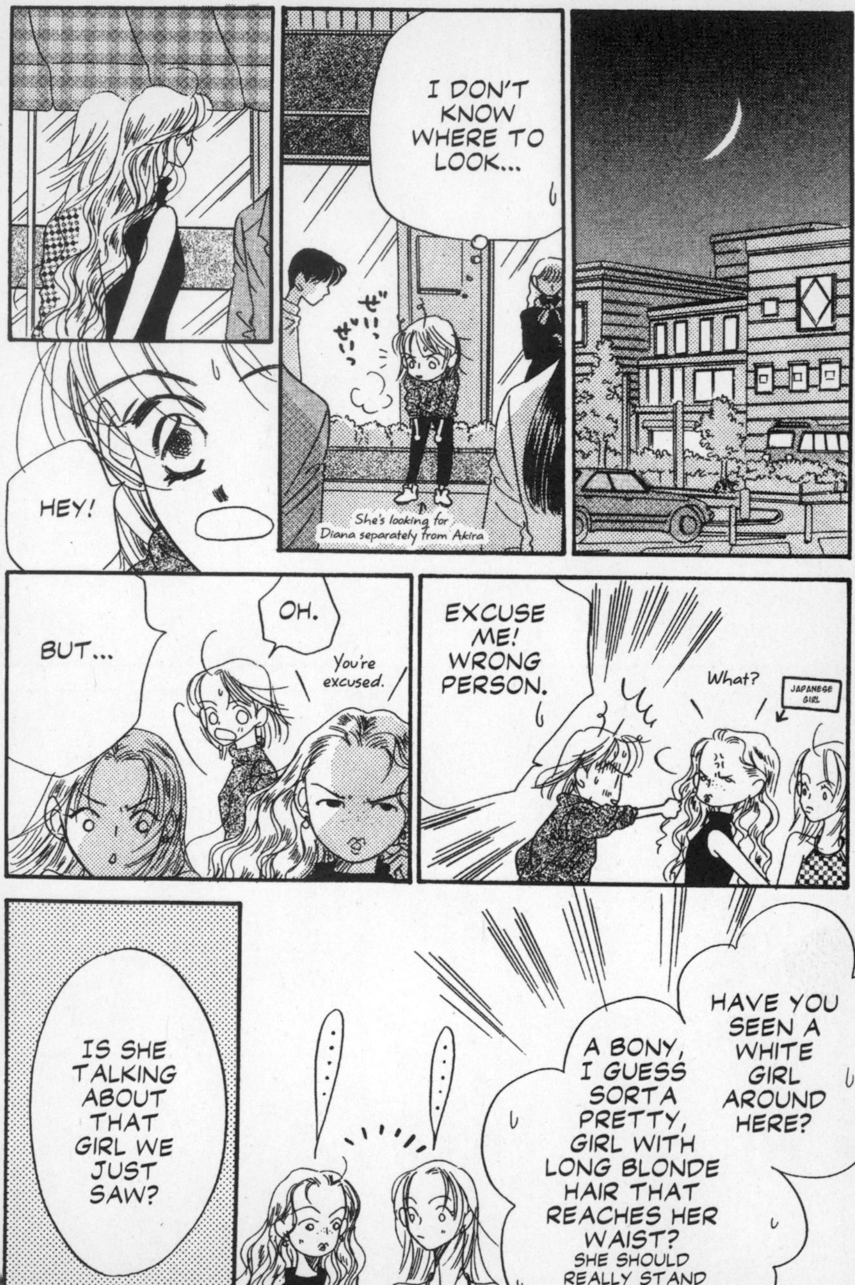
I DON'T KNOW WHERE TO LOOK...
ぜい、ぜい
She's looking for Diana separately from Akira
HEY!
EXCUSE ME! WRONG PERSON.
What?
JAPANESE GIRL
OH.
You're excused.
BUT...
HAVE YOU SEEN A WHITE GIRL AROUND HERE?
A BONY, I GUESS SORTA PRETTY, GIRL WITH LONG BLONDE HAIR THAT REACHES HER WAIST? SHE SHOULD REALLY STAND OUT.
IS SHE TALKING ABOUT THAT GIRL WE JUST SAW?

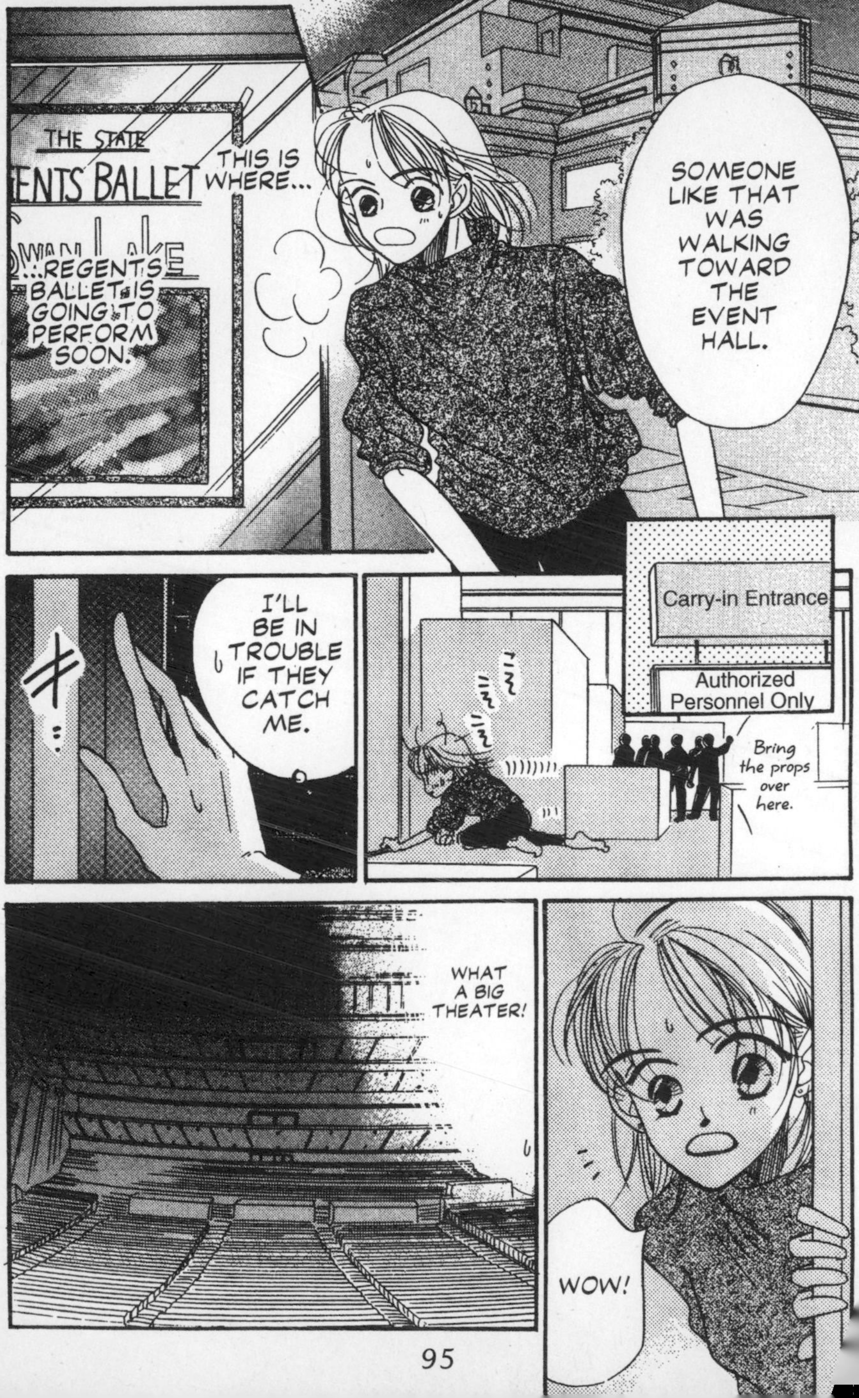
SOMEONE LIKE THAT WAS WALKING TOWARD THE EVENT HALL.
THIS IS WHERE...
THE STATE
...REGENTS BALLET IS GOING TO PERFORM SOON.
Carry-in Entrance
Authorized Personnel Only
Bring the props over here.
I'LL BE IN TROUBLE IF THEY CATCH ME.
WOW!
WHAT A BIG THEATER!

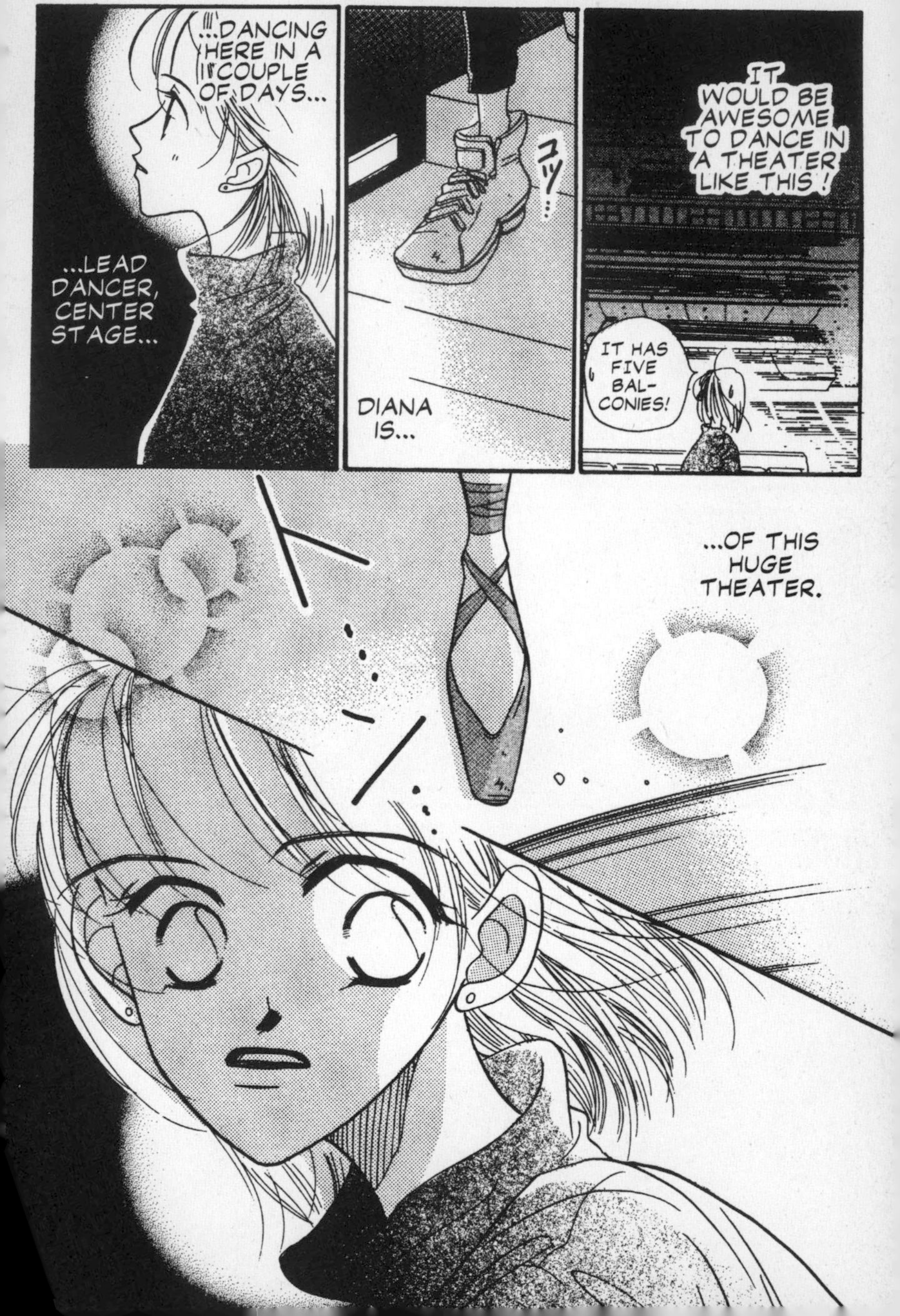
IT WOULD BE AWESOME TO DANCE IN A THEATER LIKE THIS!
IT HAS FIVE BAL-CONIES!
コッ…
DIANA IS...
...DANCING HERE IN A COUPLE OF DAYS...
...LEAD DANCER, CENTER STAGE...
...OF THIS HUGE THEATER.

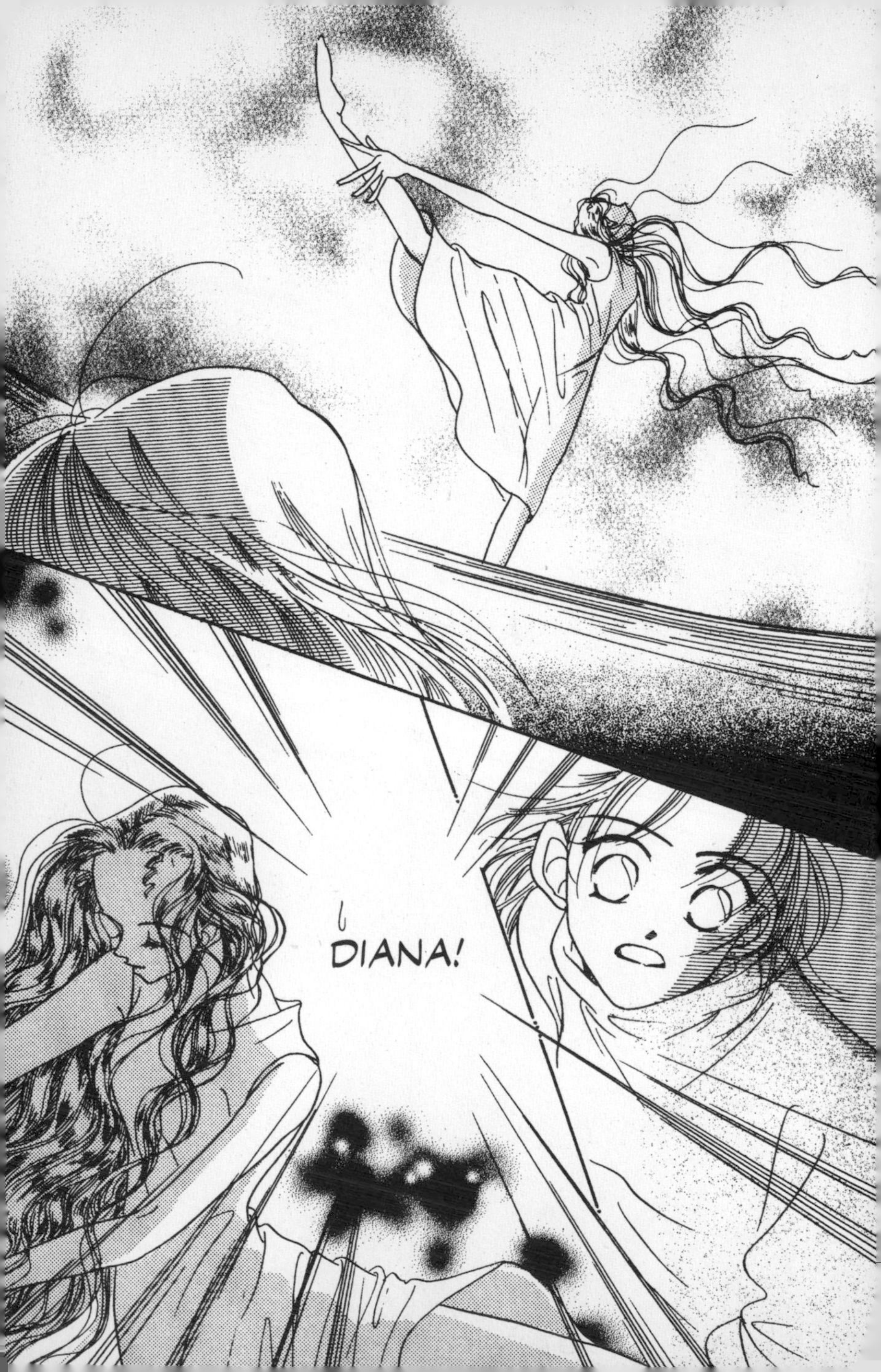
DIANA!

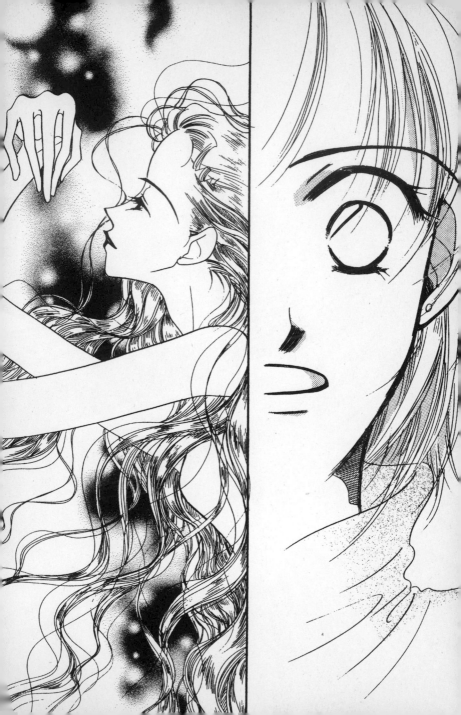

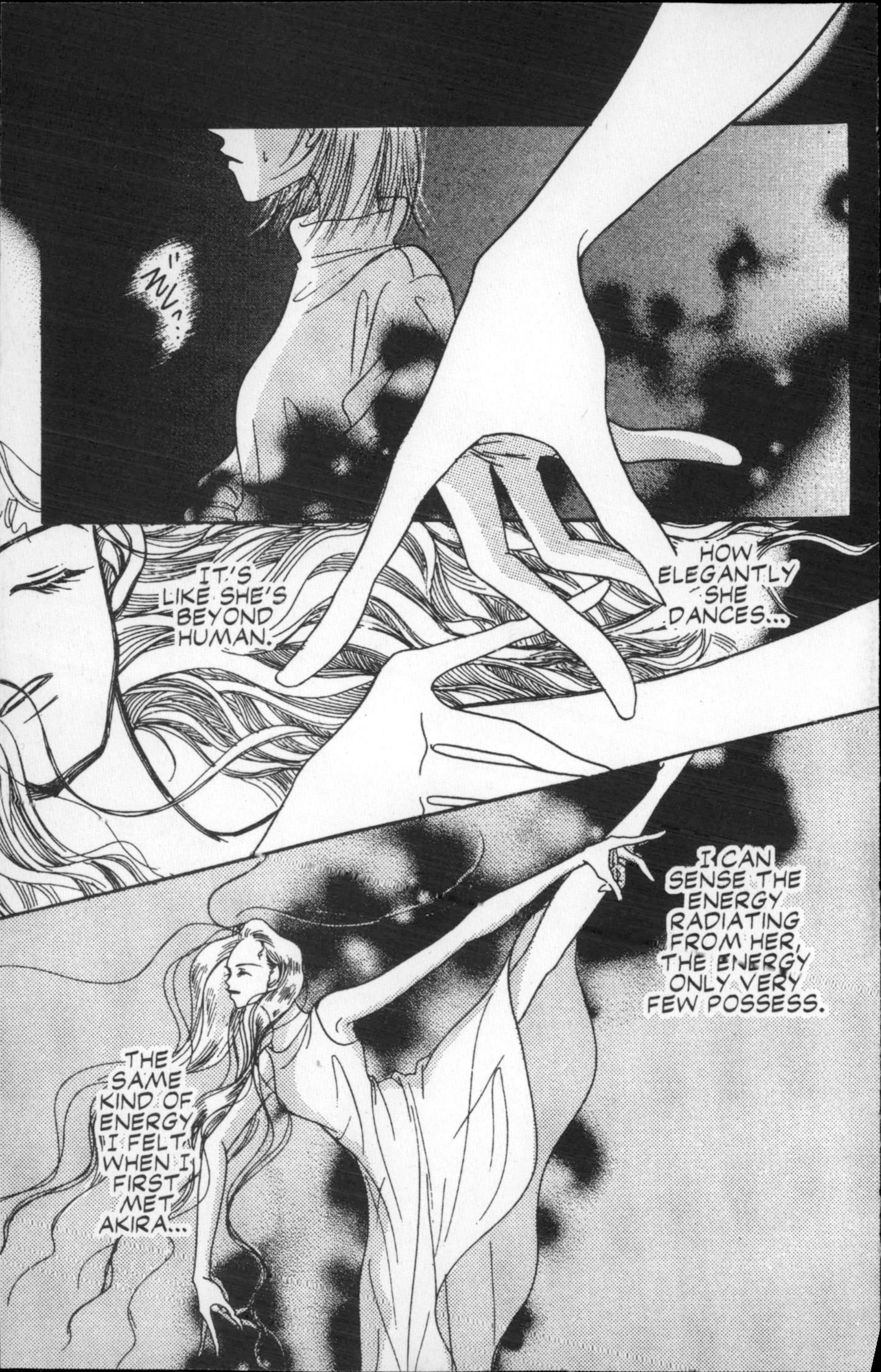
HOW ELEGANTLY SHE DANCES...
IT'S LIKE SHE'S BEYOND HUMAN.
I CAN SENSE THE ENERGY RADIATING FROM HER, THE ENERGY ONLY VERY FEW POSSESS.
THE SAME KIND OF ENERGY I FELT WHEN I FIRST MET AKIRA...

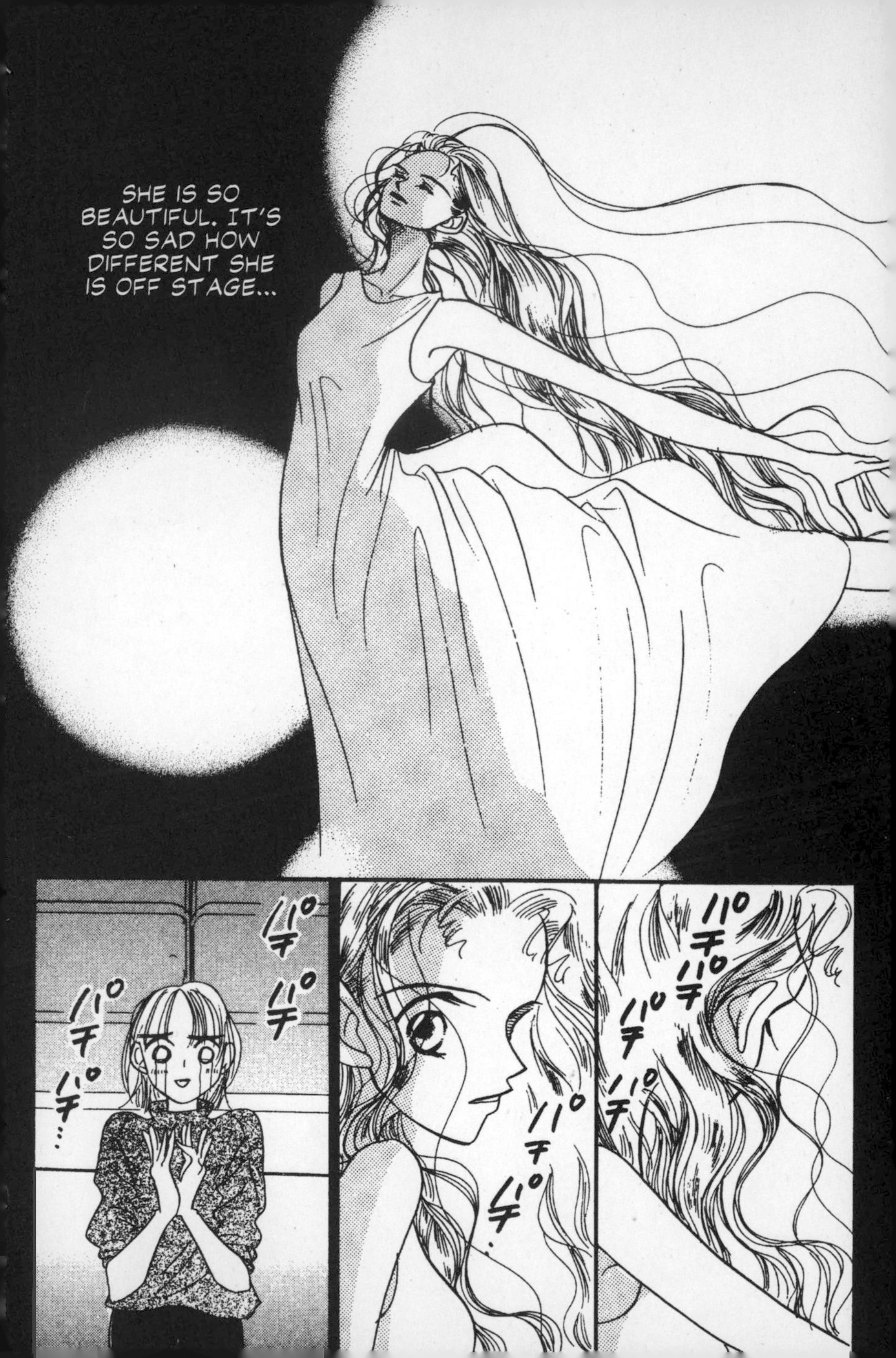
SHE IS SO BEAUTIFUL. IT'S SO SAD HOW DIFFERENT SHE IS OFF STAGE...
パチパチ
パチ
パチ
パチパチ...
パチ
パチ
パチ
パチ...

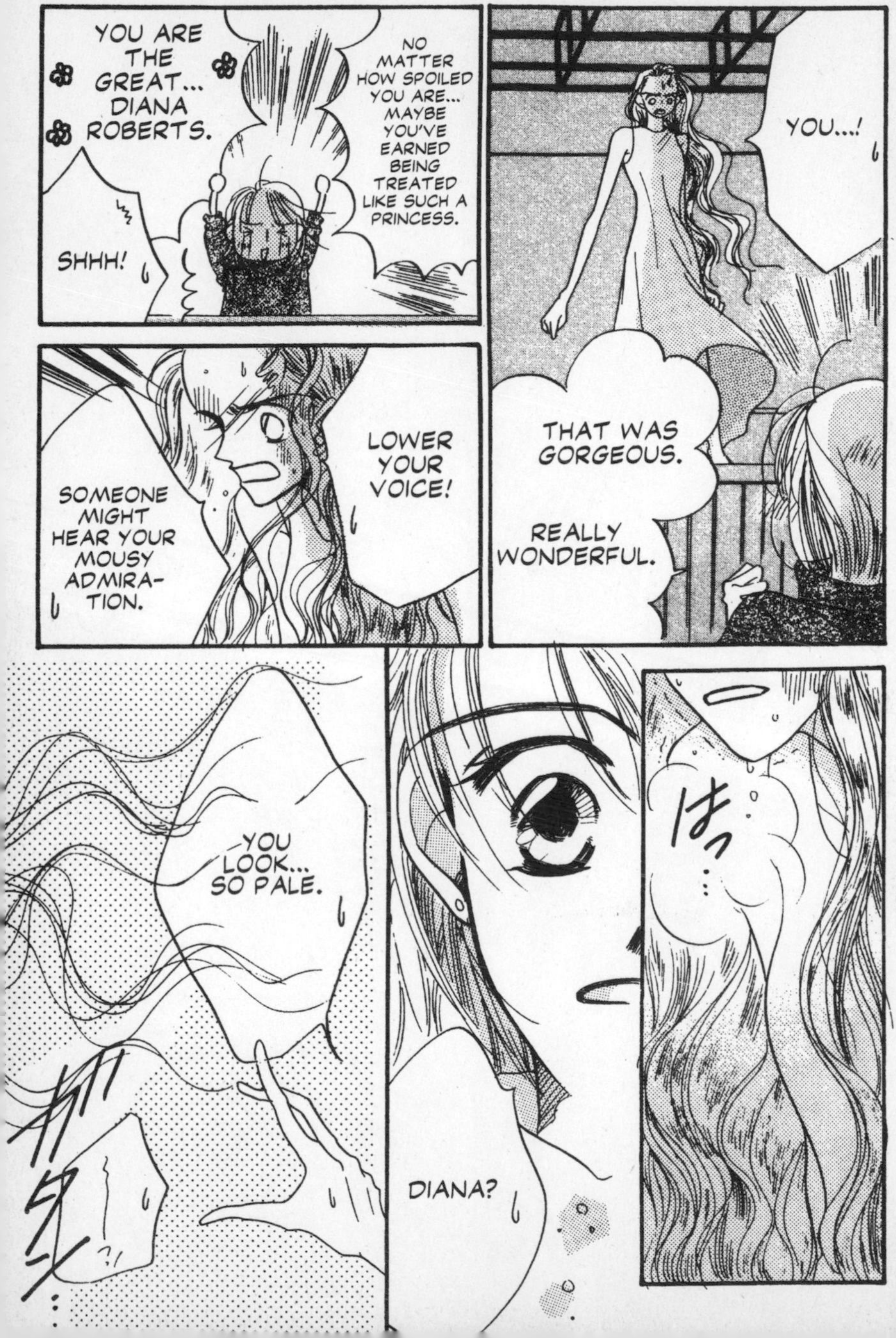
YOU...!
THAT WAS GORGEOUS.
REALLY WONDERFUL.
NO MATTER HOW SPOILED YOU ARE... MAYBE YOU'VE EARNED BEING TREATED LIKE SUCH A PRINCESS.
YOU ARE THE GREAT... DIANA ROBERTS.
SHHH!
LOWER YOUR VOICE!
SOMEONE MIGHT HEAR YOUR MOUSY ADMIRATION.
はっ…
DIANA?
YOU LOOK... SO PALE.
?!

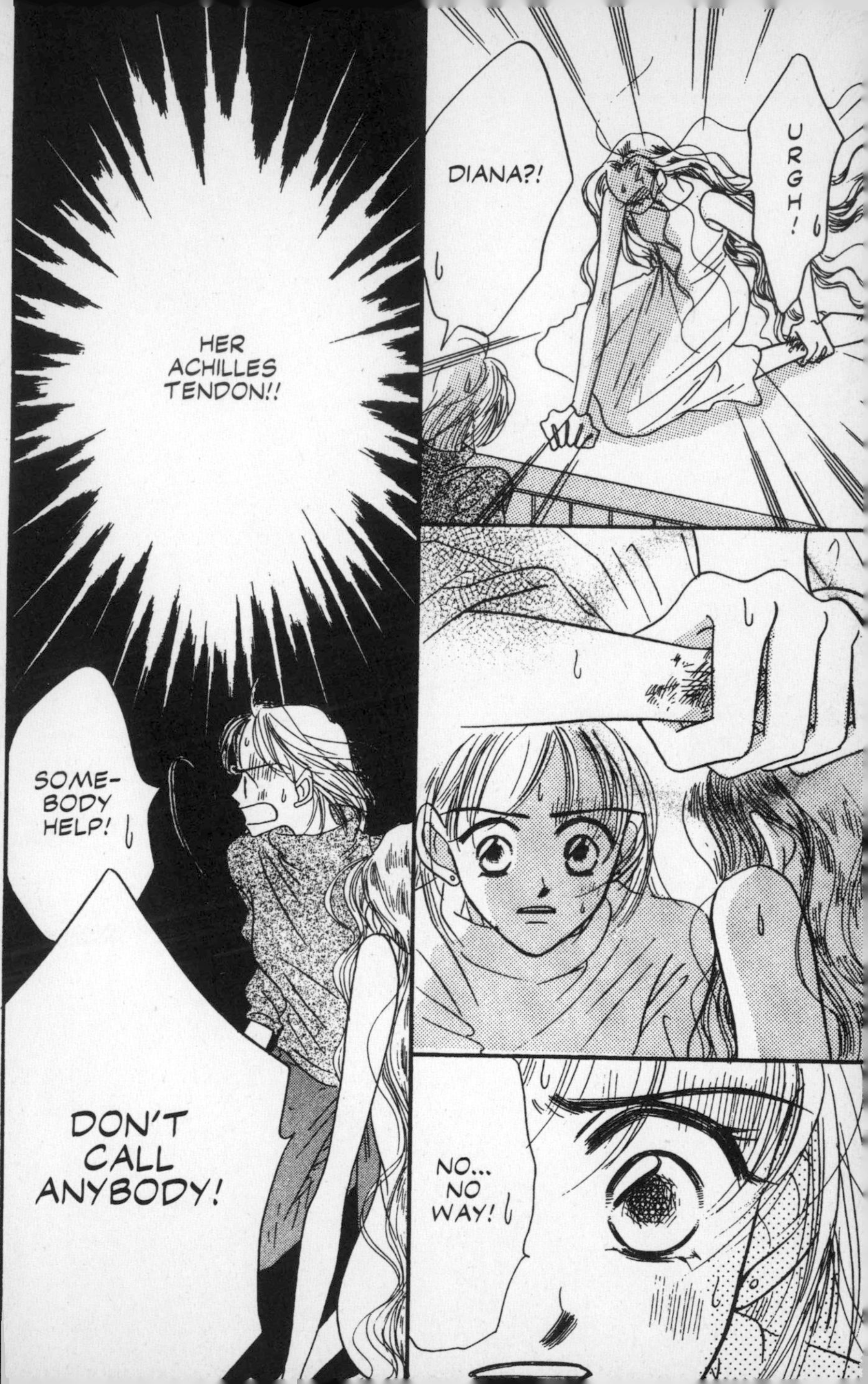
URGH!
DIANA?!
NO... NO WAY!
HER ACHILLES TENDON!!
SOME-BODY HELP!
DON'T CALL ANYBODY!

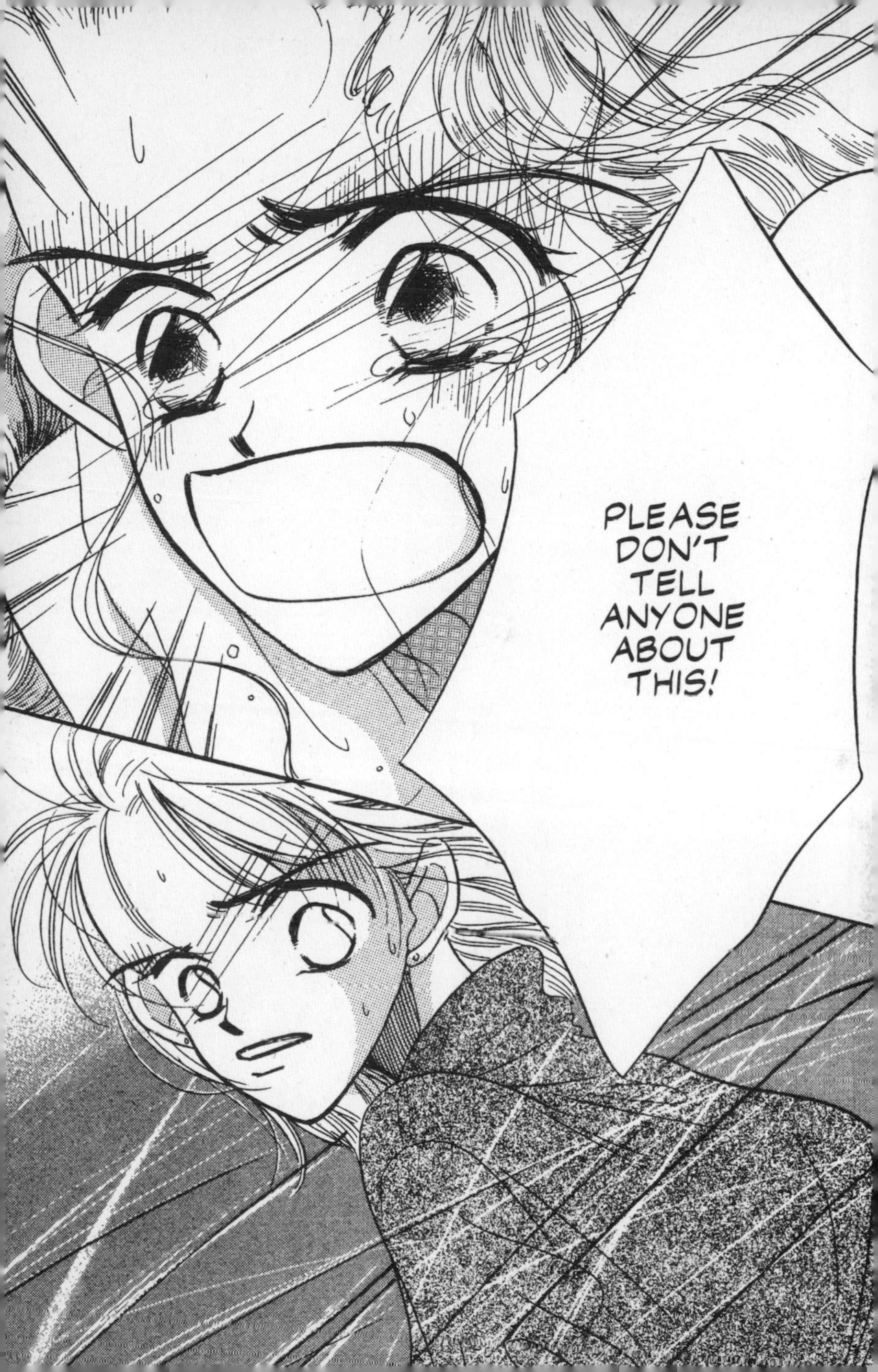
PLEASE DON'T TELL ANYONE ABOUT THIS!

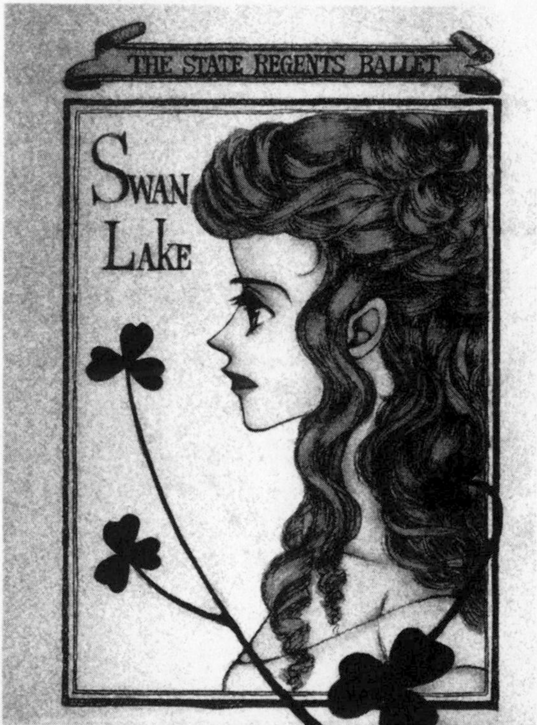
THE STATE REGENTS BALLET
SWAN
LAKE

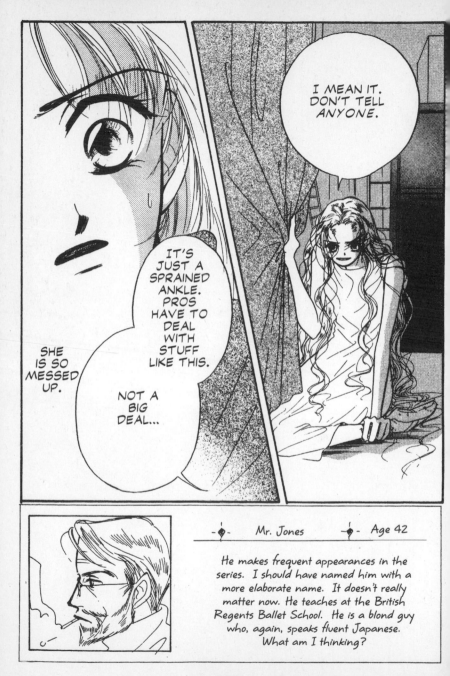

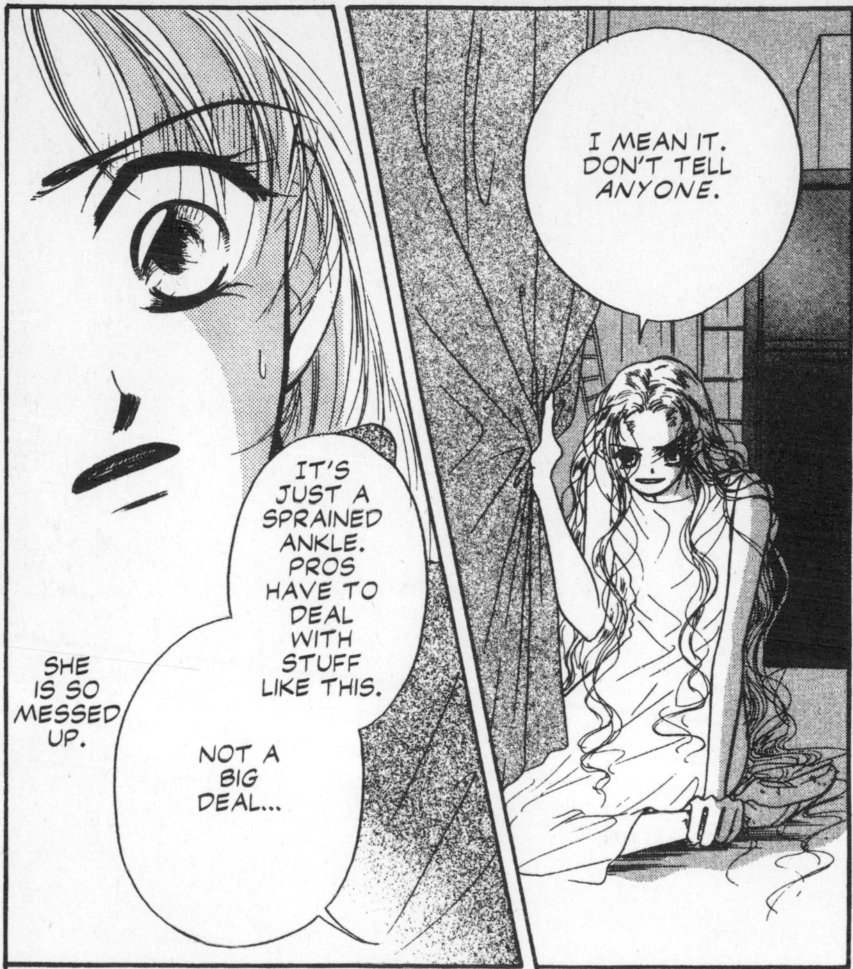
I MEAN IT. DON'T TELL ANYONE.
IT'S JUST A SPRAINED ANKLE. PROS HAVE TO DEAL WITH STUFF LIKE THIS.
NOT A BIG DEAL...
SHE IS SO MESSED UP.

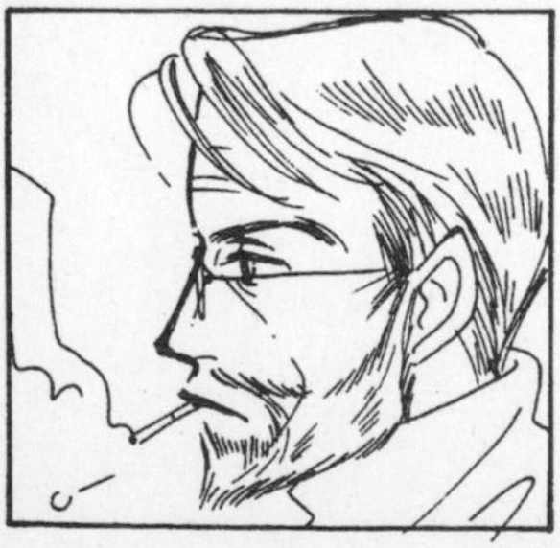

Mr. Jones — Age 42

He makes frequent appearances in the series. I should have named him with a more elaborate name. It doesn't really matter now. He teaches at the British Regents Ballet School. He is a blond guy who, again, speaks fluent Japanese. What am I thinking?

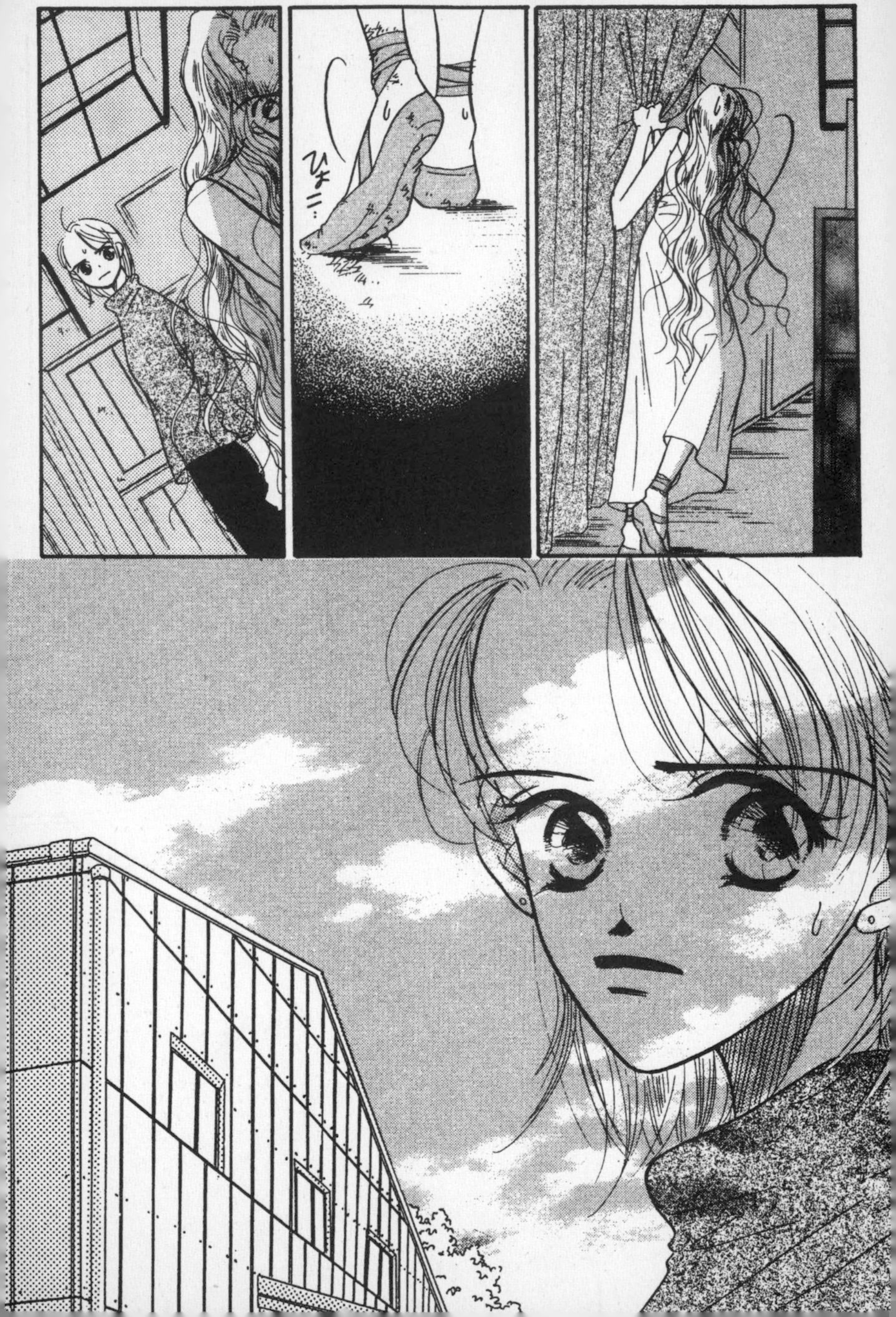
ひょこ‥

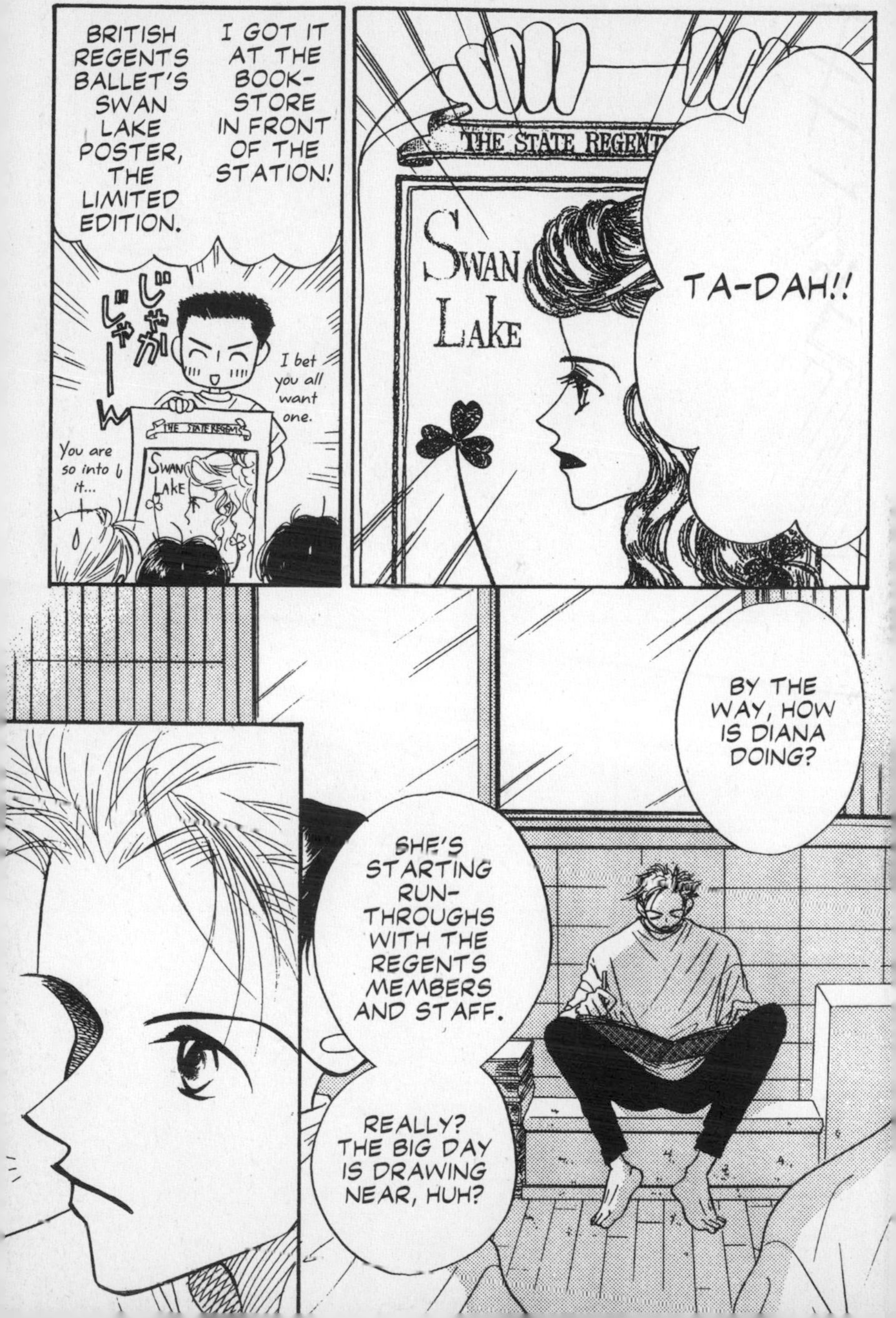
THE STATE REGENT
SWAN LAKE
TA-DAH!!
BRITISH REGENTS BALLET'S SWAN LAKE POSTER, THE LIMITED EDITION. I GOT IT AT THE BOOKSTORE IN FRONT OF THE STATION!
じゃじゃーん
I bet you all want one.
THE STATE REGENT
SWAN LAKE
You are so into it...
BY THE WAY, HOW IS DIANA DOING?
SHE'S STARTING RUN-THROUGHS WITH THE REGENTS MEMBERS AND STAFF.
REALLY? THE BIG DAY IS DRAWING NEAR, HUH?

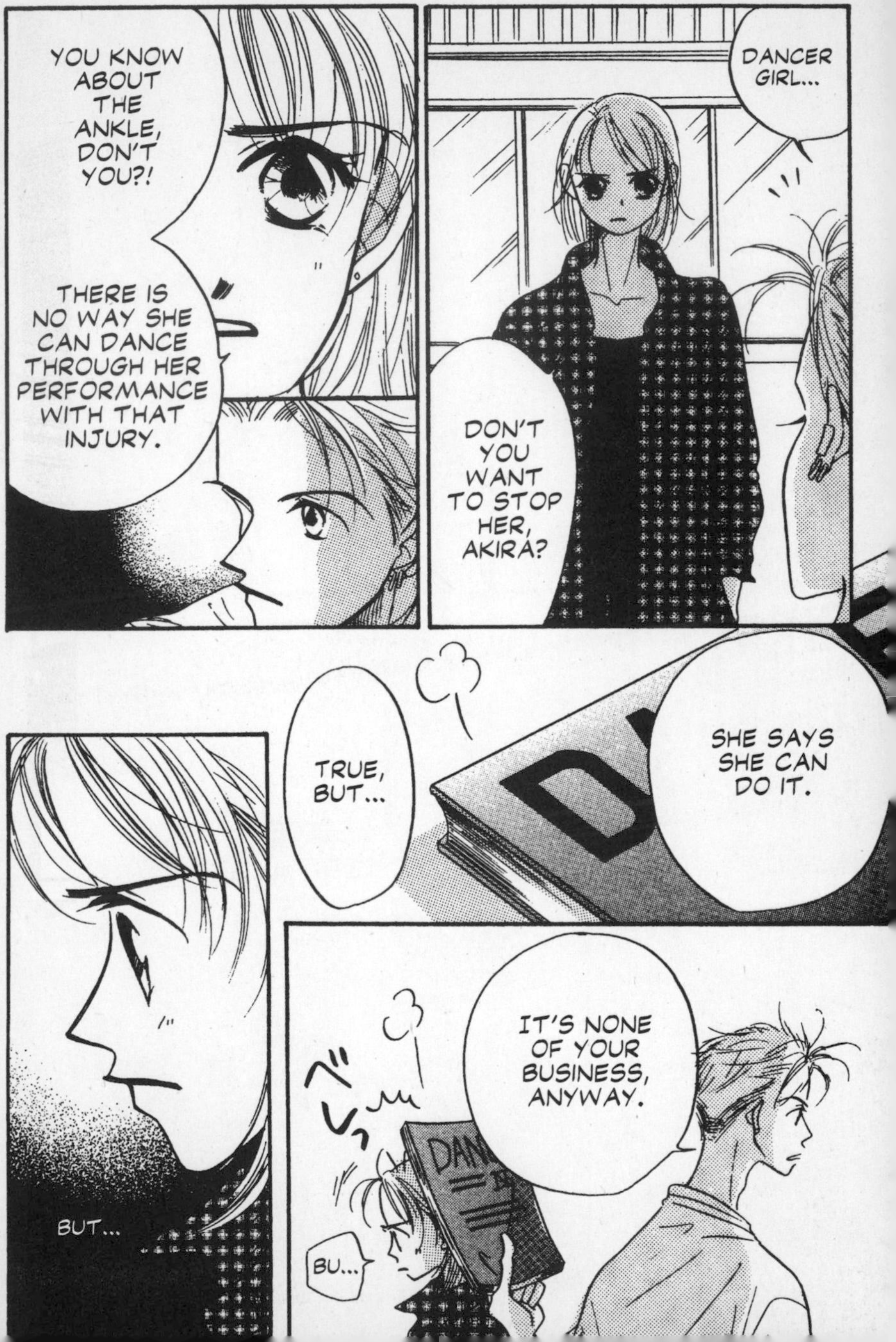
DANCER GIRL...
DON'T YOU WANT TO STOP HER, AKIRA?
YOU KNOW ABOUT THE ANKLE, DON'T YOU?!
THERE IS NO WAY SHE CAN DANCE THROUGH HER PERFORMANCE WITH THAT INJURY.
SHE SAYS SHE CAN DO IT.
TRUE, BUT...
IT'S NONE OF YOUR BUSINESS, ANYWAY.
BU...
BUT...

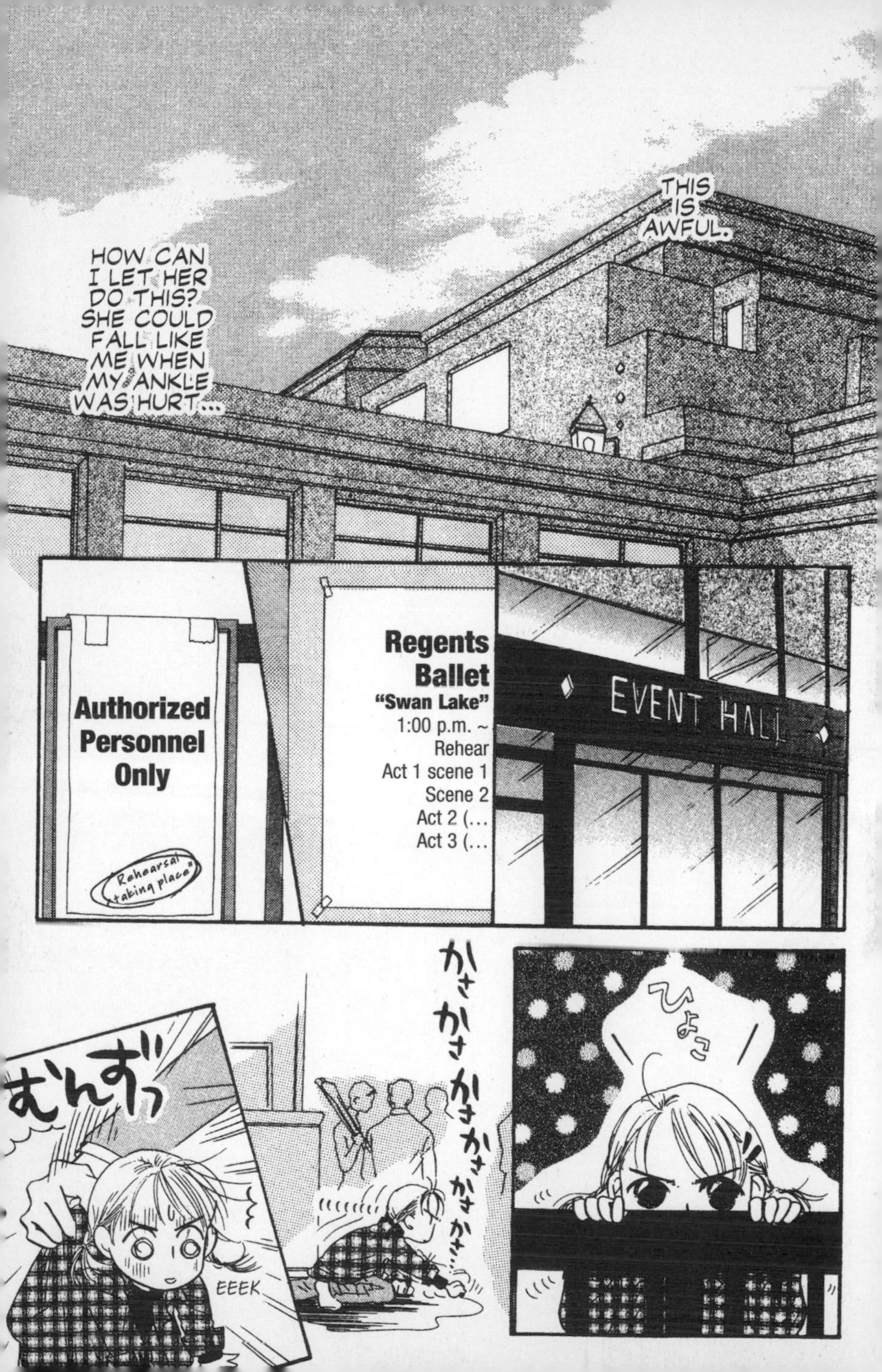
THIS IS AWFUL.
HOW CAN I LET HER DO THIS? SHE COULD FALL LIKE ME WHEN MY ANKLE WAS HURT...
EVENT HALL
Regents Ballet
"Swan Lake"
1:00 p.m. ~
Rehear
Act 1 scene 1
Scene 2
Act 2 (...
Act 3 (...
Authorized Personnel Only
Rehearsal taking place
ひょこ
かさかさかさかさかさかさかさかさ…
むんずっ
EEEK

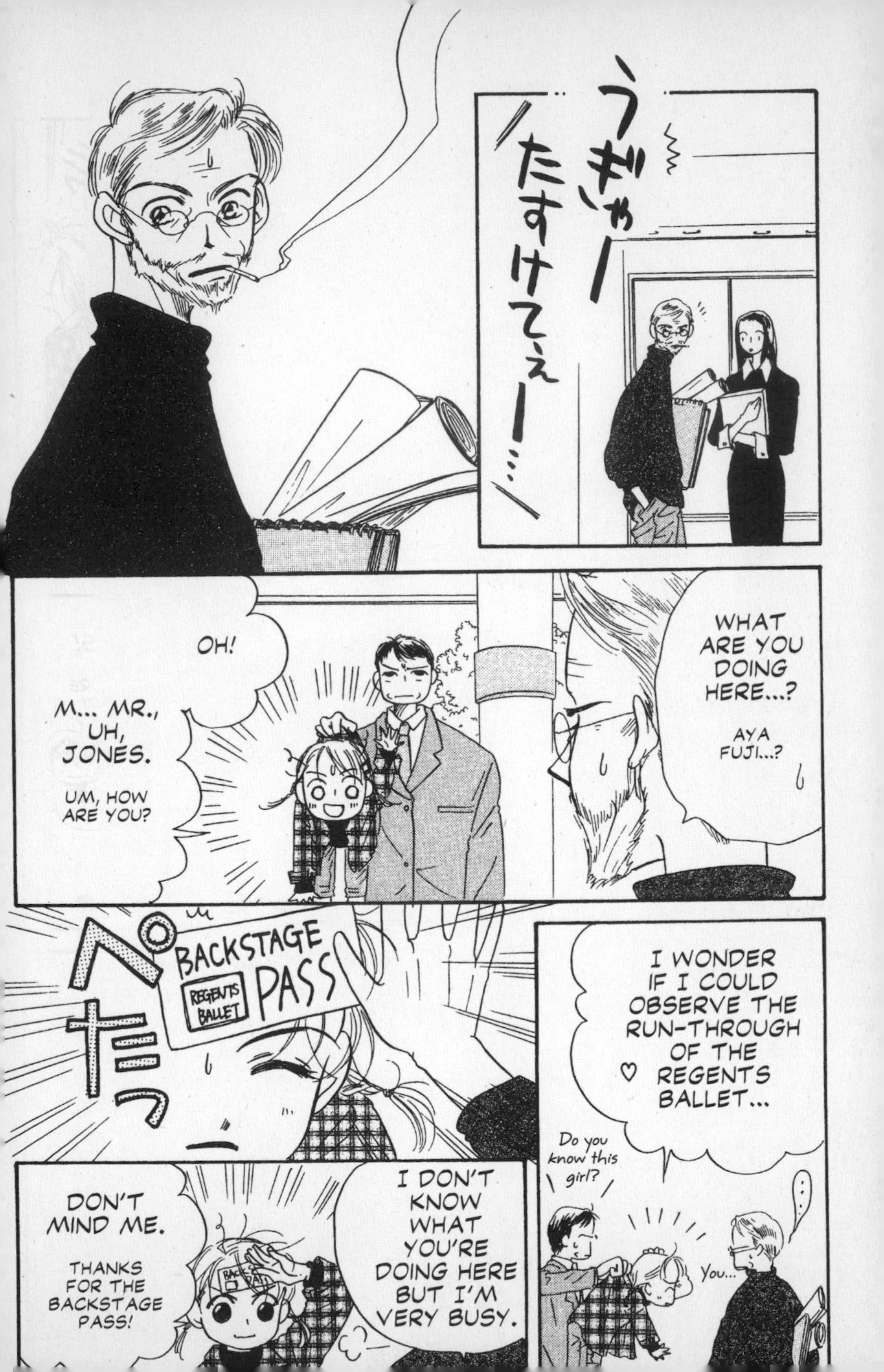
うぎゃー
たすけてぇー!…
WHAT ARE YOU DOING HERE...?
AYA FUJI...?
OH!
M... MR., UH, JONES.
UM, HOW ARE YOU?
I WONDER IF I COULD OBSERVE THE RUN-THROUGH OF THE REGENTS BALLET... ♡
Do you know this girl?
You...
...
BACKSTAGE PASS
REGENTS BALLET
I DON'T KNOW WHAT YOU'RE DOING HERE BUT I'M VERY BUSY.
DON'T MIND ME.
THANKS FOR THE BACKSTAGE PASS!

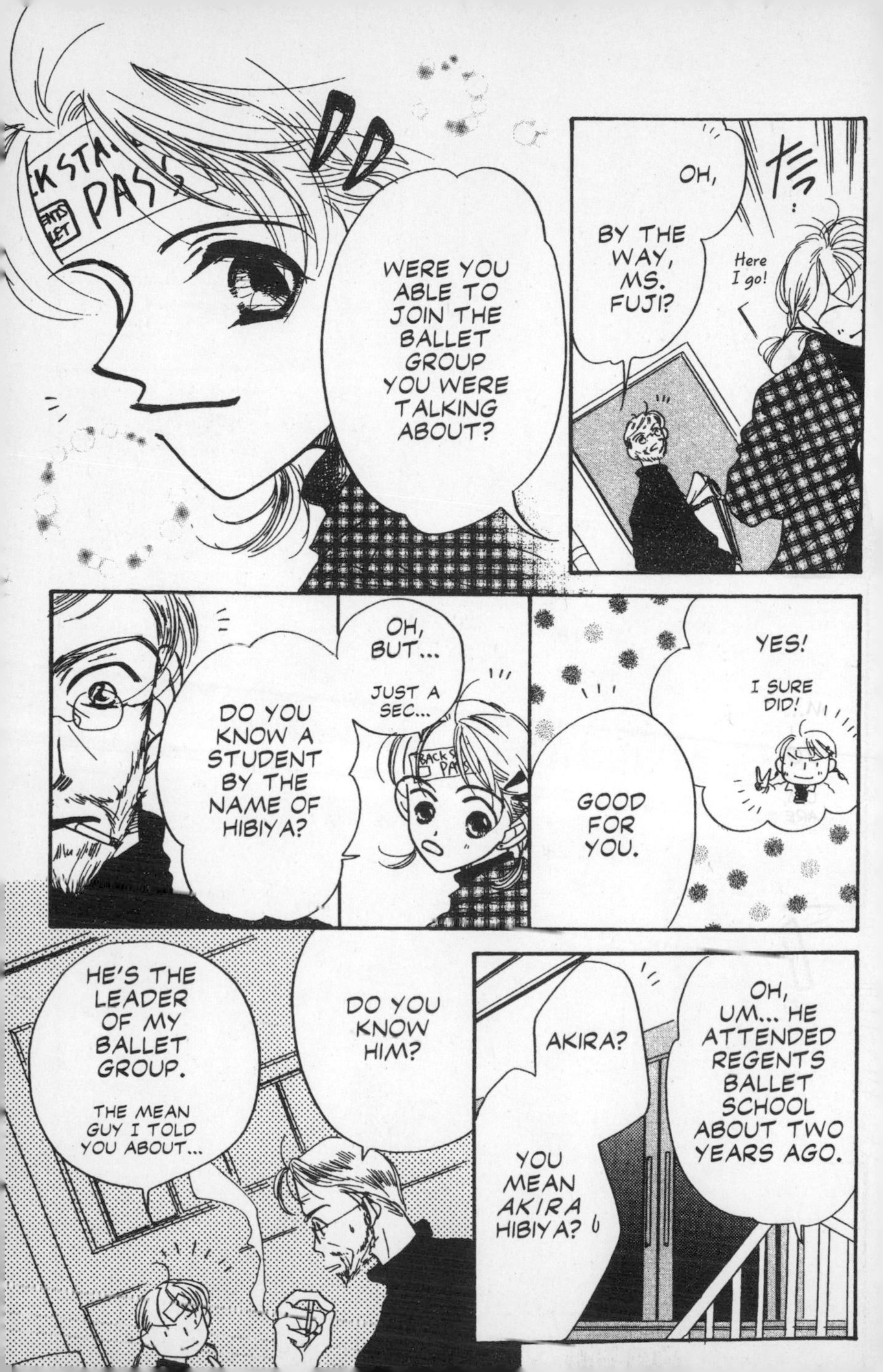
OH,
BY THE WAY, MS. FUJI?
Here I go!
WERE YOU ABLE TO JOIN THE BALLET GROUP YOU WERE TALKING ABOUT?
YES!
I SURE DID!
GOOD FOR YOU.
OH, BUT...
JUST A SEC...
DO YOU KNOW A STUDENT BY THE NAME OF HIBIYA?
OH, UM... HE ATTENDED REGENTS BALLET SCHOOL ABOUT TWO YEARS AGO.
AKIRA?
YOU MEAN AKIRA HIBIYA?
DO YOU KNOW HIM?
HE'S THE LEADER OF MY BALLET GROUP.
THE MEAN GUY I TOLD YOU ABOUT...

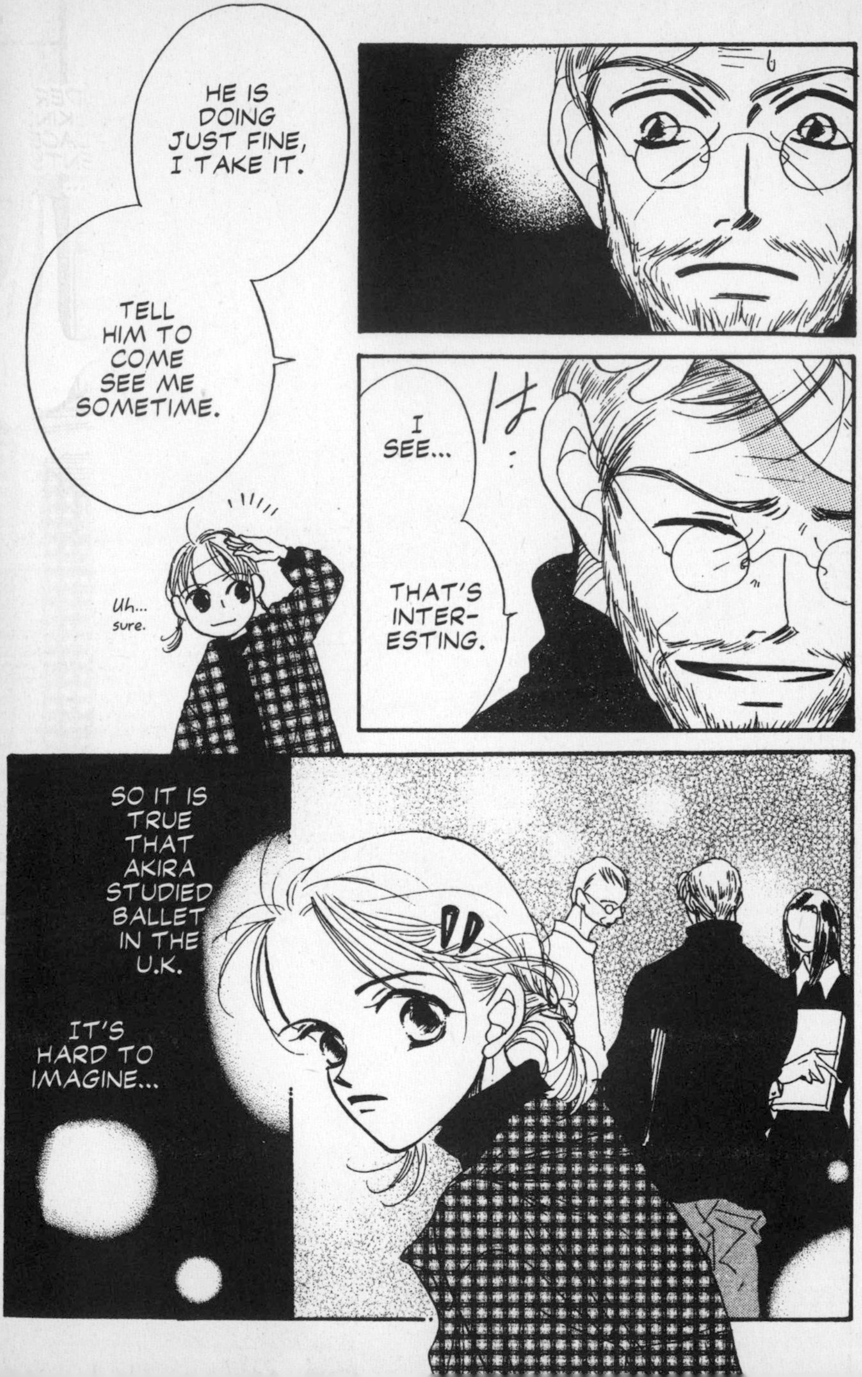
HE IS DOING JUST FINE, I TAKE IT.
TELL HIM TO COME SEE ME SOMETIME.
は
I SEE...
THAT'S INTER-ESTING.
Uh... sure.
SO IT IS TRUE THAT AKIRA STUDIED BALLET IN THE U.K.
IT'S HARD TO IMAGINE...

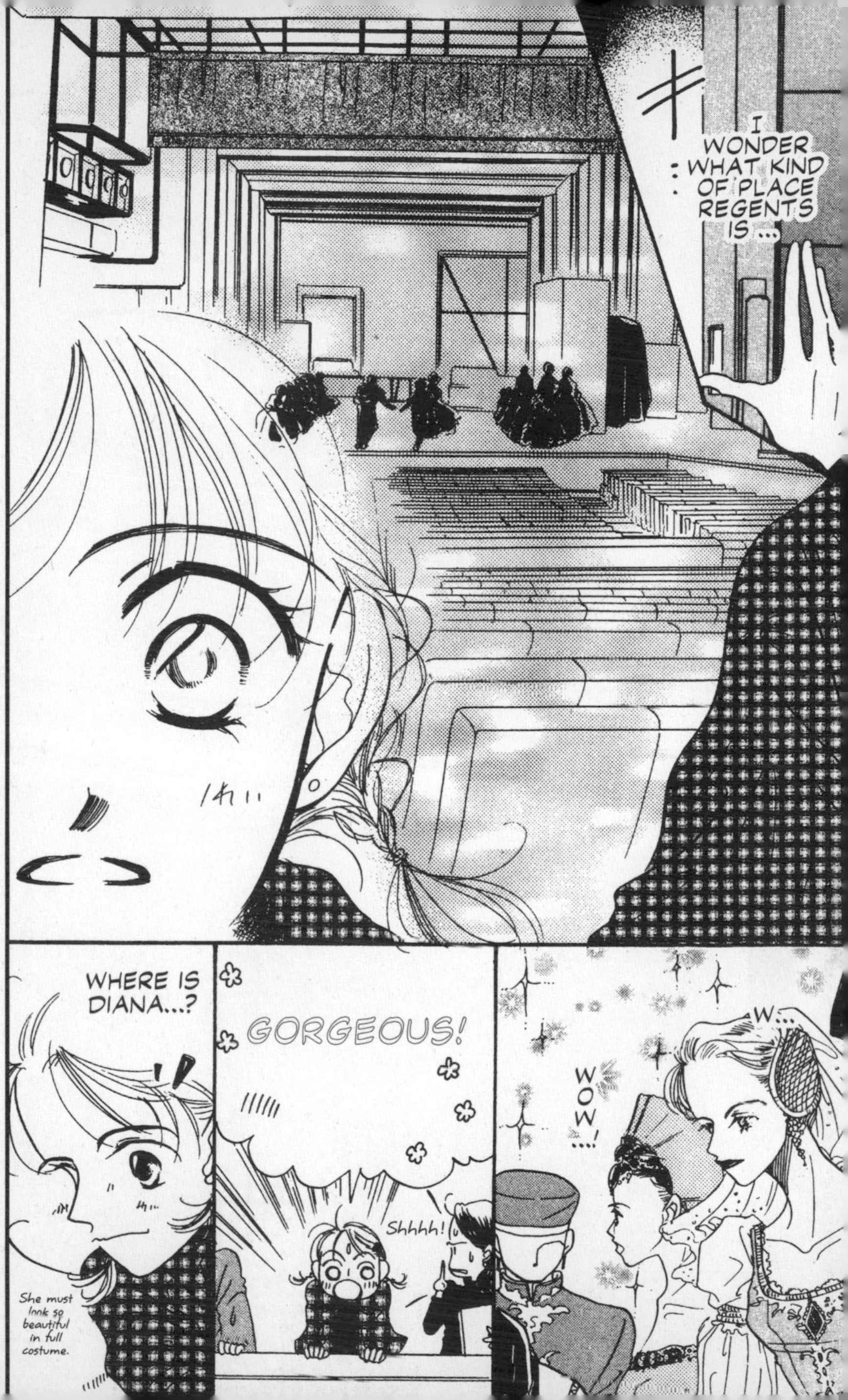
I WONDER WHAT KIND OF PLACE REGENTS IS...
W...
WOW...!
GORGEOUS!
Shhhh!
WHERE IS DIANA...?
She must look so beautiful in full costume.

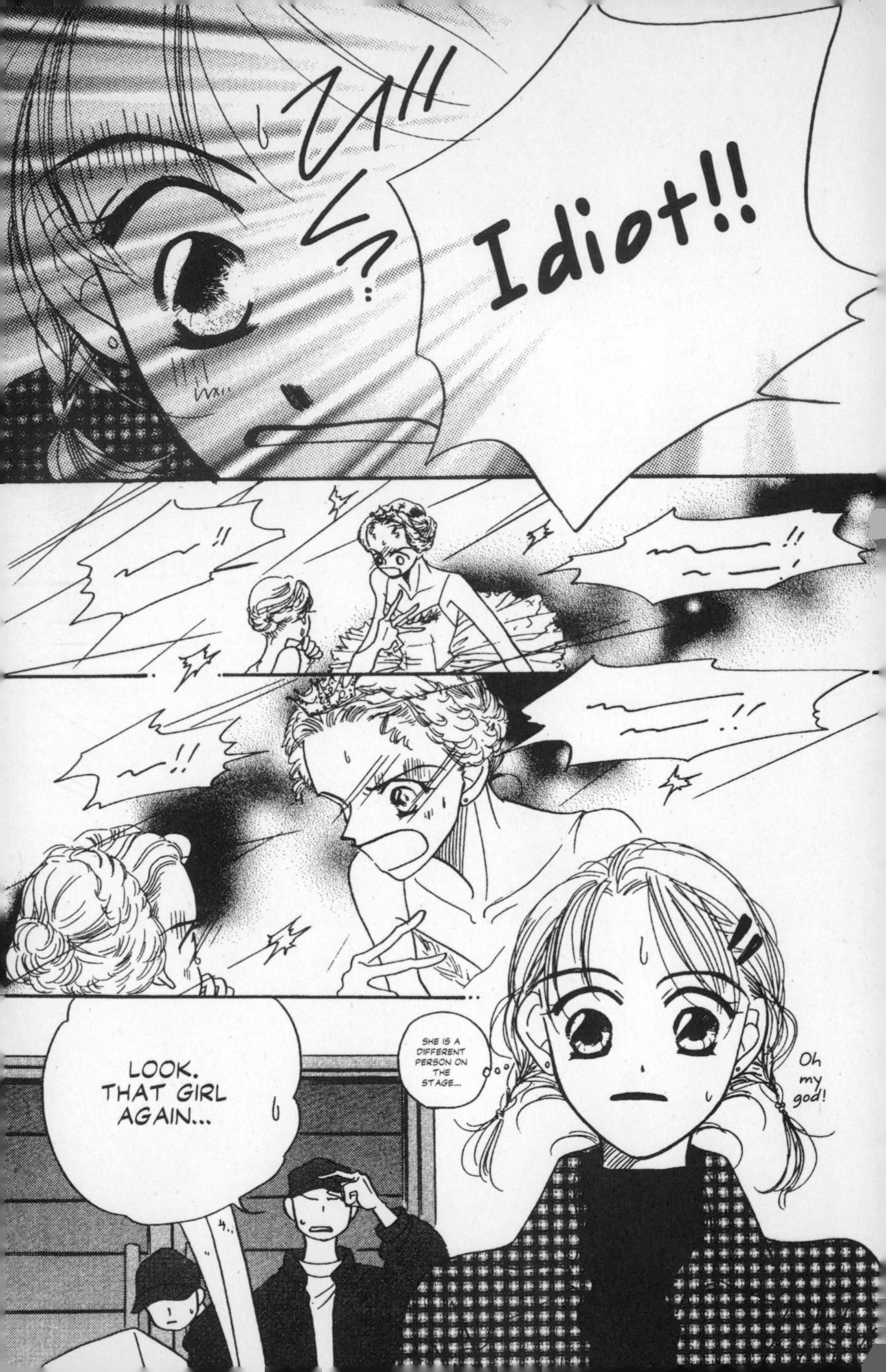
Idiot!!
Wa!!
SHE IS A DIFFERENT PERSON ON THE STAGE...
Oh my god!
LOOK. THAT GIRL AGAIN...

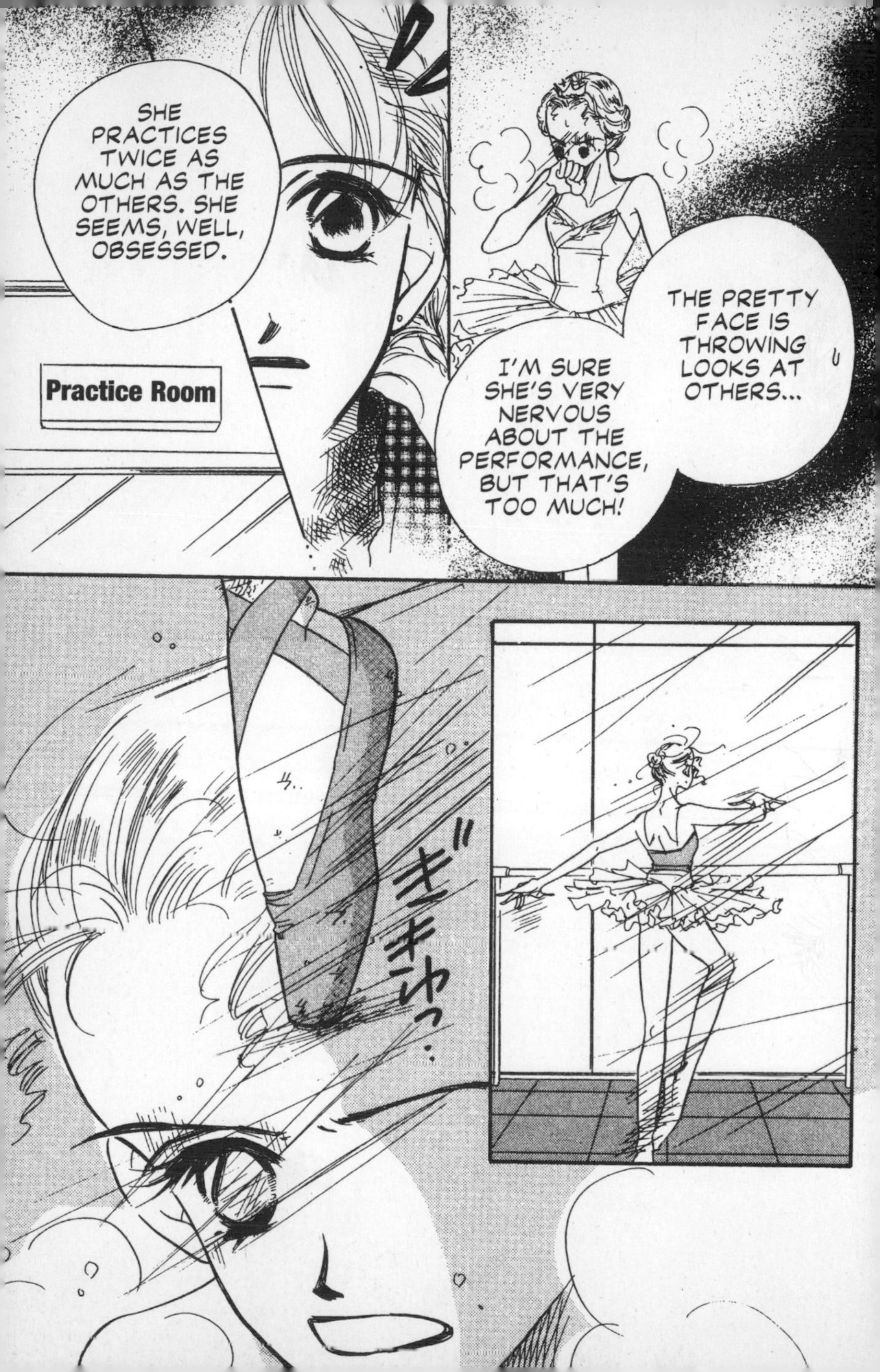
THE PRETTY FACE IS THROWING LOOKS AT OTHERS...
I'M SURE SHE'S VERY NERVOUS ABOUT THE PERFORMANCE, BUT THAT'S TOO MUCH!
Practice Room
SHE PRACTICES TWICE AS MUCH AS THE OTHERS. SHE SEEMS, WELL, OBSESSED.
ギキゅっ

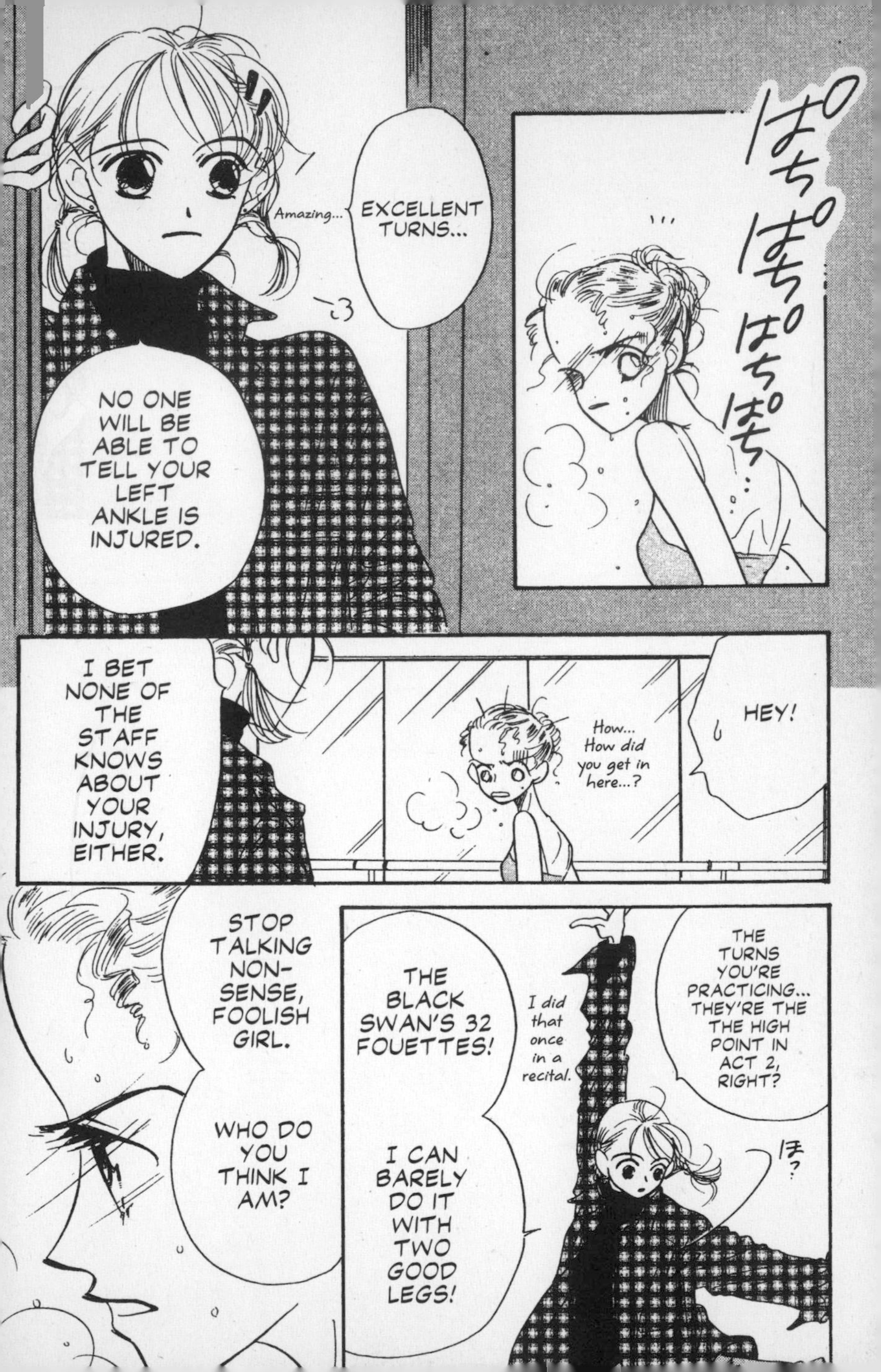
ぱちぱち
ぱちぱち
...
Amazing...
EXCELLENT TURNS...
NO ONE WILL BE ABLE TO TELL YOUR LEFT ANKLE IS INJURED.
HEY!
How... How did you get in here...?
I BET NONE OF THE STAFF KNOWS ABOUT YOUR INJURY, EITHER.
THE TURNS YOU'RE PRACTICING... THEY'RE THE THE HIGH POINT IN ACT 2, RIGHT?
ほ?
I did that once in a recital.
THE BLACK SWAN'S 32 FOUETTES!
I CAN BARELY DO IT WITH TWO GOOD LEGS!
STOP TALKING NON-SENSE, FOOLISH GIRL.
WHO DO YOU THINK I AM?

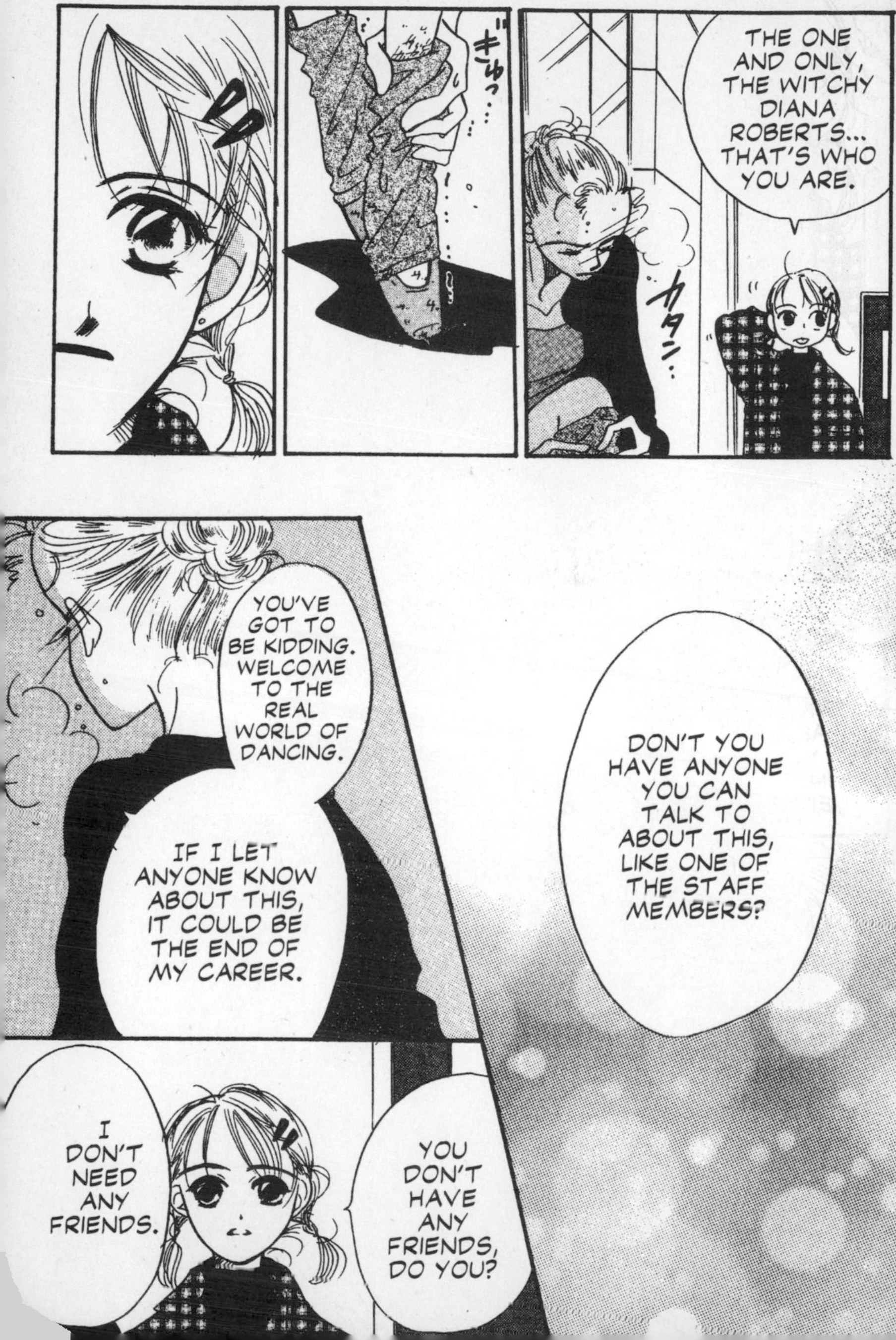
THE ONE AND ONLY, THE WITCHY DIANA ROBERTS... THAT'S WHO YOU ARE.
カタン…
ぎゅっ…
DON'T YOU HAVE ANYONE YOU CAN TALK TO ABOUT THIS, LIKE ONE OF THE STAFF MEMBERS?
YOU'VE GOT TO BE KIDDING. WELCOME TO THE REAL WORLD OF DANCING.
IF I LET ANYONE KNOW ABOUT THIS, IT COULD BE THE END OF MY CAREER.
YOU DON'T HAVE ANY FRIENDS, DO YOU?
I DON'T NEED ANY FRIENDS.

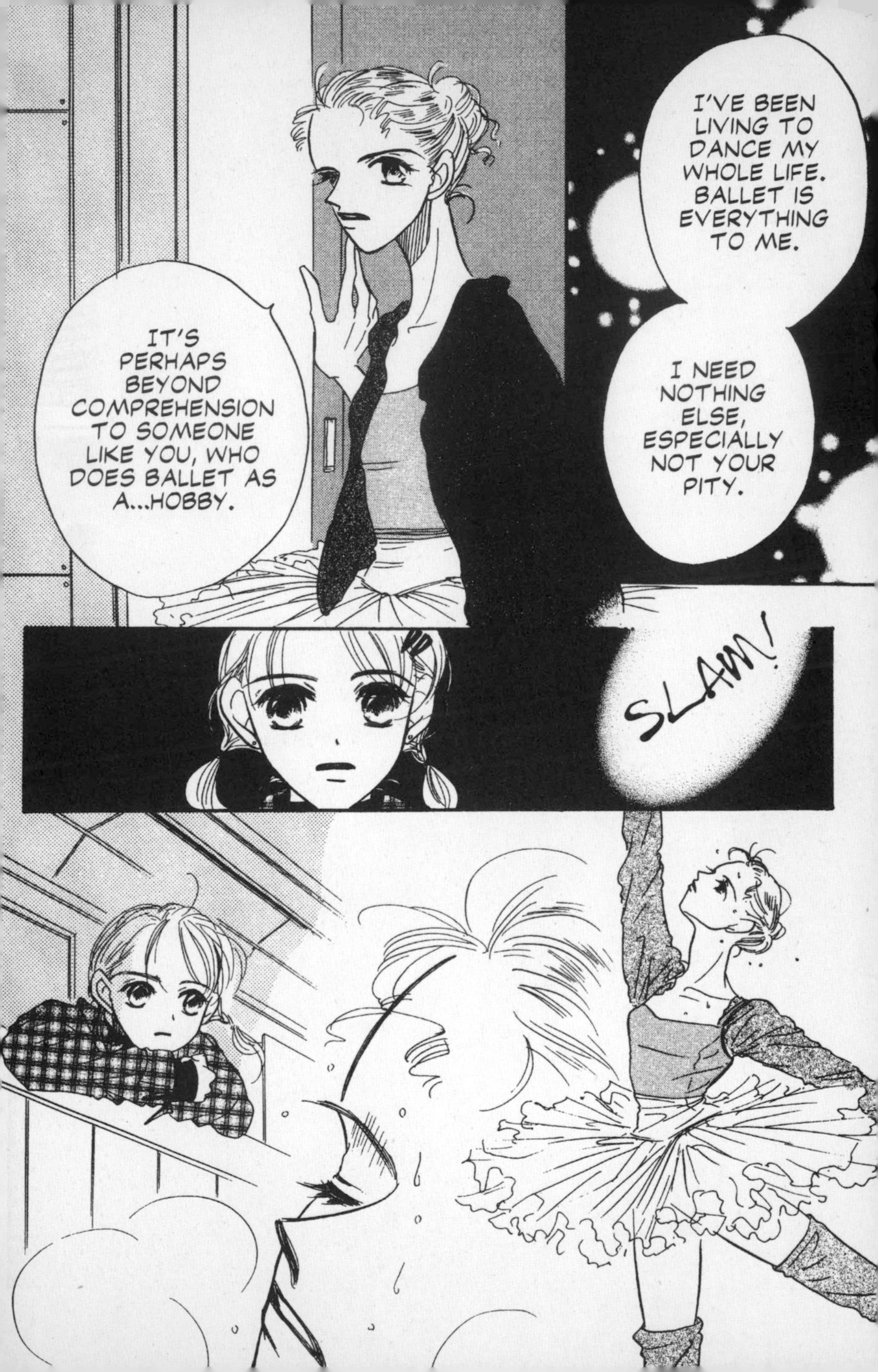
I'VE BEEN LIVING TO DANCE MY WHOLE LIFE. BALLET IS EVERYTHING TO ME.
I NEED NOTHING ELSE, ESPECIALLY NOT YOUR PITY.
IT'S PERHAPS BEYOND COMPREHENSION TO SOMEONE LIKE YOU, WHO DOES BALLET AS A...HOBBY.
SLAM!

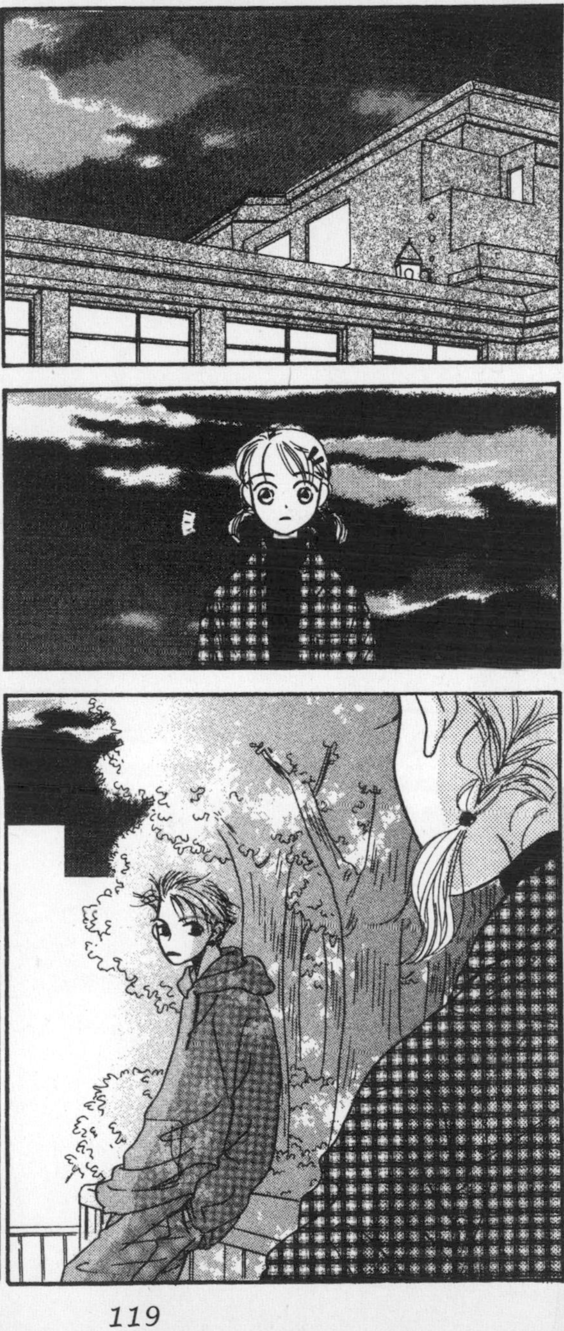

Ashihara's Diary

No. 4

Soon after I began to write Forbidden Dance and started to feel that I became familiar with ballet, I took my sister to see Royal Ballet's "Don Quixote". I enjoyed seeing how my sister reacted through the new experience more than the ballet performance itself. First, she was surprised to look at the lady who was dressed up in a formal dress.

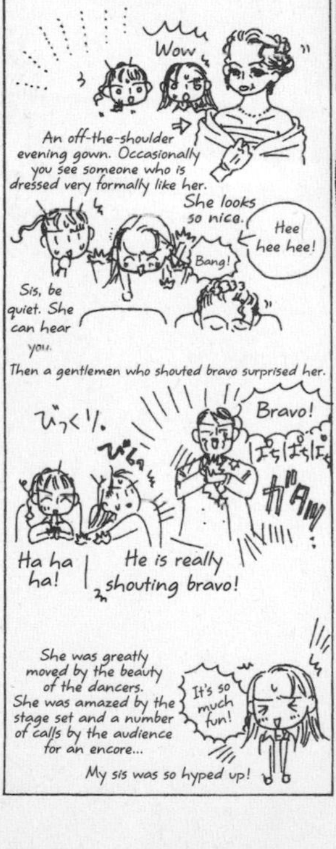
Wow
An off-the-shoulder evening gown. Occasionally you see someone who is dressed very formally like her.
She looks so nice.
Hee hee hee!
Bang!
Sis, be quiet. She can hear you.
Then a gentlemen who shouted bravo surprised her.
Bravo!
Ha ha ha!
He is really shouting bravo!
She was greatly moved by the beauty of the dancers. She was amazed by the stage set and a number of calls by the audience for an encore...
It's so much fun!
My sis was so hyped up!

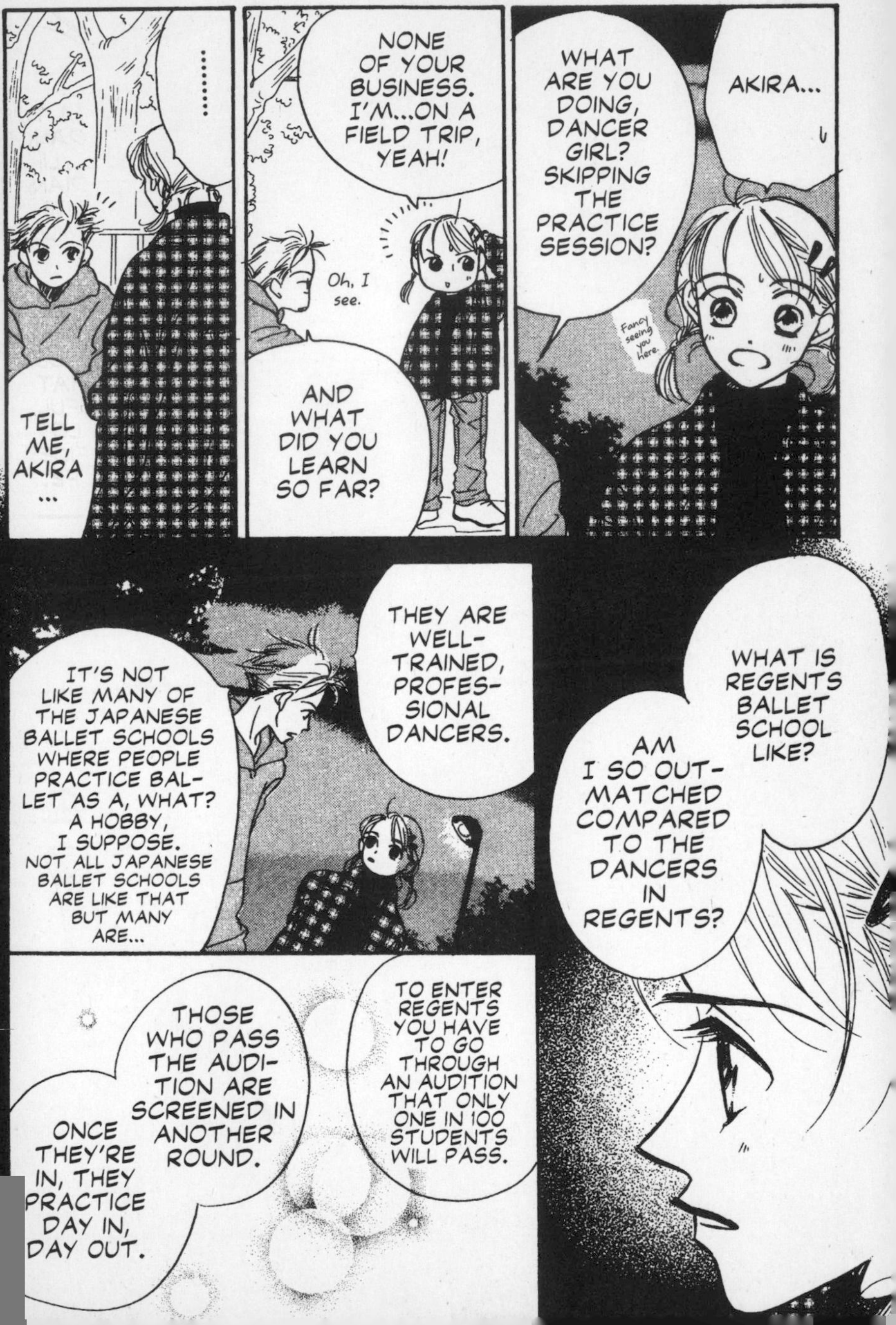
AKIRA...
WHAT ARE YOU DOING, DANCER GIRL? SKIPPING THE PRACTICE SESSION?
Fancy seeing you here.
NONE OF YOUR BUSINESS. I'M...ON A FIELD TRIP, YEAH!
Oh, I see.
AND WHAT DID YOU LEARN SO FAR?
....
TELL ME, AKIRA ...
WHAT IS REGENTS BALLET SCHOOL LIKE?
AM I SO OUT-MATCHED COMPARED TO THE DANCERS IN REGENTS?
THEY ARE WELL-TRAINED, PROFES-SIONAL DANCERS.
IT'S NOT LIKE MANY OF THE JAPANESE BALLET SCHOOLS WHERE PEOPLE PRACTICE BAL-LET AS A, WHAT? A HOBBY, I SUPPOSE.
NOT ALL JAPANESE BALLET SCHOOLS ARE LIKE THAT BUT MANY ARE...
TO ENTER REGENTS YOU HAVE TO GO THROUGH AN AUDITION THAT ONLY ONE IN 100 STUDENTS WILL PASS.
THOSE WHO PASS THE AUDI-TION ARE SCREENED IN ANOTHER ROUND.
ONCE THEY'RE IN, THEY PRACTICE DAY IN, DAY OUT.

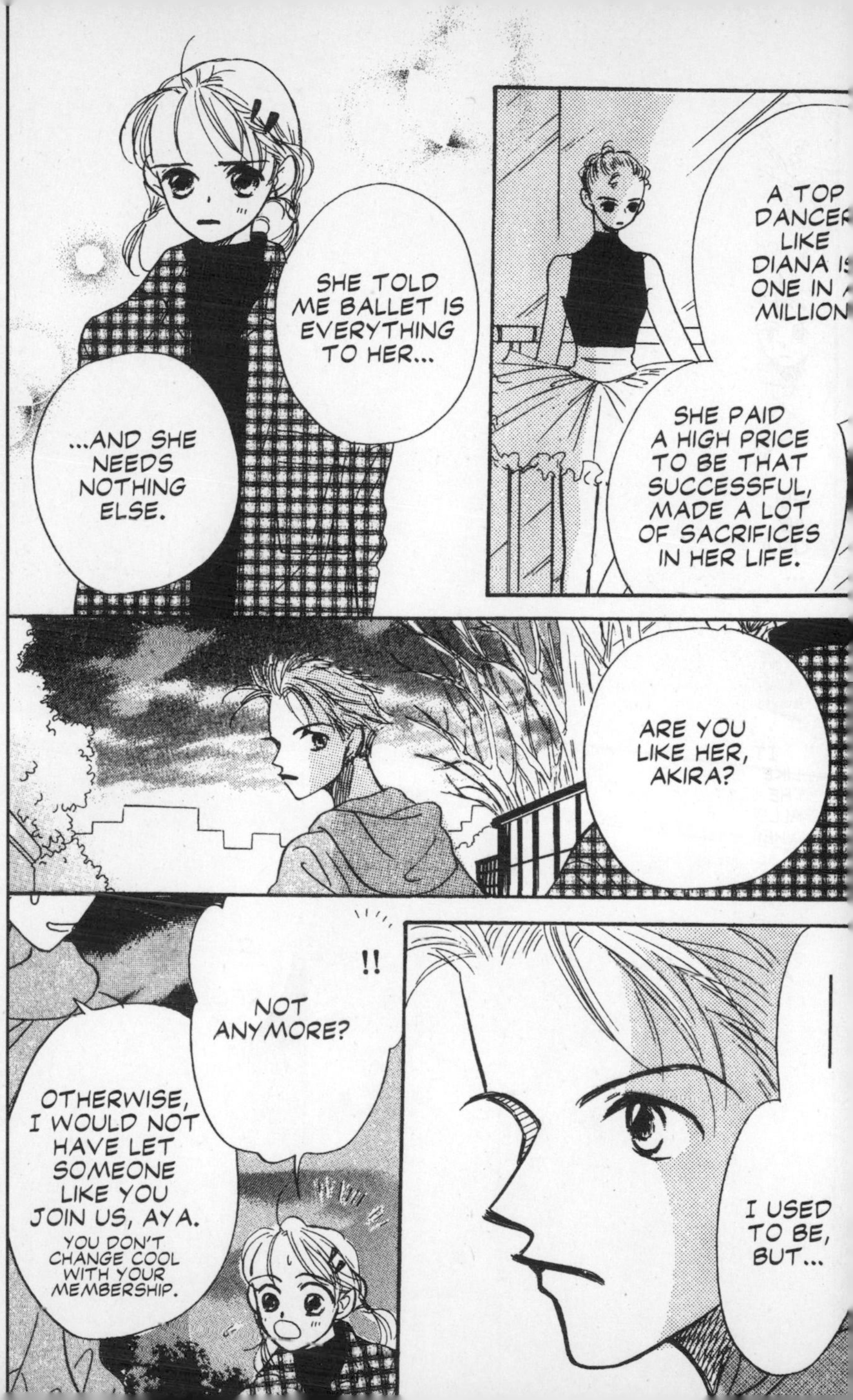
A TOP DANCER LIKE DIANA IS ONE IN A MILLION
SHE PAID A HIGH PRICE TO BE THAT SUCCESSFUL, MADE A LOT OF SACRIFICES IN HER LIFE.
SHE TOLD ME BALLET IS EVERYTHING TO HER...
...AND SHE NEEDS NOTHING ELSE.
ARE YOU LIKE HER, AKIRA?
I USED TO BE, BUT...
!!
NOT ANYMORE?
OTHERWISE, I WOULD NOT HAVE LET SOMEONE LIKE YOU JOIN US, AYA.
YOU DON'T CHANGE COOL WITH YOUR MEMBERSHIP.

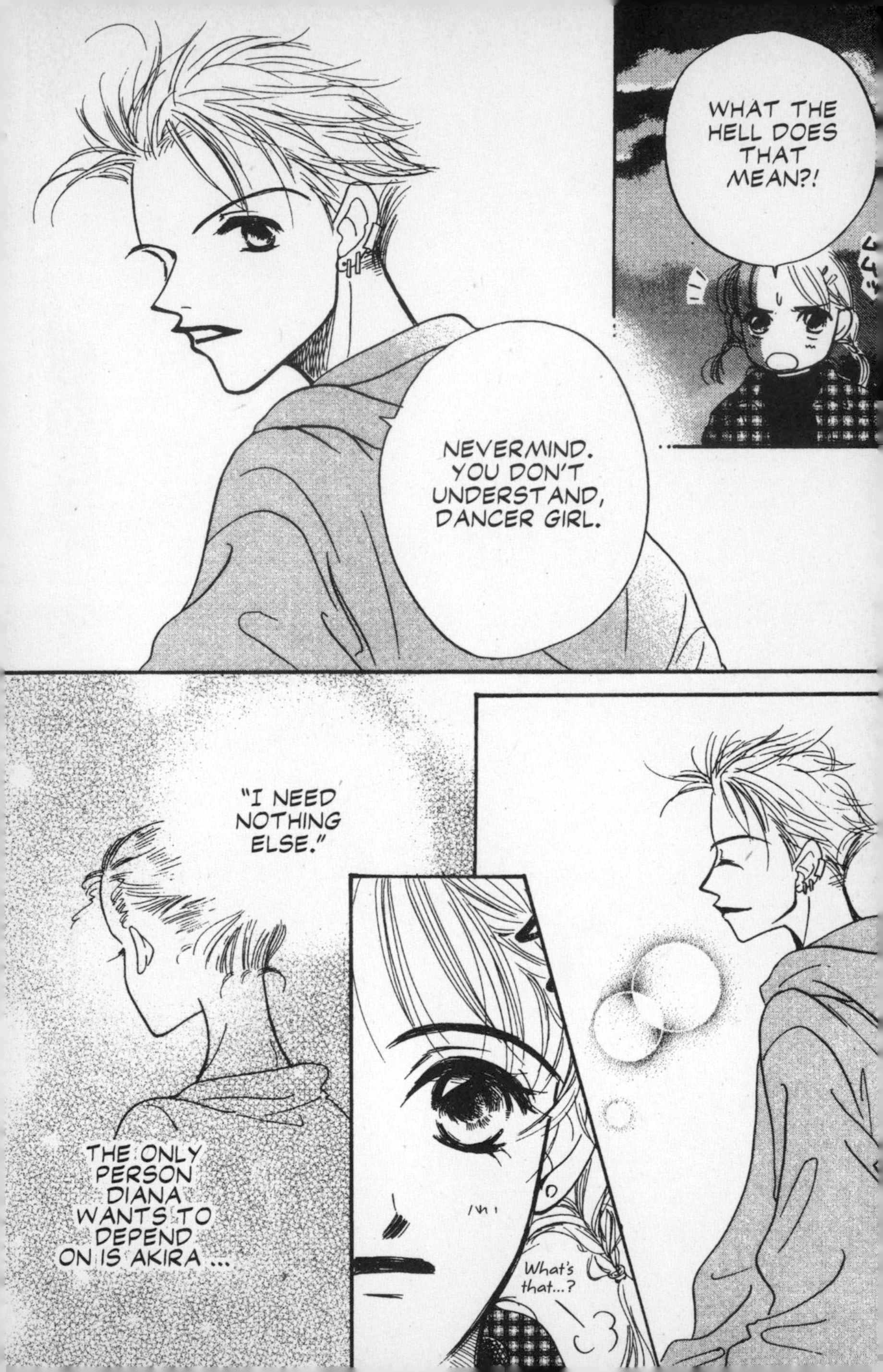
WHAT THE HELL DOES THAT MEAN?!
NEVERMIND. YOU DON'T UNDERSTAND, DANCER GIRL.
What's that...?
"I NEED NOTHING ELSE."
THE ONLY PERSON DIANA WANTS TO DEPEND ON IS AKIRA ...

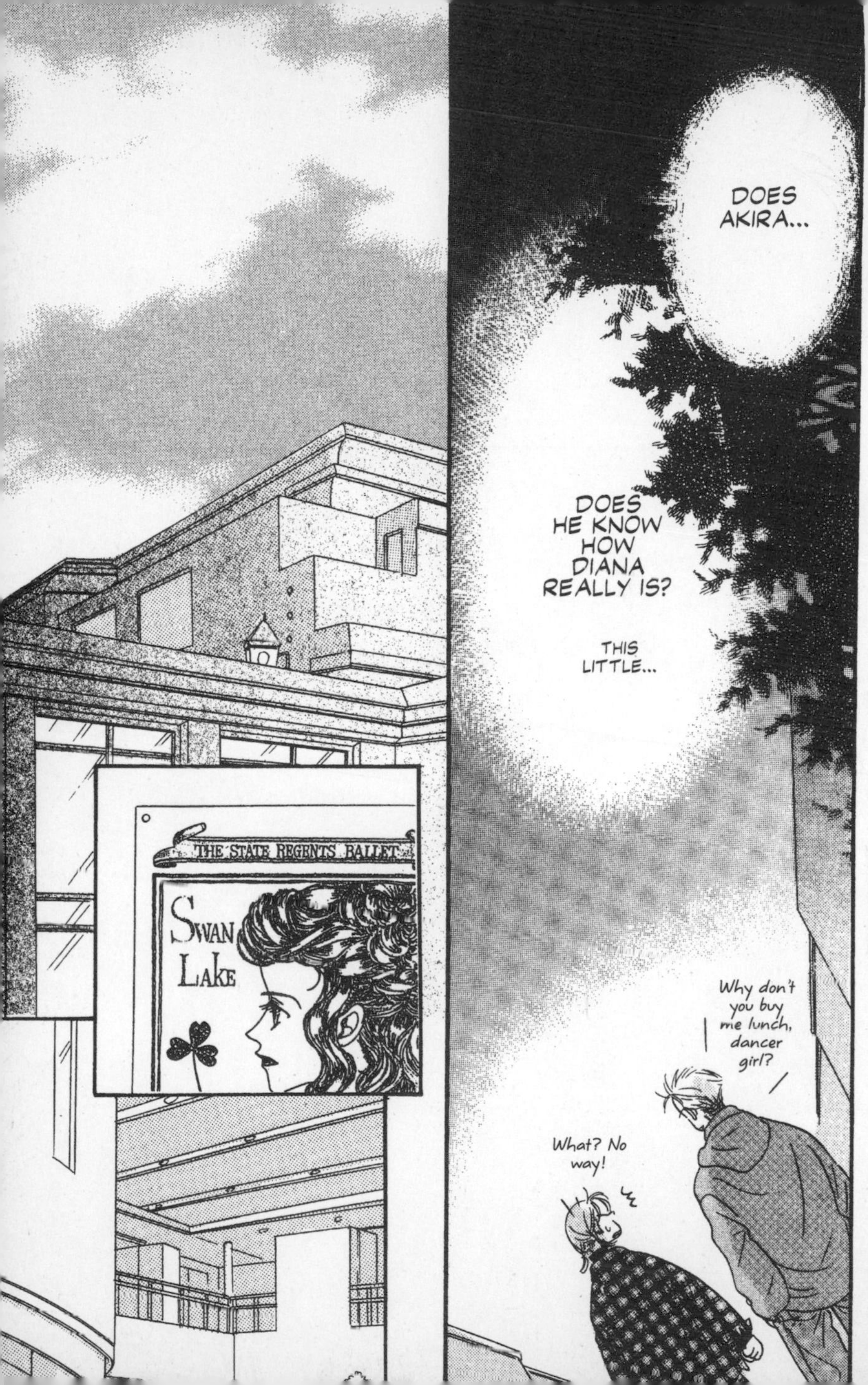
DOES AKIRA...
DOES HE KNOW HOW DIANA REALLY IS?
THIS LITTLE...
Why don't you buy me lunch, dancer girl?
What? No way!
THE STATE REGENTS BALLET
SWAN LAKE

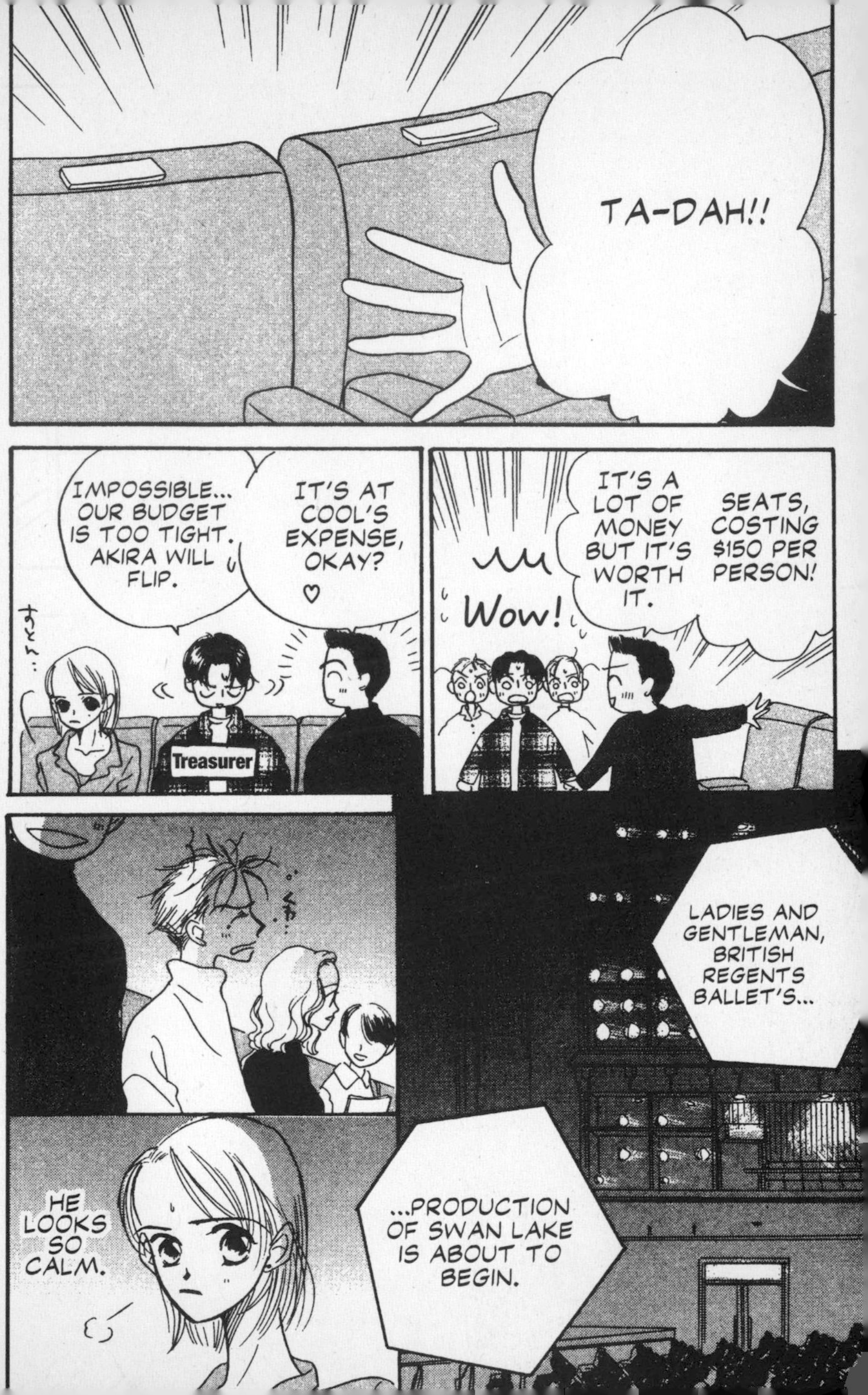
TA-DAH!!
SEATS, COSTING $150 PER PERSON!
IT'S A LOT OF MONEY BUT IT'S WORTH IT.
Wow!
IT'S AT COOL'S EXPENSE, OKAY?
IMPOSSIBLE... OUR BUDGET IS TOO TIGHT. AKIRA WILL FLIP.
Treasurer
LADIES AND GENTLEMAN, BRITISH REGENTS BALLET'S...
...PRODUCTION OF SWAN LAKE IS ABOUT TO BEGIN.
HE LOOKS SO CALM.

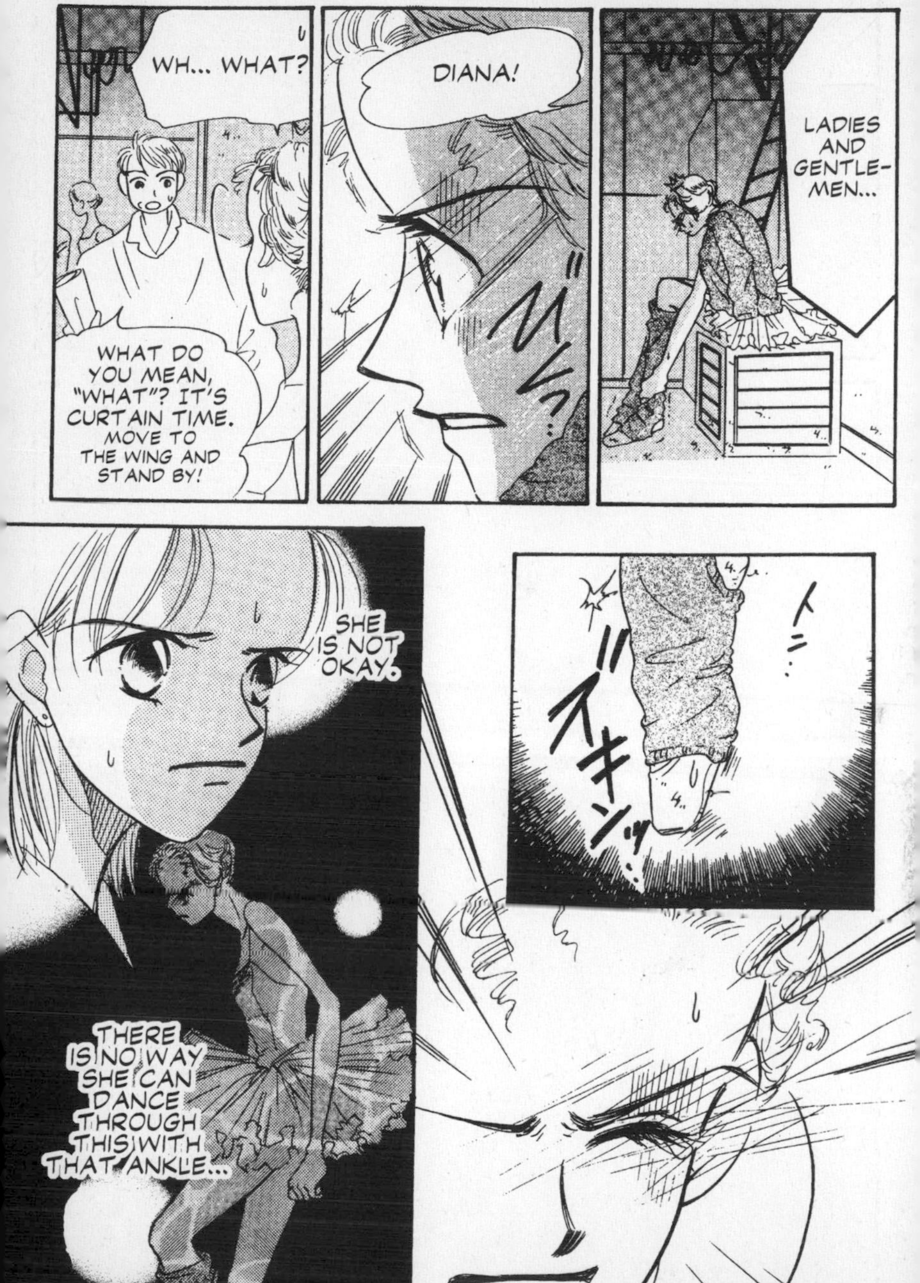
LADIES AND GENTLEMEN...
DIANA!
WH... WHAT?
WHAT DO YOU MEAN, "WHAT"? IT'S CURTAIN TIME. MOVE TO THE WING AND STAND BY!
ズキンッ
SHE IS NOT OKAY.
THERE IS NO WAY SHE CAN DANCE THROUGH THIS WITH THAT ANKLE...

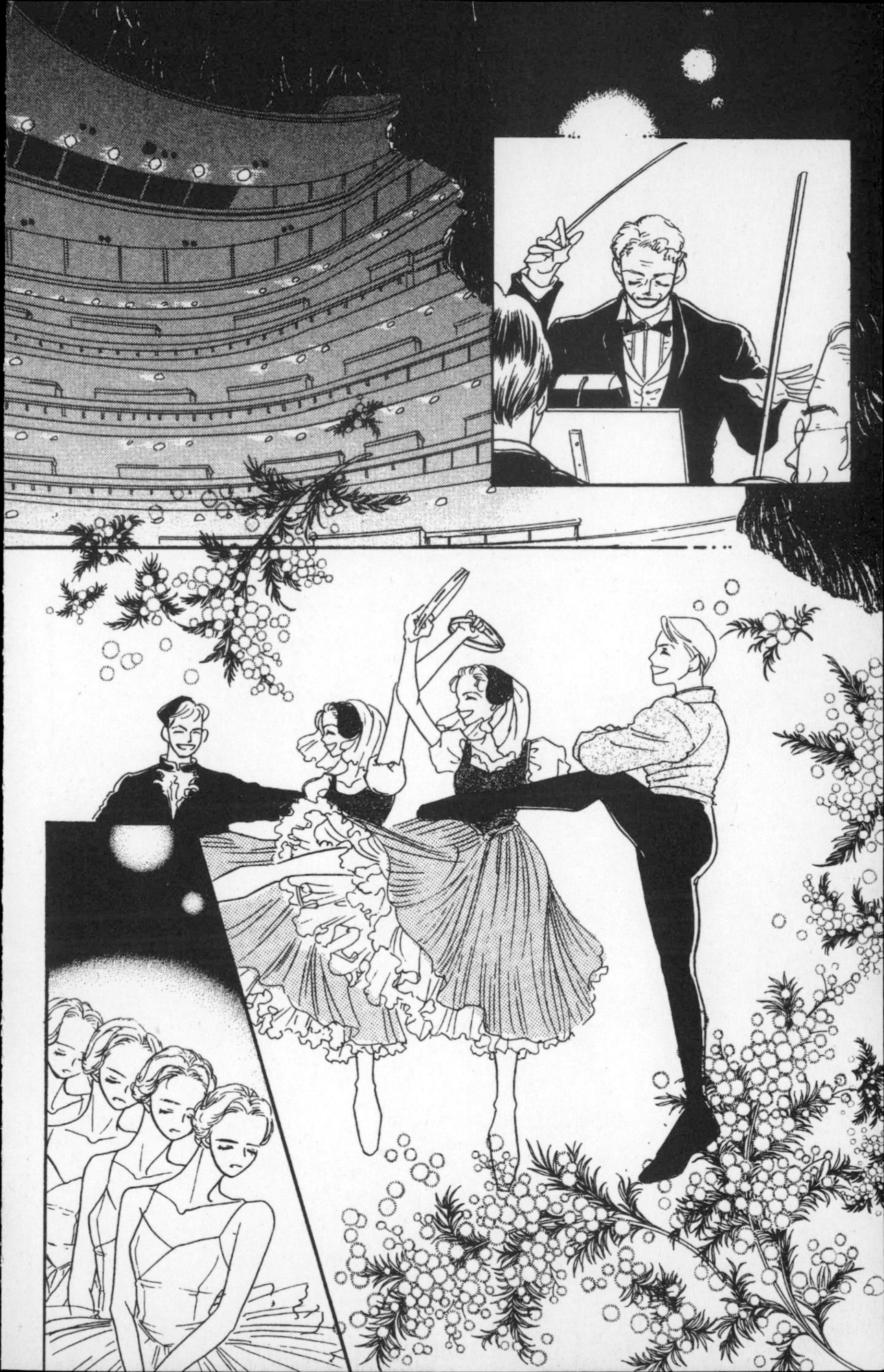

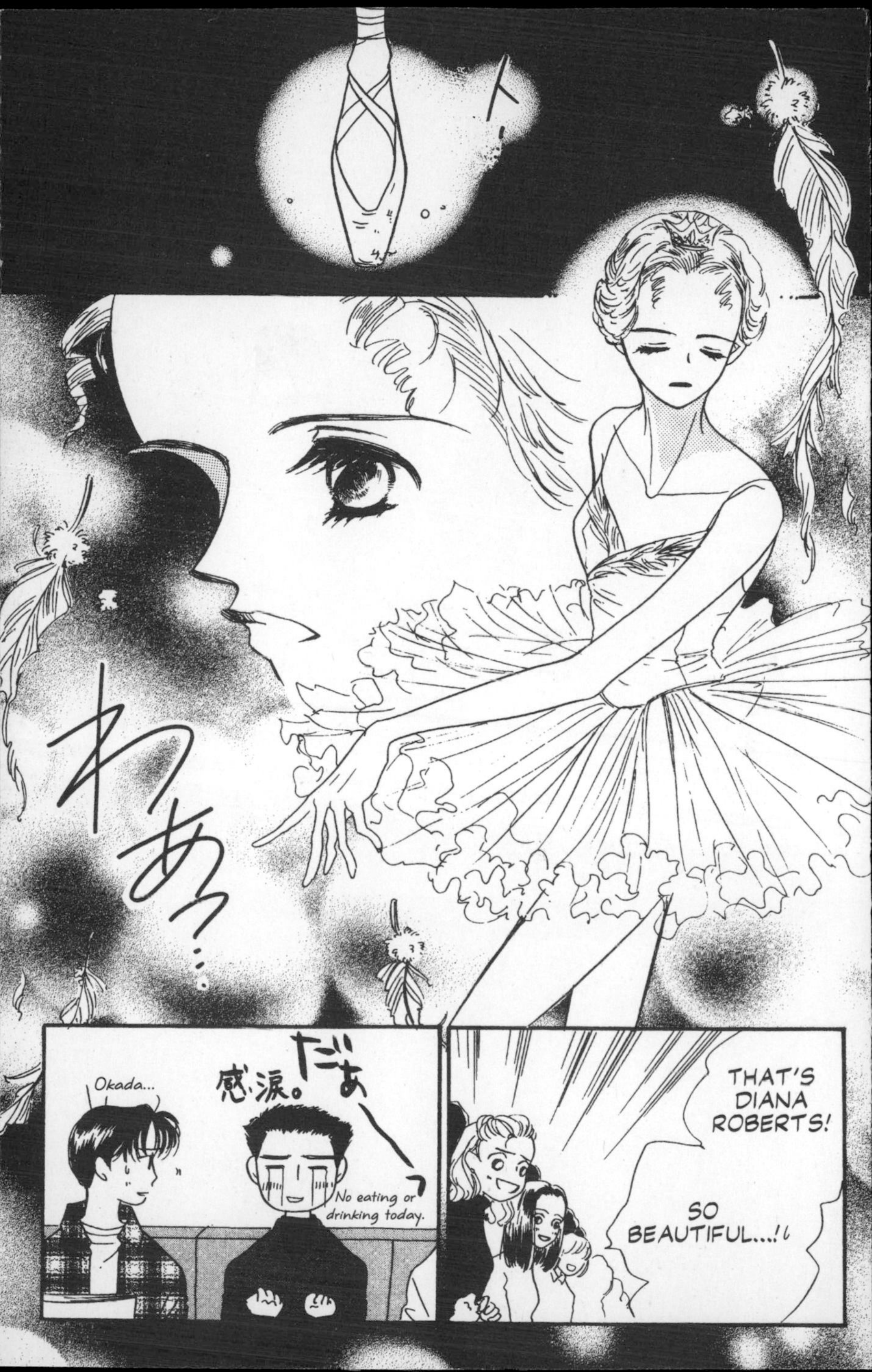
ト…
わあっ…
THAT'S DIANA ROBERTS!
SO BEAUTIFUL...!!
感涙。だあ～
No eating or drinking today.
Okada...

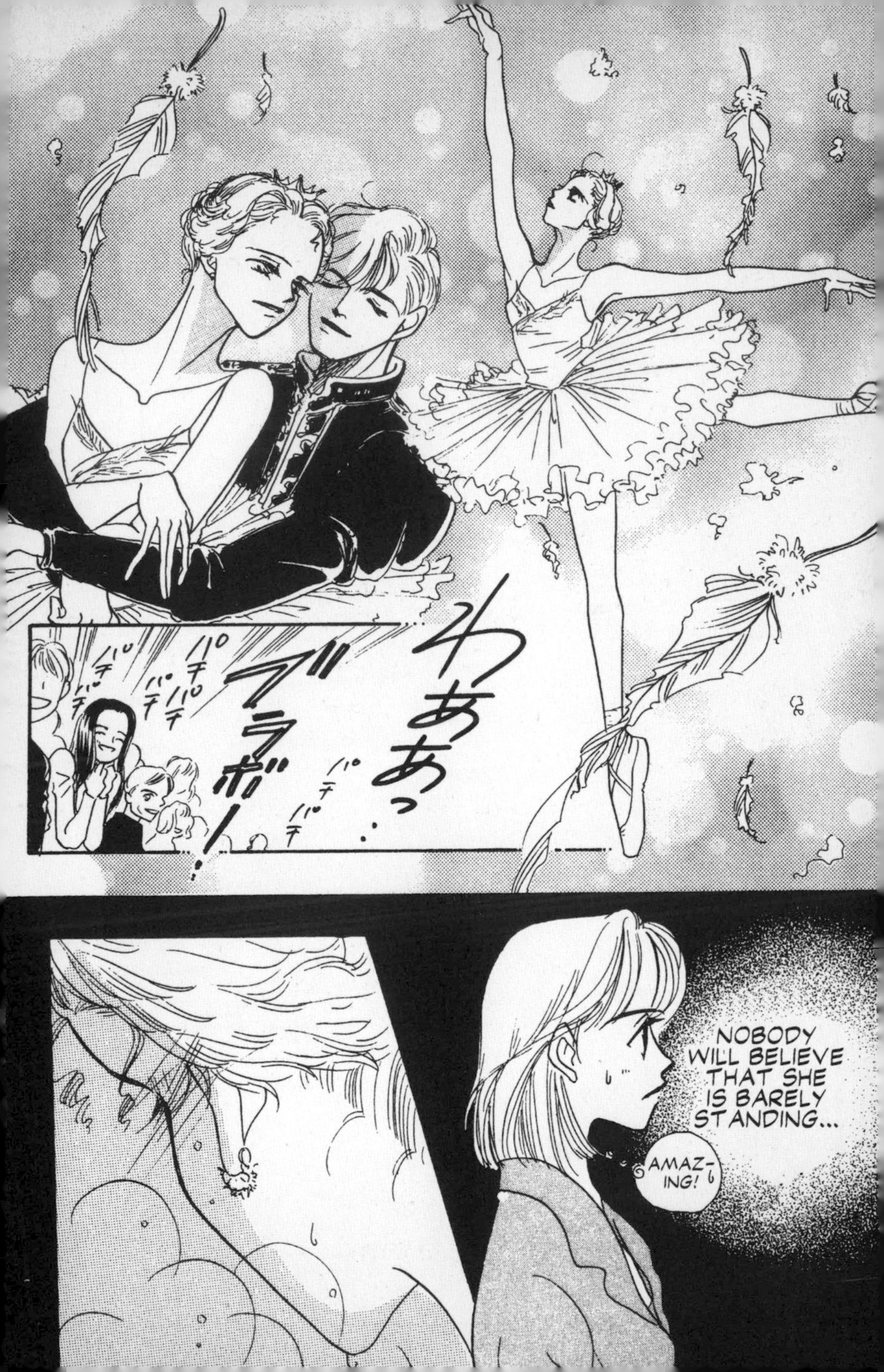
わああっ…
ブラボー!!
パチパチ
パチパチ
パチパチ
パチパチ
NOBODY WILL BELIEVE THAT SHE IS BARELY STANDING...
AMAZ-ING!

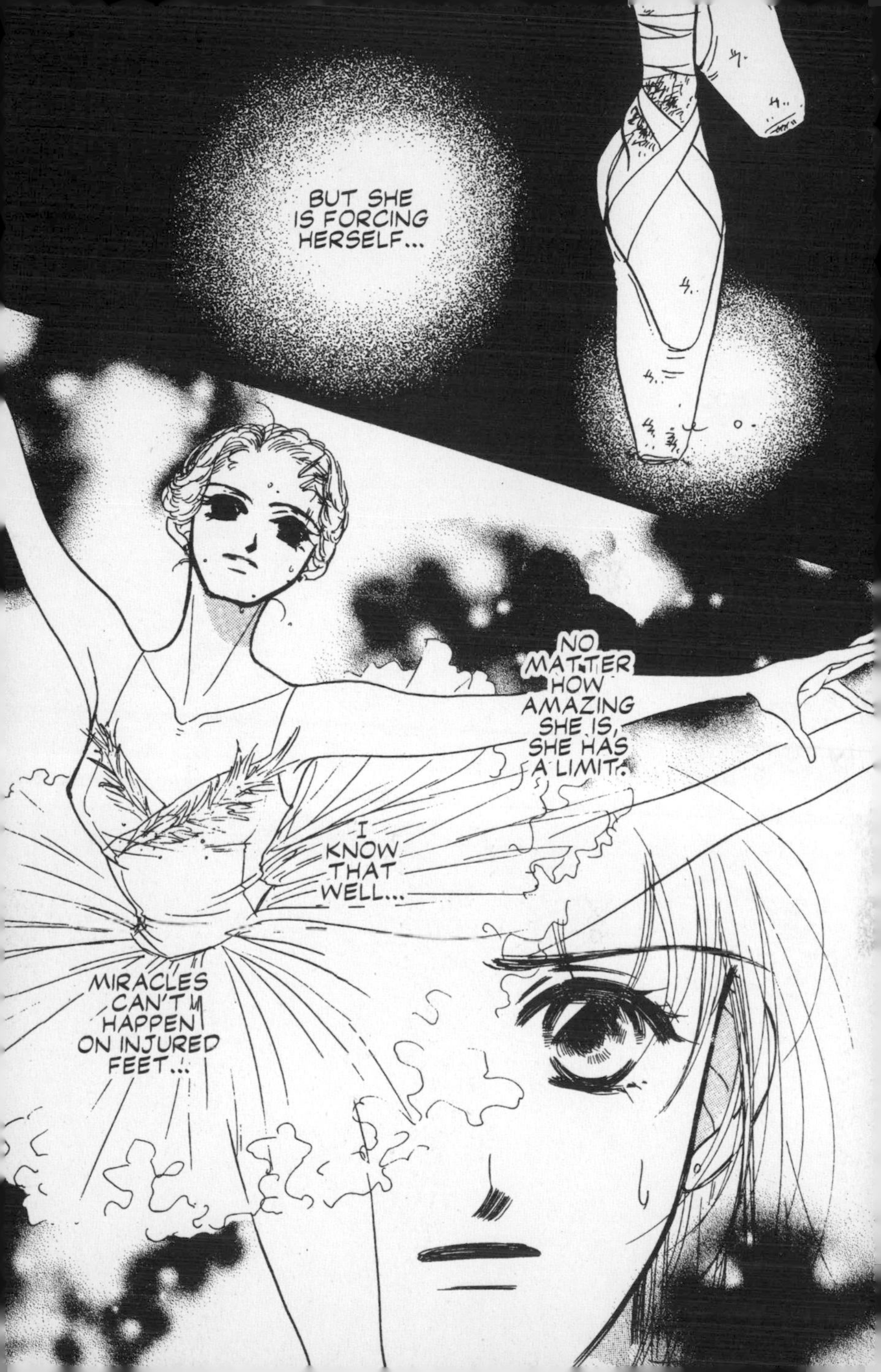
BUT SHE IS FORCING HERSELF...
NO MATTER HOW AMAZING SHE IS, SHE HAS A LIMIT.
I KNOW THAT WELL...
MIRACLES CAN'T HAPPEN ON INJURED FEET...

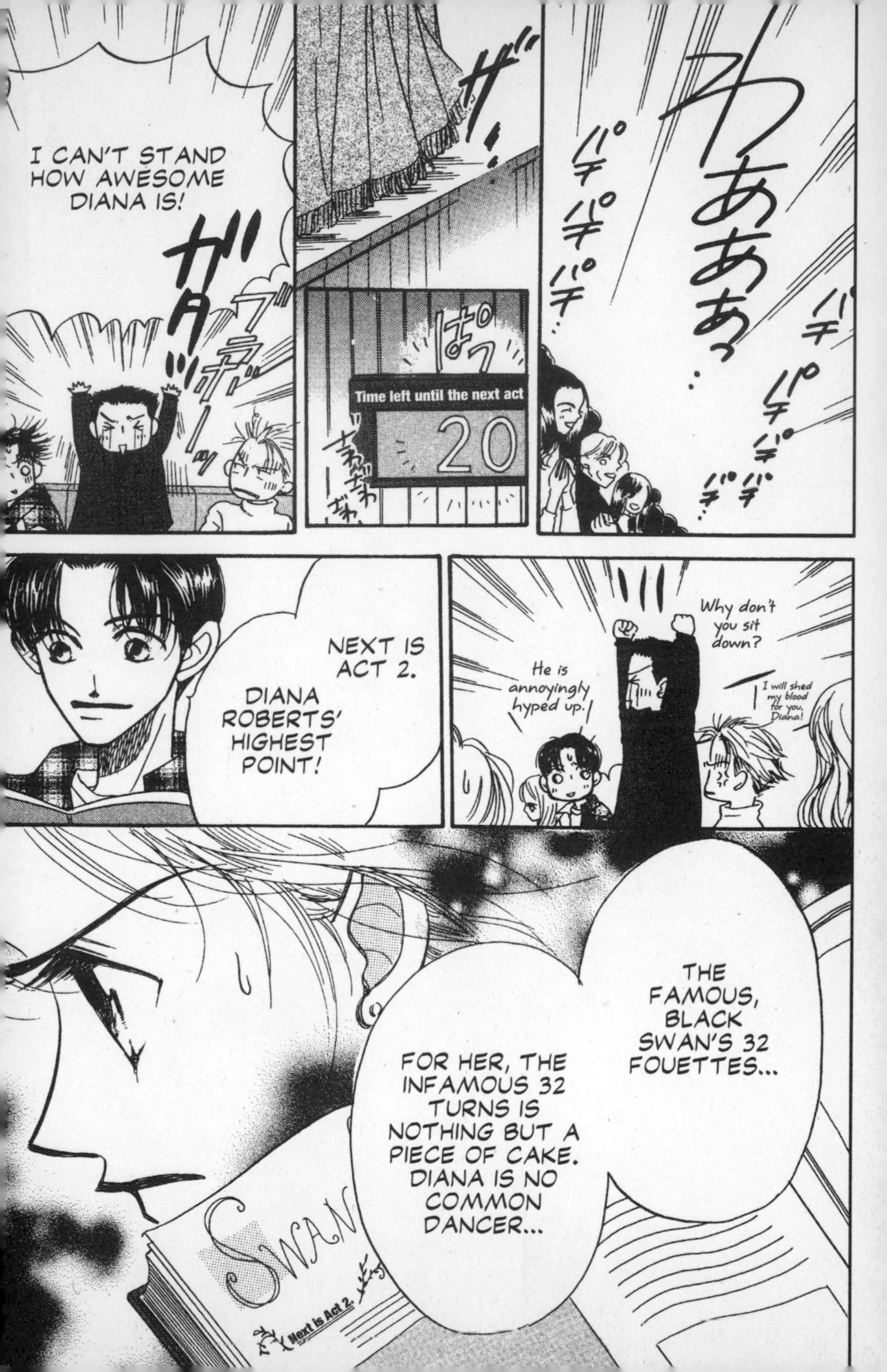
わあああっ…
パチパチパチパチ…
パチパチパチパチ…
ザッ
ぱっ
Time left until the next act
20
ざわざわ
I CAN'T STAND HOW AWESOME DIANA IS!
ガタッ
ブラボーッ
Why don't you sit down?
I will shed my blood for you, Diana!
He is annoyingly hyped up.
NEXT IS ACT 2.
DIANA ROBERTS' HIGHEST POINT!
THE FAMOUS, BLACK SWAN'S 32 FOUETTES...
FOR HER, THE INFAMOUS 32 TURNS IS NOTHING BUT A PIECE OF CAKE. DIANA IS NO COMMON DANCER...
SWAN
Next is Act 2.

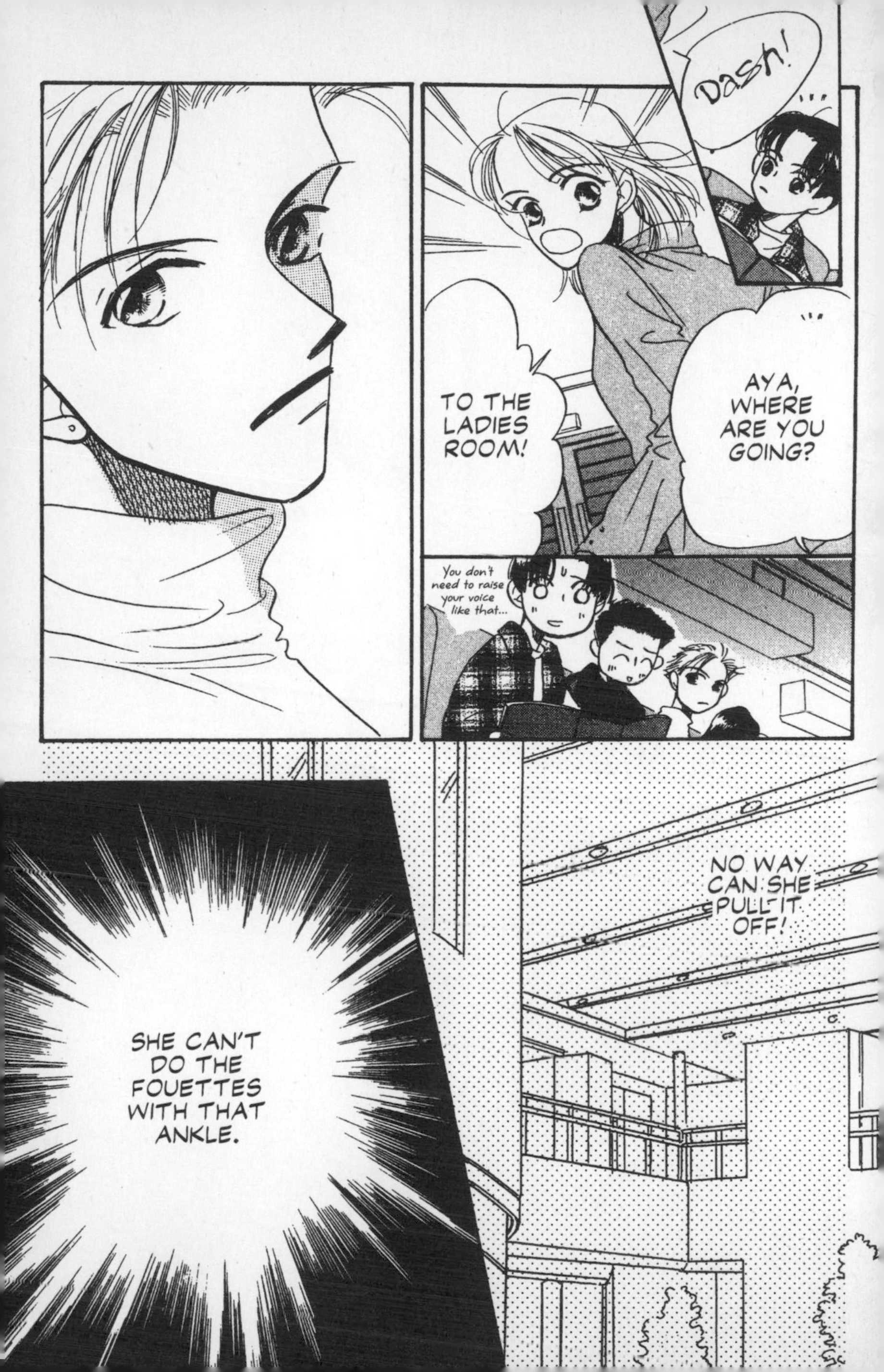
Dash!
AYA, WHERE ARE YOU GOING?
TO THE LADIES ROOM!
You don't need to raise your voice like that...
NO WAY CAN SHE PULL IT OFF!
SHE CAN'T DO THE FOUETTES WITH THAT ANKLE.

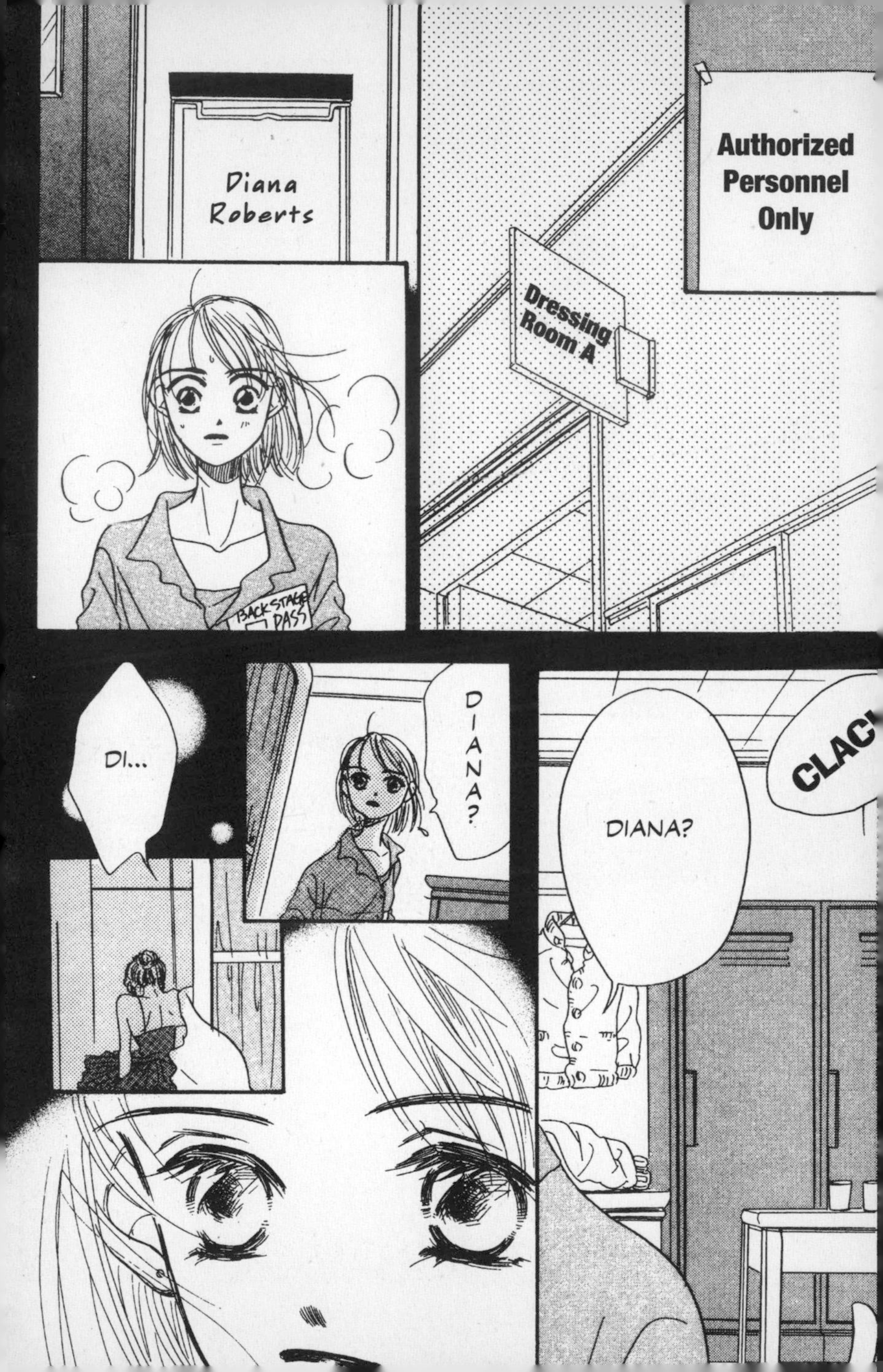
Authorized Personnel Only
Dressing Room A
Diana Roberts
BACKSTAGE PASS
CLAC
DIANA?
DIANA?
DI...

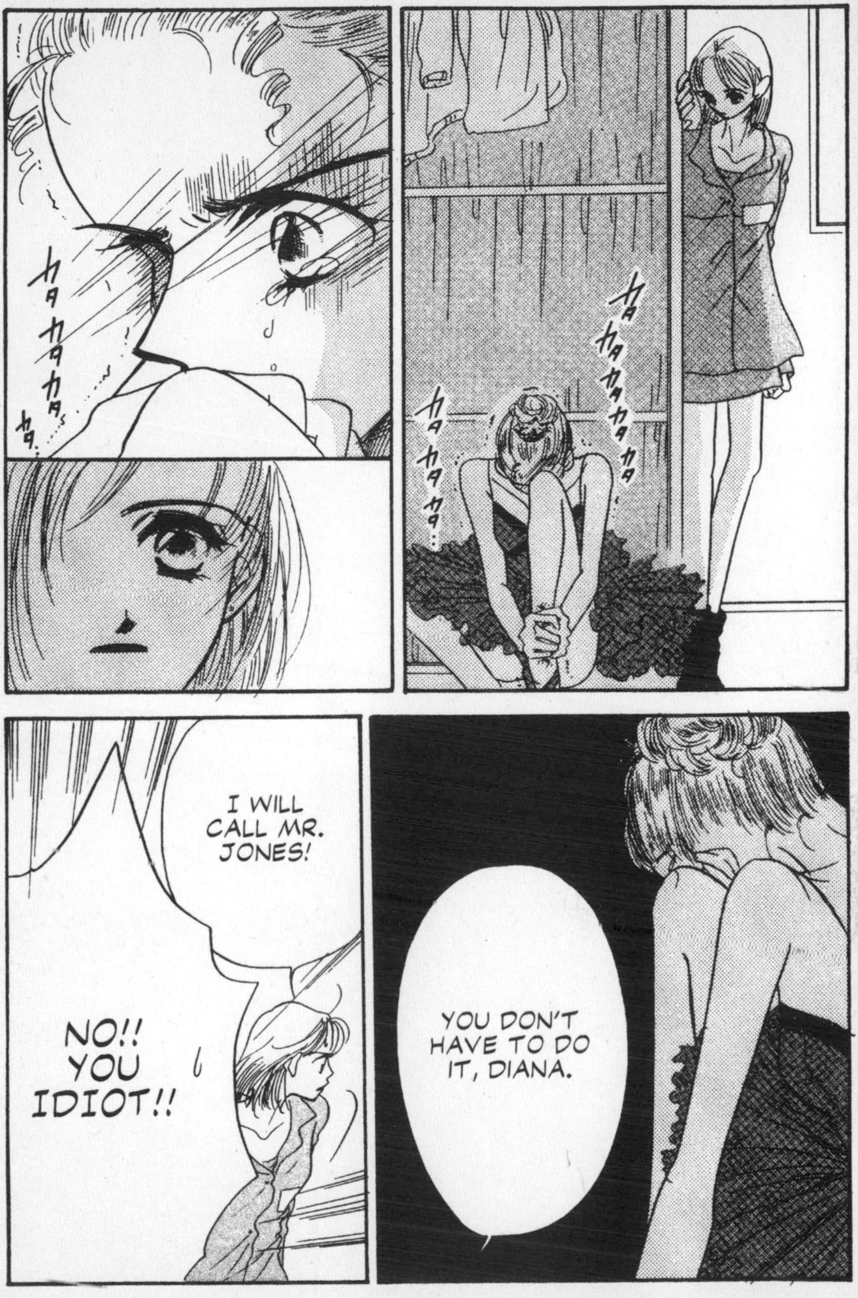
カタカタカタカタカタ
カタカタカタ…
カタカタカタカタ…
カタ…
YOU DON'T HAVE TO DO IT, DIANA.
I WILL CALL MR. JONES!
NO!! YOU IDIOT!!

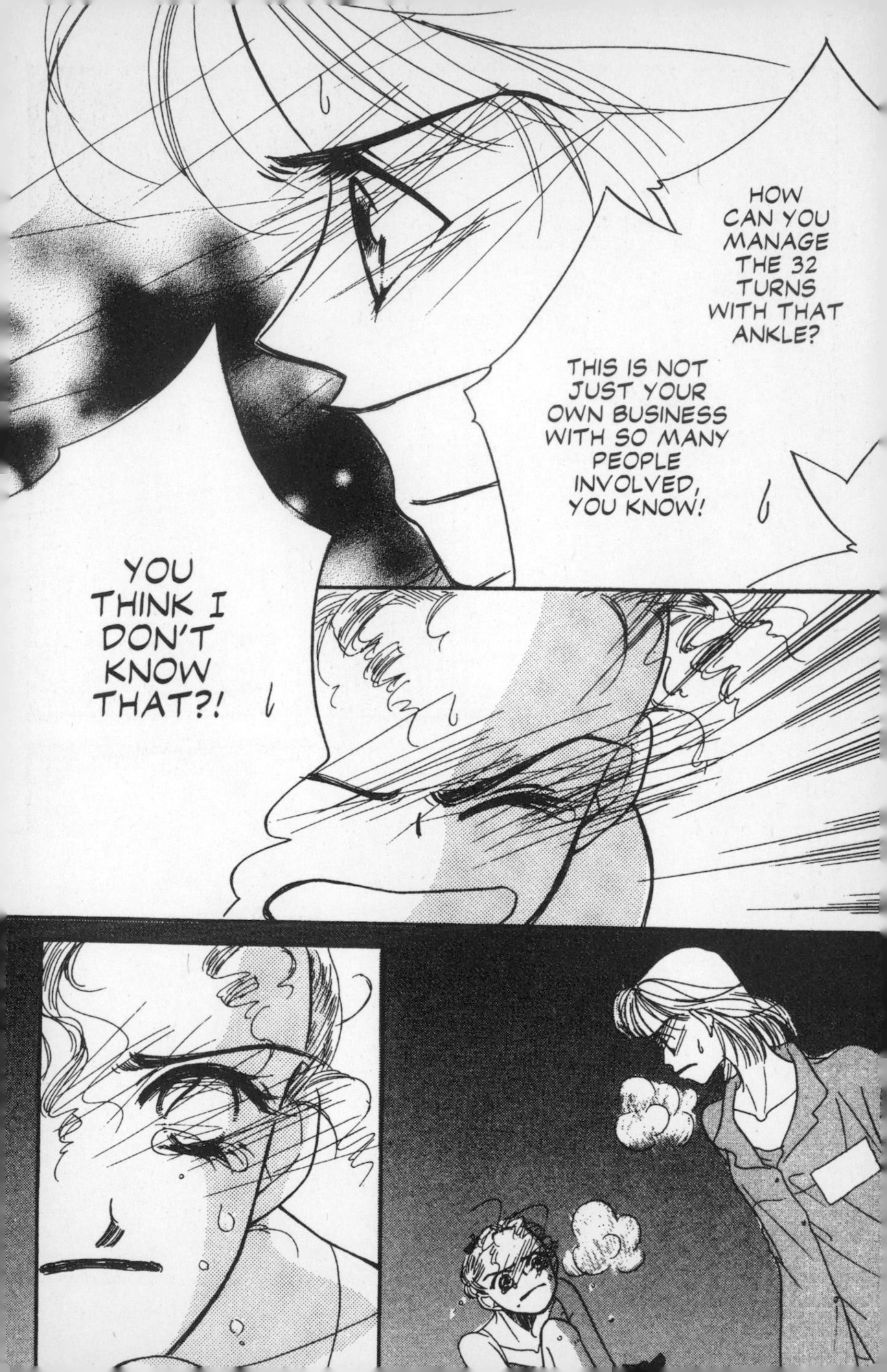
HOW CAN YOU MANAGE THE 32 TURNS WITH THAT ANKLE?
THIS IS NOT JUST YOUR OWN BUSINESS WITH SO MANY PEOPLE INVOLVED, YOU KNOW!
YOU THINK I DON'T KNOW THAT?!

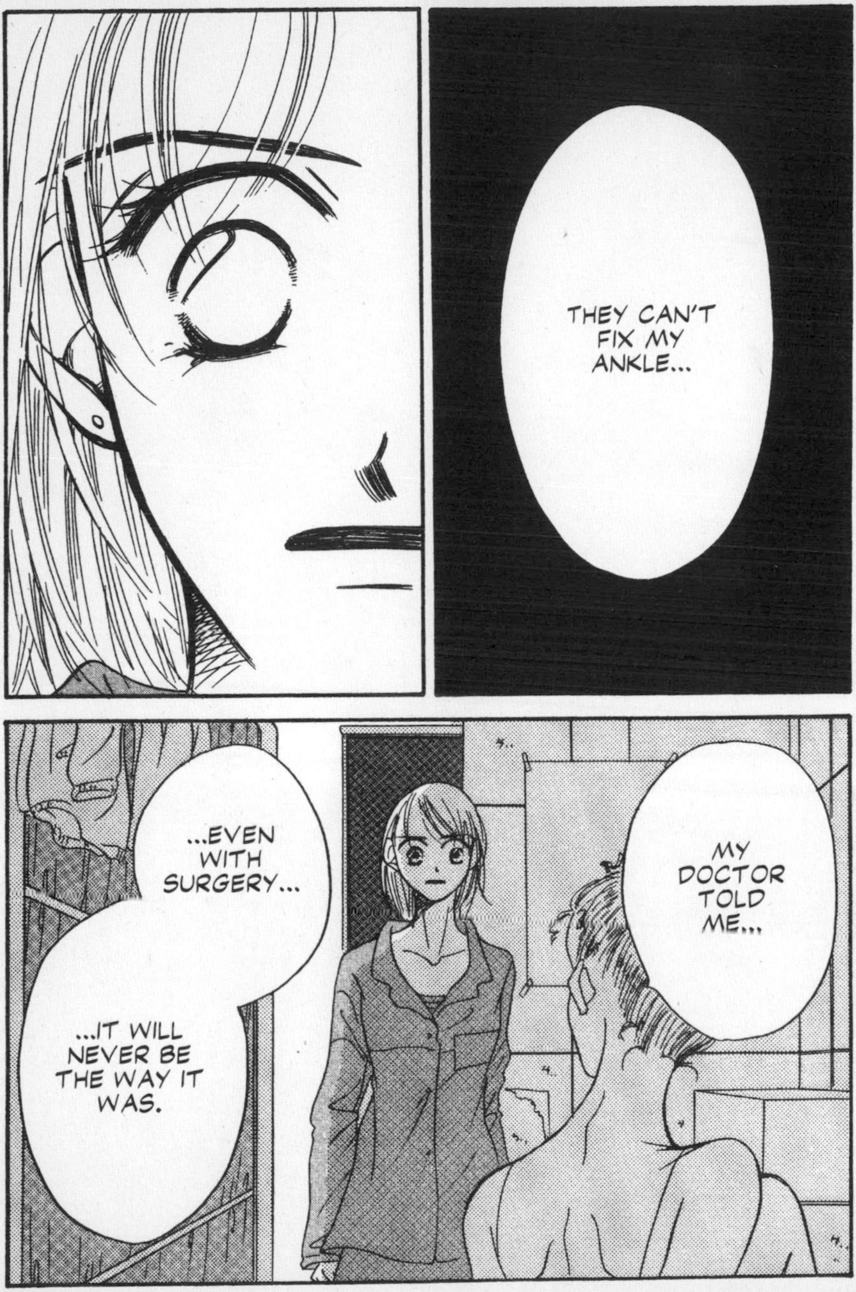
THEY CAN'T FIX MY ANKLE...
MY DOCTOR TOLD ME...
...EVEN WITH SURGERY...
...IT WILL NEVER BE THE WAY IT WAS.

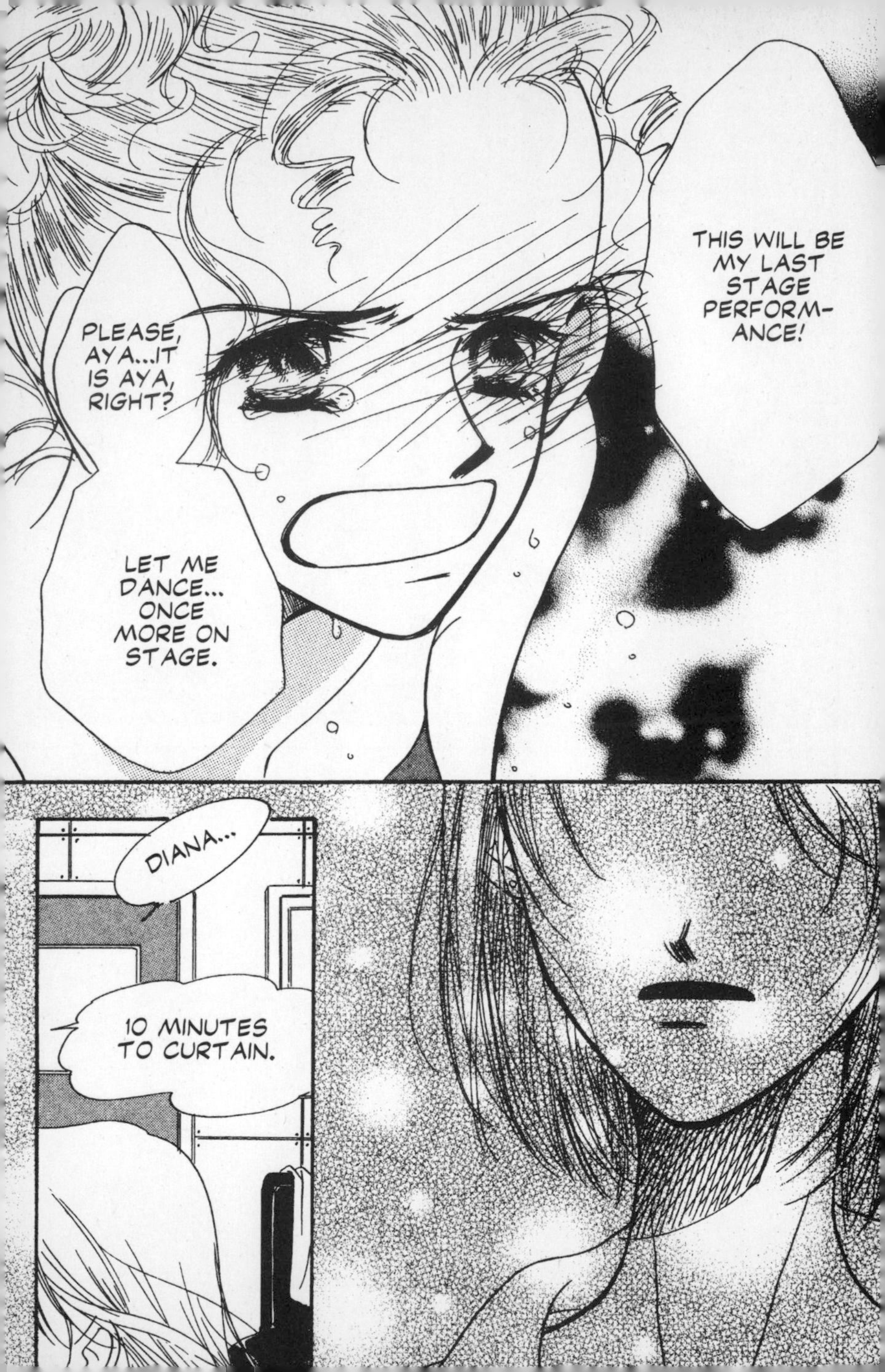
THIS WILL BE MY LAST STAGE PERFORM-ANCE!
PLEASE, AYA...IT IS AYA, RIGHT?
LET ME DANCE... ONCE MORE ON STAGE.
DIANA...
10 MINUTES TO CURTAIN.

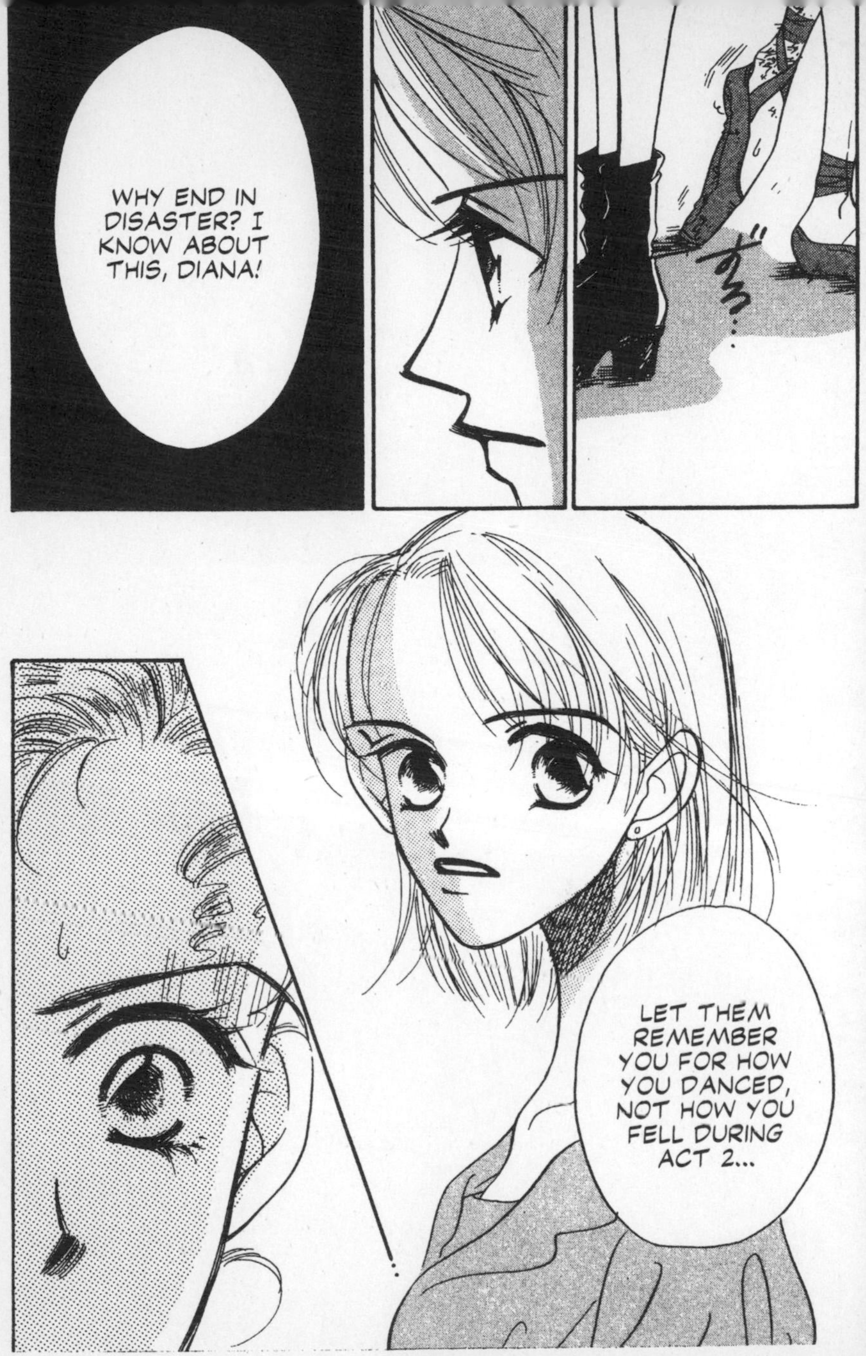
WHY END IN DISASTER? I KNOW ABOUT THIS, DIANA!
LET THEM REMEMBER YOU FOR HOW YOU DANCED, NOT HOW YOU FELL DURING ACT 2...

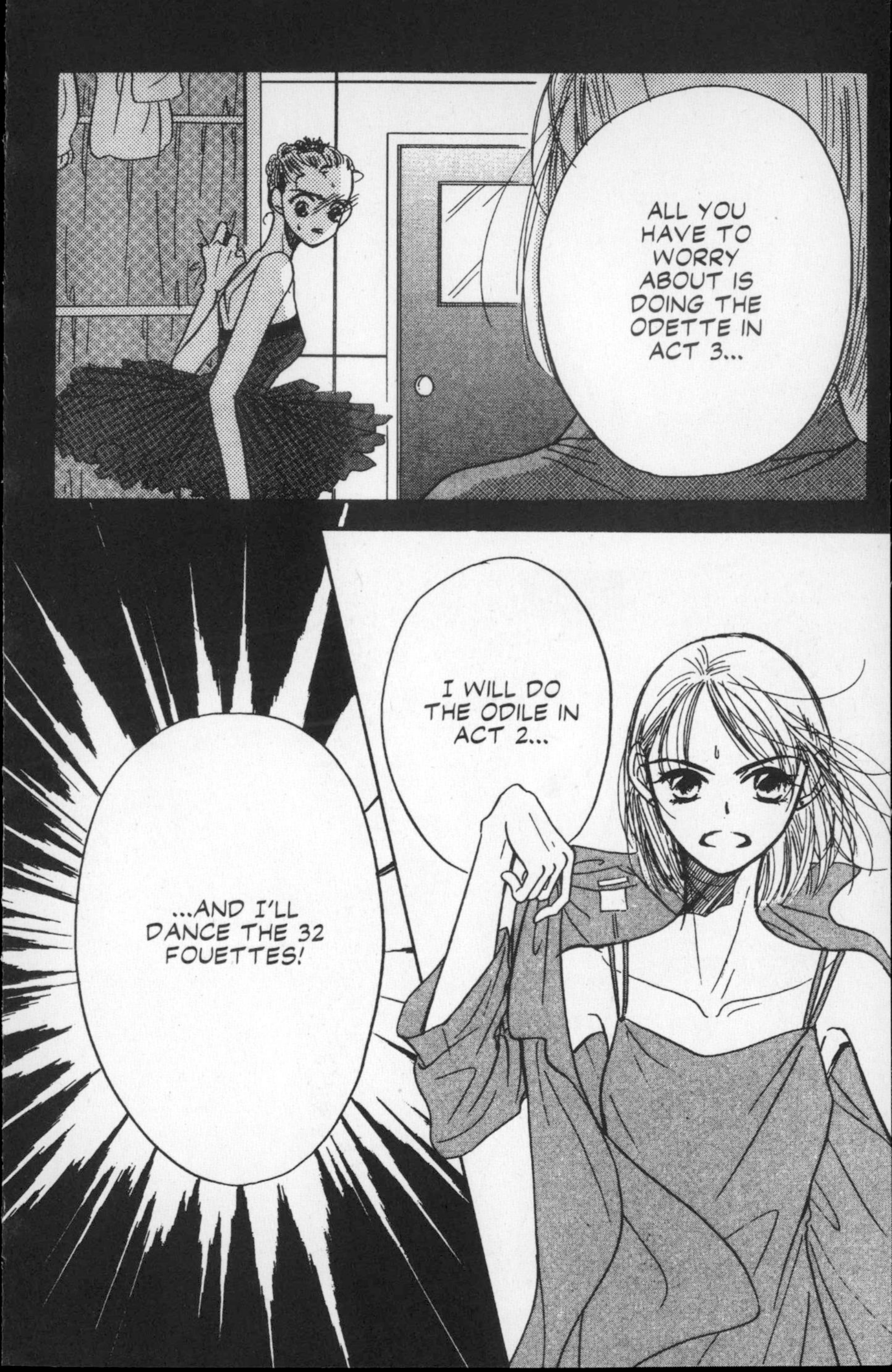
ALL YOU HAVE TO WORRY ABOUT IS DOING THE ODETTE IN ACT 3...
I WILL DO THE ODILE IN ACT 2...
...AND I'LL DANCE THE 32 FOUETTES!

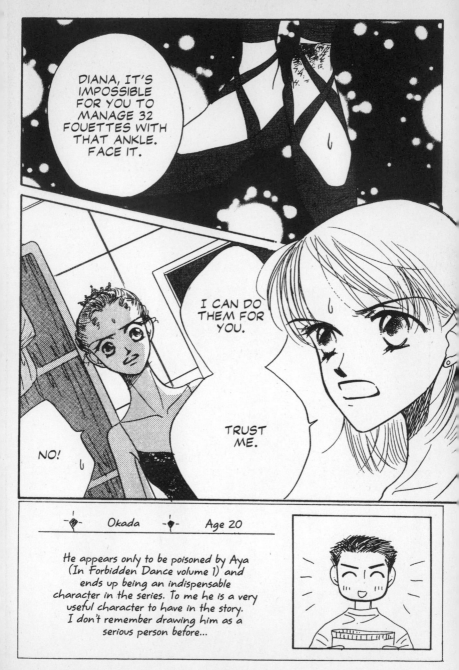

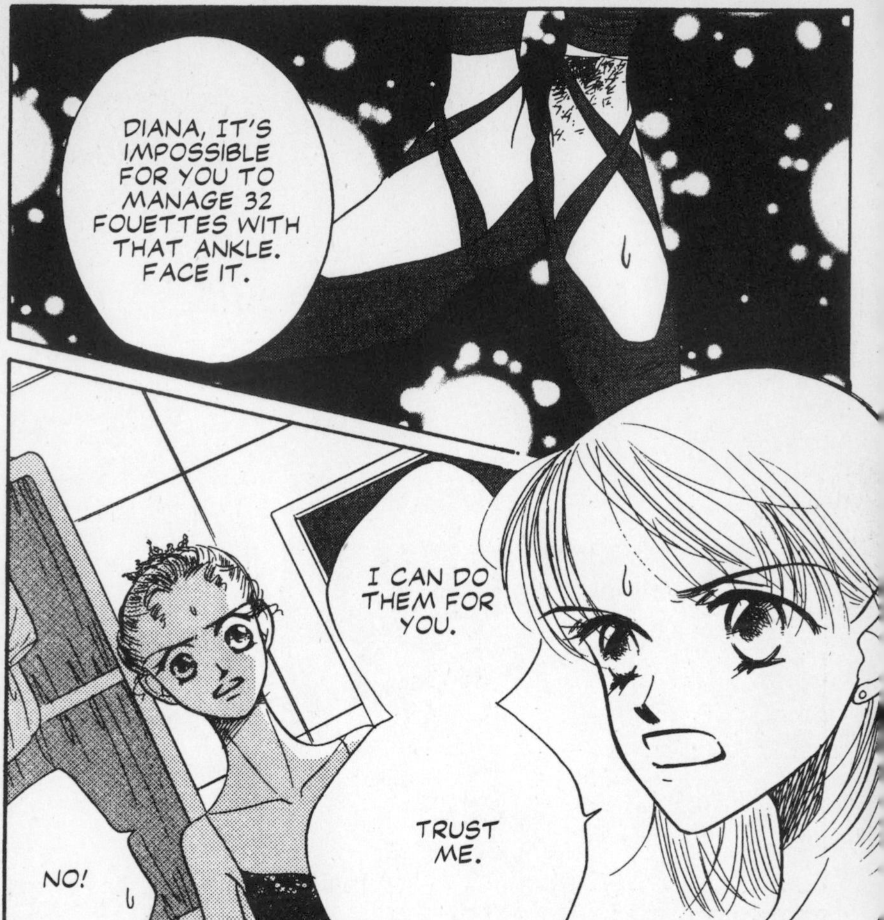
DIANA, IT'S IMPOSSIBLE FOR YOU TO MANAGE 32 FOUETTES WITH THAT ANKLE. FACE IT.
I CAN DO THEM FOR YOU.
TRUST ME.
NO!

Okada — Age 20

He appears only to be poisoned by Aya (In Forbidden Dance volume 1) and ends up being an indispensable character in the series. To me he is a very useful character to have in the story. I don't remember drawing him as a serious person before...

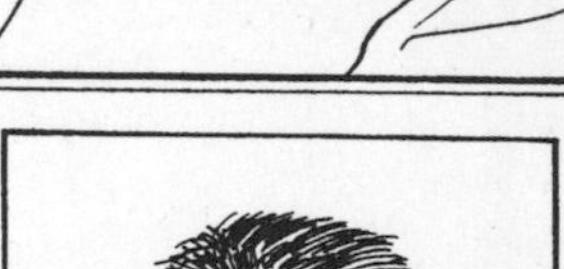

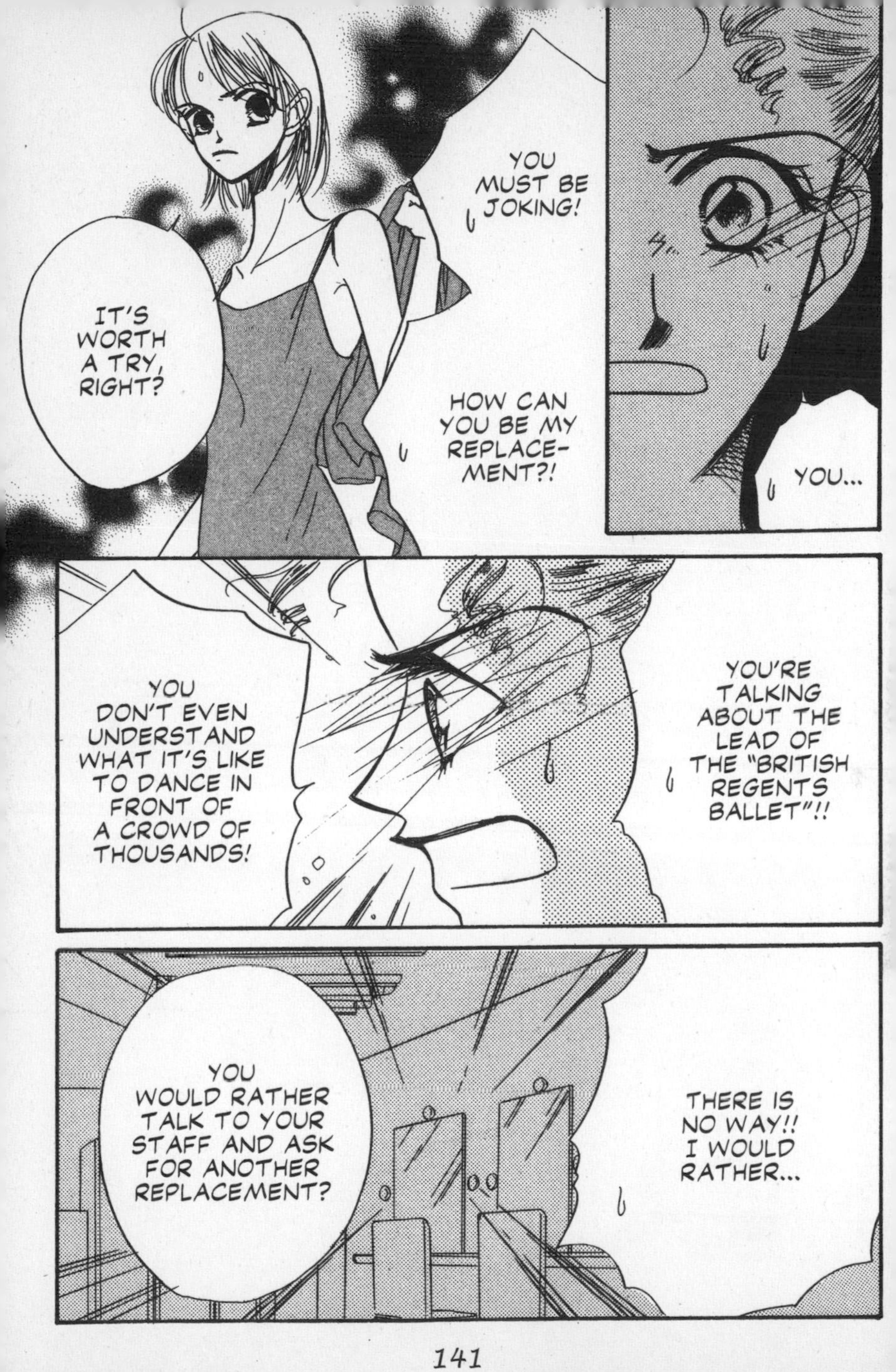
YOU...
YOU MUST BE JOKING!
HOW CAN YOU BE MY REPLACEMENT?!
IT'S WORTH A TRY, RIGHT?
YOU'RE TALKING ABOUT THE LEAD OF THE "BRITISH REGENTS BALLET"!!
YOU DON'T EVEN UNDERSTAND WHAT IT'S LIKE TO DANCE IN FRONT OF A CROWD OF THOUSANDS!
THERE IS NO WAY!! I WOULD RATHER...
YOU WOULD RATHER TALK TO YOUR STAFF AND ASK FOR ANOTHER REPLACEMENT?

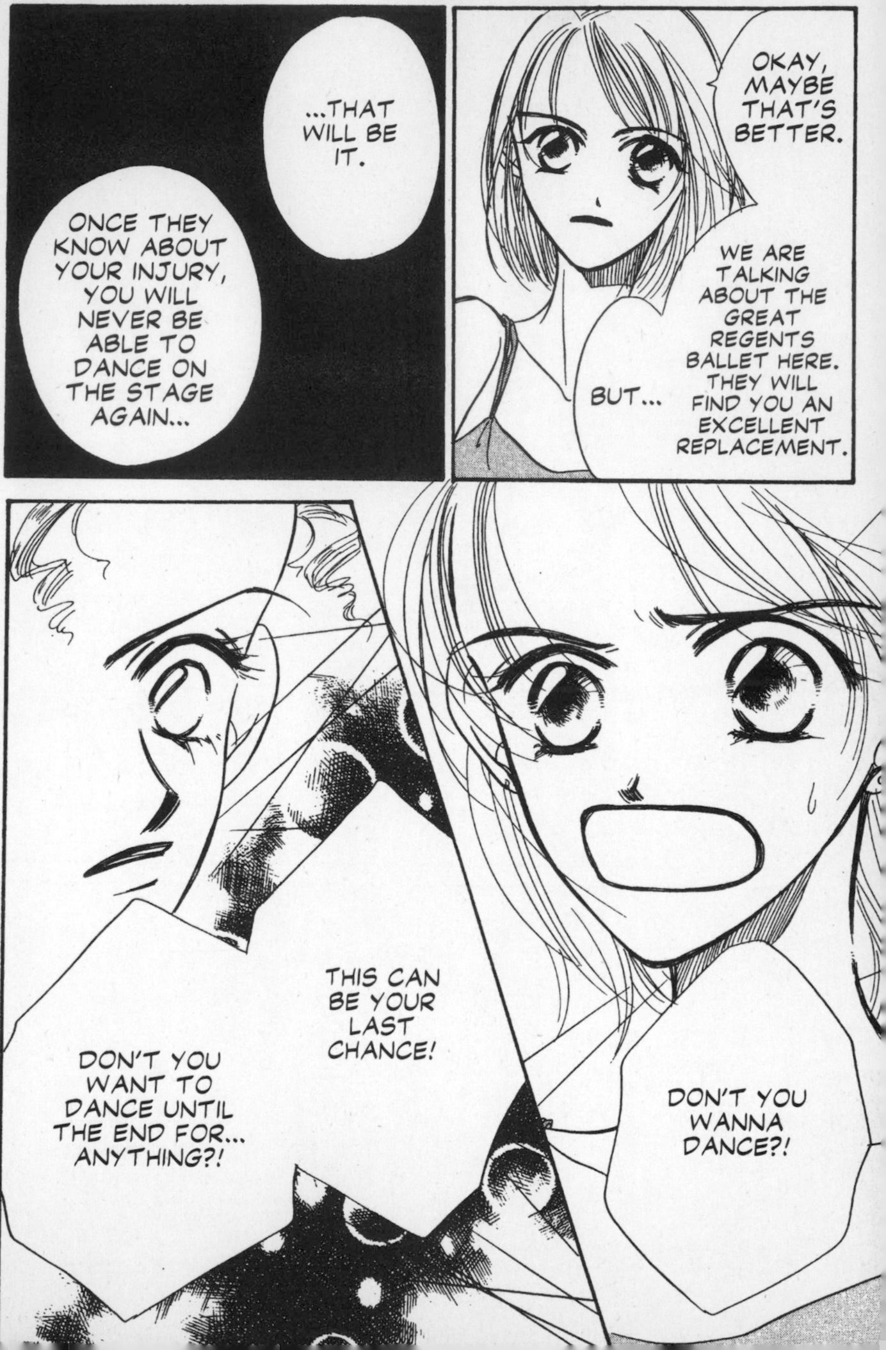
OKAY, MAYBE THAT'S BETTER.
WE ARE TALKING ABOUT THE GREAT REGENTS BALLET HERE. THEY WILL FIND YOU AN EXCELLENT REPLACEMENT.
BUT...
...THAT WILL BE IT.
ONCE THEY KNOW ABOUT YOUR INJURY, YOU WILL NEVER BE ABLE TO DANCE ON THE STAGE AGAIN...
DON'T YOU WANNA DANCE?!
THIS CAN BE YOUR LAST CHANCE!
DON'T YOU WANT TO DANCE UNTIL THE END FOR... ANYTHING?!

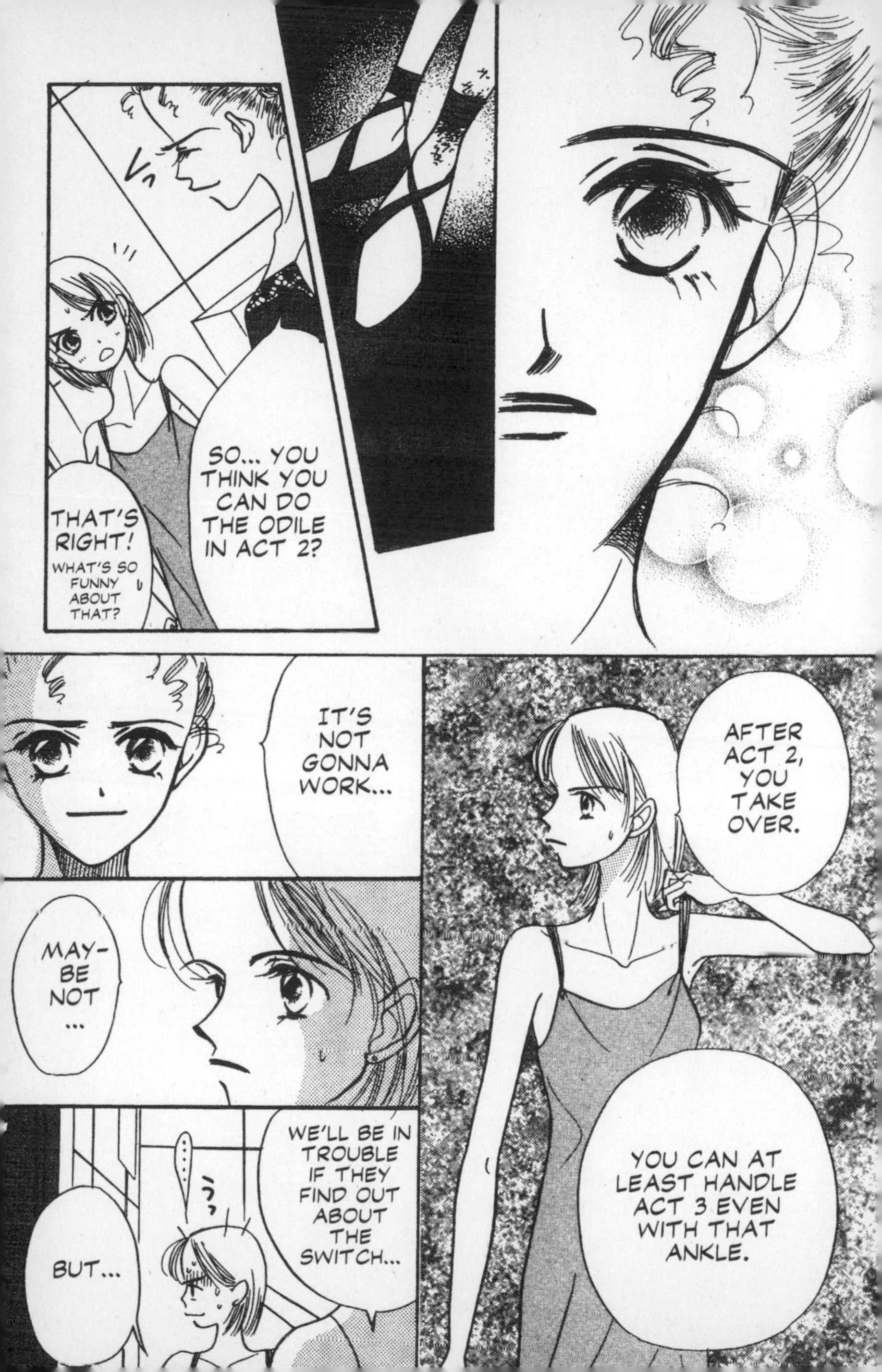
SO... YOU THINK YOU CAN DO THE ODILE IN ACT 2?
THAT'S RIGHT! WHAT'S SO FUNNY ABOUT THAT?
AFTER ACT 2, YOU TAKE OVER.
YOU CAN AT LEAST HANDLE ACT 3 EVEN WITH THAT ANKLE.
IT'S NOT GONNA WORK...
MAY-BE NOT ...
WE'LL BE IN TROUBLE IF THEY FIND OUT ABOUT THE SWITCH...
BUT...

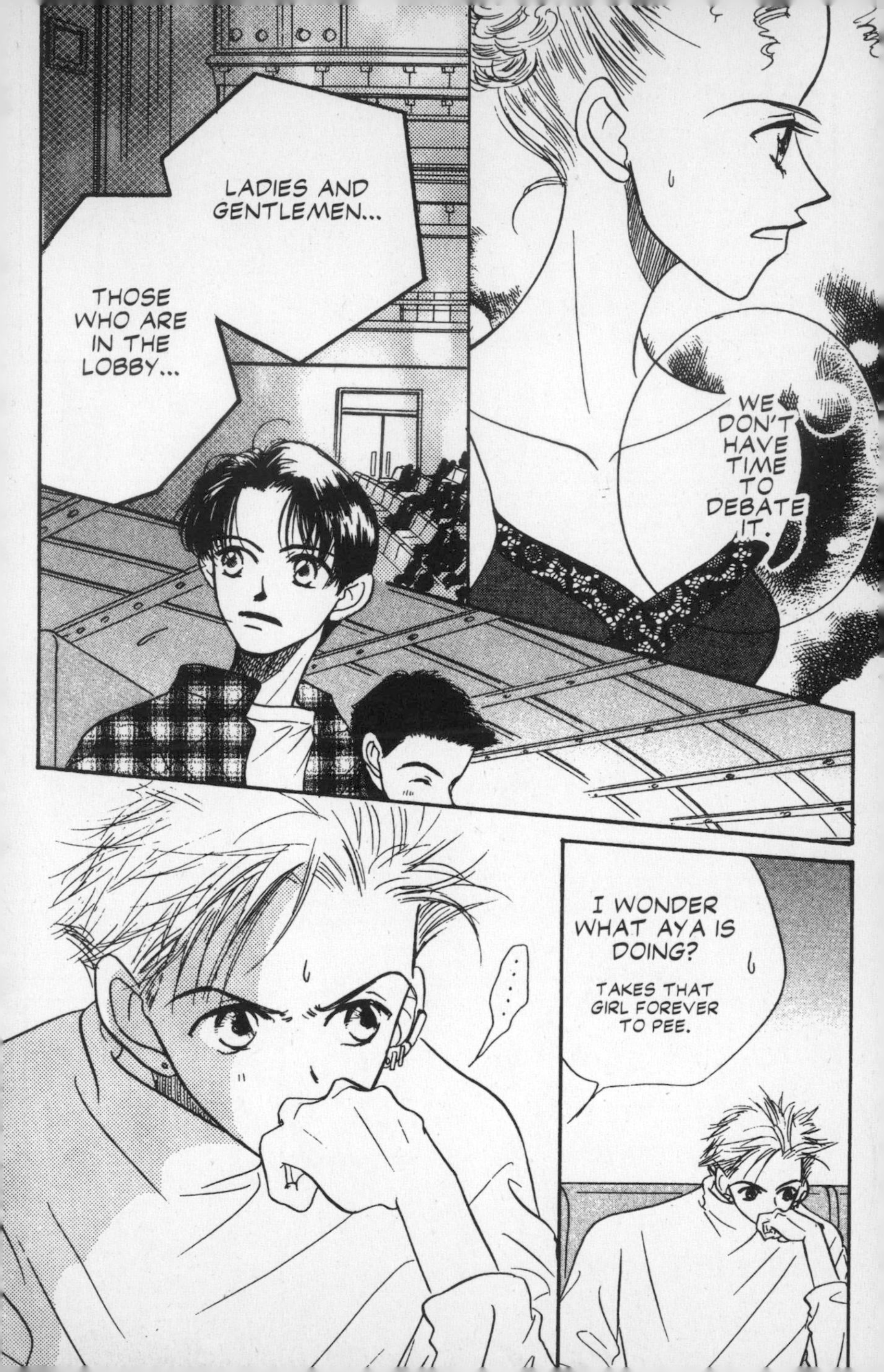
WE DON'T HAVE TIME TO DEBATE IT.
LADIES AND GENTLEMEN...
THOSE WHO ARE IN THE LOBBY...
I WONDER WHAT AYA IS DOING?
TAKES THAT GIRL FOREVER TO PEE.
....

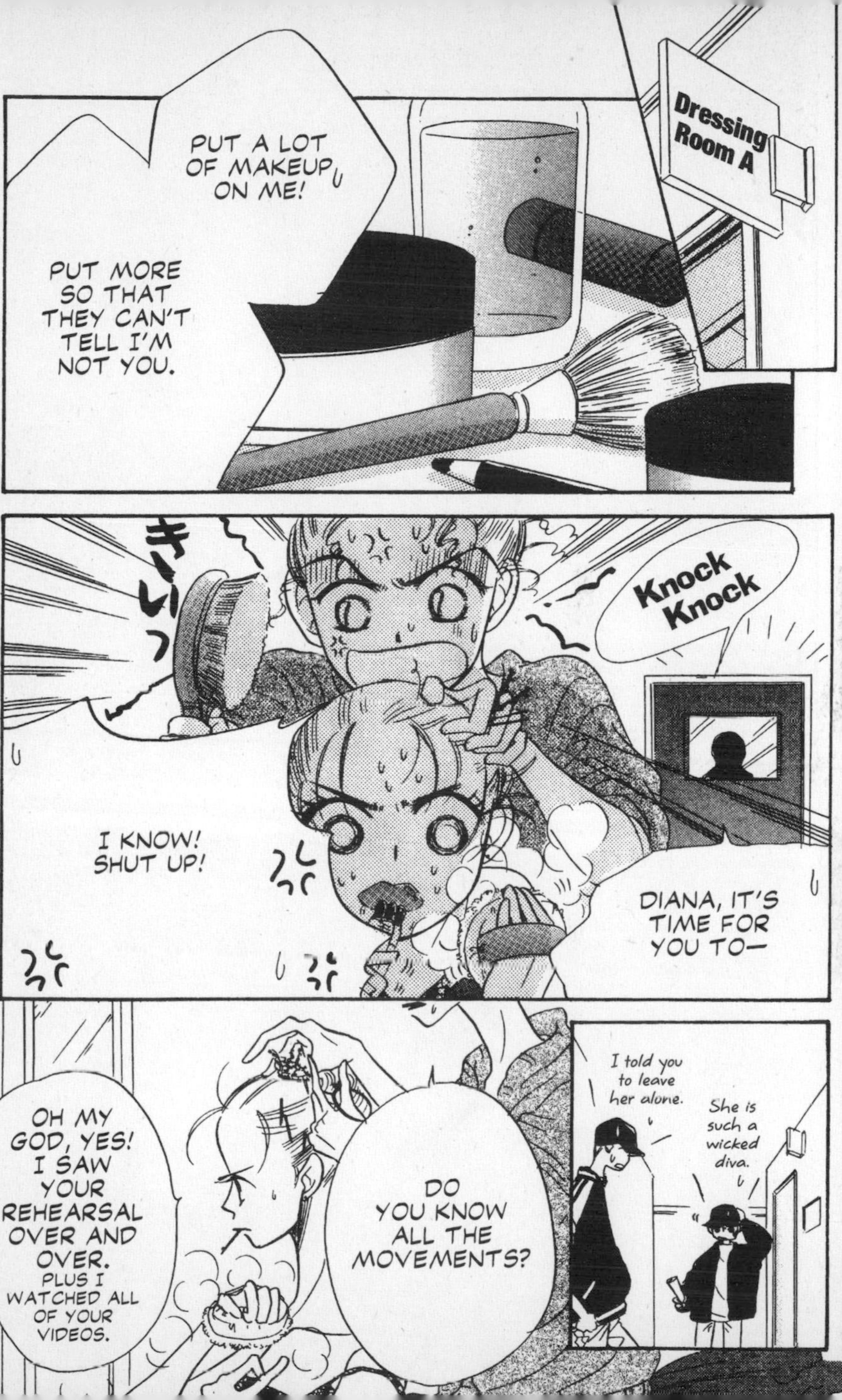
Dressing Room A
PUT A LOT OF MAKEUP ON ME!
PUT MORE SO THAT THEY CAN'T TELL I'M NOT YOU.
Knock Knock
DIANA, IT'S TIME FOR YOU TO—
I KNOW! SHUT UP!
I told you to leave her alone.
She is such a wicked diva.
DO YOU KNOW ALL THE MOVEMENTS?
OH MY GOD, YES! I SAW YOUR REHEARSAL OVER AND OVER. PLUS I WATCHED ALL OF YOUR VIDEOS.

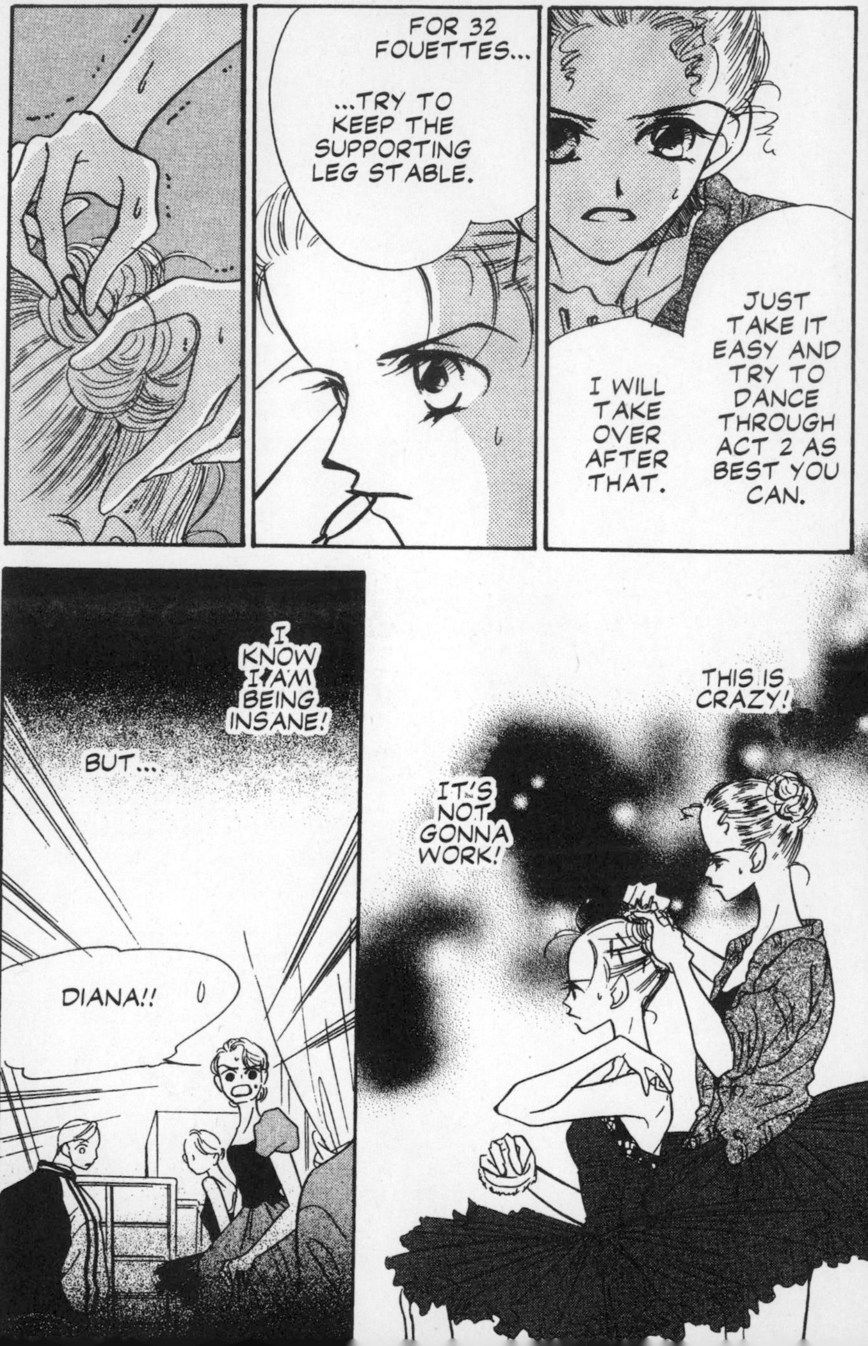
JUST TAKE IT EASY AND TRY TO DANCE THROUGH ACT 2 AS BEST YOU CAN.
I WILL TAKE OVER AFTER THAT.
FOR 32 FOUETTES...
...TRY TO KEEP THE SUPPORTING LEG STABLE.
THIS IS CRAZY!
IT'S NOT GONNA WORK!
I KNOW I AM BEING INSANE!
BUT...
DIANA!!

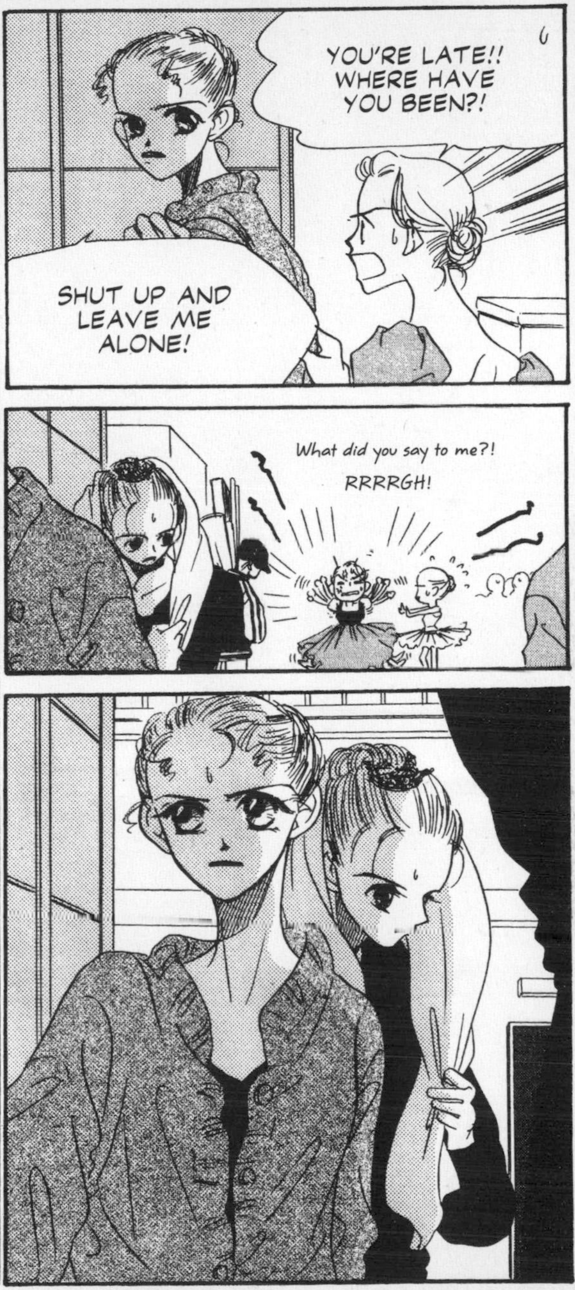
YOU'RE LATE!! WHERE HAVE YOU BEEN?!
SHUT UP AND LEAVE ME ALONE!
What did you say to me?!
RRRRGH!

Ashihara's Diary

No. 5

Because my sister had no interest in ballet, I was wondering if she would really enjoy the performance. But it turned out that she loved it very much.

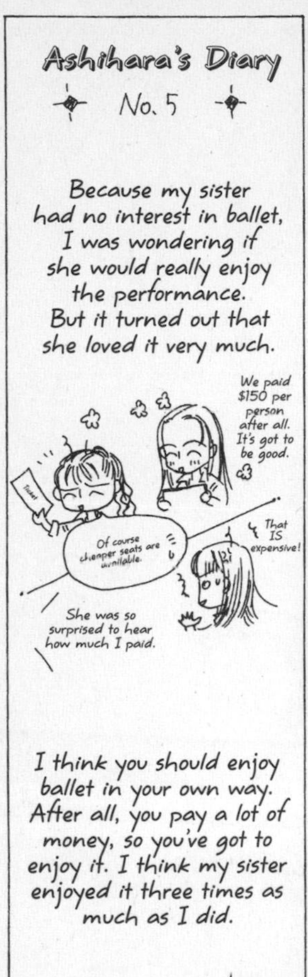
We paid $150 per person after all. It's got to be good.
Ticket
That IS expensive!
Of course cheaper seats are available.
She was so surprised to hear how much I paid.

I think you should enjoy ballet in your own way. After all, you pay a lot of money, so you've got to enjoy it. I think my sister enjoyed it three times as much as I did.

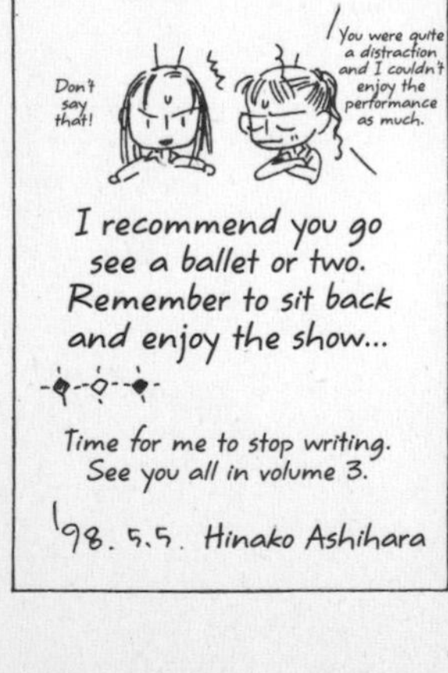
You were quite a distraction and I couldn't enjoy the performance as much.
Don't say that!

I recommend you go see a ballet or two. Remember to sit back and enjoy the show...

Time for me to stop writing. See you all in volume 3.

'98. 5. 5. Hinako Ashihara

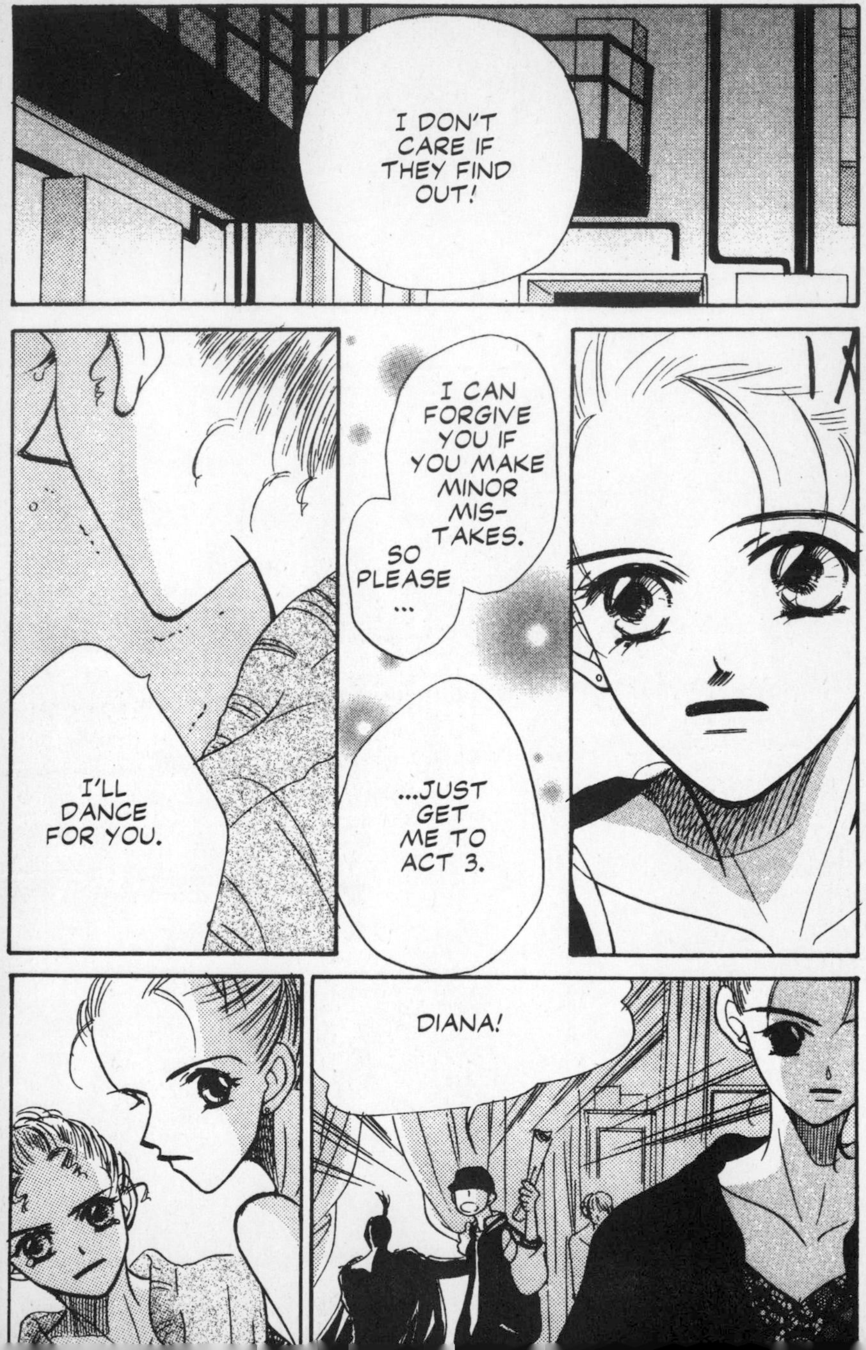
I DON'T CARE IF THEY FIND OUT!
I CAN FORGIVE YOU IF YOU MAKE MINOR MIS-TAKES.
SO PLEASE ...
...JUST GET ME TO ACT 3.
I'LL DANCE FOR YOU.
DIANA!

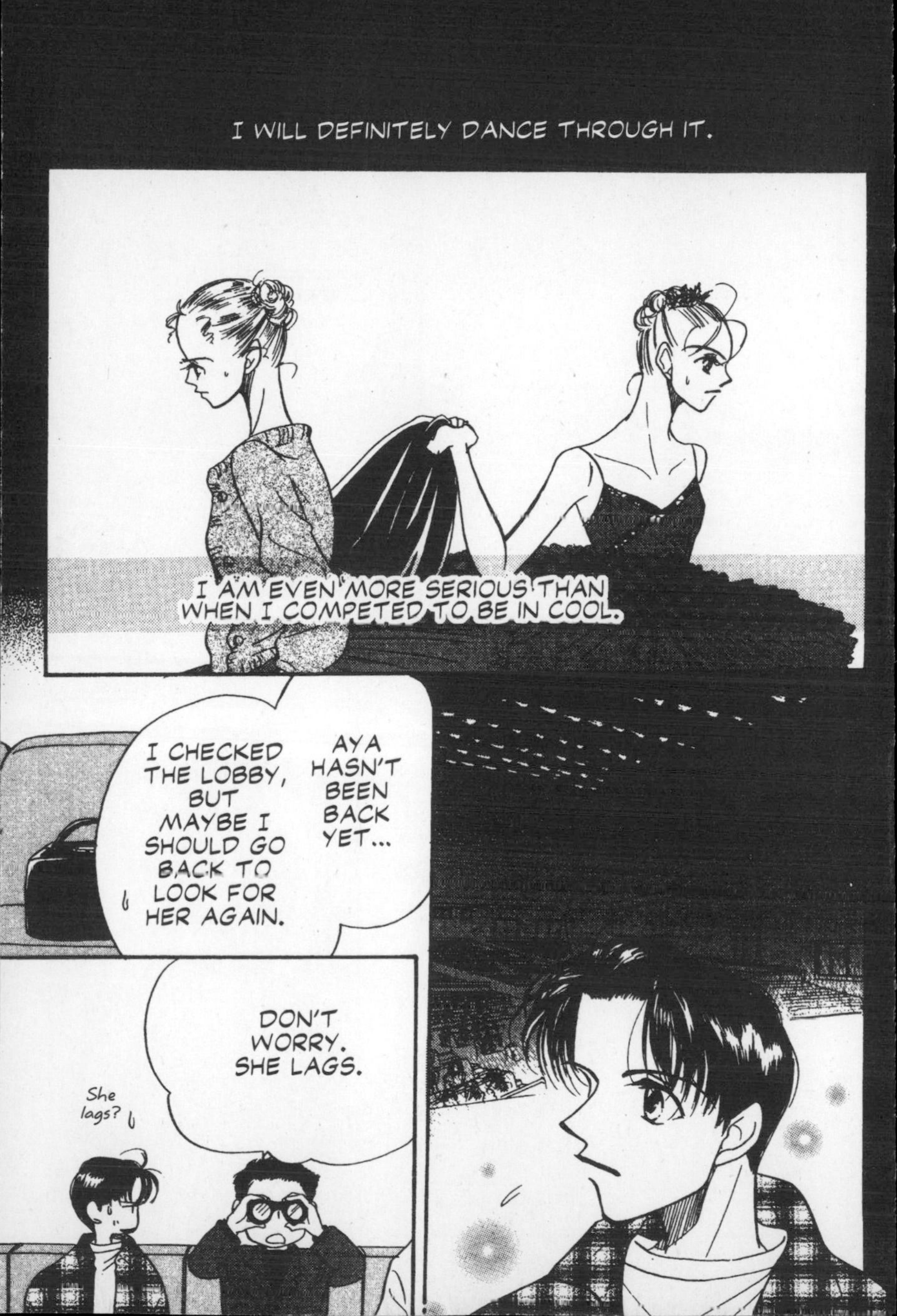
I WILL DEFINITELY DANCE THROUGH IT.
I AM EVEN MORE SERIOUS THAN WHEN I COMPETED TO BE IN COOL.
AYA HASN'T BEEN BACK YET...
I CHECKED THE LOBBY, BUT MAYBE I SHOULD GO BACK TO LOOK FOR HER AGAIN.
DON'T WORRY. SHE LAGS.
She lags?

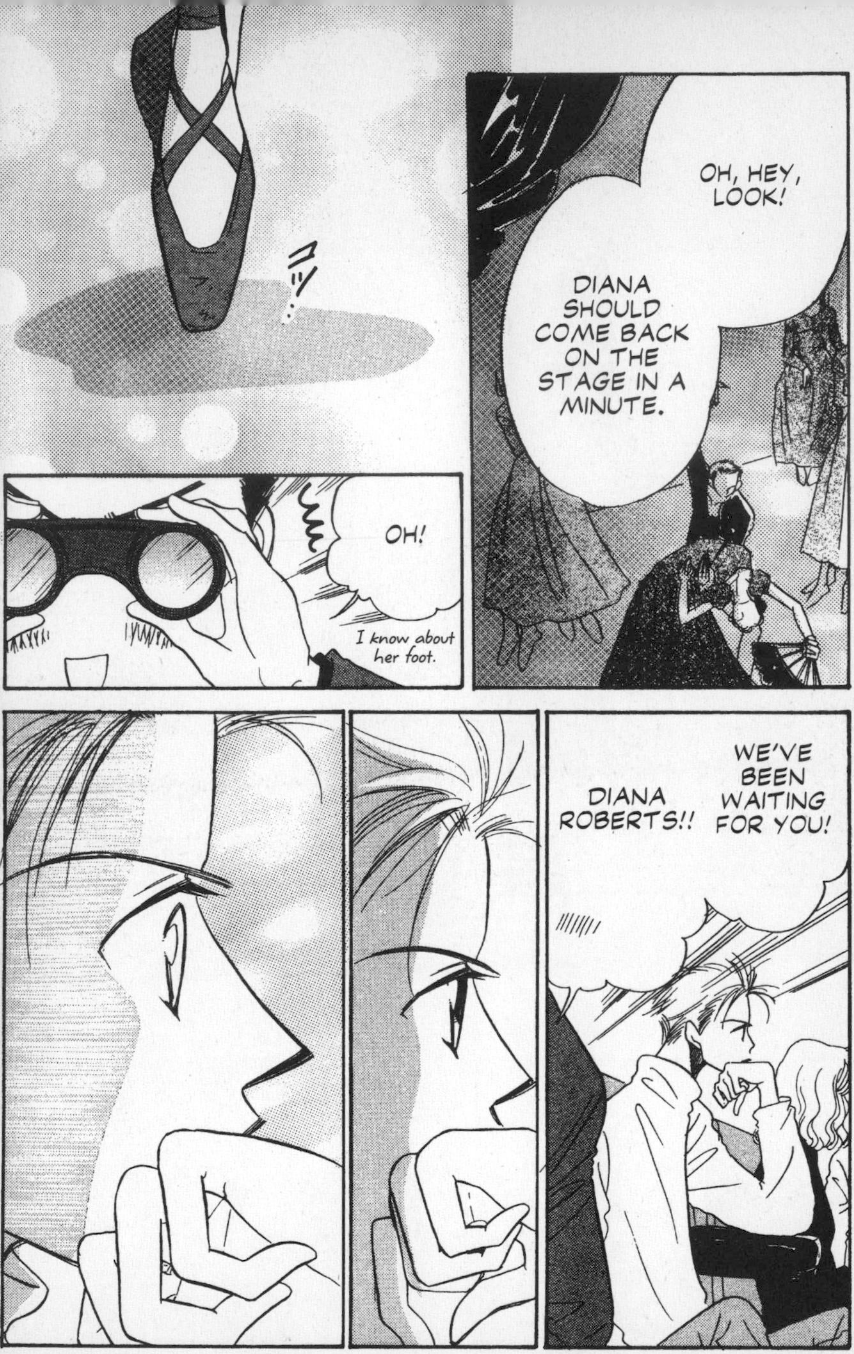
OH, HEY, LOOK!
DIANA SHOULD COME BACK ON THE STAGE IN A MINUTE.
OH!
I know about her foot.
DIANA ROBERTS!! WE'VE BEEN WAITING FOR YOU!

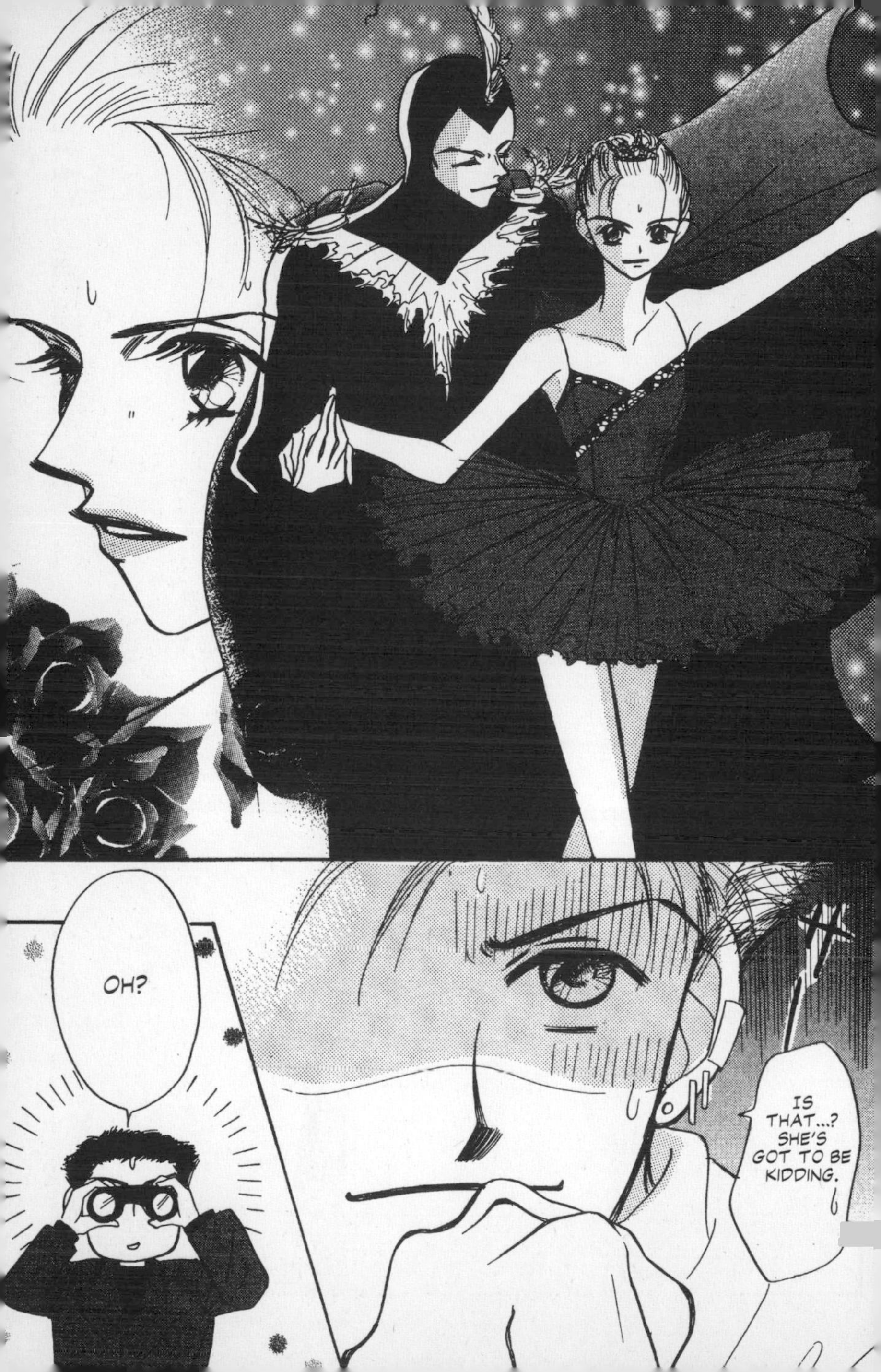
IS THAT...? SHE'S GOT TO BE KIDDING.
OH?

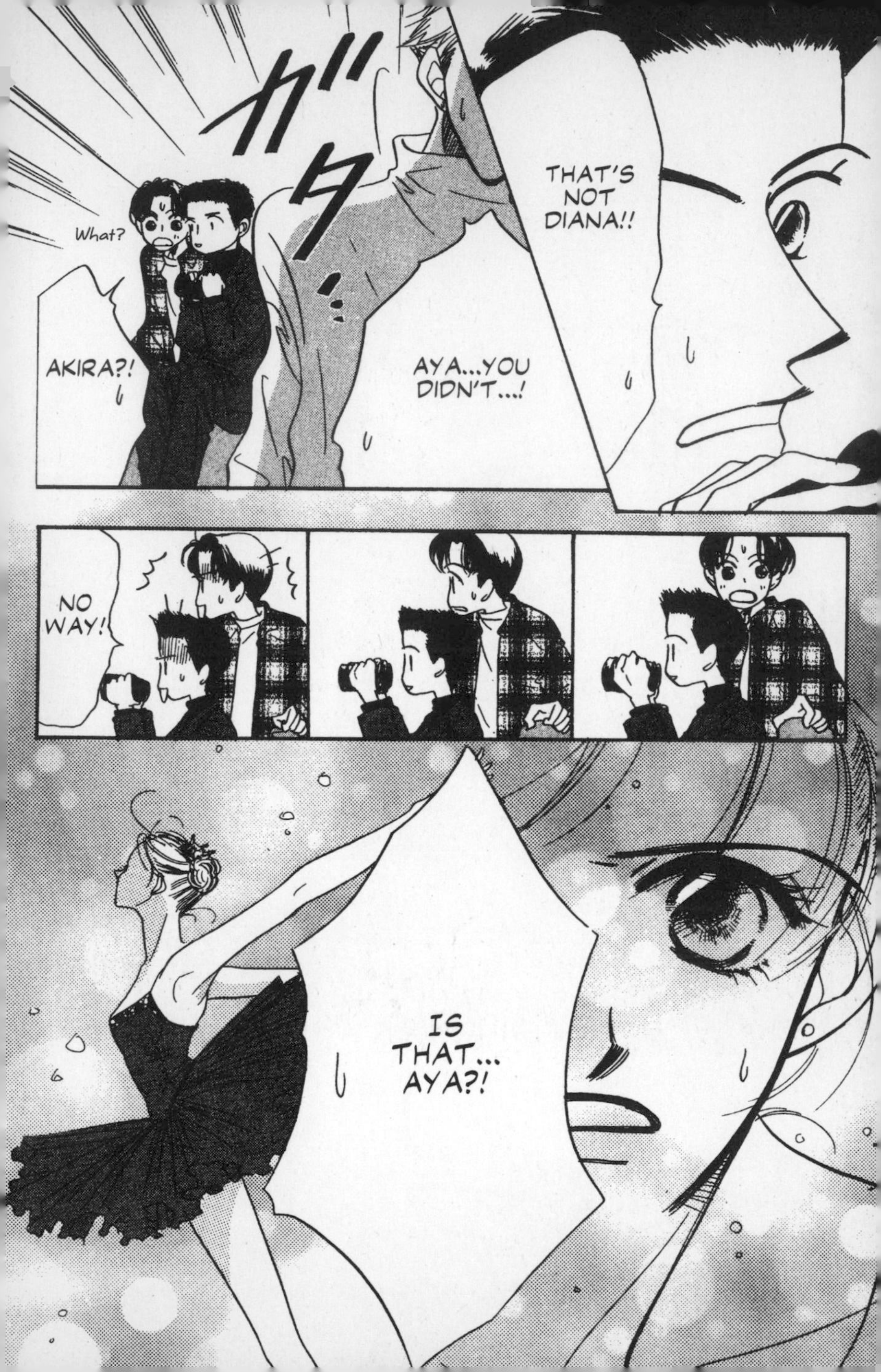
THAT'S NOT DIANA!!
ガタ
AYA...YOU DIDN'T...!
What?
AKIRA?!
NO WAY!
IS THAT... AYA?!

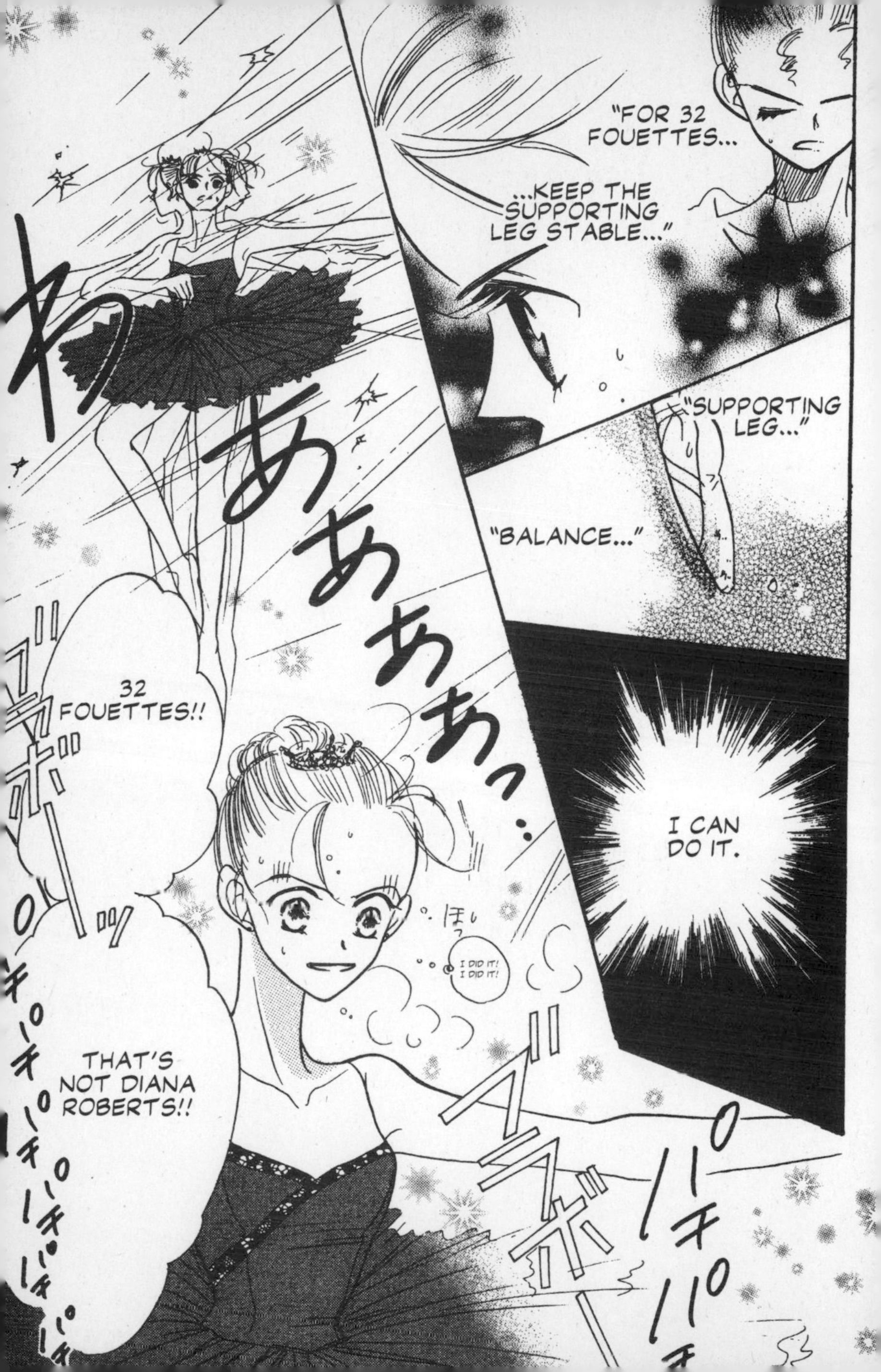
"FOR 32 FOUETTES...
...KEEP THE SUPPORTING LEG STABLE..."
"SUPPORTING LEG..."
"BALANCE..."
I CAN DO IT.
32 FOUETTES!!
I DID IT! I DID IT!
THAT'S NOT DIANA ROBERTS!!

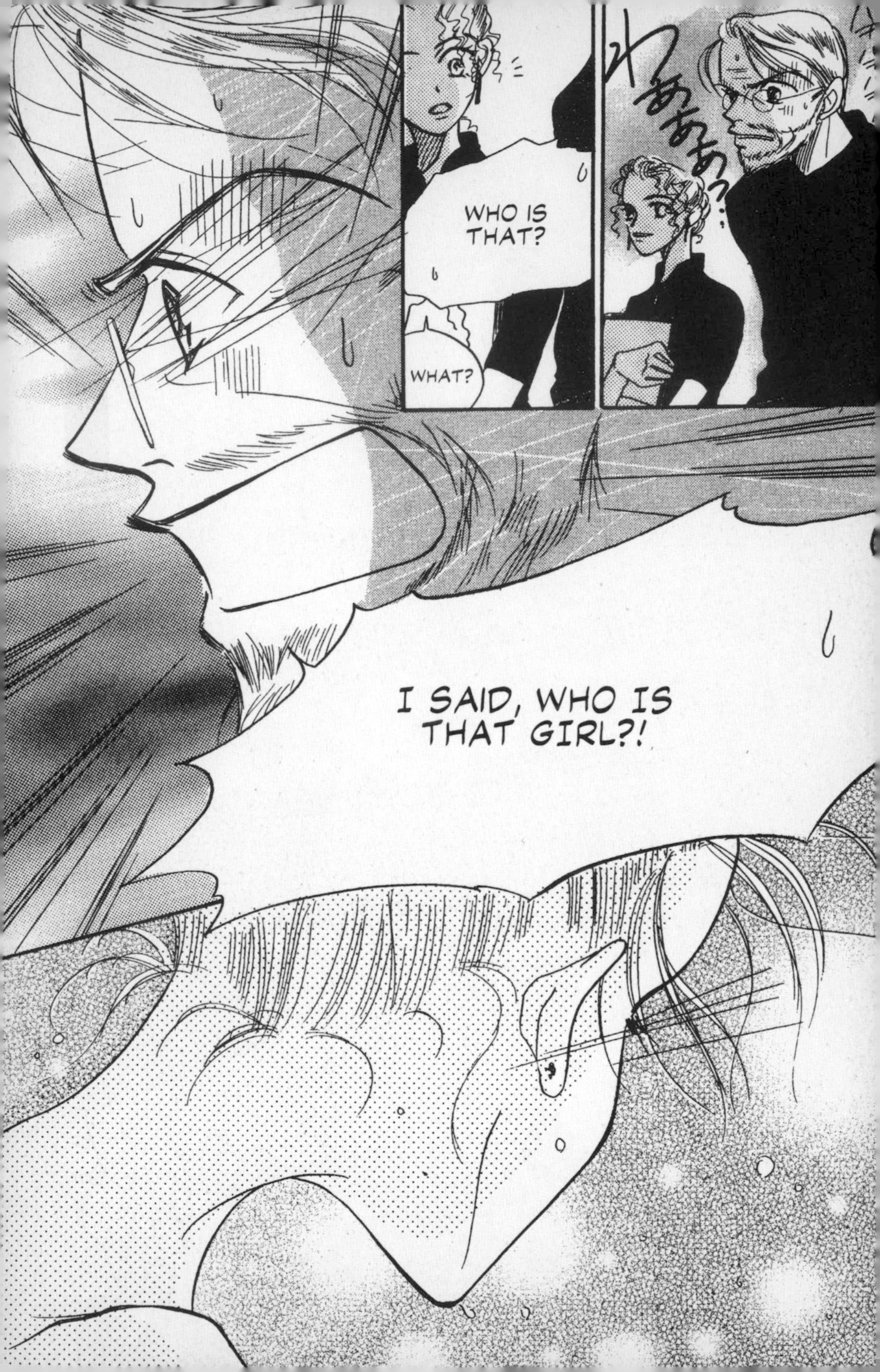
WHO IS THAT?
WHAT?
I SAID, WHO IS THAT GIRL?!

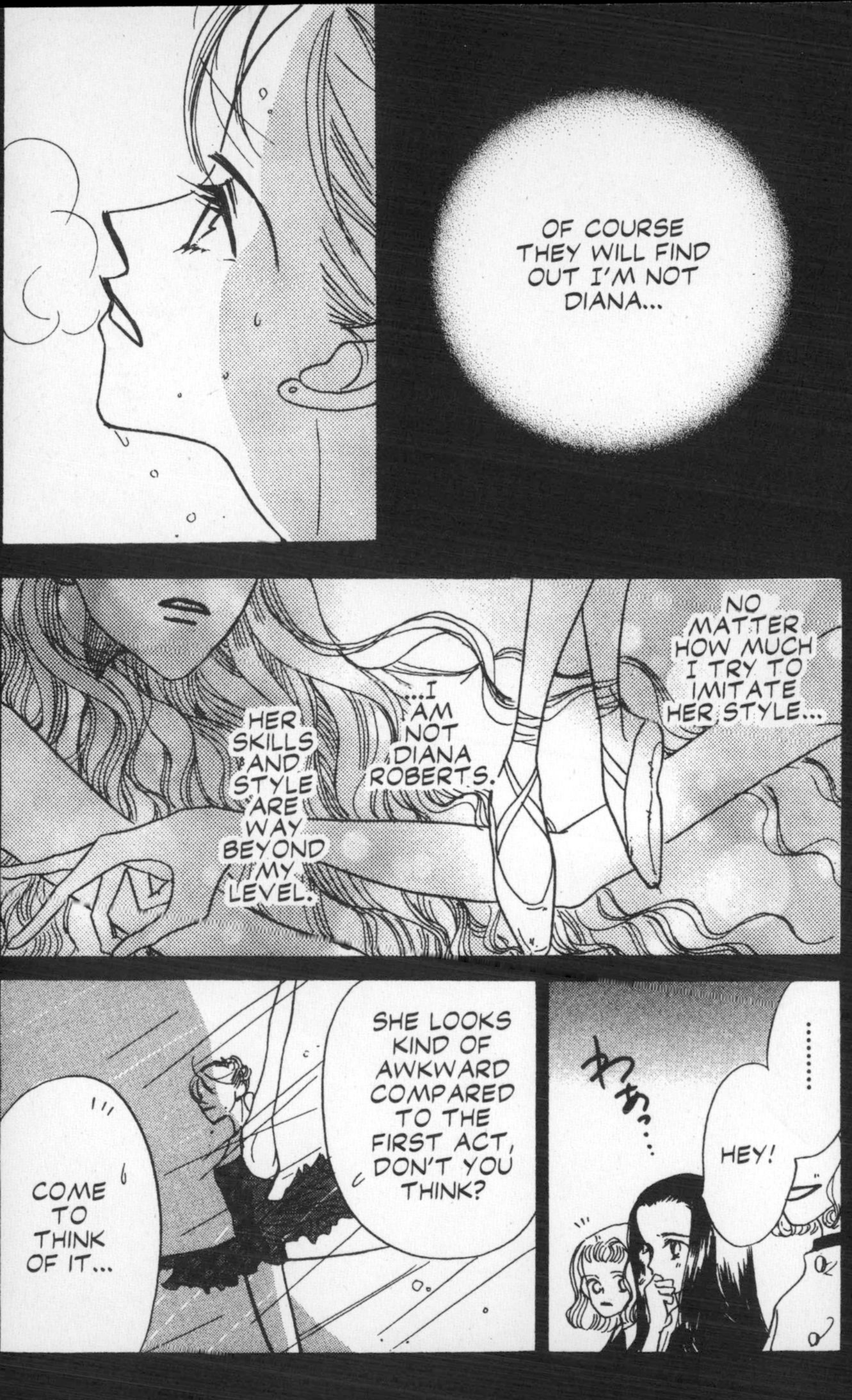
OF COURSE THEY WILL FIND OUT I'M NOT DIANA...
NO MATTER HOW MUCH I TRY TO IMITATE HER STYLE...
...I AM NOT DIANA ROBERTS.
HER SKILLS AND STYLE ARE WAY BEYOND MY LEVEL.
....
HEY!
わあっ…
SHE LOOKS KIND OF AWKWARD COMPARED TO THE FIRST ACT, DON'T YOU THINK?
COME TO THINK OF IT...

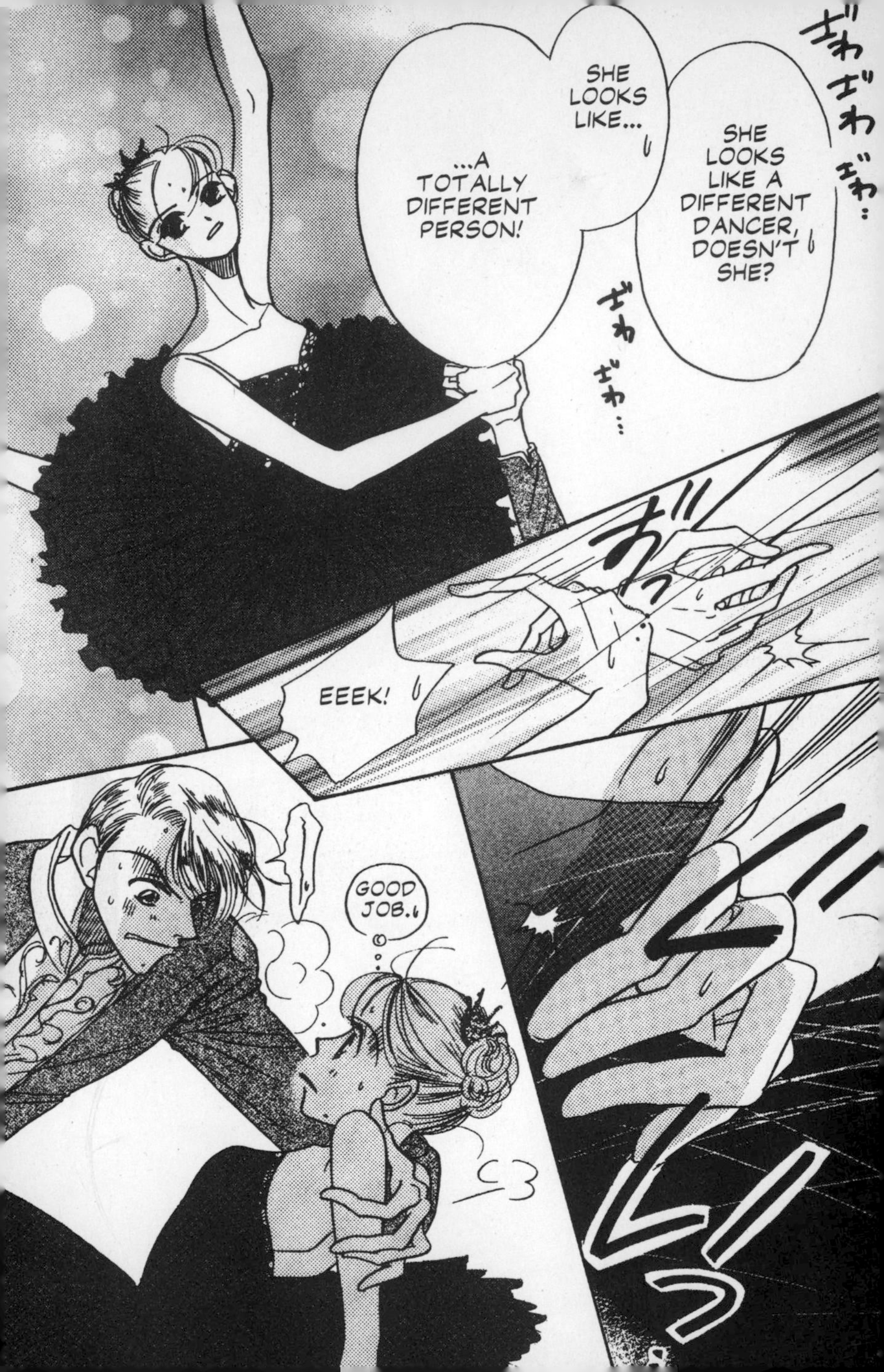
SHE LOOKS LIKE A DIFFERENT DANCER, DOESN'T SHE?
SHE LOOKS LIKE...
...A TOTALLY DIFFERENT PERSON!
EEEK!
GOOD JOB.

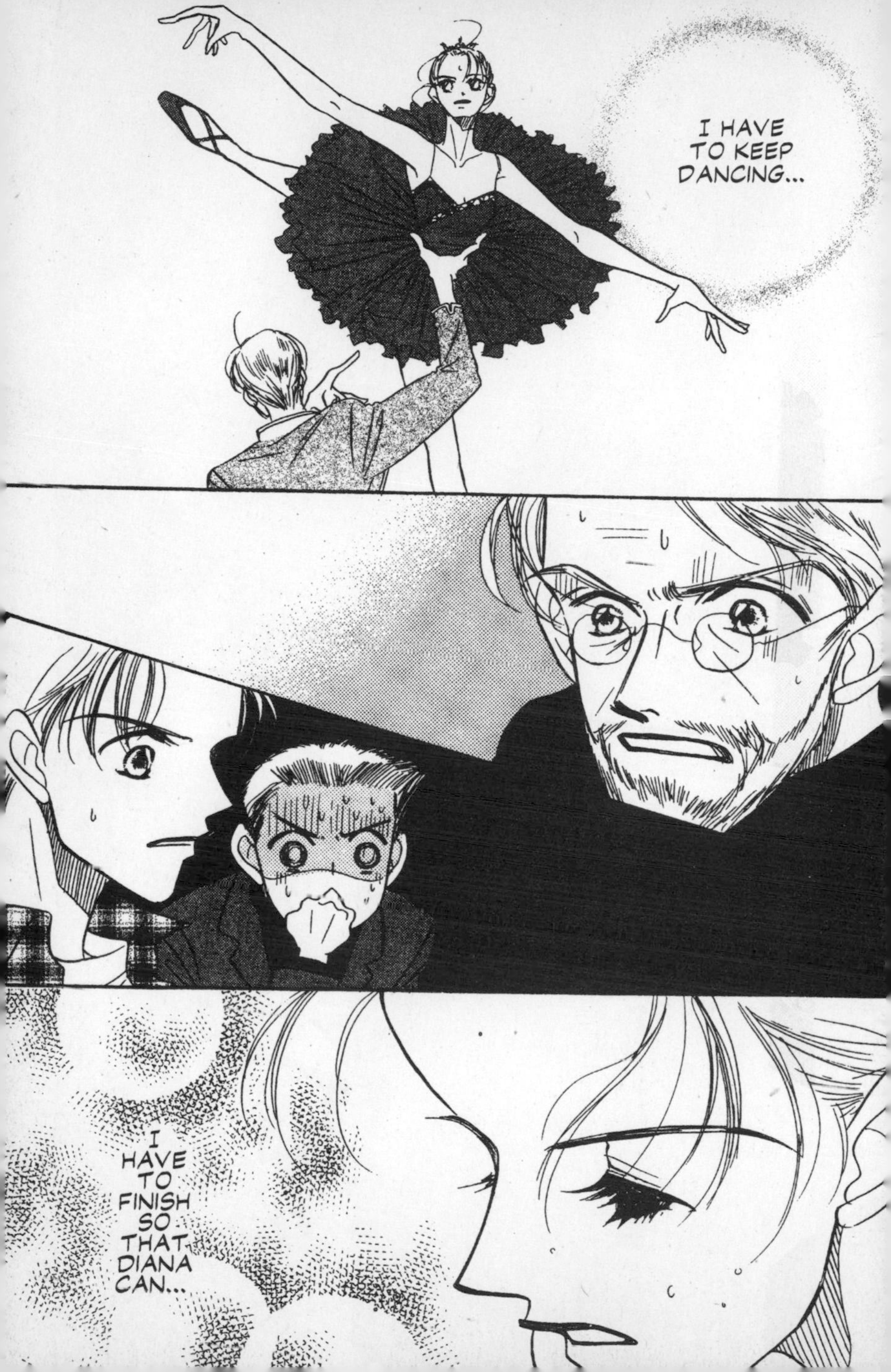
I HAVE TO KEEP DANCING...
I HAVE TO FINISH SO THAT DIANA CAN...

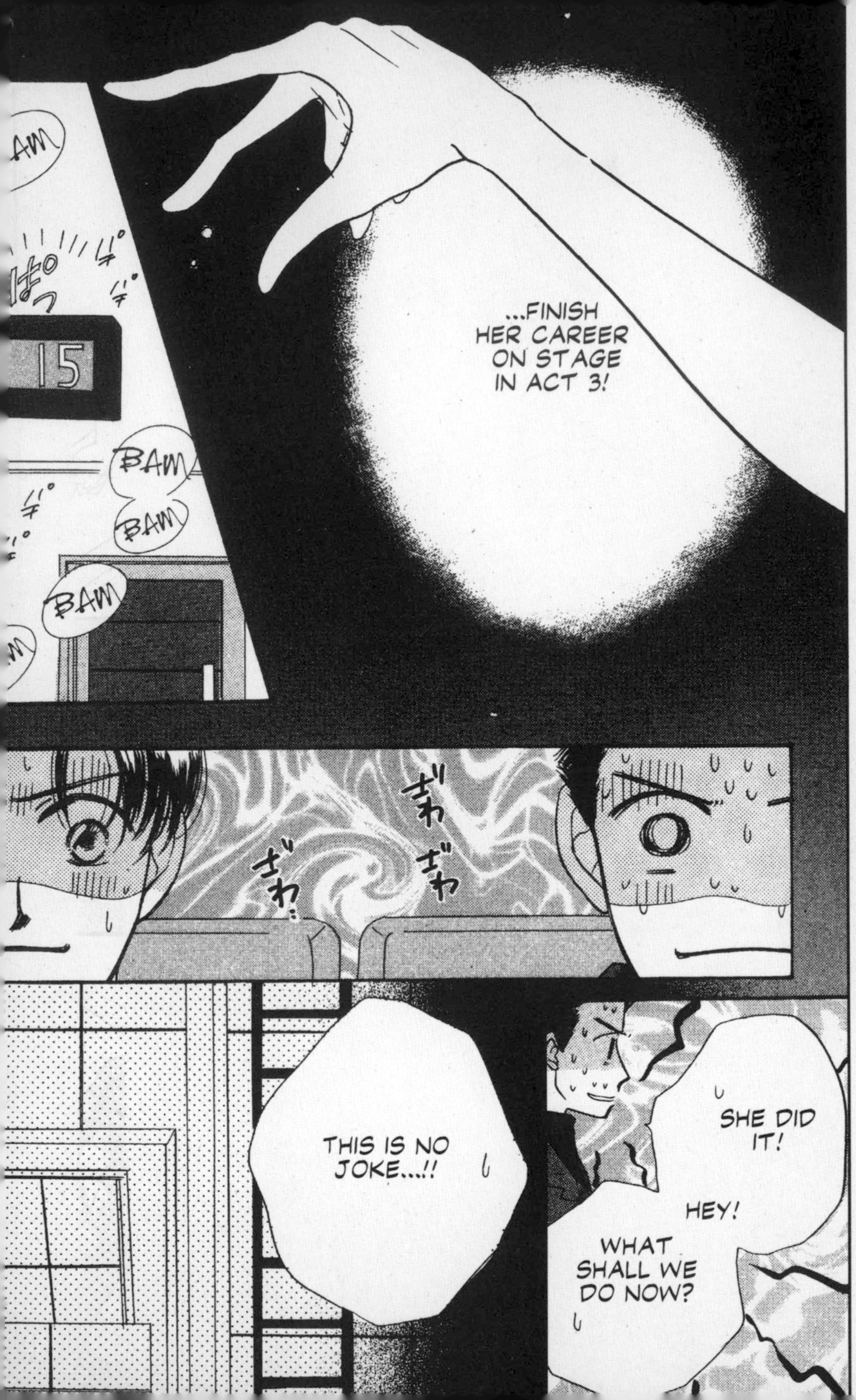
...FINISH HER CAREER ON STAGE IN ACT 3!
BAM
BAM
BAM
ざわ ざわ
ざわ...
SHE DID IT!
HEY!
WHAT SHALL WE DO NOW?
THIS IS NO JOKE...!!

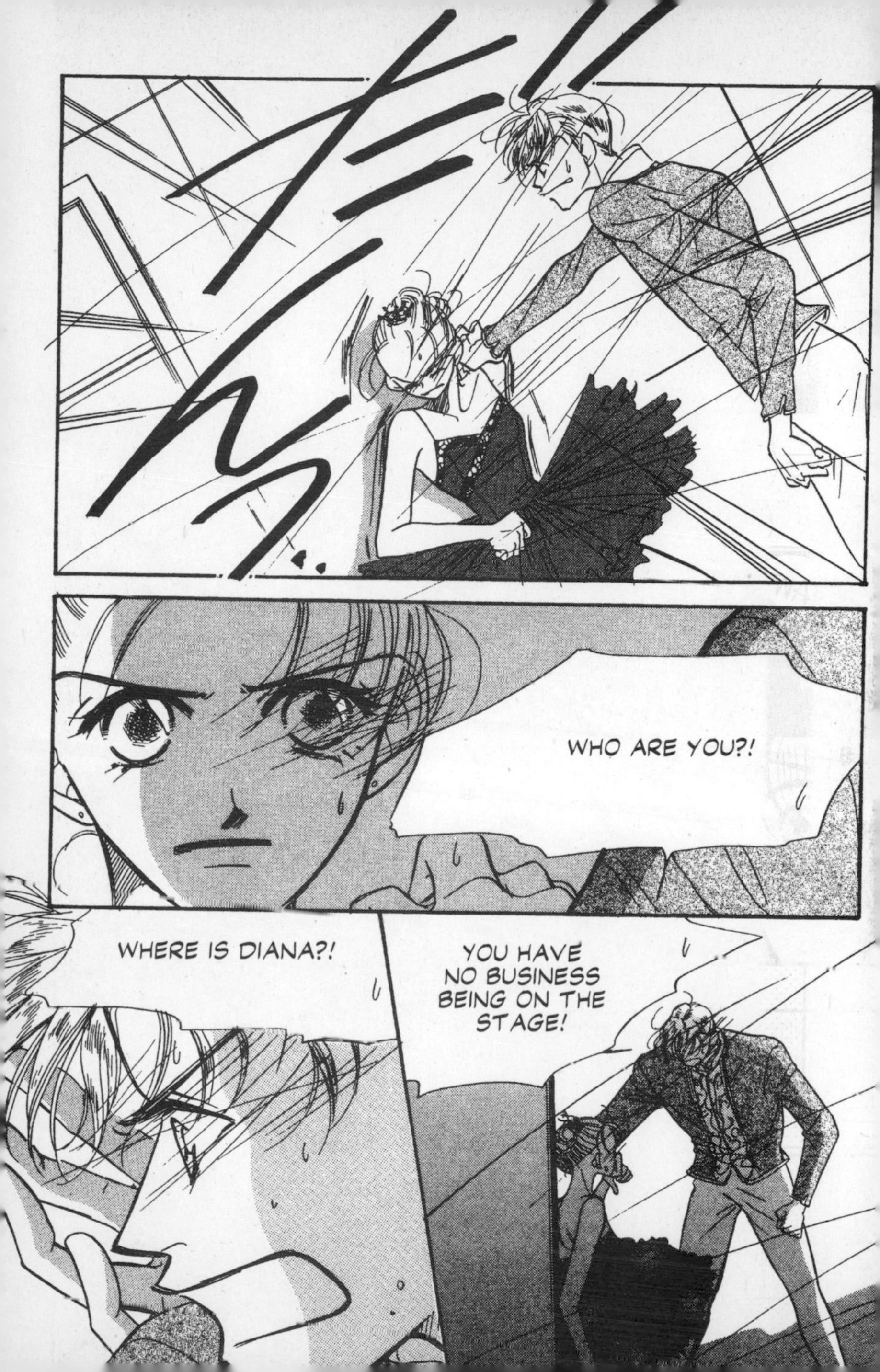
WHO ARE YOU?!
YOU HAVE NO BUSINESS BEING ON THE STAGE!
WHERE IS DIANA?!

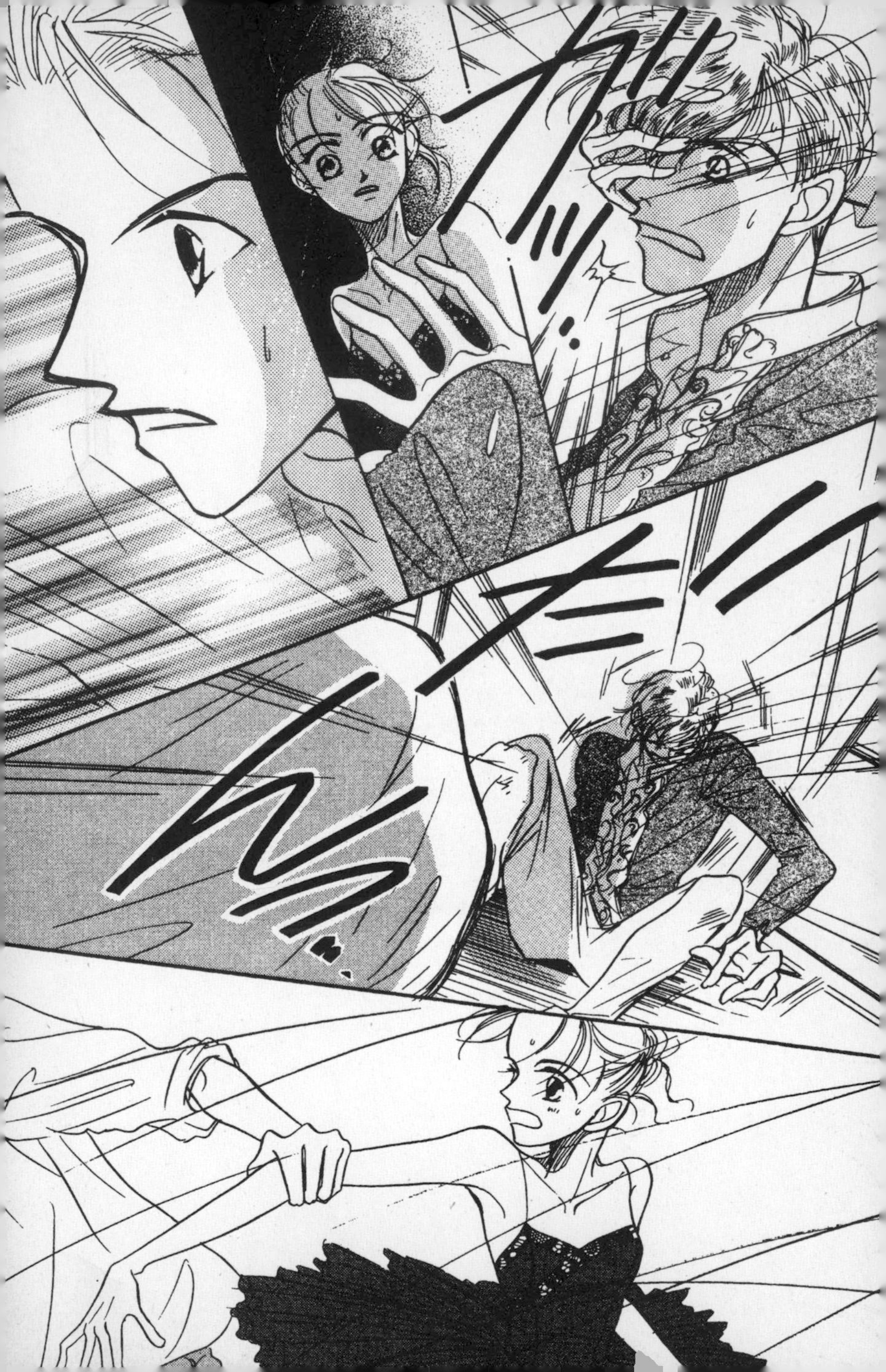
ガッ…

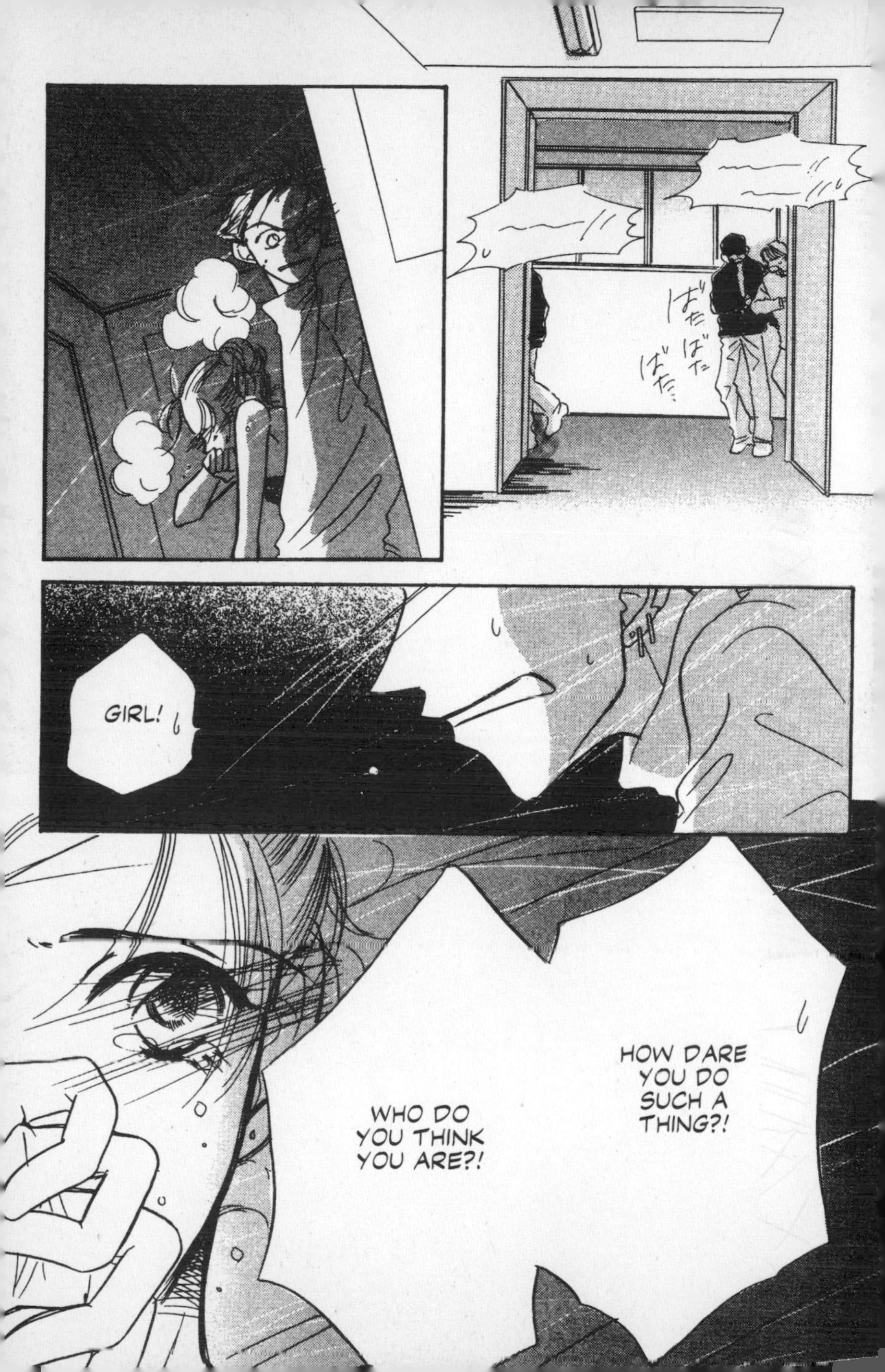
ばたばた
ばた…
GIRL!
HOW DARE YOU DO SUCH A THING?!
WHO DO YOU THINK YOU ARE?!

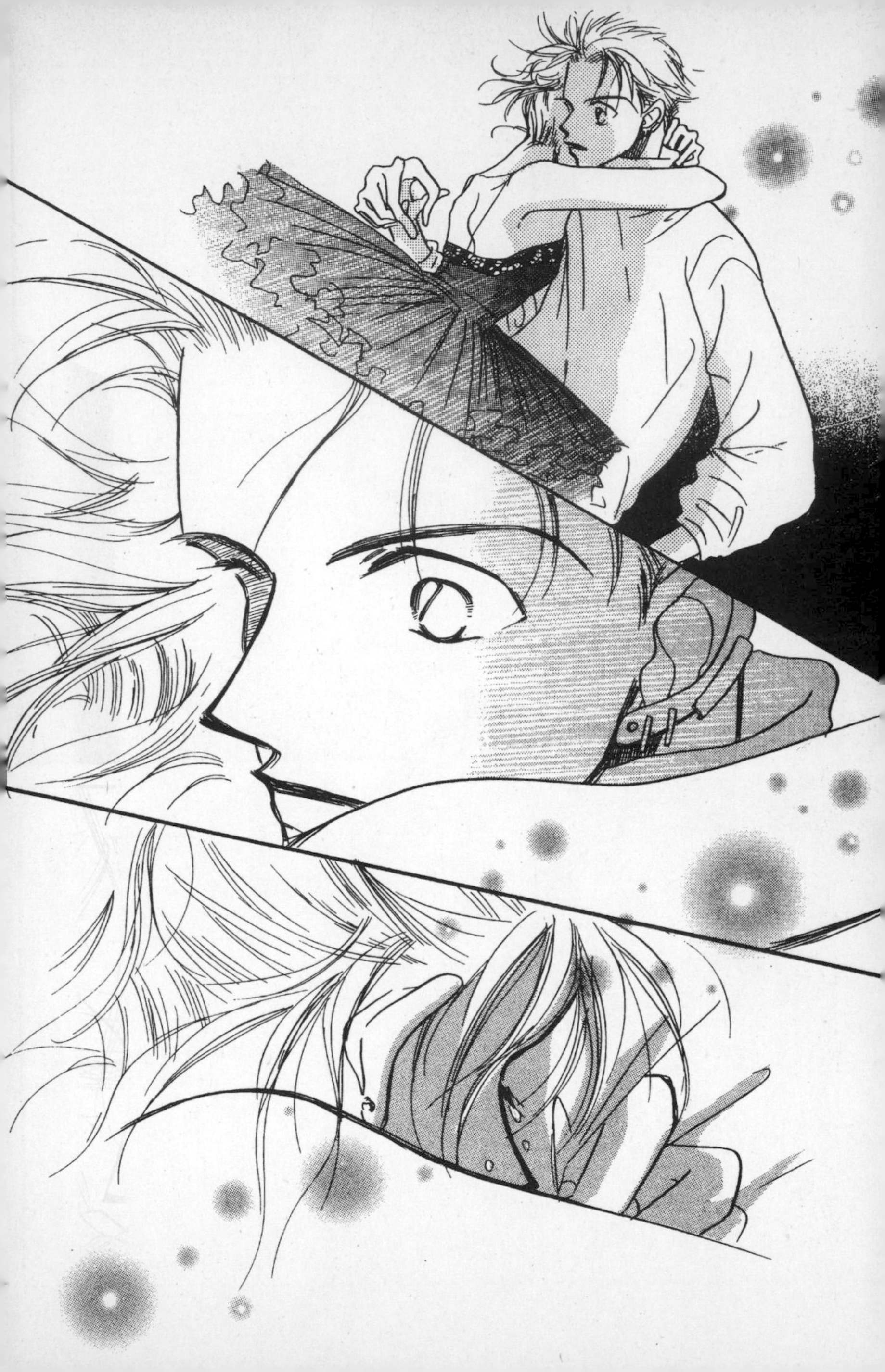

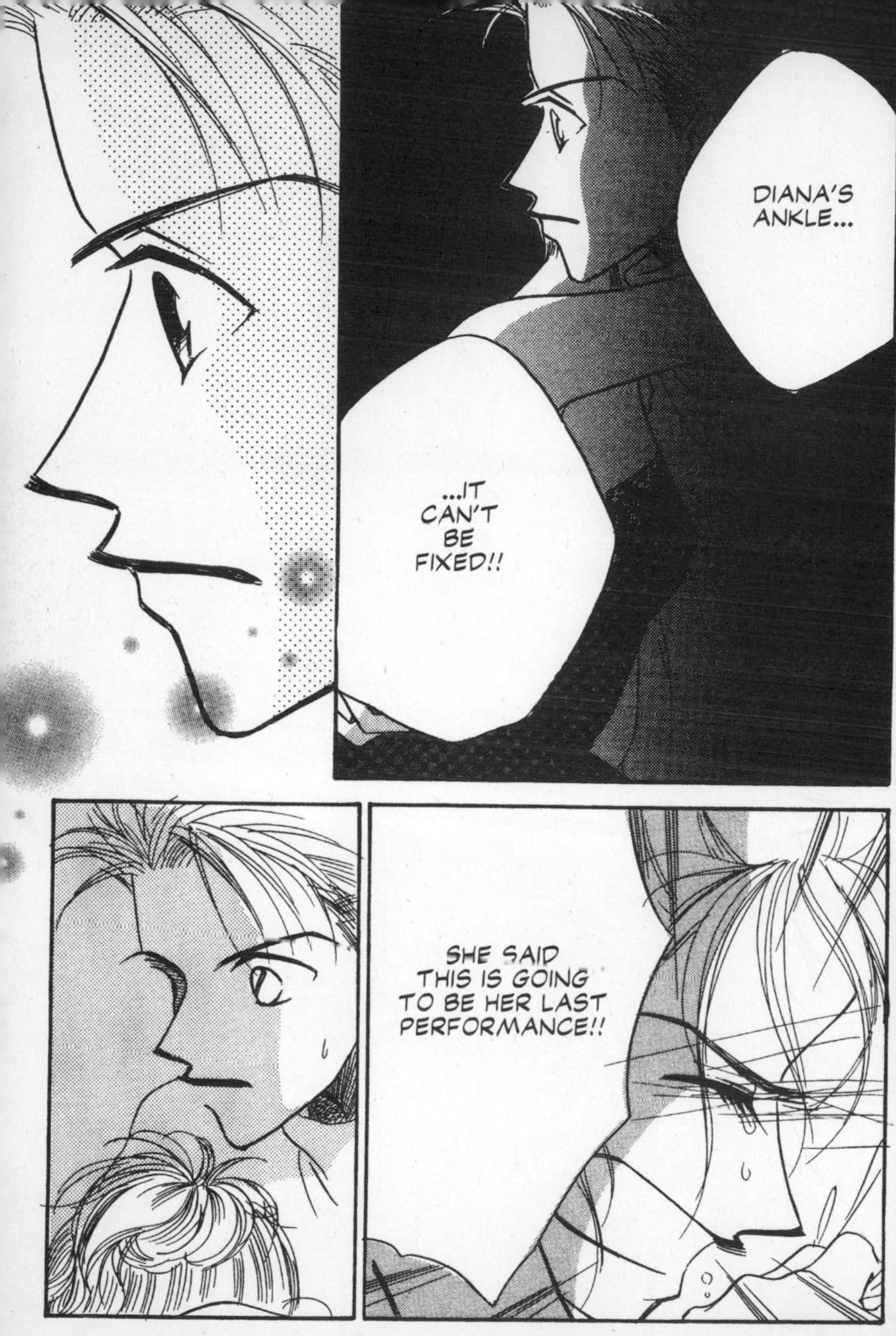
DIANA'S ANKLE...
...IT CAN'T BE FIXED!!
SHE SAID THIS IS GOING TO BE HER LAST PERFORMANCE!!

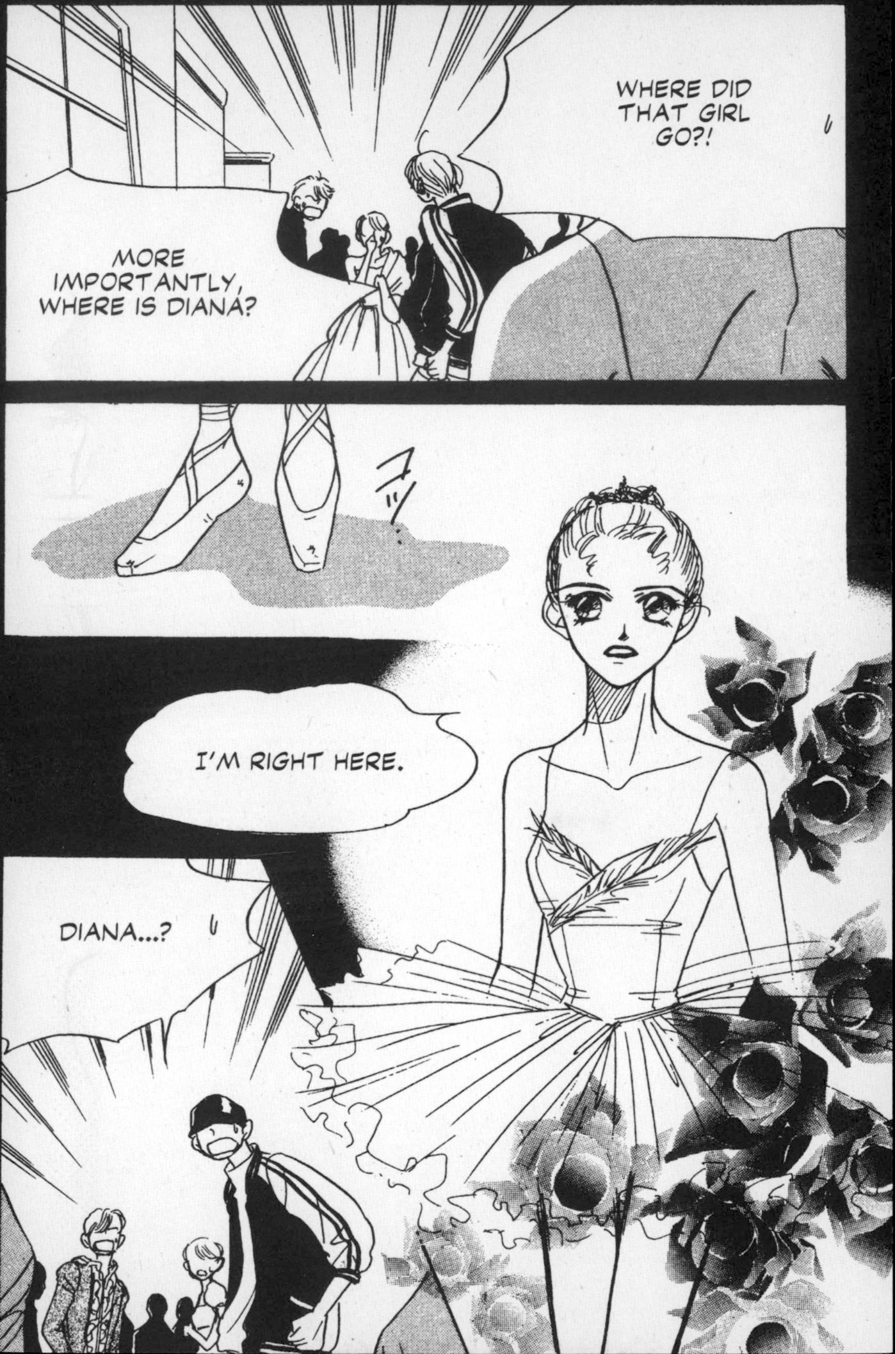
WHERE DID THAT GIRL GO?!
MORE IMPORTANTLY, WHERE IS DIANA?
I'M RIGHT HERE.
DIANA...?

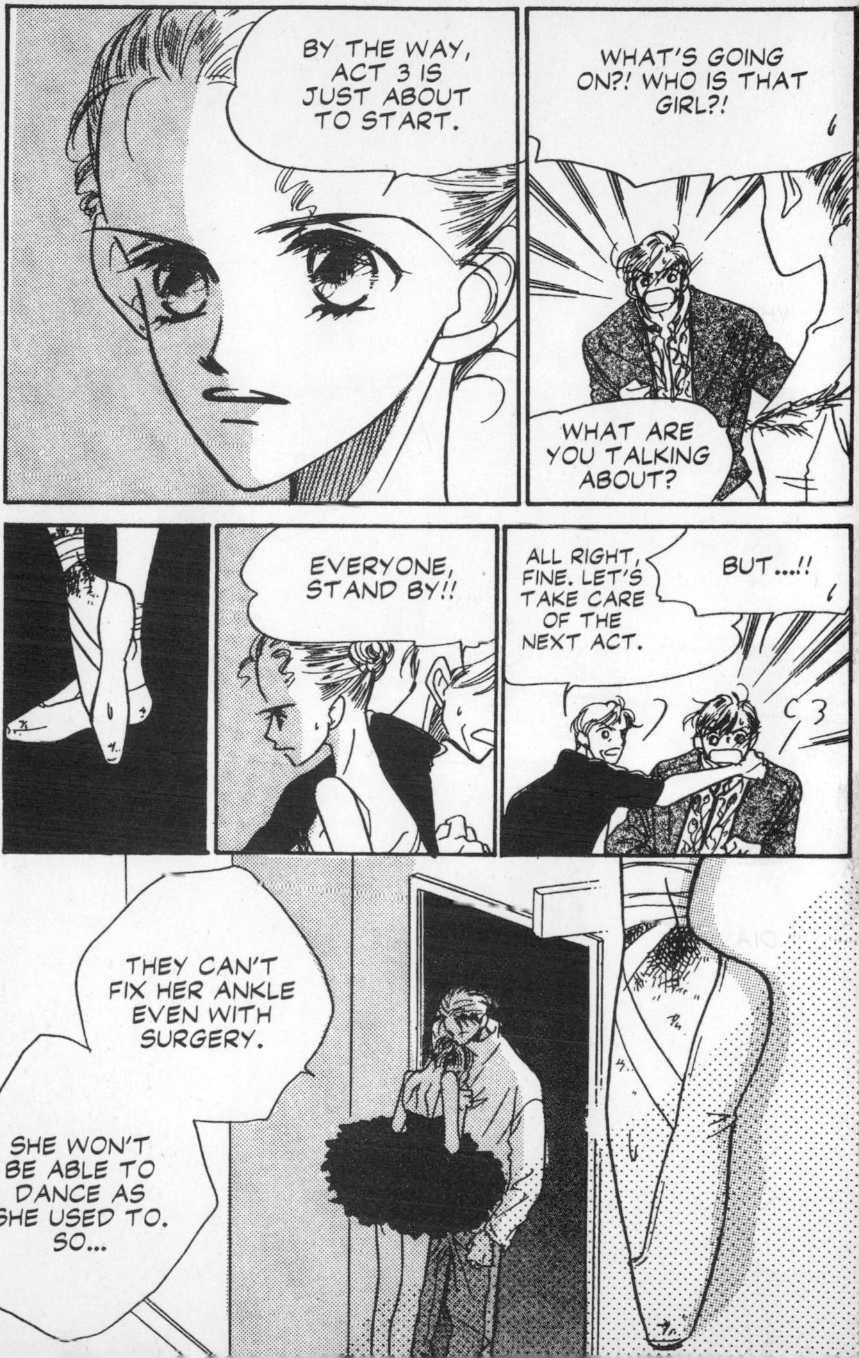
WHAT'S GOING ON?! WHO IS THAT GIRL?!
WHAT ARE YOU TALKING ABOUT?
BY THE WAY, ACT 3 IS JUST ABOUT TO START.
ALL RIGHT, FINE. LET'S TAKE CARE OF THE NEXT ACT.
BUT....!!
EVERYONE, STAND BY!!
THEY CAN'T FIX HER ANKLE EVEN WITH SURGERY.
SHE WON'T BE ABLE TO DANCE AS SHE USED TO. SO...

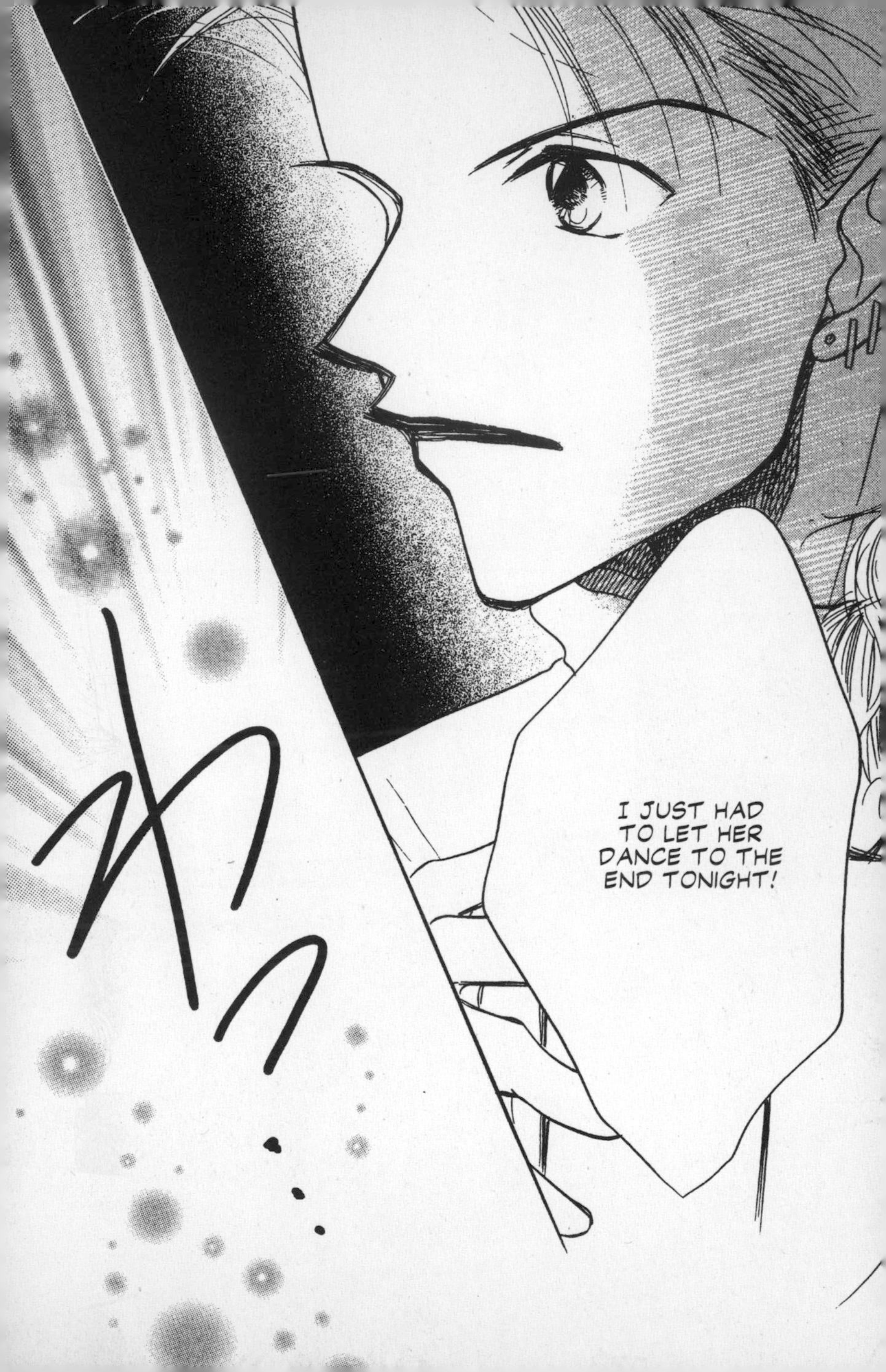
I JUST HAD TO LET HER DANCE TO THE END TONIGHT!

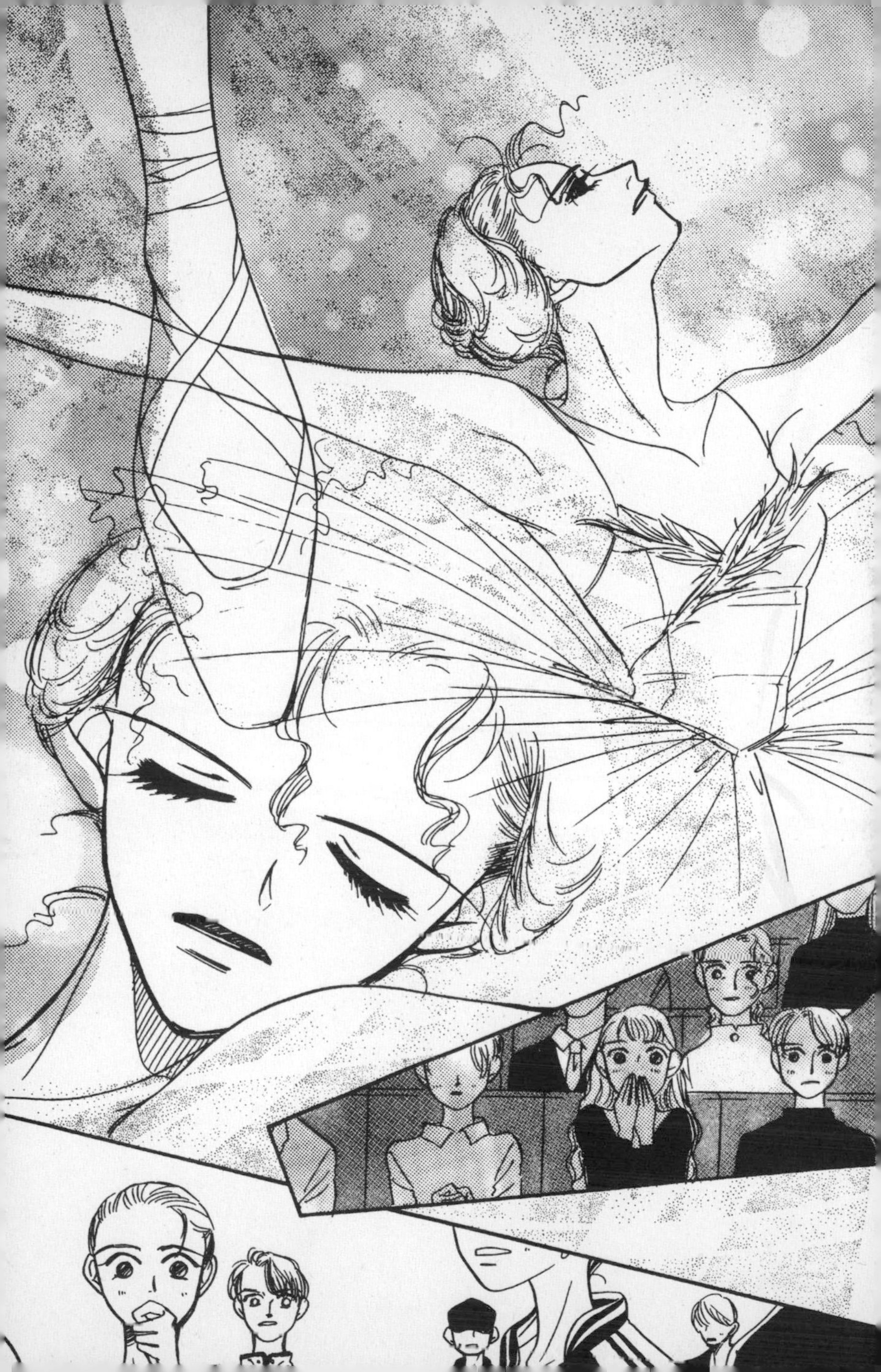

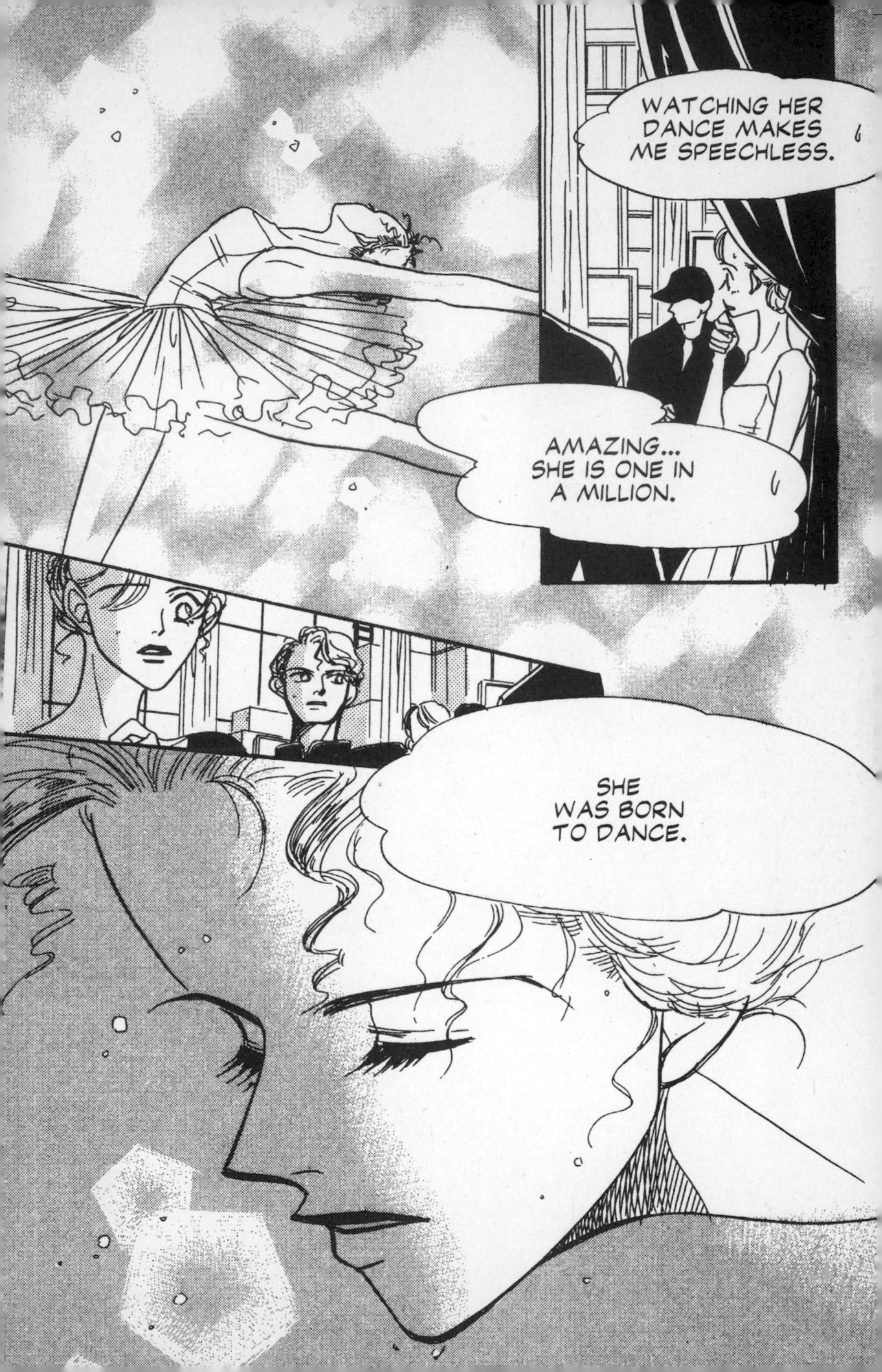
WATCHING HER DANCE MAKES ME SPEECHLESS.
AMAZING... SHE IS ONE IN A MILLION.
SHE WAS BORN TO DANCE.

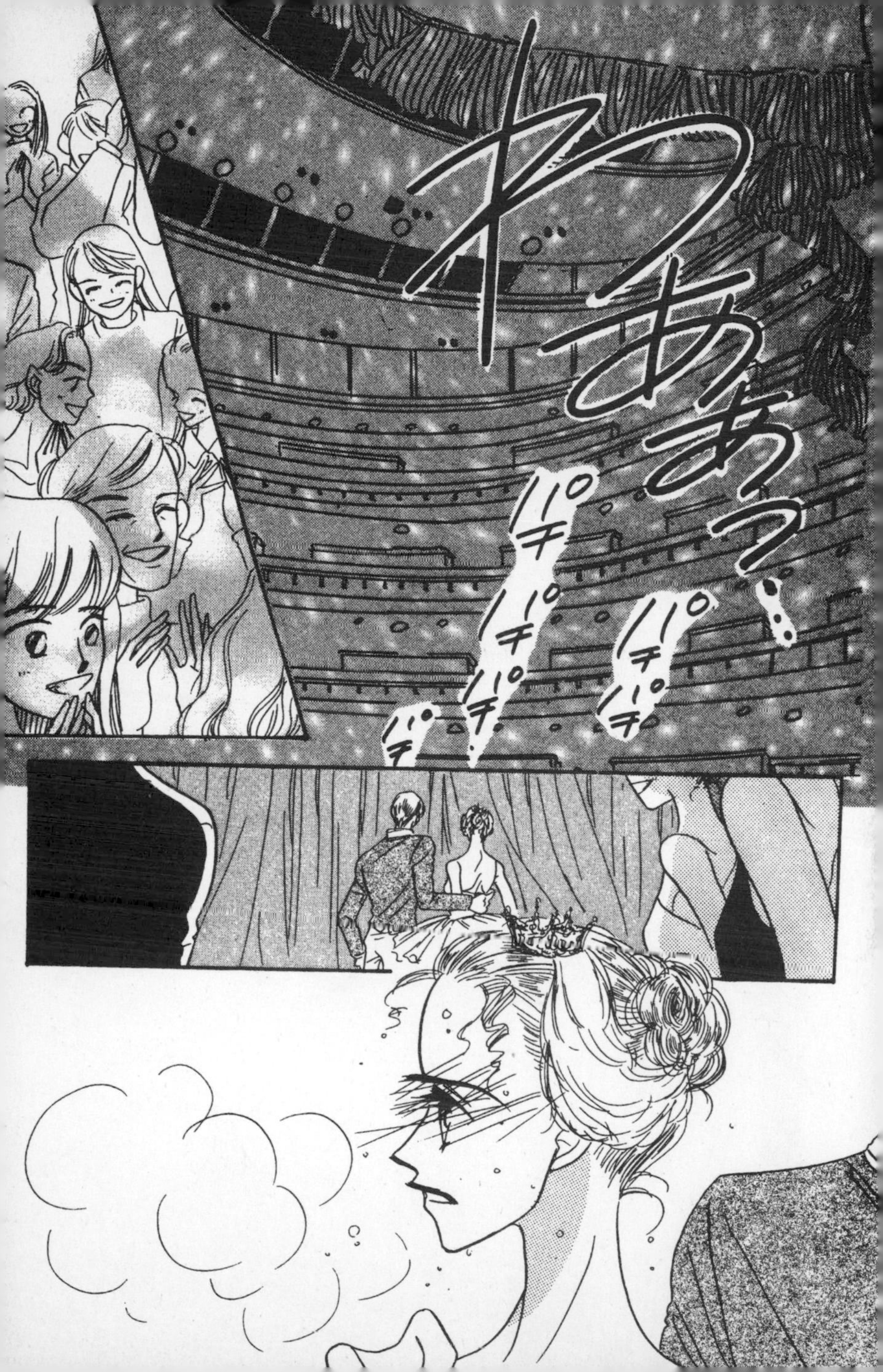

わああっ…
パチパチ
パチパチパチ
パチ

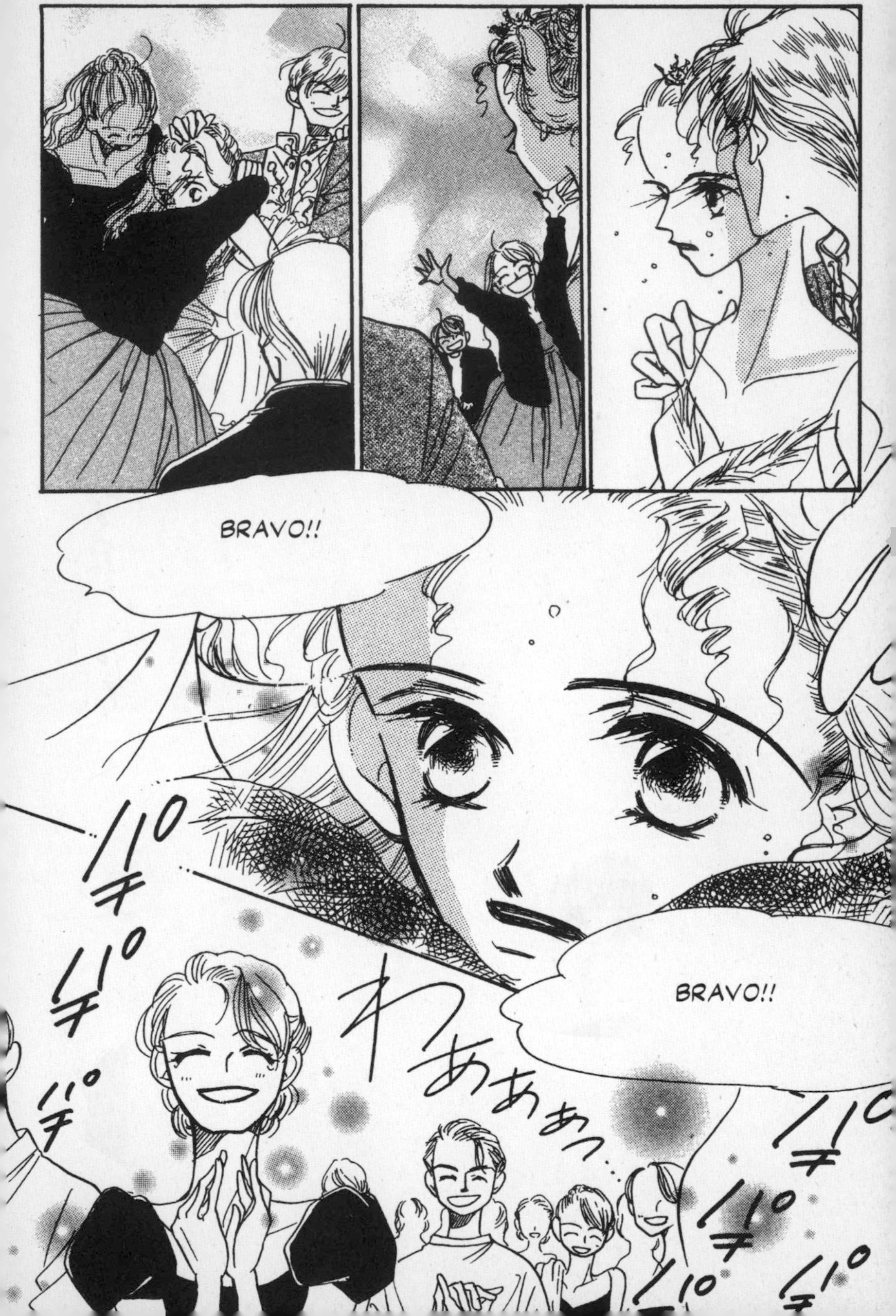
BRAVO!!
パチパチ
パチ
BRAVO!!
わあああっ…
パチパチパチ

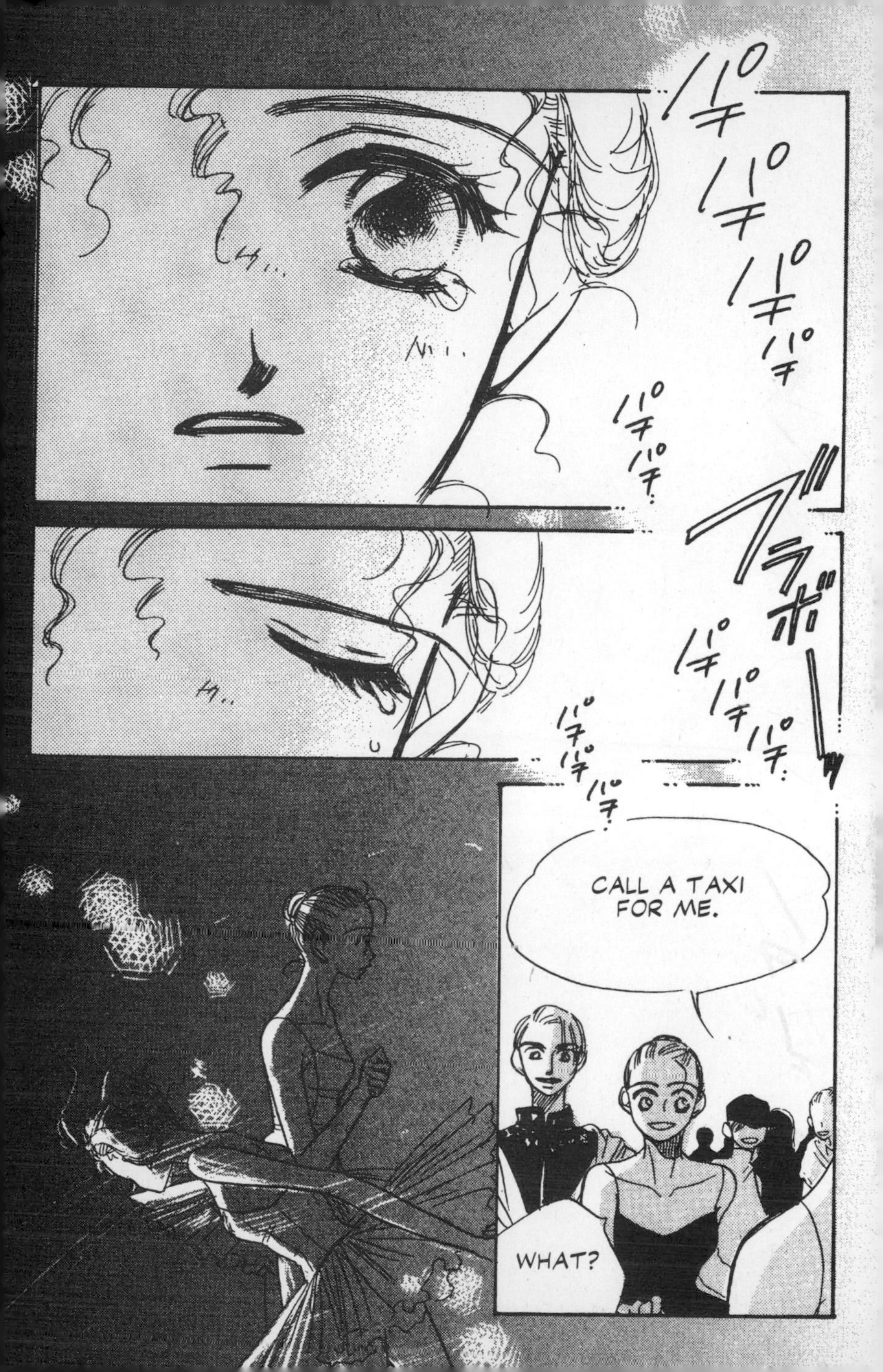
パチパチパチパチ
パチパチ
ブラボー
パチパチパチ
パチパチパチ
CALL A TAXI FOR ME.
WHAT?

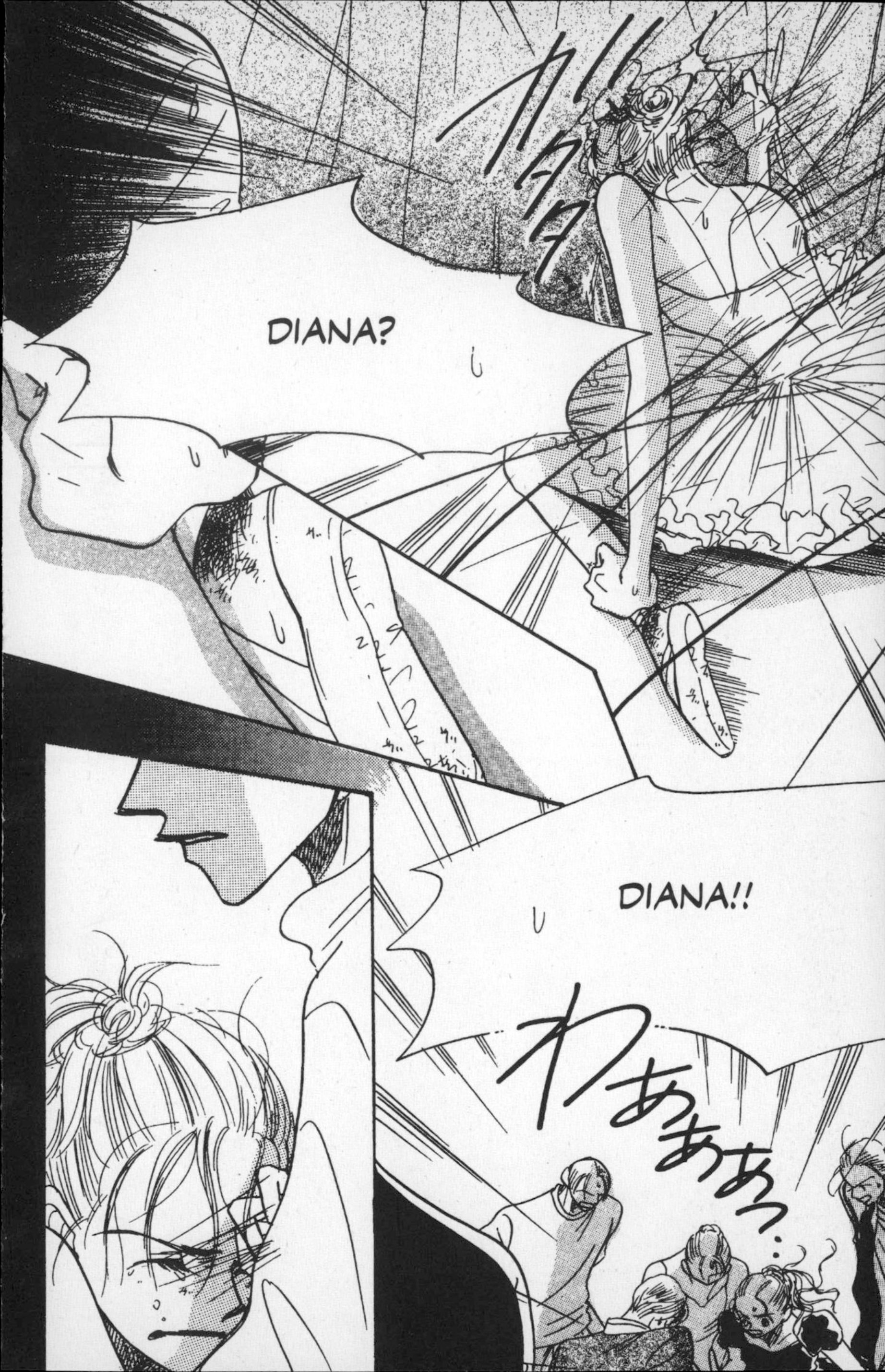
DIANA?
DIANA!!
わあああっ…

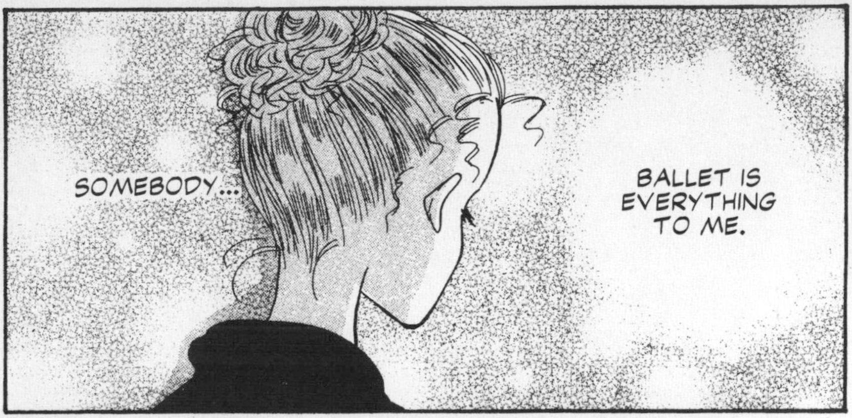
BALLET IS EVERYTHING TO ME.
SOMEBODY...

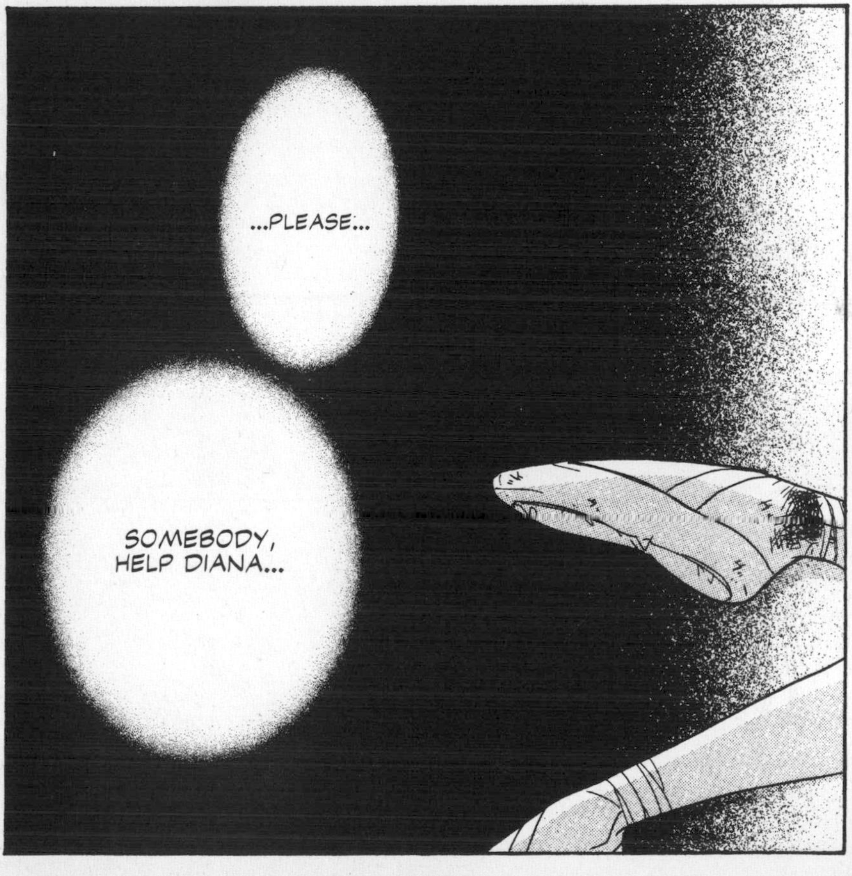
...PLEASE...
SOMEBODY, HELP DIANA...

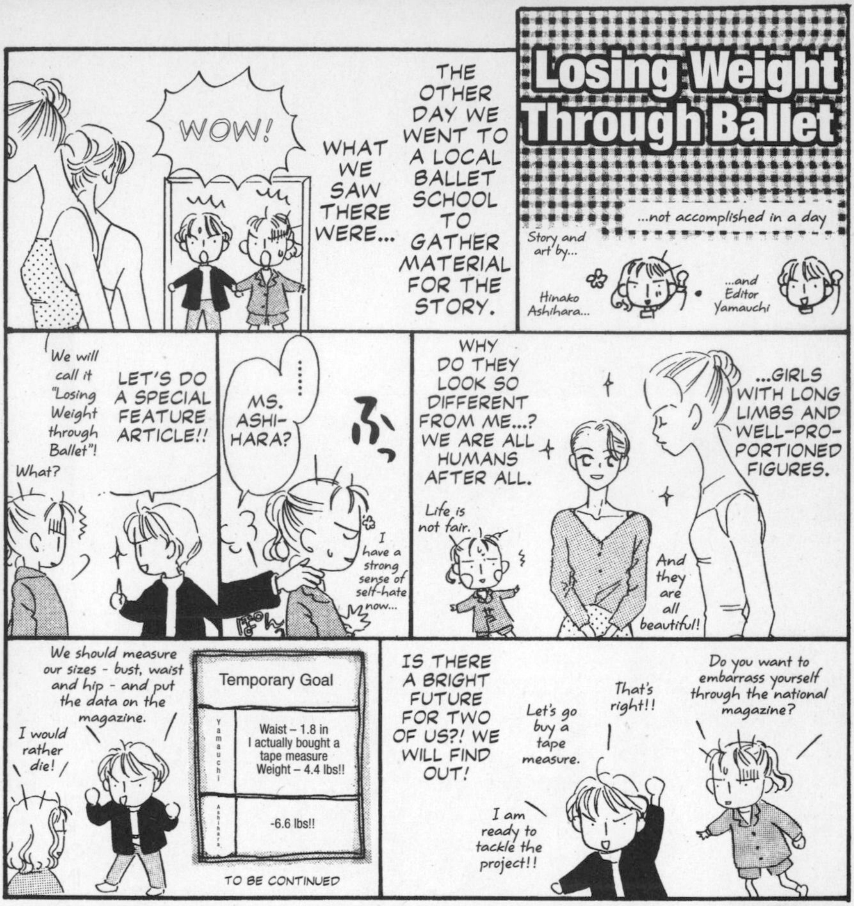
Losing Weight Through Ballet
...not accomplished in a day
Story and art by...
Hinako Ashihara...
...and Editor Yamauchi
THE OTHER DAY WE WENT TO A LOCAL BALLET SCHOOL TO GATHER MATERIAL FOR THE STORY.
WHAT WE SAW THERE WERE...
WOW!
...GIRLS WITH LONG LIMBS AND WELL-PROPORTIONED FIGURES.
WHY DO THEY LOOK SO DIFFERENT FROM ME...? WE ARE ALL HUMANS AFTER ALL.
And they are all beautiful!
Life is not fair.
......
MS. ASHIHARA?
ふっ
I have a strong sense of self-hate now...
LET'S DO A SPECIAL FEATURE ARTICLE!!
We will call it "Losing Weight through Ballet"!
What?
Do you want to embarrass yourself through the national magazine?
That's right!!
Let's go buy a tape measure.
IS THERE A BRIGHT FUTURE FOR TWO OF US?! WE WILL FIND OUT!
I am ready to tackle the project!!
We should measure our sizes - bust, waist and hip - and put the data on the magazine.
I would rather die!
Temporary Goal
Yamauchi
Waist – 1.8 in
I actually bought a tape measure
Weight – 4.4 lbs!!
Ashihara
-6.6 lbs!!
TO BE CONTINUED

★ THIS IS A SPECIAL FEATURE ARTICLE FOR GIRLS!!

YOU CAN TRY TO LOSE WEIGHT WITH HINAKO ASHIHARA!!

(LOSING WEIGHT THROUGH BALLET)

BALLET DE DIET

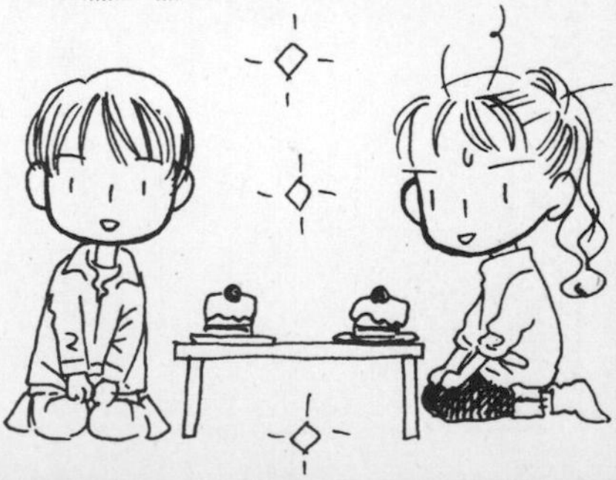

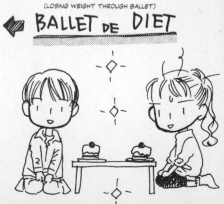

Exercise One

BALLERINAS HAVE BEAUTIFUL POSTURE! USE BASIC BALLET MOVEMENTS IN YOUR EVERYDAY LIFE AND ACHIEVE A WELL-PROPORTIONED FIGURE. HERE IS LESSON ONE.

♥

BREATHE FROM YOUR ABDOMEN AND GET RID OF THAT BULGE.

1

THIS IS AN EXERCISE WHICH ALLOWS YOU TO STRENGTHEN YOUR LOWER ABDOMINAL MUSCLES IN THE BATHTUB BY BREATHING FROM THE ABDOMEN.

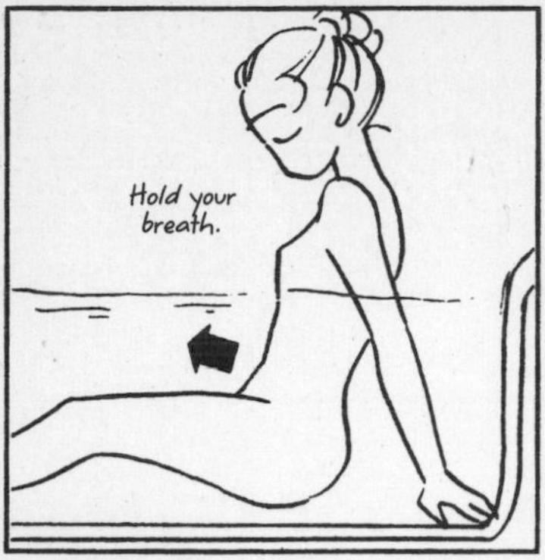
Hold your breath.

FIRST, SOAK IN THE BATHTUB, SIT AND RELAX. YOU CAN SIT WITH YOUR LEGS EITHER FOLDED OR UNFOLDED. THEN HOLD YOUR BREATH AND TRY TO STICK YOUR STOMACH OUT. TRY TO USE THE MUSCLES IN THE STOMACH AND WAIST TO STICK THE BELLY OUT, NOT BY BREATHING. REMEMBER TO KEEP YOUR BACK STRAIGHT.

2

AFTER DOING (1), KEEP BREATHING IN AND TIGHTEN THE MUSCLES IN THE STOMACH AND WAIST EVEN FURTHER. YOUR STOMACH TENDS TO STICK OUT WHEN YOU BREATHE IN, BUT YOU HAVE TO TRY TO KEEP IT IN. REPEAT (1) AND (2) FIVE TIMES ALTERNATELY. AFTER YOU MASTER THIS EXERCISE, YOU WILL FIND IT EASIER TO CONTROL YOUR ABDOMINAL MUSCLES. TRY THIS IN THE BATHTUB EVERYDAY!

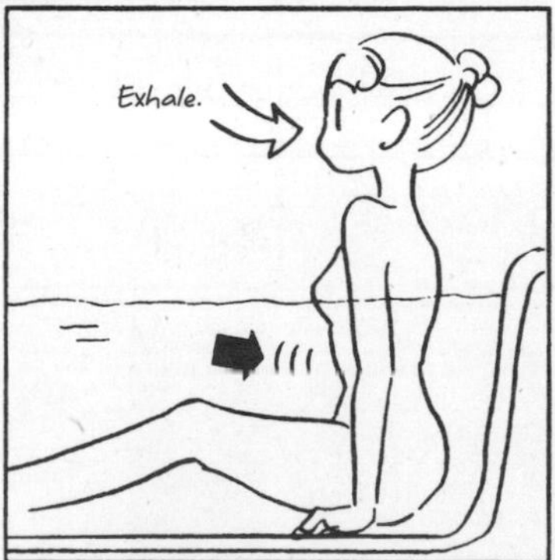
Exhale.

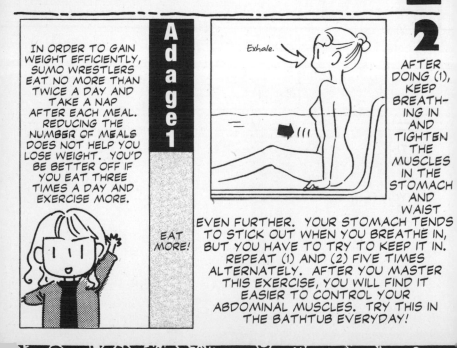

Adage 1

IN ORDER TO GAIN WEIGHT EFFICIENTLY, SUMO WRESTLERS EAT NO MORE THAN TWICE A DAY AND TAKE A NAP AFTER EACH MEAL. REDUCING THE NUMBER OF MEALS DOES NOT HELP YOU LOSE WEIGHT. YOU'D BE BETTER OFF IF YOU EAT THREE TIMES A DAY AND EXERCISE MORE.

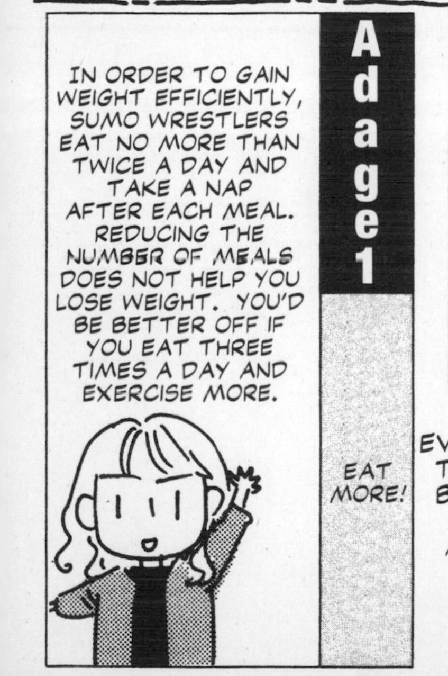

EAT MORE!

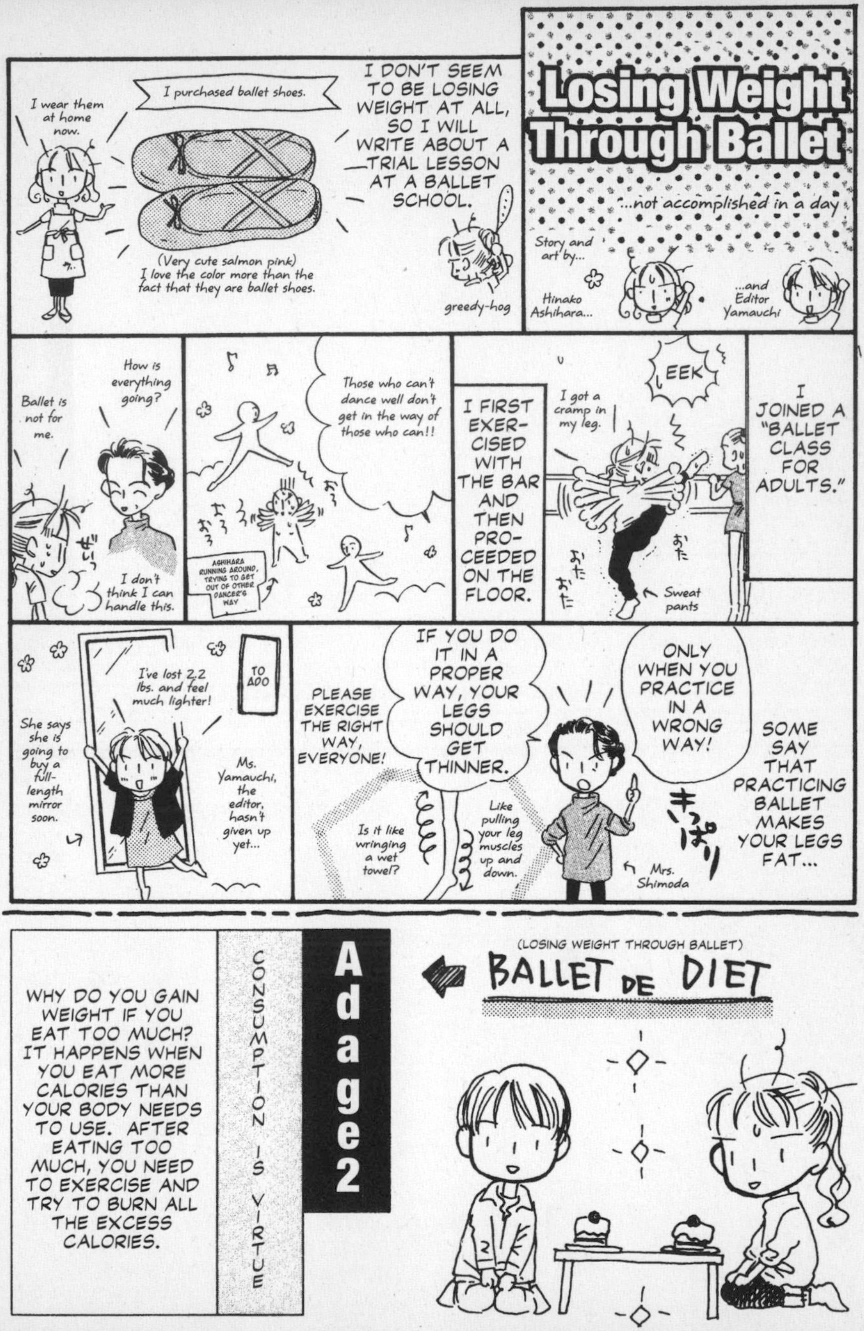
Losing Weight Through Ballet
...not accomplished in a day
Story and art by...
Hinako Ashihara...
...and Editor Yamauchi
I DON'T SEEM TO BE LOSING WEIGHT AT ALL, SO I WILL WRITE ABOUT A TRIAL LESSON AT A BALLET SCHOOL.
greedy-hog
I purchased ballet shoes.
(Very cute salmon pink) I love the color more than the fact that they are ballet shoes.
I wear them at home now.
I JOINED A "BALLET CLASS FOR ADULTS."
EEK
I got a cramp in my leg.
おた おた おた
Sweat pants
I FIRST EXERCISED WITH THE BAR AND THEN PROCEEDED ON THE FLOOR.
Those who can't dance well don't get in the way of those who can!!
おろ おろ おろ
ASHIHARA RUNNING AROUND, TRYING TO GET OUT OF OTHER DANCER'S WAY
How is everything going?
Ballet is not for me.
ぜいっ
I don't think I can handle this.
SOME SAY THAT PRACTICING BALLET MAKES YOUR LEGS FAT...
ONLY WHEN YOU PRACTICE IN A WRONG WAY!
きっぱり
Mrs. Shimoda
IF YOU DO IT IN A PROPER WAY, YOUR LEGS SHOULD GET THINNER.
PLEASE EXERCISE THE RIGHT WAY, EVERYONE!
Like pulling your leg muscles up and down.
Is it like wringing a wet towel?
TO ADO
I've lost 2.2 lbs. and feel much lighter!
She says she is going to buy a full-length mirror soon.
Ms. Yamauchi, the editor, hasn't given up yet...
(LOSING WEIGHT THROUGH BALLET)
BALLET DE DIET
Adage2
CONSUMPTION IS VIRTUE
WHY DO YOU GAIN WEIGHT IF YOU EAT TOO MUCH? IT HAPPENS WHEN YOU EAT MORE CALORIES THAN YOUR BODY NEEDS TO USE. AFTER EATING TOO MUCH, YOU NEED TO EXERCISE AND TRY TO BURN ALL THE EXCESS CALORIES.

Exercise Two

HERE IS LESSON 2. INCORPORATES BALLET MOVEMENTS INTO YOUR EVERYDAY LIFE AND BUILDS A BEAUTIFUL BODY! TRY IT AND SAY FAREWELL TO THAT EXCESS FAT. ♥

EXERCISE TO BURN THAT EXTRA FAT.

TARGET: ANKLE

♥

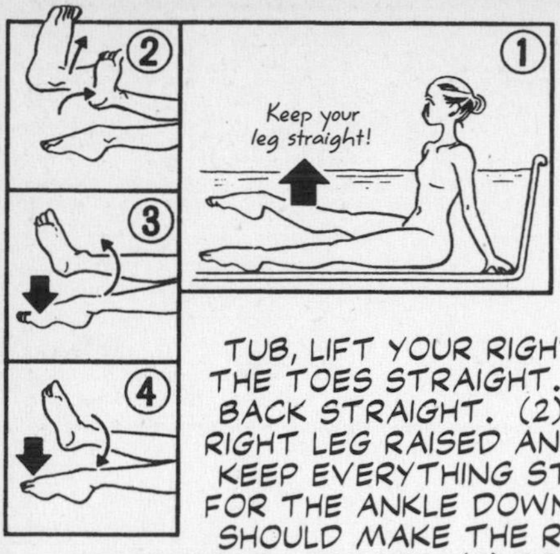

Keep your leg straight!

TO REDUCE FAT AROUND THE ANKLE (1) SIT IN THE BATHTUB, LIFT YOUR RIGHT LEG WITH THE TOES STRAIGHT. KEEP YOUR BACK STRAIGHT. (2) WITH YOUR RIGHT LEG RAISED AND STRAIGHT, KEEP EVERYTHING STILL EXCEPT FOR THE ANKLE DOWN. THE FOOT SHOULD MAKE THE RIGHT ANGLE WITH YOUR LEFT LEG. (3) ROTATE THE ENTIRE LENGTH OF YOUR RIGHT LEG CLOCKWISE, RELAX, AND LOWER THE LEG. DO THE SAME THING (FROM 1 TO 3) WITH THE LEFT LEG. KEEP THE ANGLE BETWEEN YOUR FOOT AND LEG AT 90 DEGREES. (4) LIFT YOUR RIGHT LEG AGAIN AND ROTATE IT COUNTER-CLOCKWISE, THEN RELAX AND LOWER THE LEG. DO THE SAME WITH THE LEFT LEG. REPEAT (1) TO (4) FOUR TIMES.

BUST-UP EXERCISE

TARGET CHEST

♥

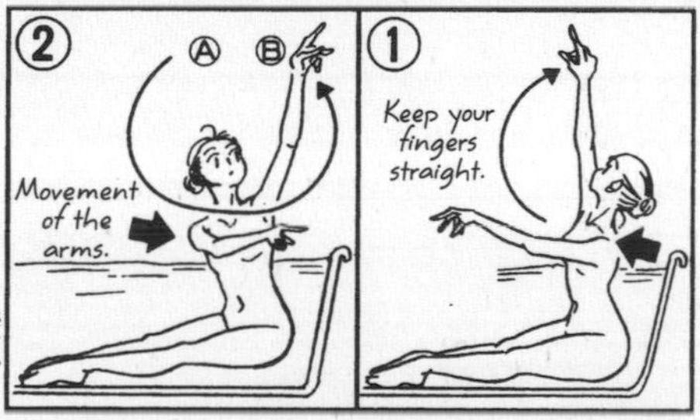

Keep your fingers straight.
Movement of the arms.

(1) SIT IN THE BATHTUB, AND BRING YOUR RIGHT ARM UPWARDS TO THE RIGHT AND BRING YOUR LEFT ARM IN FRONT OF YOUR CHEST. AT THE SAME TIME, THROW YOUR CHEST OUT. (2) TWIST YOUR BODY AROUND THE BLADE BONE AND BRING YOUR RIGHT ARM TO THE LOWER LEFT AND YOUR LEFT ARM UPWARDS BY GIVING IT MOMENTUM. DON'T FORGET TO KEEP YOUR CHEST LIFTED. KEEP YOUR EYES ON YOUR FINGER TIPS. REPEAT (1) TO (2) EIGHT TIMES.

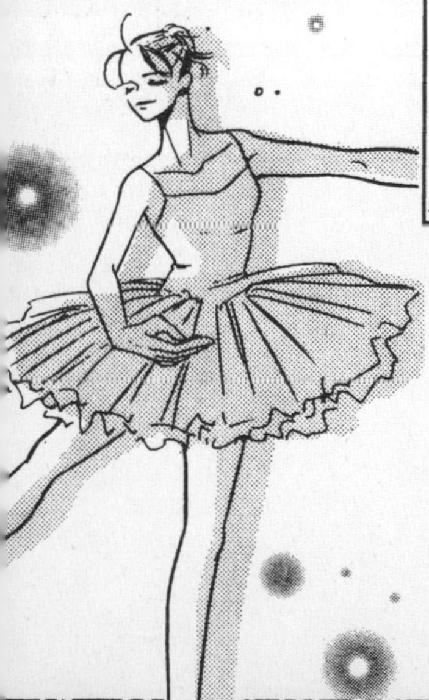

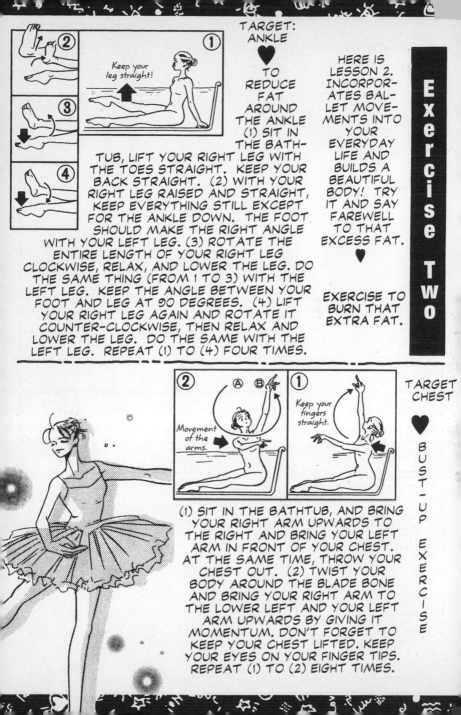

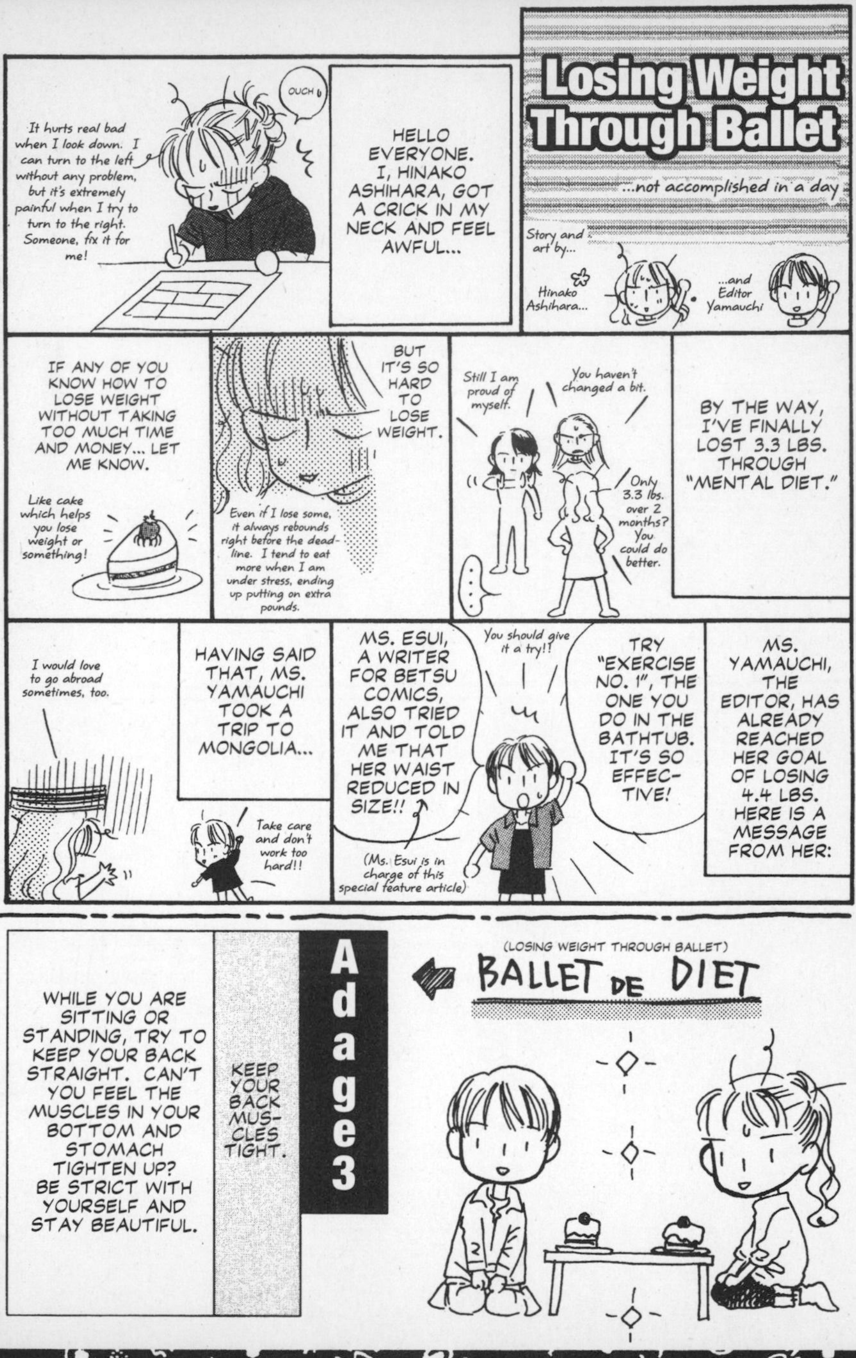
Losing Weight Through Ballet
...not accomplished in a day
Story and art by...
Hinako Ashihara...
...and Editor Yamauchi
HELLO EVERYONE. I, HINAKO ASHIHARA, GOT A CRICK IN MY NECK AND FEEL AWFUL...
OUCH
It hurts real bad when I look down. I can turn to the left without any problem, but it's extremely painful when I try to turn to the right. Someone, fix it for me!
BY THE WAY, I'VE FINALLY LOST 3.3 LBS. THROUGH "MENTAL DIET."
You haven't changed a bit.
Still I am proud of myself.
Only 3.3 lbs. over 2 months? You could do better.
...
BUT IT'S SO HARD TO LOSE WEIGHT.
Even if I lose some, it always rebounds right before the deadline. I tend to eat more when I am under stress, ending up putting on extra pounds.
IF ANY OF YOU KNOW HOW TO LOSE WEIGHT WITHOUT TAKING TOO MUCH TIME AND MONEY... LET ME KNOW.
Like cake which helps you lose weight or something!
MS. YAMAUCHI, THE EDITOR, HAS ALREADY REACHED HER GOAL OF LOSING 4.4 LBS. HERE IS A MESSAGE FROM HER:
TRY "EXERCISE NO. 1", THE ONE YOU DO IN THE BATHTUB. IT'S SO EFFECTIVE!
You should give it a try!!
MS. ESUI, A WRITER FOR BETSU COMICS, ALSO TRIED IT AND TOLD ME THAT HER WAIST REDUCED IN SIZE!!
(Ms. Esui is in charge of this special feature article)
HAVING SAID THAT, MS. YAMAUCHI TOOK A TRIP TO MONGOLIA...
Take care and don't work too hard!!
I would love to go abroad sometimes, too.
(LOSING WEIGHT THROUGH BALLET)
BALLET DE DIET
Adage 3
KEEP YOUR BACK MUSCLES TIGHT.
WHILE YOU ARE SITTING OR STANDING, TRY TO KEEP YOUR BACK STRAIGHT. CAN'T YOU FEEL THE MUSCLES IN YOUR BOTTOM AND STOMACH TIGHTEN UP? BE STRICT WITH YOURSELF AND STAY BEAUTIFUL.

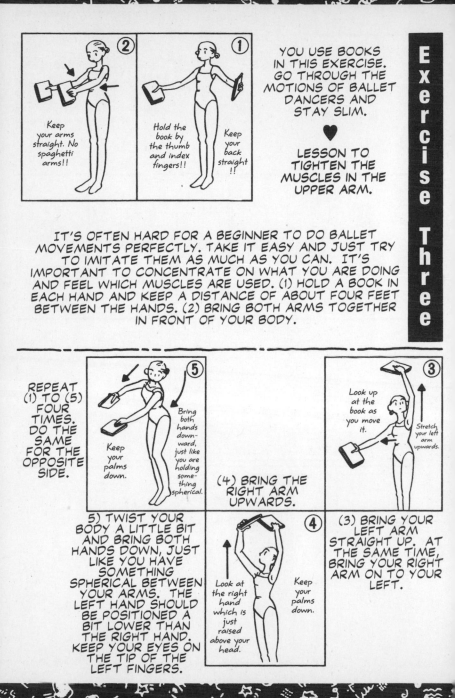

Exercise Three

YOU USE BOOKS IN THIS EXERCISE. GO THROUGH THE MOTIONS OF BALLET DANCERS AND STAY SLIM.

♥

LESSON TO TIGHTEN THE MUSCLES IN THE UPPER ARM.

1
Keep your back straight !!
Hold the book by the thumb and index fingers!!
2
Keep your arms straight. No spaghetti arms!!

IT'S OFTEN HARD FOR A BEGINNER TO DO BALLET MOVEMENTS PERFECTLY. TAKE IT EASY AND JUST TRY TO IMITATE THEM AS MUCH AS YOU CAN. IT'S IMPORTANT TO CONCENTRATE ON WHAT YOU ARE DOING AND FEEL WHICH MUSCLES ARE USED. (1) HOLD A BOOK IN EACH HAND AND KEEP A DISTANCE OF ABOUT FOUR FEET BETWEEN THE HANDS. (2) BRING BOTH ARMS TOGETHER IN FRONT OF YOUR BODY.

3
Stretch your left arm upwards.
Look up at the book as you move it.

(3) BRING YOUR LEFT ARM STRAIGHT UP. AT THE SAME TIME, BRING YOUR RIGHT ARM ON TO YOUR LEFT.

(4) BRING THE RIGHT ARM UPWARDS.

4
Keep your palms down.
Look at the right hand which is just raised above your head.

5
Bring both hands down-ward, just like you are holding some-thing spherical.
Keep your palms down.

5) TWIST YOUR BODY A LITTLE BIT AND BRING BOTH HANDS DOWN, JUST LIKE YOU HAVE SOMETHING SPHERICAL BETWEEN YOUR ARMS. THE LEFT HAND SHOULD BE POSITIONED A BIT LOWER THAN THE RIGHT HAND. KEEP YOUR EYES ON THE TIP OF THE LEFT FINGERS.

REPEAT (1) TO (5) FOUR TIMES. DO THE SAME FOR THE OPPOSITE SIDE.

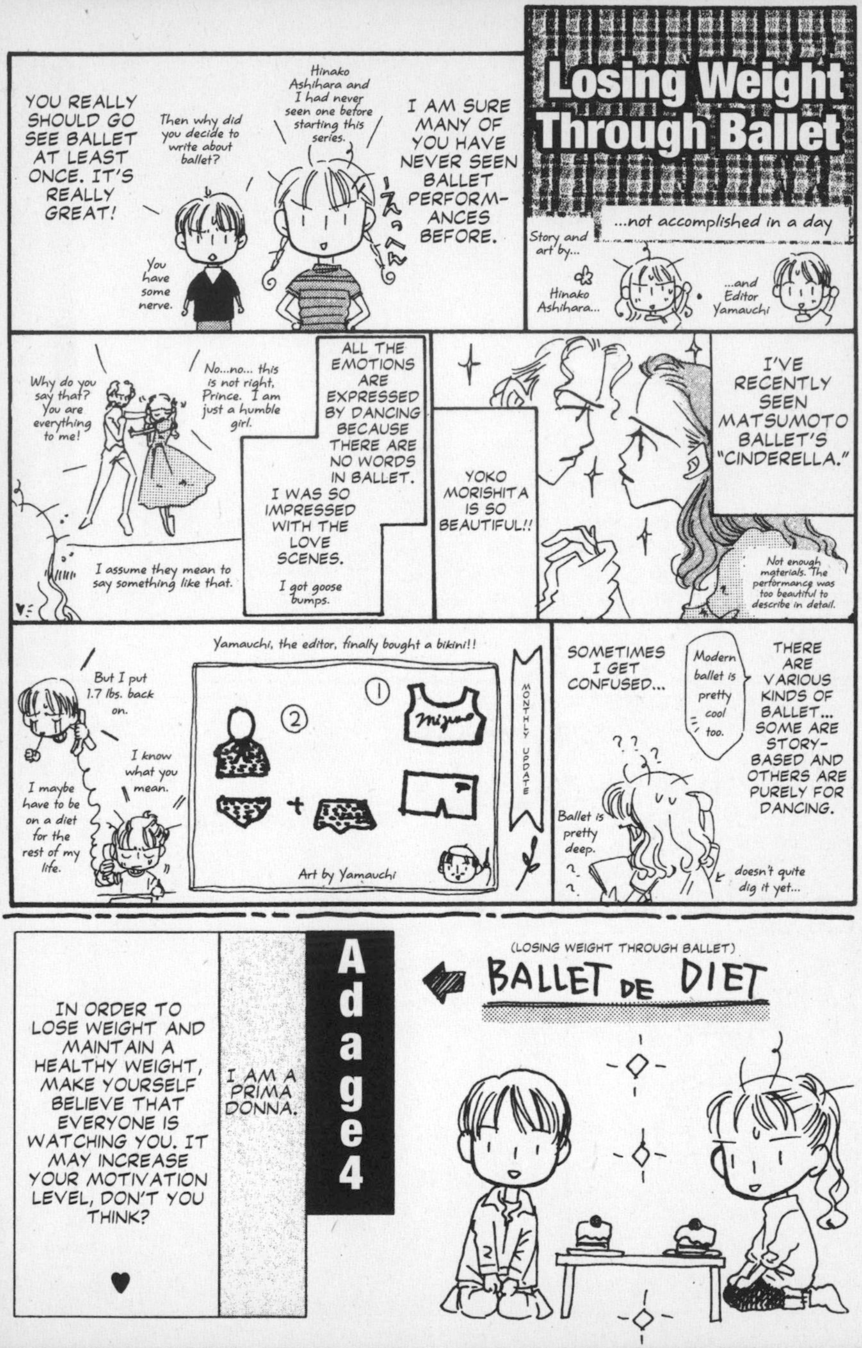

Losing Weight Through Ballet
...not accomplished in a day
Story and art by...
Hinako Ashihara...
...and Editor Yamauchi
I AM SURE MANY OF YOU HAVE NEVER SEEN BALLET PERFORMANCES BEFORE.
Hinako Ashihara and I had never seen one before starting this series.
えっへん
Then why did you decide to write about ballet?
YOU REALLY SHOULD GO SEE BALLET AT LEAST ONCE. IT'S REALLY GREAT!
You have some nerve.
I'VE RECENTLY SEEN MATSUMOTO BALLET'S "CINDERELLA."
YOKO MORISHITA IS SO BEAUTIFUL!!
Not enough materials. The performance was too beautiful to describe in detail.
ALL THE EMOTIONS ARE EXPRESSED BY DANCING BECAUSE THERE ARE NO WORDS IN BALLET.
I WAS SO IMPRESSED WITH THE LOVE SCENES.
I got goose bumps.
No...no... this is not right, Prince. I am just a humble girl.
Why do you say that? You are everything to me!
I assume they mean to say something like that.
THERE ARE VARIOUS KINDS OF BALLET... SOME ARE STORY-BASED AND OTHERS ARE PURELY FOR DANCING.
Modern ballet is pretty cool too.
SOMETIMES I GET CONFUSED...
doesn't quite dig it yet...
Ballet is pretty deep.
MONTHLY UPDATE
Yamauchi, the editor, finally bought a bikini!!
1
mizuno
2
Art by Yamauchi
But I put 1.7 lbs. back on.
I know what you mean.
I maybe have to be on a diet for the rest of my life.
(LOSING WEIGHT THROUGH BALLET)
BALLET DE DIET
Adage 4
I AM A PRIMA DONNA.
IN ORDER TO LOSE WEIGHT AND MAINTAIN A HEALTHY WEIGHT, MAKE YOURSELF BELIEVE THAT EVERYONE IS WATCHING YOU. IT MAY INCREASE YOUR MOTIVATION LEVEL, DON'T YOU THINK?

Exercise Four

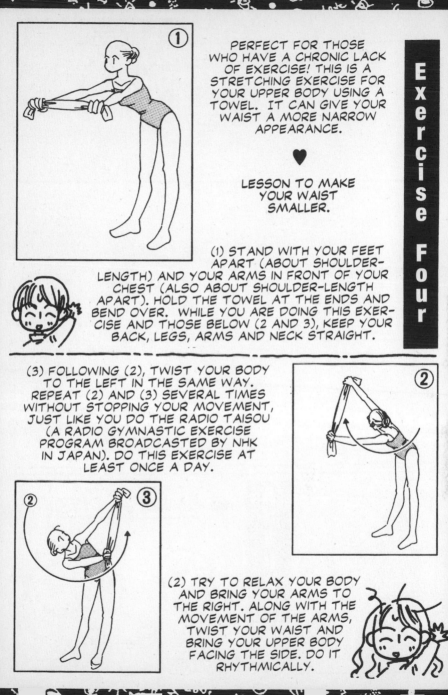

PERFECT FOR THOSE WHO HAVE A CHRONIC LACK OF EXERCISE! THIS IS A STRETCHING EXERCISE FOR YOUR UPPER BODY USING A TOWEL. IT CAN GIVE YOUR WAIST A MORE NARROW APPEARANCE.

♥

LESSON TO MAKE YOUR WAIST SMALLER.

1

(1) STAND WITH YOUR FEET APART (ABOUT SHOULDER-LENGTH) AND YOUR ARMS IN FRONT OF YOUR CHEST (ALSO ABOUT SHOULDER-LENGTH APART). HOLD THE TOWEL AT THE ENDS AND BEND OVER. WHILE YOU ARE DOING THIS EXERCISE AND THOSE BELOW (2 AND 3), KEEP YOUR BACK, LEGS, ARMS AND NECK STRAIGHT.

2

(2) TRY TO RELAX YOUR BODY AND BRING YOUR ARMS TO THE RIGHT. ALONG WITH THE MOVEMENT OF THE ARMS, TWIST YOUR WAIST AND BRING YOUR UPPER BODY FACING THE SIDE. DO IT RHYTHMICALLY.

(3) FOLLOWING (2), TWIST YOUR BODY TO THE LEFT IN THE SAME WAY. REPEAT (2) AND (3) SEVERAL TIMES WITHOUT STOPPING YOUR MOVEMENT, JUST LIKE YOU DO THE RADIO TAISOU (A RADIO GYMNASTIC EXERCISE PROGRAM BROADCASTED BY NHK IN JAPAN). DO THIS EXERCISE AT LEAST ONCE A DAY.

3
2

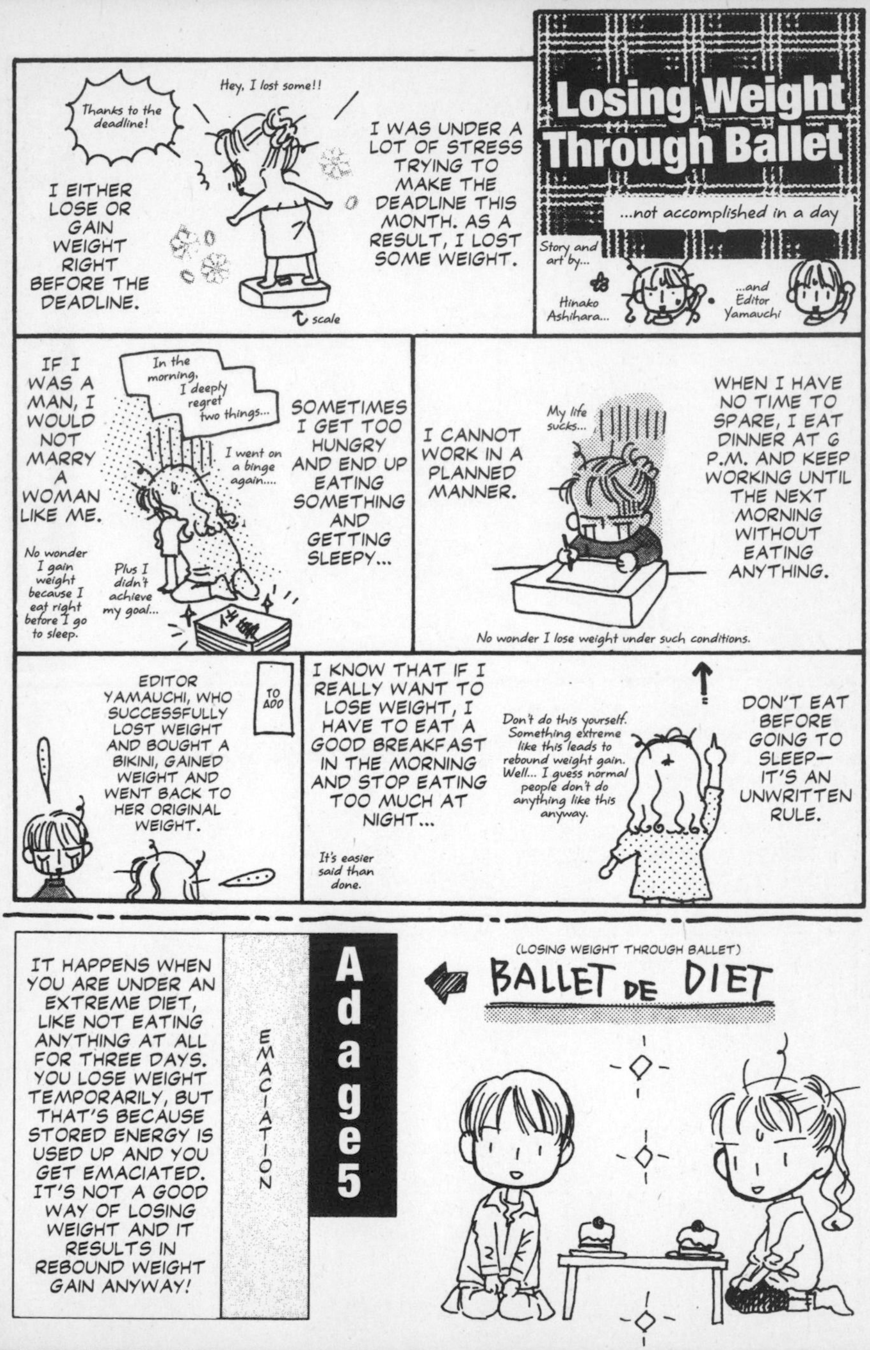

Losing Weight Through Ballet
...not accomplished in a day
Story and art by...
Hinako Ashihara...
...and Editor Yamauchi
I WAS UNDER A LOT OF STRESS TRYING TO MAKE THE DEADLINE THIS MONTH. AS A RESULT, I LOST SOME WEIGHT.
Hey, I lost some!!
Thanks to the deadline!
I EITHER LOSE OR GAIN WEIGHT RIGHT BEFORE THE DEADLINE.
scale
WHEN I HAVE NO TIME TO SPARE, I EAT DINNER AT 6 P.M. AND KEEP WORKING UNTIL THE NEXT MORNING WITHOUT EATING ANYTHING.
My life sucks...
I CANNOT WORK IN A PLANNED MANNER.
No wonder I lose weight under such conditions.
SOMETIMES I GET TOO HUNGRY AND END UP EATING SOMETHING AND GETTING SLEEPY...
I went on a binge again....
In the morning, I deeply regret two things...
IF I WAS A MAN, I WOULD NOT MARRY A WOMAN LIKE ME.
Plus I didn't achieve my goal...
No wonder I gain weight because I eat right before I go to sleep.
DON'T EAT BEFORE GOING TO SLEEP— IT'S AN UNWRITTEN RULE.
Don't do this yourself. Something extreme like this leads to rebound weight gain. Well... I guess normal people don't do anything like this anyway.
I KNOW THAT IF I REALLY WANT TO LOSE WEIGHT, I HAVE TO EAT A GOOD BREAKFAST IN THE MORNING AND STOP EATING TOO MUCH AT NIGHT...
It's easier said than done.
TO ADD
EDITOR YAMAUCHI, WHO SUCCESSFULLY LOST WEIGHT AND BOUGHT A BIKINI, GAINED WEIGHT AND WENT BACK TO HER ORIGINAL WEIGHT.
(LOSING WEIGHT THROUGH BALLET)
BALLET DE DIET
Adage 5
EMACIATION
IT HAPPENS WHEN YOU ARE UNDER AN EXTREME DIET, LIKE NOT EATING ANYTHING AT ALL FOR THREE DAYS. YOU LOSE WEIGHT TEMPORARILY, BUT THAT'S BECAUSE STORED ENERGY IS USED UP AND YOU GET EMACIATED. IT'S NOT A GOOD WAY OF LOSING WEIGHT AND IT RESULTS IN REBOUND WEIGHT GAIN ANYWAY!

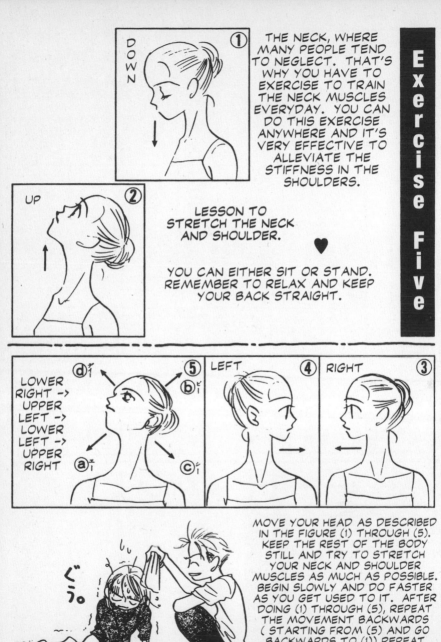

① DOWN

THE NECK, WHERE MANY PEOPLE TEND TO NEGLECT. THAT'S WHY YOU HAVE TO EXERCISE TO TRAIN THE NECK MUSCLES EVERYDAY. YOU CAN DO THIS EXERCISE ANYWHERE AND IT'S VERY EFFECTIVE TO ALLEVIATE THE STIFFNESS IN THE SHOULDERS.

② UP

LESSON TO STRETCH THE NECK AND SHOULDER.

♥

YOU CAN EITHER SIT OR STAND. REMEMBER TO RELAX AND KEEP YOUR BACK STRAIGHT.

⑤

LOWER RIGHT –> UPPER LEFT –> LOWER LEFT –> UPPER RIGHT

ⓓ ⓑ ⓐ ⓒ

LEFT **④**

RIGHT **③**

MOVE YOUR HEAD AS DESCRIBED IN THE FIGURE (1) THROUGH (5). KEEP THE REST OF THE BODY STILL AND TRY TO STRETCH YOUR NECK AND SHOULDER MUSCLES AS MUCH AS POSSIBLE. BEGIN SLOWLY AND DO FASTER AS YOU GET USED TO IT. AFTER DOING (1) THROUGH (5), REPEAT THE MOVEMENT BACKWARDS (STARTING FROM (5) AND GO BACKWARDS TO (1)) REPEAT EACH DIRECTION FOUR TIMES. DO THE EXERCISE EVERYDAY.

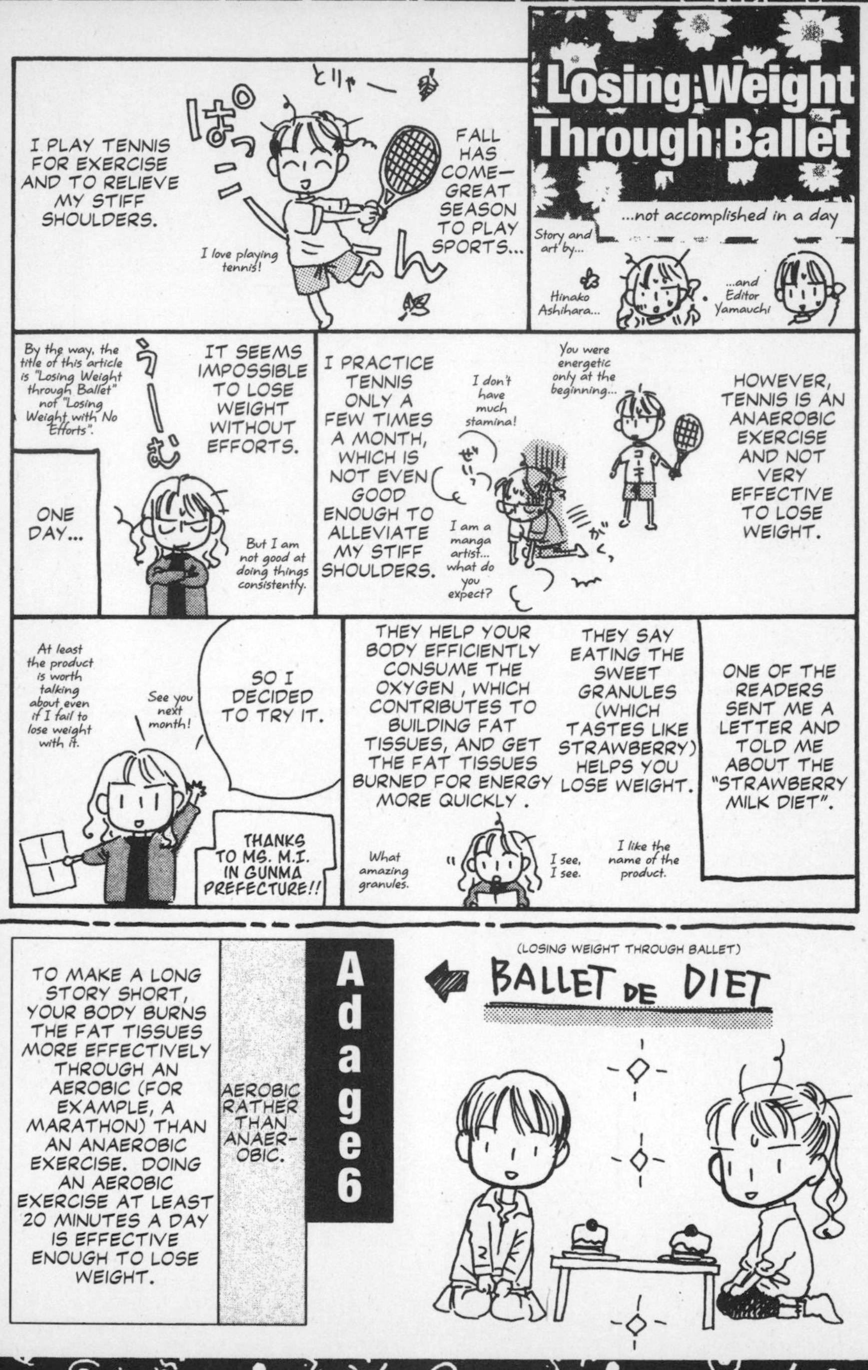
Losing Weight Through Ballet
...not accomplished in a day
Story and art by...
Hinako Ashihara...
...and Editor Yamauchi
FALL HAS COME—GREAT SEASON TO PLAY SPORTS...
とりゃー
ぱっこーん
I PLAY TENNIS FOR EXERCISE AND TO RELIEVE MY STIFF SHOULDERS.
I love playing tennis!
HOWEVER, TENNIS IS AN ANAEROBIC EXERCISE AND NOT VERY EFFECTIVE TO LOSE WEIGHT.
You were energetic only at the beginning...
I don't have much stamina!
ぜー
がくっ
I am a manga artist... what do you expect?
I PRACTICE TENNIS ONLY A FEW TIMES A MONTH, WHICH IS NOT EVEN GOOD ENOUGH TO ALLEVIATE MY STIFF SHOULDERS.
IT SEEMS IMPOSSIBLE TO LOSE WEIGHT WITHOUT EFFORTS.
うーむ
By the way, the title of this article is "Losing Weight through Ballet" not "Losing Weight with No Efforts".
But I am not good at doing things consistently.
ONE DAY...
ONE OF THE READERS SENT ME A LETTER AND TOLD ME ABOUT THE "STRAWBERRY MILK DIET".
THEY SAY EATING THE SWEET GRANULES (WHICH TASTES LIKE STRAWBERRY) HELPS YOU LOSE WEIGHT.
THEY HELP YOUR BODY EFFICIENTLY CONSUME THE OXYGEN , WHICH CONTRIBUTES TO BUILDING FAT TISSUES, AND GET THE FAT TISSUES BURNED FOR ENERGY MORE QUICKLY .
I like the name of the product.
I see, I see.
What amazing granules.
SO I DECIDED TO TRY IT.
See you next month!
At least the product is worth talking about even if I fail to lose weight with it.
THANKS TO MS. M.I. IN GUNMA PREFECTURE!!
(LOSING WEIGHT THROUGH BALLET)
BALLET DE DIET
Adage 6
AEROBIC RATHER THAN ANAEROBIC.
TO MAKE A LONG STORY SHORT, YOUR BODY BURNS THE FAT TISSUES MORE EFFECTIVELY THROUGH AN AEROBIC (FOR EXAMPLE, A MARATHON) THAN AN ANAEROBIC EXERCISE. DOING AN AEROBIC EXERCISE AT LEAST 20 MINUTES A DAY IS EFFECTIVE ENOUGH TO LOSE WEIGHT.

Exercise Six

TO ACHIEVE A BEAUTIFUL POSTURE, TRY THIS STRETCHING EXERCISE THAT INCORPORATES BALLET MOVEMENTS. IT'S VERY EASY AND YOU CAN DO IT WHILE YOU ARE SITTING.

♥

STRETCH EXERCISE ON THE CHAIR.

STRETCHING THE BACK AND NECK

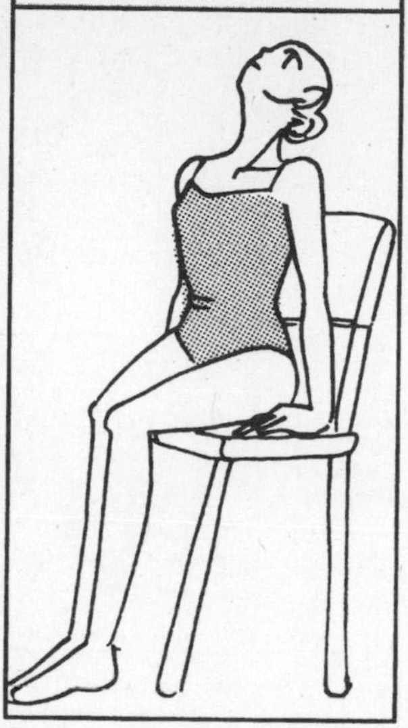

(1) SIT ON A CHAIR WITH YOUR BACK AND NECK STRAIGHT. (2) SIT WITH YOUR ARMS STRAIGHT ON YOUR SIDE. (3) THROW BACK YOUR SHOULDERS AND MAKE YOUR BACK MUSCLES CONTRACT. THROW OUT YOUR CHEST. AT THE SAME TIME, YOUR FACE LOOKS UP. (4) RELAX AND GO BACK TO THE INITIAL POSITION. REPEAT (1) TO (4) FOUR TIMES.

TWIST THE WAIST

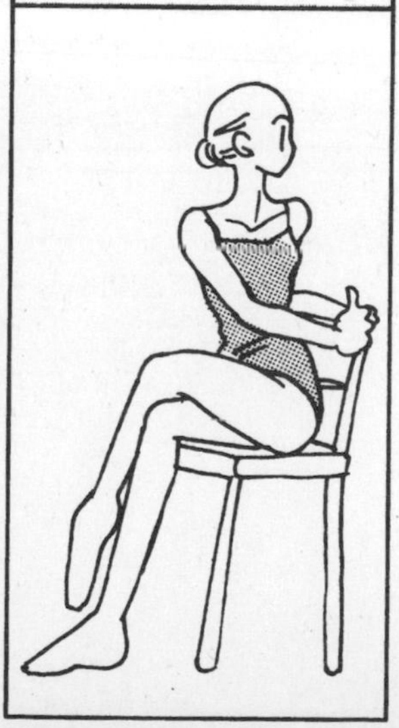

(1) SIT ON A CHAIR WITH A BACKREST. CROSS YOUR LEGS WITH YOUR LEFT LEG ON TOP OF YOUR RIGHT. TRY TO KEEP YOUR BACK STRAIGHT AND TIGHTEN THE MUSCLES IN THE ENTIRE LENGTH OF THE LEGS. (2) PLACE BOTH HANDS ONTO THE LEFT SIDE OF THE BACKREST AND TWIST YOUR BODY TO THE LEFT. TRY TO LOOK RIGHT BEHIND YOU AS YOU DO THIS. (3) GO BACK TO THE INITIAL POSITION SLOWLY. DO THE SAME THING WITH THE OTHER SIDE. CROSS YOUR LEGS WITH THE RIGHT LEG ON TOP OF THE LEFT AND TWIST YOUR BODY TO THE RIGHT. REPEAT THE MOVEMENT FOUR TIMES ON BOTH SIDES.

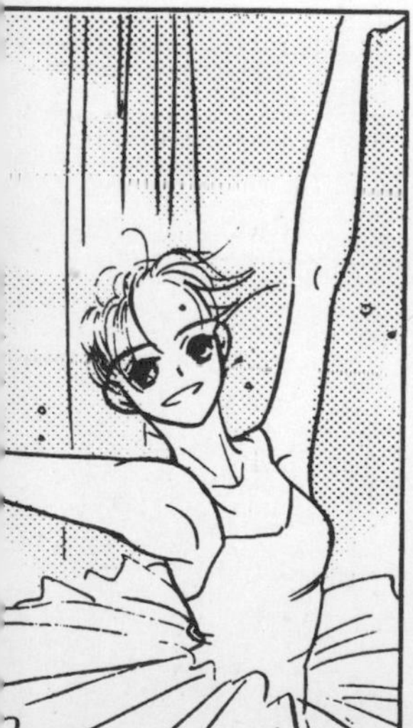

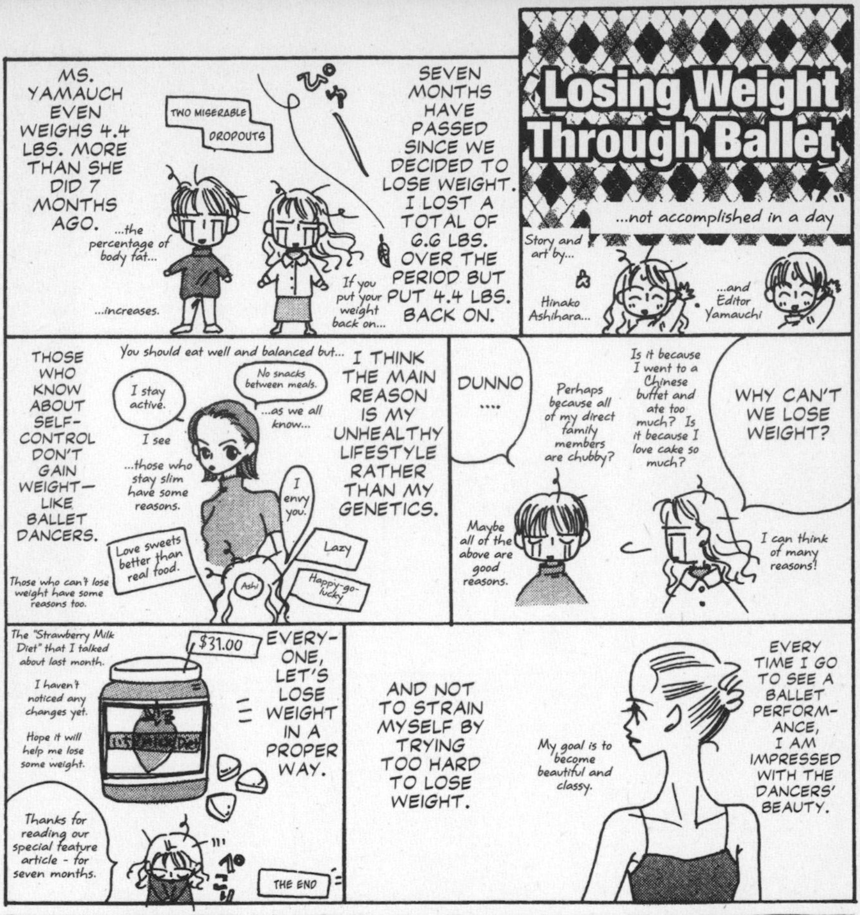
Losing Weight Through Ballet
...not accomplished in a day
Story and art by... Hinako Ashihara...
...and Editor Yamauchi
SEVEN MONTHS HAVE PASSED SINCE WE DECIDED TO LOSE WEIGHT. I LOST A TOTAL OF 6.6 LBS. OVER THE PERIOD BUT PUT 4.4 LBS. BACK ON.
If you put your weight back on...
TWO MISERABLE DROPOUTS
...the percentage of body fat...
...increases.
MS. YAMAUCH EVEN WEIGHS 4.4 LBS. MORE THAN SHE DID 7 MONTHS AGO.
WHY CAN'T WE LOSE WEIGHT?
I can think of many reasons!
Is it because I went to a Chinese buffet and ate too much? Is it because I love cake so much?
Perhaps because all of my direct family members are chubby?
DUNNO ....
Maybe all of the above are good reasons.
I THINK THE MAIN REASON IS MY UNHEALTHY LIFESTYLE RATHER THAN MY GENETICS.
You should eat well and balanced but...
No snacks between meals.
...as we all know...
I stay active.
I see
...those who stay slim have some reasons.
I envy you.
Lazy
Happy-go-lucky
Love sweets better than real food.
Ashi
THOSE WHO KNOW ABOUT SELF-CONTROL DON'T GAIN WEIGHT—LIKE BALLET DANCERS.
Those who can't lose weight have some reasons too.
EVERY TIME I GO TO SEE A BALLET PERFORMANCE, I AM IMPRESSED WITH THE DANCERS' BEAUTY.
My goal is to become beautiful and classy.
AND NOT TO STRAIN MYSELF BY TRYING TOO HARD TO LOSE WEIGHT.
EVERYONE, LET'S LOSE WEIGHT IN A PROPER WAY.
$31.00
The "Strawberry Milk Diet" that I talked about last month.
I haven't noticed any changes yet.
Hope it will help me lose some weight.
Thanks for reading our special feature article - for seven months.
THE END

★ THAT'S IT. IT WAS THE BONUS PAGES FOR GOOD GIRLS WHO WOULD LOVE TO LOSE WEIGHT BY EMULATING BALLET DANCERS. HOPE YOU ENJOYED IT!!

(LOSING WEIGHT THROUGH BALLET)

BALLET DE DIET

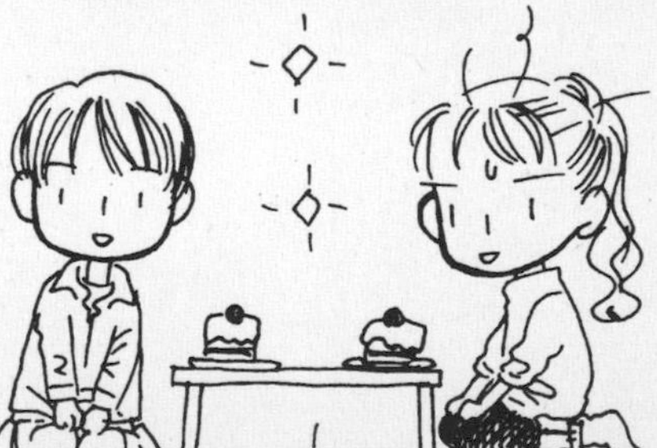

Exercise Seven

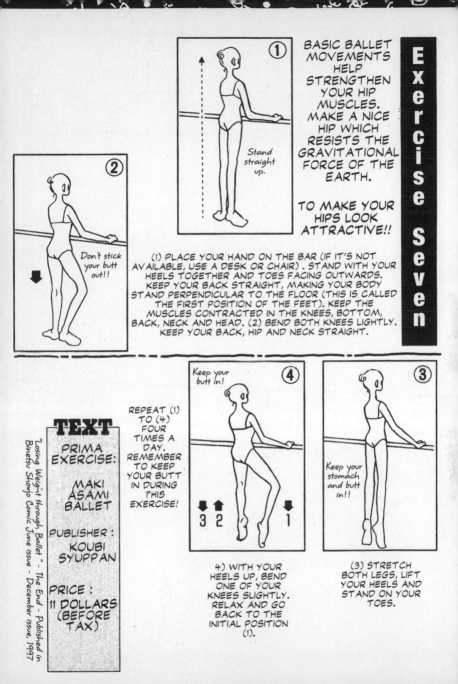

BASIC BALLET MOVEMENTS HELP STRENGTHEN YOUR HIP MUSCLES. MAKE A NICE HIP WHICH RESISTS THE GRAVITATIONAL FORCE OF THE EARTH.

TO MAKE YOUR HIPS LOOK ATTRACTIVE!!

1
Stand straight up.

2
Don't stick your butt out!!

(1) PLACE YOUR HAND ON THE BAR (IF IT'S NOT AVAILABLE, USE A DESK OR CHAIR) . STAND WITH YOUR HEELS TOGETHER AND TOES FACING OUTWARDS. KEEP YOUR BACK STRAIGHT, MAKING YOUR BODY STAND PERPENDICULAR TO THE FLOOR (THIS IS CALLED THE FIRST POSITION OF THE FEET). KEEP THE MUSCLES CONTRACTED IN THE KNEES, BOTTOM, BACK, NECK AND HEAD. (2) BEND BOTH KNEES LIGHTLY. KEEP YOUR BACK, HIP AND NECK STRAIGHT.

3
Keep your stomach and butt in!!

(3) STRETCH BOTH LEGS, LIFT YOUR HEELS AND STAND ON YOUR TOES.

4
Keep your butt in!
1
2
3

4) WITH YOUR HEELS UP, BEND ONE OF YOUR KNEES SLIGHTLY. RELAX AND GO BACK TO THE INITIAL POSITION (1).

REPEAT (1) TO (4) FOUR TIMES A DAY. REMEMBER TO KEEP YOUR BUTT IN DURING THIS EXERCISE!

TEXT

PRIMA EXERCISE:

MAKI ASAMI BALLET

PUBLISHER : KOUBI SYUPPAN

PRICE : 11 DOLLARS (BEFORE TAX)

"Losing Weight through Ballet" - The End - Published in Binetsu Shoujo Comic June issue - December issue, 1997

My Trip to England

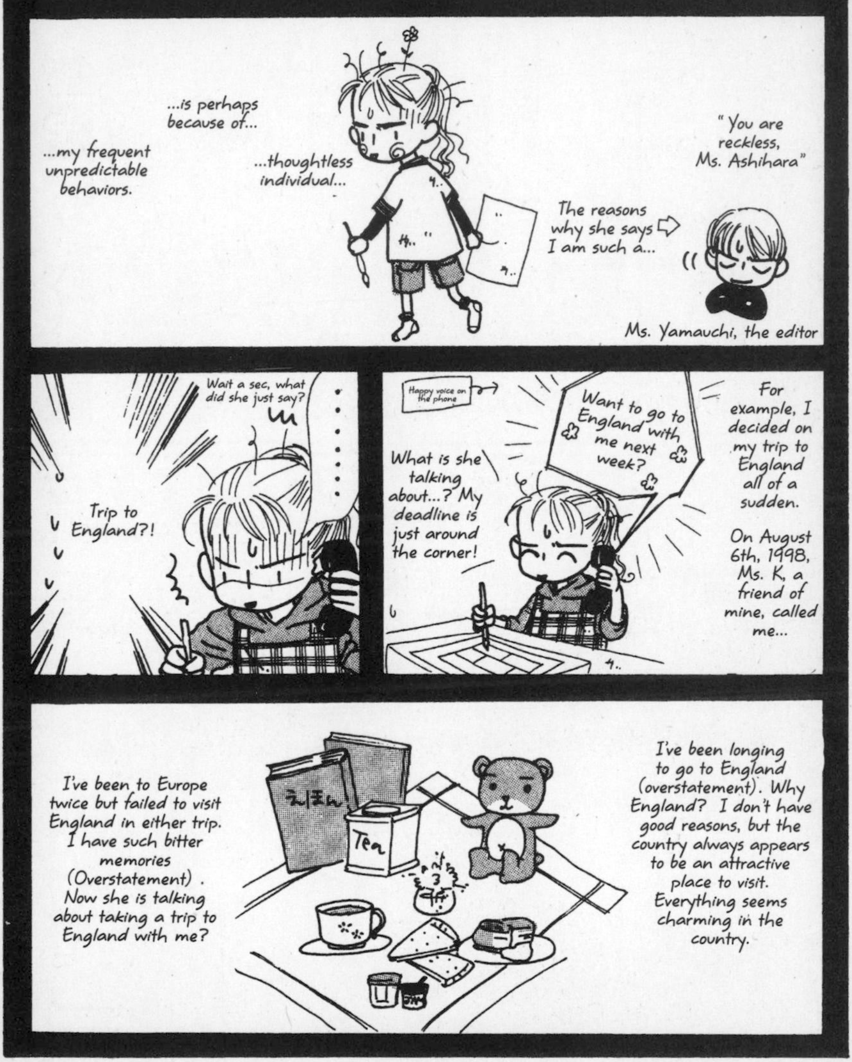
"You are reckless, Ms. Ashihara"
The reasons why she says I am such a...
...thoughtless individual...
...is perhaps because of...
...my frequent unpredictable behaviors.
Ms. Yamauchi, the editor
For example, I decided on my trip to England all of a sudden.
On August 6th, 1998, Ms. K, a friend of mine, called me...
Want to go to England with me next week?
Happy voice on the phone
What is she talking about...? My deadline is just around the corner!
Wait a sec, what did she just say?
Trip to England?!
I've been longing to go to England (overstatement). Why England? I don't have good reasons, but the country always appears to be an attractive place to visit. Everything seems charming in the country.
Tea
I've been to Europe twice but failed to visit England in either trip. I have such bitter memories (Overstatement). Now she is talking about taking a trip to England with me?

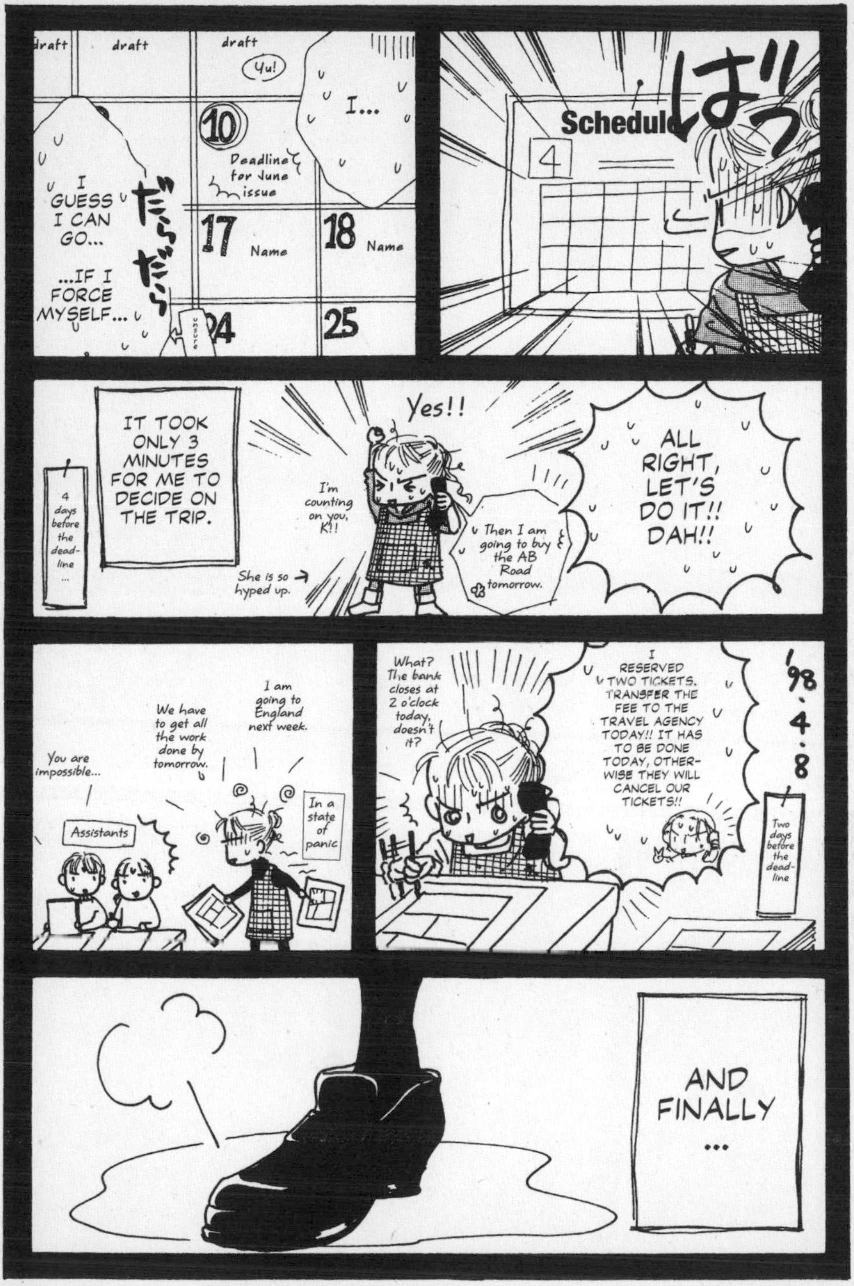

Schedule
はっ
draft
draft
draft
Yu!
I...
10
Deadline for June issue
I GUESS I CAN GO...
だらだら
17
Name
18
Name
...IF I FORCE MYSELF...
24
25
ALL RIGHT, LET'S DO IT!! DAH!!
Yes!!
Then I am going to buy the AB Road tomorrow.
I'm counting on you, K!!
She is so hyped up.
IT TOOK ONLY 3 MINUTES FOR ME TO DECIDE ON THE TRIP.
4 days before the deadline ...
'98.4.8
Two days before the deadline
I RESERVED TWO TICKETS. TRANSFER THE FEE TO THE TRAVEL AGENCY TODAY!! IT HAS TO BE DONE TODAY, OTHERWISE THEY WILL CANCEL OUR TICKETS!!
What? The bank closes at 2 o'clock today, doesn't it?
In a state of panic
I am going to England next week.
We have to get all the work done by tomorrow.
You are impossible...
Assistants
AND FINALLY ...

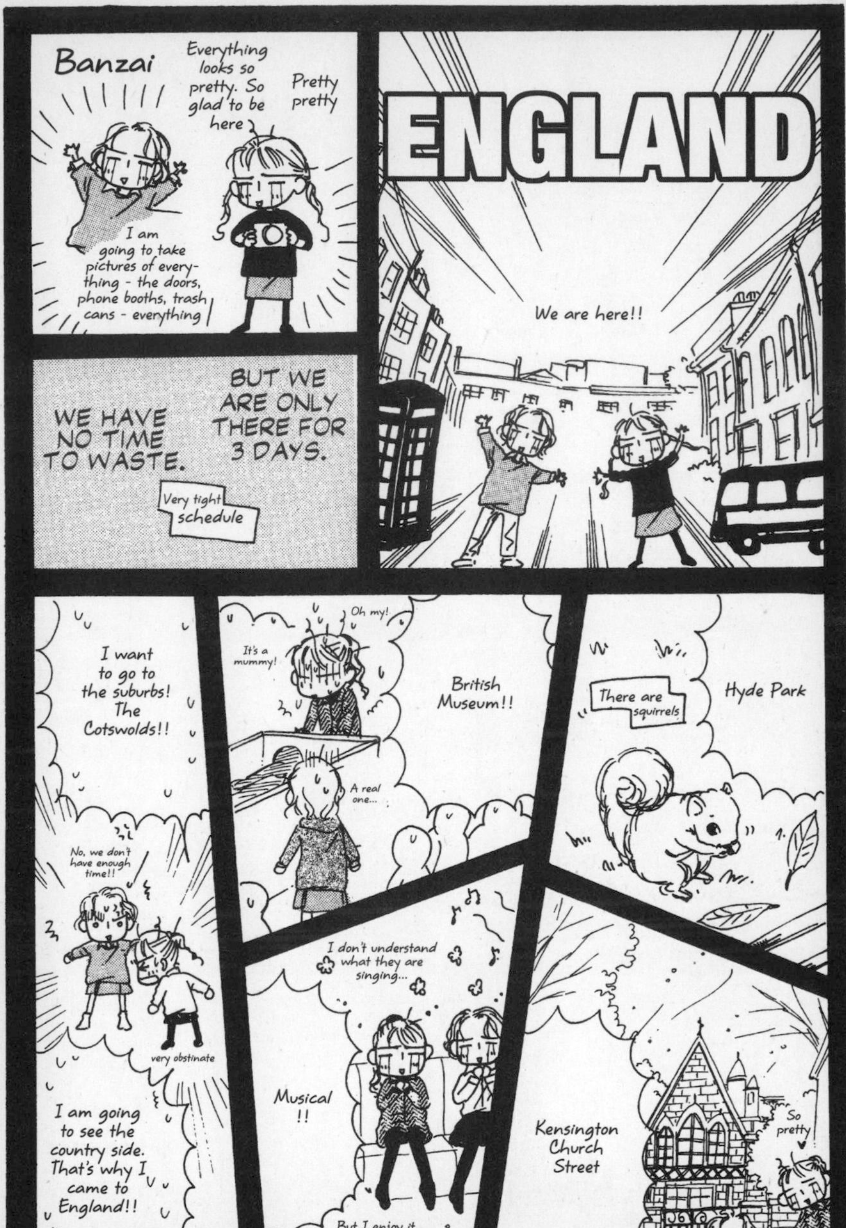
ENGLAND
We are here!!
Pretty pretty
Everything looks so pretty. So glad to be here
Banzai
I am going to take pictures of every-thing - the doors, phone booths, trash cans - everything
BUT WE ARE ONLY THERE FOR 3 DAYS.
WE HAVE NO TIME TO WASTE.
Very tight schedule
Hyde Park
There are squirrels
Oh my!
British Museum!!
It's a mummy!
A real one...
So pretty
Kensington Church Street
I don't understand what they are singing...
Musical !!
But I enjoy it very much
I want to go to the suburbs! The Cotswolds!!
No, we don't have enough time!!
very obstinate
I am going to see the country side. That's why I came to England!!

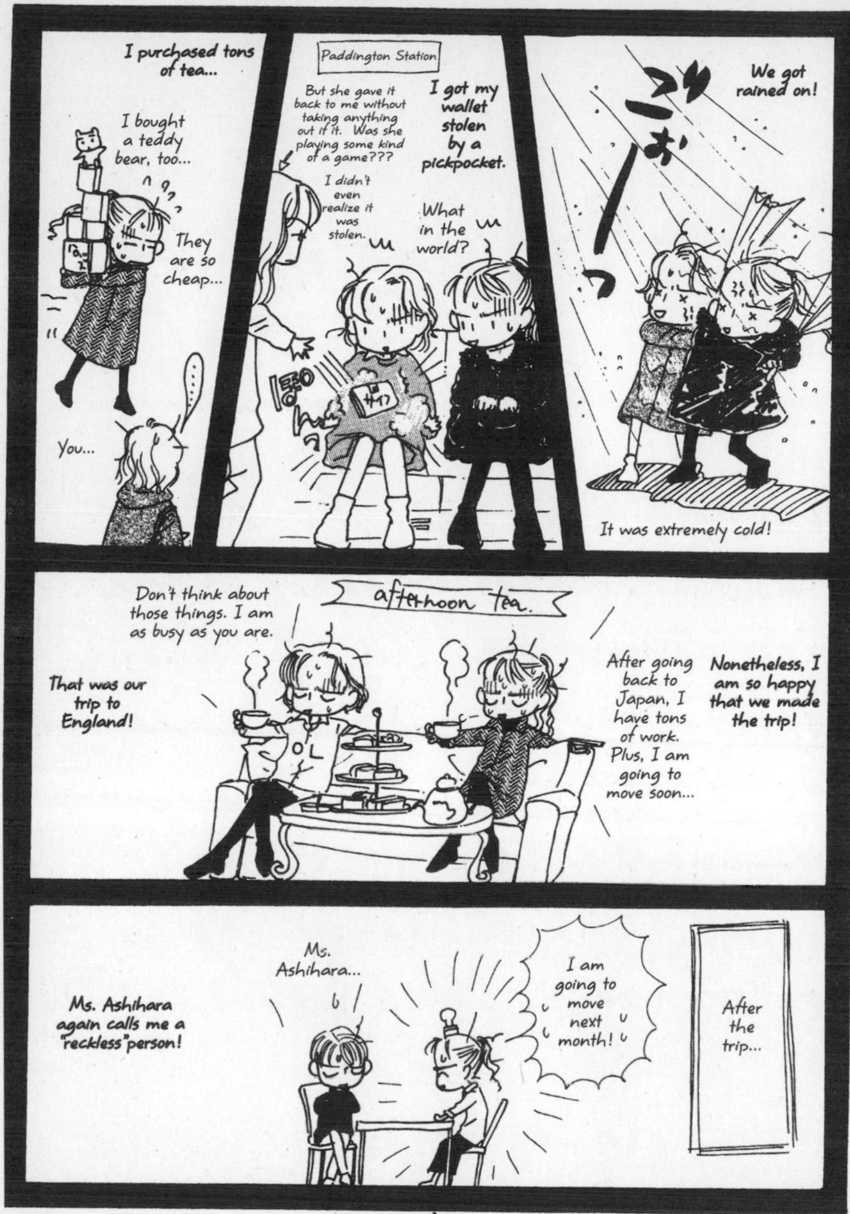
We got rained on!
It was extremely cold!
Paddington Station
I got my wallet stolen by a pickpocket.
But she gave it back to me without taking anything out it it. Was she playing some kind of a game???
I didn't even realize it was stolen.
What in the world?
サイフ
I purchased tons of tea...
I bought a teddy bear, too...
They are so cheap...
You...
afternoon tea.
Nonetheless, I am so happy that we made the trip!
After going back to Japan, I have tons of work. Plus, I am going to move soon...
Don't think about those things. I am as busy as you are.
That was our trip to England!
OL
After the trip...
I am going to move next month!
Ms. Ashihara...
Ms. Ashihara again calls me a "reckless" person!

The End

In the next volume

of...

Forbidden Dance

After Diana's fall, it's difficult to say if she'll ever dance again. In the meantime, COOL needs a sponsor for its upcoming anniversary performance. Mr. Harukichi Suehiro agrees to sponsor them on the condition that Aya not be in the performance. Akira agrees, but Aya has a harder time coming to terms with these conditions.

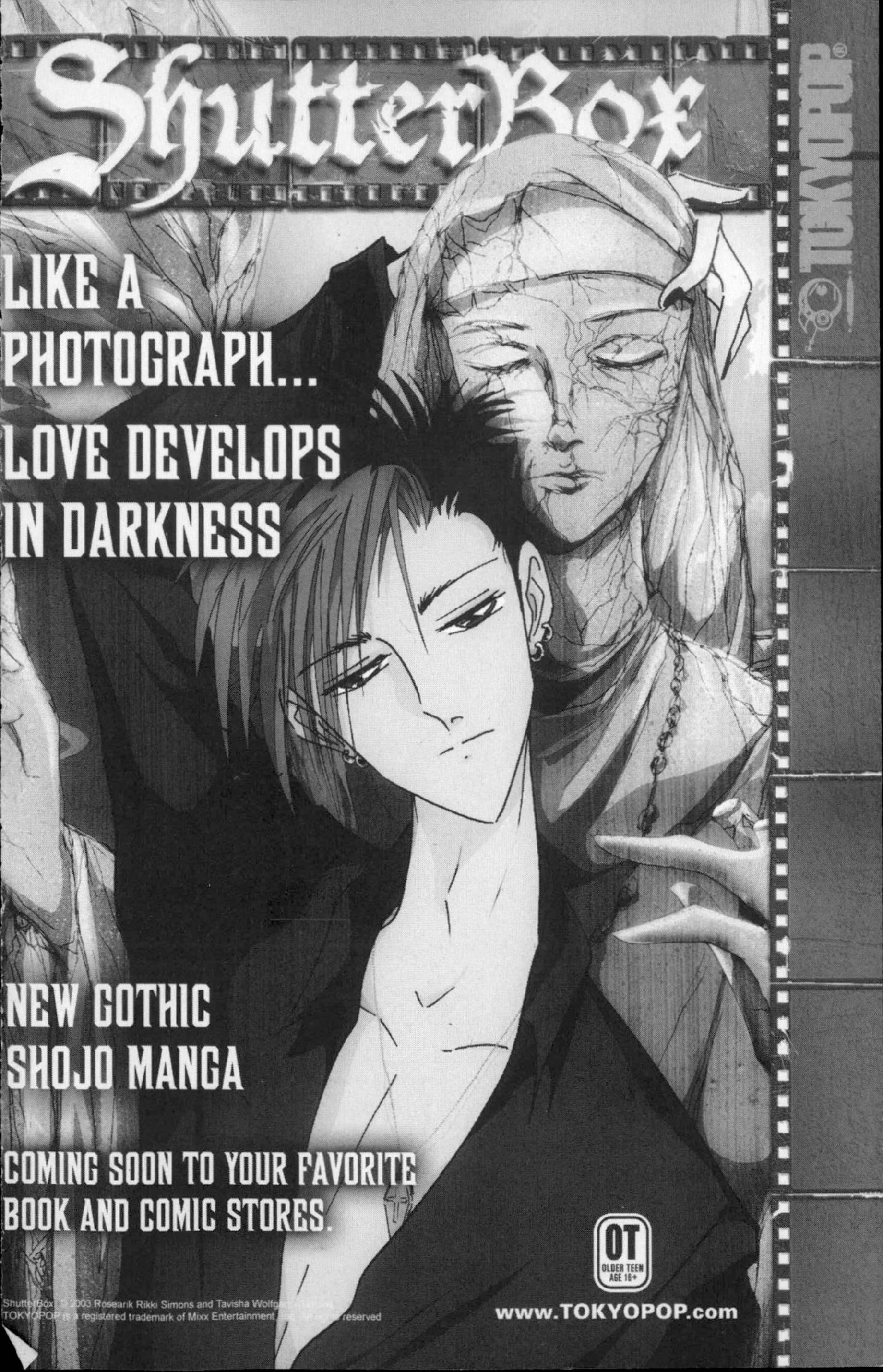

ShutterBox
TOKYOPOP
LIKE A PHOTOGRAPH...
LOVE DEVELOPS IN DARKNESS
NEW GOTHIC SHOJO MANGA
COMING SOON TO YOUR FAVORITE BOOK AND COMIC STORES.
OT
OLDER TEEN AGE 16+
ShutterBox © 2003 Rosearik Rikki Simons and Tavisha
TOKYOPOP is a registered trademark of Mixx Entertainment reserved
www.TOKYOPOP.com